Lee and Saralee Rosenberg's

50 Fabulous Places to Retire in America

Second Edition

By
Ken Stern, CFP

CAREER PRESS
3 Tice Road
P.O. Box 687
Franklin Lakes, NJ 07417
1-800-CAREER-1
201-848-0310 (NJ and outside U.S.)
FAX: 201-848-1727

Copyright © 1996 by The Career Press, Inc.

LEE AND SARALEE ROSENBERG'S 50 FABULOUS PLACES TO RETIRE IN AMERICA, SECOND EDITION
Cover design by Dean Johnson Design, Inc.
Cover photo by Stephen Marks, Inc./Image Bank
Printed in the U.S.A. by Book-mart Press

To order this title, please call toll-free 1-800-CAREER-1 (NJ and Canada: 201-848-0310) to order using VISA or MasterCard, or for further information on books from Career Press.

Library of Congress Cataloging-in-Publication Data

Stern, Ken.
    Lee and Saralee Rosenberg's 50 fabulous places to retire in America.--2nd ed./by Ken Stern.
        p.   cm.
    Includes index.
    ISBN 1-56414-260-4 (pbk.)
    1. Retirement, Places of--United States.   I. Rosenberg, Lee, 1952-   50 fabulous places to retire in America.   II. Title.
HQ1063.2.U6S73   1996
646.7'9'0973--dc20   96-28346

Acknowledgments

A task of this magnitude is not simple. My thanks to Career Press for giving me the authority; Anne Robinson for her months of research, writing and attention to tedious detail that this overwhelming project demanded; all my associates at Asset Planning Solutions who contributed to this manuscript; my dear friend Shirley Sunde, for her moral support; Dan Clark; Leslie Bailey, for her editing expertise; and, of course, all of you, the readers, who now have the adventure of a lifetime before you—the adventure of retirement.

—Kenneth A. Stern, CFP

Contents

Introduction

Extra! Extra!
Every day, almost 6,000 Americans celebrate their 65th birthdays

The good news is *we are living longer than ever before.* One of the most visible demographic trends in the United States during the next decade will be the "graying" of the population. According to the U.S. Census Bureau, the sector of the population age 55 and up grows twice as fast as the total population. *Twice as fast!* In 1950, this segment accounted for 17 percent of our population. Already, one out of five Americans is over 55. By the turn of the century, this number should increase to about 25 percent—one in four.

A longer life span means an increased number of those of us who will be retired, as well as an increase in the number of years we will spend in retirement. On the bright side, this should give us more time to savor the "golden years" by exploring new hobbies, traveling and visiting family. Retirement will also give us the opportunity to experience living in a new location.

The catch

With increased life spans come, naturally, increased costs. It is not uncommon to be retired for as many as 20 to 30 years. Now more than ever, many of the costs associated with retirement—medical expenses, tourism, travel, housing—will be ours to bear, along with general increases in the cost of living. Simultaneously, we will also experience a decrease in entitlements such as Social Security.

For most retirees, costs associated with housing comprise the largest percentage of retirement expenses—and these are expenses that will continue to rise substantially with our increased longevity.

The solution

Fortunately, there is one way to withstand the financial challenges of retirement while maximizing your enjoyment of this period of your life. The answer? Plan ahead.

One aspect of retirement most people look forward to is deciding where to live. This, however, will have a profound effect on all aspects of your life, including your happiness, health and the health of your pocketbook. With prudent planning and some handy guidelines set forth in this book, you should be able to retire on *your* terms, with the lifestyle to which you are accustomed, and in the location you desire.

The question: where to retire

Every year, more than 500,000 adults 55 and older move out of the state they worked in, as reported by the U.S. Census Bureau. And now, in addition to traditionally popular retirement states such as Florida, California, Arizona, Texas, North Carolina and Georgia, increasing numbers of retirees are choosing states such as Washington, Oregon, Nevada, Alabama and South Carolina.

Another major change is that relocating, once thought to be only for the rich, is now done by middle class retirees, who often relocate to a new state to *save* money. It is increasingly possible to find locations that both suit your needs and save you money—on housing, taxes or cost of living.

Of course, the traditional reasons for finding a new location during retirement still exist. Most retirees want to leave big cities and move to places where they may enjoy a better climate, more activities and meeting people with similar interests.

Regardless of the reasons for moving, there is almost universal agreement as to what constitutes an ideal retirement spot. The consensus is that a retirement spot should have mild seasons, beautiful scenery, affordable living costs, abundant culture and recreation, low crime, low taxes, a healthy economy and enough activity to entice the kids to visit.

Therein lies the need for an updated version of *50 Fabulous Places to Retire in America:* to provide retirees, and those preparing for retirement, the most current facts, figures and features of the places from coast to coast that could give retirees what they are looking for. Most people would be happy to find just one place to fit the bill. Here are 50!

Criteria for the 50 fabulous places

1. Great scenic beauty nearby.
2. Three to four seasons of glorious weather.
3. A diversified housing market with wide ranges of affordability.
4. An overall reduced tax burden compared to the major metropolitan areas from which retirees are migrating.
5. Affordable living costs.
6. An economically healthy area, offering desirable housing.

7. An abundance of culture, recreation and entertainment.

8. Access to quality medical care, as well as reasonable health care costs.

9. A thriving economy that offers job and business opportunities (about 25 percent of retirees go back to work).

10. Proximity to major highways and airports to make vacation travel and trips back home convenient.

11. Availability of continuing education and volunteer programs.

12. Ample attractions and events to entertain visiting family and friends.

13. Availability of quality services for seniors, including social, physical and emotional support.

14. An area where residents feel safe because of low crime rates and excellent police and fire protection.

15. A warm, friendly community where newcomers feel welcome.

Needless to say, there are a few exceptions. Santa Barbara and Palm Springs are two of the country's most expensive areas to live, but also two of the most beautiful and fantasy-filled; if you can afford them, count your blessings. Rochester, Minnesota, can get blistering cold, but there are those of you who thrive on "invigorating" climates. San Diego and San Antonio are big cities with their fair share of crime, but their climates and amenities are so extraordinary that they couldn't be eliminated.

The 50 that made the final cut are a diverse bunch. They include fabulous college towns (Bloomington, Ind.), military towns (Colorado Springs, Colo.), state capitals (Austin, Texas), golf capitals (Palm Springs, Calif.) and ski capitals (Santa Fe, N.M.—we kid you not). Why, you'll even discover a place where you can golf and ski on the same day (Clayton, Ga.)! You'll be able to check out big cities and tiny towns. The bases are also covered in terms of climate. What's your pleasure? Tropical, semitropical, desert, semiarid, four mild seasons?

If you've been dreaming of a particular retirement lifestyle, but aren't sure where it exists, this book will help you find the best place. This raises the most frequently asked question: "Which is the best place?"

This, my friends, is for you to decide. But you can be assured that the 50 included in this volume have enough outstanding attributes to be worthy of your consideration. With all due respect to the popular guides that rank and rate an assortment of lifestyle factors, throw in a year's supply of statistics and then assign each area a final score, I never understood how that was valuable. Fort Myers may emerge as the number-one choice mathematically, but if you would be miserable in a place that had 12 months of summer, would it be your first choice? Probably not.

That's why *50 Fabulous Places to Retire* won't inundate you with numbers. Instead, you'll be given relevant facts, inside information, and a feel for what it's like to live in each area. For example, the profiles won't bore you with the numbers of hospitals in the community, but instead will identify them and describe the level of available care. You won't be bombarded with FBI crime statistics; instead, you'll learn whether a community is a safe place to live and why. Also, the profiles are laid out in such a way that you can read them in their entirety or "cherry pick" by subjects of interest (climate, recreation, etc.). You be the judge.

Most Americans work very hard toward retirement. Sometimes hard work, however, is not *smart* work. To make your retirement journey as sweet as retirement itself, I encourage you to promise yourself something: that you will plan and not wait until the last minute!

Getting your finances in order is critical. You can do this in many ways. However, most ways are so complicated they scare many people off, resulting in nothing getting done. Although it is not as exciting as reading about fabulous places to live, I urge you to read the chapters, "Getting ready for retirement" and "Making your money work so you don't have to." These commonsense "short courses" offer hundreds of great ideas to save you headaches, heartache and money. To be sure, this planning will help ensure you will be able to enjoy the retirement goal in the manner that you are dreaming of.

The next step is even more fun. Your job is to thoroughly research all the areas that you are considering moving to. You will, of course, learn how to do that by reading this book. Again, it is easy to dream of living in new and exotic locations. If you do your homework, the reality should be even better than the dream.

Good luck! And remember, a dream is only a dream, and will only be a reality with careful planning.

## Chapter 1

50 fabulous ways to get ready for retirement

You are close to the longest vacation of your life! Possibly 20, 30 or even 40 years of retirement. Sound farfetched? It isn't. A man retiring at age 54 has a life expectancy exceeding 80 years—and the number is getting higher.

Typical retirees have devoted an average of 90,000 hours of their lives to earning a living, and an even greater amount of time to raising a family. Retirement is the chance to finally change gears. Some may be looking to slow the pace, while others will feel like horses at the starting gate. At the sound of the gun they will be off and running, enjoying hobbies, socializing, traveling, pursuing new interests, starting businesses—the possibilities are endless.

However, despite the universal perception that life will be blissful once the stress of working and raising a family is gone, hard work doesn't guarantee successful retirement. Retirement requires serious planning—how and where to spend time, and how to balance money and family concerns. It always amazes me that people will spend hours planning for a one-week trip, and yet attempt retirement without careful and methodical research—research that should start years before retirement actually occurs. Unfortunately, if you fail to take into consideration a myriad of factors such as health care, money and estate planning, your retirement reality might fall short of your expectations.

We all have different attitudes about retirement—but one thing is for sure: Just as with a vacation or a dinner party, a successful retirement is only as good as the preparation behind it. With one-third of your life ahead of you, the only prudent course of action is to leave as little to chance as possible.

50 important questions to ask yourself

Would you think about driving across the country without a road map? Probably not. Without a map and some thorough planning, you are liable to come across roadblocks you will not know how to get around to maintain your course. The same can be said of retirement. Thankfully, most of the obstacles that typically arise during retirement can be easily dealt with when anticipated.

Addressing these issues now will help prevent problems later. These are the four most common obstacles to a happy retirement:

- No general plan.
- Not happy with retirement location.
- No health-related planning.
- Not enough money.

Take some time to explore the following questions, roughly grouped in four categories corresponding to the topics above. Keep in mind that there is some necessary overlap among topics—for example, issues relating to money may also affect your choice of location or your ability to provide for your health care. Highlight the numbers that you feel are most relevant to you.

What is your general plan?

1. **What's your timing?** Have you decided exactly when you will retire? Will you and your spouse be retiring at the same time? If not, have you considered how the one who retires first will handle free time while the other still works?

2. **How do you handle change?** What will the change of going from working to sudden retirement be like for you? Can you ease into retirement by either working part-time or taking longer vacations?

3. **What do your loved ones think?** Openly share your thoughts on retirement with your spouse, children and friends. If your loved ones raise strong disagreements, be open-minded to their objections.

4. **What are your dreams?** Is there something you have waited your whole life to do? Do you want a fishing boat, or maybe to buy a mobile home and tour the United States? Sketch out specific dates and the associated costs to see if it will be financially feasible.

5. **How do you currently spend your free time?** Do you baby-sit grandchildren? Are there certain activities that you can do only in the area where you currently live? How will this change if you move?

6. **How do you hope to spend your days?** Do you want to work part-time (perhaps at a senior organization)? Will you golf three days a week? Describe your ideal day, week and even year.

7. **What about your social life?** Do you currently have an active social life or do you prefer quite, solitary days? If you relocate, how will you handle leaving the security of your home and friends?

8. **What are your hobbies?** What do you enjoy doing most in your spare time? Do you hope to develop these skills and hobbies more in your retirement?

9. **Do you plan to learn new tricks?** It's never too late to learn and develop hobbies. Are you considering taking up new activities? Do you have access to the knowledge, resources and tools necessary for your new interests?

10. **Have you thought about school?** Now that you have the time, are you thinking about taking up a foreign language or a current events class?

11. **Will you join a club?** Do you plan to become active in clubs, organizations or civic groups?

12. **Could you give a little back?** Would like to get involved in helping others in their communities? Through what organizations in your new community can you volunteer your talents and services?

13. **Do you love culture?** Are you a theater, opera or dance buff? Would you prefer to live in an area that has ongoing cultural events, or would it be acceptable to drive an hour to take in a show?

14. **Do you plan to travel?** Do you plan on taking trips or joining an Elderhostel? Are you looking at areas that are close to major highways and airports? Do many airlines serve the area?

15. **Play ball!?** If you are an avid sports fan, are there plenty of sporting events in the area you are considering? Also, find out about participating in open senior sports teams.

16. **What about your parents?** How much of your time will your parents require? Will you need to assist in physically caring for them? Also, consider how it would be if you moved away from them.

17. **Suddenly single?** Although it is not a pleasant subject, you should consider how the possible loss of your spouse may affect you. If you move to a new location void of family, how will it affect you?

What do you look for in a location?

18. **Weather or not?** Weather is one of the biggest factors in considering where to live. How do you react to humid climates? Do you have problems with allergies? How about dry heat?

19. **The sea or not the sea?** You may want to live close to the sea for the beauty and serenity of it. But consider increased property and rent prices, congestion and noise.

20. **One place or two?** Often, people enjoy two locations during retirement. Consider aspects such as commuting costs, who will watch over your things and your home when you are not there, and which state you will officially reside in.

21. **How's the community?** Do you seek the communal living, clubs and planned activities of a retirement community, or a diverse, more independent community with working people and families?

22. **Do you want seclusion?** If you want to live off the beaten path, have emergency plans in order. What are the roads like in the winter? How close is medical care?

23. **What about religion?** Make sure you can find an acceptable house of worship and a religious community near your new home.

24. **What about man's best friend?** Many people acquire pets after retirement. This requires planning, too, because condominiums, mobile homes and retirement communities often do not accommodate pets.

25. **Are you wary of homeowners' associations?** Carefully check into a potential community's homeowners' association. Check their balance sheet for a history of rising fees or charging of special assessments. Be sure they are not overly intrusive. Get the facts in advance.

26. **Will you be driving?** How close are you going to be to shopping and friends? What if the time comes to choose not to drive on the freeways? Will you still have access to what you need?

27. **Do you have children living in different areas of the country?** Do you need to consider a central location to accommodate visits to and from family and friends?

28. **What might the future hold?** A place that seems charming today might not be so charming 10 years from now. How is the area you are considering planning to handle growth? What can you expect as far as congestion, traffic and pollution?

How will you take care of your health?

29. **Have you checked the hospitals?** Are they close enough? Do they offer the specialty areas you may need?

30. **What type of care is available?** In the future, finding top-notch assisted-living, continuing care and even home health-care providers will be an important consideration.

31. **What is the quality of the HMOs?** Many of us may soon be forced to use HMOs as a low-cost alternative for medical care. Make sure the area you are retiring to has HMOs that meet your medical requirements. Consider the following questions: Are the doctors you wish to use members of the HMO you can join? Does the HMO you are considering have all the coverage you need?

32. **New health insurance?** If you have to change HMOs, Medicare or supplemental insurance plans, are there any contingencies? Will you be denied coverage for pre-existing conditions?

33. **What climates are best for your health?** Often, people's health can be affected by the climate they live in. Before moving anywhere permanently, make sure it won't have a negative effect on you.

34. **What's up, doc?** Have you asked your family, friends and doctors if they can refer you to a physician in your new town? Although most places have a physician referral service, it's always better to start out with personal recommendations.

35. **Are you eating right and exercising?** Our physical decline as we get older is often caused by lack of exercise and poor eating habits. Have you changed your habits to compensate for a slower metabolism and greater risk of disease? Are you considering areas where you can incorporate physical activity into your daily regimen?

How will you make sure you have enough money?

36. **Have you started a budget?** The financial aspects of where you wish to live is a big retirement consideration. If you don't budget, you may not be able to manage expenses during your retirement.

37. **Have you figured out what your income will be?** People often think they know their income, but many fail to take all the factors into account. For example, if you plan on working during retirement, did you consider how it might reduce your Social Security benefits?

38. **How is your new state's economy?** Although you might be more concerned about your own finances than the state's, a poor state economy could affect many aspects of your retirement, such as your part-time work, real estate values and taxes.

39. **Is your prospective state more costly or less costly?** Look at all of your regular expenses. Check your current grocery prices, utilities and housing costs against those for the place you are considering.

40. **Are you aware of tax differences?** Different states have different ways to tax you. Be very mindful of this. For example, a state that does not have a property tax may tax Social Security benefits.

41. **Will you still own or retain assets in the state that you move from?** If you decide to keep real estate in both states, you will have to consider the laws of both states. If you do plan on keeping assets in both states, consider a revocable living trust as a way of titling assets.

42. **Which taxes will affect you?** In addition to state taxes, there are county taxes, taxes on Social Security income (in some states), property taxes and even death taxes. Which taxes are going to affect you?

43. **If you move somewhere part-time, where will you be domiciled?** Many states have different titling laws (such as community property as opposed to joint tenancy), so make sure your assets are titled properly in order to take advantage of all the state laws.

44. **Are you minding your business?** If starting a business is part of your retirement plan, make sure there is a need for the type of business you want to start.

45. **Do you plan to work some?** Part-time work is common during retirement. Is the area you are considering open to hiring retirees? Check the classifieds for job availability.

46. **How will the climate affect your expenses?** Hot states usually have higher air conditioning bills. Cold states often mean more costly heating bills. Factor this into your decision.

47. **Can you afford the state's attractions?** You might like Colorado because you are an avid skier, but this will do you little good if you can't afford the cost of skiing!

48. **Will you go home for the holidays?** Make sure to factor in the costs of being with your loved ones during special times of the year.

49. **Will you own or rent?** If interest rates are low and you feel property will appreciate, you might consider buying a home. Otherwise, some people are happy not to have the burden of home ownership and the corresponding chores and costs.

50. **Do you have expensive hobbies?** Don't forget to factor in the costs of your favorite activities.

What if you decide to move back home?

Just as an increasing number of people are moving to new locations, some are changing their minds and deciding to move back to their home towns. We call this the *boomerang* phenomenon. One reason is people retire to a place only to find out that life there isn't for them. Another involves people who have lost a loved one and return home for the support of their family.

To make sure moving is right for you, give it plenty of thought before you make this huge commitment. If your children start having families, will you be able to stand being away from your grandchildren? What if your spouse dies? Can you leave the familiar places and customs you know and love?

If you find a place you like, don't simply pick up and move. Visit the area several times and during different times of the year. Consider moving on a trial basis, perhaps renting for a year without making a final decision. This will not only give you time to explore the area, but it will allow the novelty of the new area to wear off. Then you can you truly tell if a certain location will work for you.

A decision to move home will require just as much thought as your original decision to move away. Before moving back:

1. Talk about it with friends and family before you make a decision.

2. Clearly determine how this will affect you financially.

3. Visit the area to which you are considering returning. Think very carefully before selling your current home or buying a new one. Consider renting.

4. Don't fool yourself. Consider how you will spend your time in the "old neighborhood." Are your memories of the good times a bit glorified?

5. If you are not happy, moving home could be a viable option. In order to be happy with this decision do thorough research.

Situations sometimes arise that require you to either move back home or somewhere else. Remember the exercises you performed when you moved to the new location? Perform them again. Review everything that is important to you—from medical needs to the type of home you wish to live in. If the new location passes your strict requirements, why not move again?

Living in the area that is right for you is among the most important aspects of a successful retirement. If you are not happy with your surroundings it will affect other aspects of your life. Make sure you are happy in your new home and you will be one step closer to the retirement of your dreams.

## Chapter 2

How much money will you need?

Will Rogers once said, "It's not the return *on* my money, rather the return *of* my money." He had a good point. It is important to not simply make more money, but rather to make your money work harder, more efficiently and smarter. The key is to maximize every dollar and to protect your savings.

Unfortunately, most Americans spend more time shopping for a car or planning for a vacation than they do planning for their retirement. Yet, no retiree wants to spend his or her last dollar—before his or her last day. The best way to beat the retirement busters is to have a plan. A very generic plan involves three key principles:

1. I want to keep control of my money. If I am sick or if I die, I don't want strangers, in-laws, courts or attorneys making decisions about my money.

2. I want to invest wisely and maximize my earning potential.

3. I want to preserve my money from unnecessary income, capital gain or estate taxes. In addition, I want to preserve my estate from long-term care costs or other forces that could use up my money.

Your pre-retirement financial checklist

Before creating your plan or investing, you need to know what is and is not important. The following checklist outlines 18 important questions you will need to answer in order to prepare financially for your retirement. I am often asked when this checklist should be done. My answer is, *right now!* This checklist should be done years before retirement and constantly updated. Please review these points and place a big "X" by all those that require *immediate* attention.

1. ____Do you know the size of your retirement nest egg?

2. ____Have you contacted your employer(s) regarding the amount vested in your pension plan(s)? Have you decided how the funds will be disbursed?

3. ____Have you contacted Social Security to determine your estimated retirement benefits? Have you informed them that you are ready to receive benefits?

4. ____If you plan to work and collect benefits after retirement, are you aware of the income limitations established by Social Security?

5. ____Are you making arrangements to move some of your liquid and equity assets into income-producing vehicles?

6. ____Once you know the sources of your retirement income, do you know how much you will need to make on your invested money to generate your required income during retirement?

7. ____Are you aware of the most current tax laws and how they will affect your retirement income?

8. ____Have you estimated your living expenses after retirement?

9. ____Have you figured out how much gross income you will need throughout retirement? This should take into account inflation, taxes and your cost of living during retirement.

10. ____Are you aware of how much it costs you to live now?

11. ____Are you cutting back on your living expenses now so that you don't carry unnecessary debts into retirement?

12. ___Have you reviewed your insurance policies to determine which policies can be restructured or canceled?

13. ___Do you have estate-planning documents such as a will or a living trust? Further, do you have an understanding of the laws pertaining to inheritances, taxes and probate?

14. ___Does your spouse, child, relative or close friend have power-of-attorney for you in case you become incapacitated? Does this include power-of-attorney for both financial and medical concerns?

15. ___Does your spouse, child, relative or close friend know where important records are kept? (For that matter, do *you* know where all these records are?)

16. ___Have you figured into your budget higher medical costs and less coverage from Medicare? Have you included home health care or long-term care?

17. ___Do you know where you want to live after retirement?

18. ___Have you discussed your retirement needs with a certified financial planner?

5 steps to simplify your financial retirement plan

Now that you have completed the checklist, you are ready to begin your retirement plan. Remember, your goal is to control, maximize and preserve your retirement. I once had a friend tell me he would like to spend his last dollar on his last day. The problem is, we don't know when that day will come. We need a strategy. Here are the five steps to simplifying your financial retirement plan:

1. Determine your net worth.

2. Determine your income needs during retirement.

3. Take inflation into account.

4. Don't forget to consider taxes.

5. Prepare for the eventual costs of health care.

Retiring is like opening night at the theater: There are no more dress rehearsals and you can't do it over. When you were working, if you made a mistake and spent too much money or lost money on an investment, you could simply make more money. When you retire, it is more difficult to make more money.

Before retiring, you need to know your assets and liabilities. When you review assets, you start to get a sense of which assets can be converted to income and which assets will be left to appreciate for years to come.

In this section, you'll find out how much you'll have to live on each year, how much to reinvest and how much to save. Armed with this information, you and your financial advisors can develop the best strategy to ensure that your money will stand the test of time. Ultimately, the goal is to accurately determine the retirement lifestyle you can afford.

Step 1: Determine your net worth

Your net worth can be figured many different ways. The first thing to look at is the value of your combined assets, including your home, investments, pension(s) and savings. At the same time, you must appraise your liabilities, such as mortgages and installment loans. When you subtract what you *owe* from what you *own*, this is your net worth.

Here's how to prepare your personal net worth statement.

1. Cash reserve assets

Add up your cash or near-cash resources such as checking accounts, savings accounts and money market funds. These are your "liquid" assets because they can be liquidated quickly without penalties.

It's also possible to include the cash value of a life insurance policy, as well as a bank Certificate of Deposit (CD). These are liquid to the extent that it's possible to tap into them in an emergency. However, doing so may result in penalties for early withdrawal. Or, as in the case of borrowing from the cash value of a life insurance policy, it may trigger interest charges on the value of the loan.

Between 15 and 20 percent of your total assets should be liquid, and there should be enough ready cash to cover your living expenses for a minimum of three months, preferably six.

2. Equity/retirement assets

Generally, the most valuable asset in your portfolio is the equity in your home. But ideally, you will also have a combination of other investment assets, including stocks and options, mutual funds, taxable and tax-free bonds, T-bills, annuities, investment property (not your residence) and/or equity in a business.

Retirement assets also include IRA/Keogh Plans, 401(k)s, vested pension plans, employee savings and stock option programs. In tandem, these should represent 50 to 60 percent of your total assets. Keep in mind that if you do sell off investment assets, this will more than likely trigger tax liabilities and possible penalties for early withdrawal.

To establish the values of these assets, ask your insurance agent, stockbroker, real estate agent and certified financial planner for assistance. You can also refer to recent price quotes in the newspaper. Although establishing values for real estate, limited partnerships and vacation timeshares is complicated, for the purpose of this exercise, it's acceptable to place the value at the price you paid.

Finally, to determine the value of your 401(k) or other company benefit programs, ask your employee benefits department to provide the calculations.

As for personal property, such as clothing, furs, jewels, cars and furniture, appraise the value by estimating how much money an item would generate if it were sold today (only if you intend to liquidate).

Once you have compiled a list and the value of your assets, it's imperative to examine which ones can be converted into cash and/or income-producing investments. In essence, you need to figure out where you can generate more than 50 percent of your annual "salary."

3. Liabilities

Liabilities are the outstanding balances on your mortgage(s), cars, installment loans and credit cards. They also include your projected state and federal tax bill. Normally, your liabilities should represent no more than 30 percent to 50 percent of your total assets. In retirement, however, I urge clients to carry as light a load as possible with respect to debts. They add significantly to monthly living expenses at a time when income may be fixed and limited.

In addition, the interest on car loans, credit cards and installment loans is no longer deductible. And with banks charging 18-percent interest (in Florida, it can be up to 21 percent), but only paying out 3 to 4 percent on savings, it doesn't take an accountant to tell you that installment debt is a raw deal.

(If you don't have a current net worth statement, fill out the worksheet on page 23.)

Step 2: Determine your income needs during retirement

Retired people usually need at least 60 percent annually of what they earned during their last year of employment. However, I recommend calculating retirement needs at a rate of 75 percent to allow for unexpected circumstances. You must consider all facets of retirement revenues when considering your income needs during retirement. See Figure 2-1 on page 24, which shows an example of how your income sources might be broken down. Chapter 3 will provide advice on how to make the most of your income during retirement.

Your net worth statement

Assets

Cash reserve assets

checking accounts/cash $_____

savings accounts _____

money market funds _____

Certificates of Deposit _____

life insurance (cash value) _____

Equity/retirement assets

time deposits (Treasury bills) $_____

stocks and options _____

retirement savings (IRAs/Keoghs) _____

annuities (surrender value) _____

pensions (vested interest) _____

profit-sharing plans _____

collectibles _____

house (market value) _____

other real estate/limited partnerships _____

business interests _____

personal property (automobiles, jewels, etc.) _____

loans owed you _____

other assets _____

Total assets $_____

Liabilities

mortgage or rent (balance due) $_____

auto loan (balance due) _____

credit cards _____

installment loans _____

annual tax bill _____

business debts _____

student loans _____

brokerage margin loans _____

home equity loans/second or third mortgages _____

Total liabilities $_____

(Subtract total liabilities from total assets to determine your net worth.)

Total net worth $_____

Figure 2-1: Sources of income

Source of income	% of total income
Pensions, annuities, gifts, dividends, interest and other investments	50.0%
Social Security	25.0%
Sale of assets, home equity, personal savings	11.0%
Earnings (part-time work)	10.2%
Supplemental security income and public assistance	1.8%
Other	2.0%

How far will your retirement dollars go?

Once you've created a net worth statement and added your Social Security and pension benefits to the mix, you'll finally know the size of your nest egg. The next pressing matter is figuring out how long these funds can be expected to last.

To estimate the strength of your retirement account, look at the total amount of funds you're starting with. Refer to Figure 2-2 to see how many years the money will last.

Figure 2-2: How much money can you withdraw?

Size of nest egg	If you withdraw this amount each month for the following number of years, you'll have "0" balance					If you withdraw this amount each month, you won't be touching the nest egg at all
	10 yrs.	15 yrs.	20 yrs.	25 yrs.	30 yrs.	35 yrs.
$ 15,000	$ 174	$ 134	$ 118	$ 106	$ 99	$59
$ 25,000	290	224	193	176	166	118
$ 50,000	580	448	386	352	332	285
$ 80,000	928	718	620	564	532	467
$100,000	1,160	896	772	700	668	585

These figures are based on 7% net annual growth (after taxes).

As this chart clearly illustrates, even a fairly large sum of money can be used up quickly in retirement. If you're like most individuals, you may find an alarming gap between what you think you will need for a comfortable retirement and the amount of money you will actually have on hand, given your current savings plan. The worksheet on page 26 is designed to help you assess what your personal income needs will be, including steps to help you determine your retirement income gap—the difference between the monthly income you will need and the amount you expect to receive. The calculations assume that you will retire at age 65 and will require 75 percent of your preretirement income to retire comfortably.

Figure 2-3: Inflation factor

(based on an annual percentage rate of 4%)

Age in 1995	25	30	35	40	45	55	60	61	62	63	64
Year of retirement at age 65	2035	2030	2025	2020	2015	2005	2000	1999	1998	1997	1996
Inflation factor	4.80	3.95	3.24	2.67	2.19	1.48	1.22	1.17	1.12	1.08	1.04

Figure 2-4: Projected Social Security benefits

To use this table, find your age and the figure closest to your earnings in 1995. These figures will give you an estimate of your monthly retirement benefits at various ages. Or call the Social Security Administration at 800-772-1213 and ask for an estimate of the amount you will be receiving at retirement, and how the benefits are figured. Ask specifically for your *Personal Earnings and Benefits* statement. Chapter 3 will offer further discussion of Social Security benefits.

Worker's age in 1995	Worker's family	Your earnings in 1995				
		$15,000	**$24,000**	**$36,000**	**$48,000**	**$62,700 or more**
40	retiree only	$587	$802	$1,040	$1,174	$1,338
	retiree / spouse	286	391	507	572	652
50	retiree only	594	809	1,057	1,186	1,323
	retiree / spouse	291	397	519	582	650
55	retiree only	604	821	1,077	1,193	1,308
	retiree / spouse	298	406	532	589	646
62	retiree only	626	850	1,111	1,203	1,287
	retiree / spouse	313	425	555	601	643
65	retiree only	622	845	1,100	1,179	1,248
	retiree / spouse	311	422	550	589	624

Step 3: Take inflation into account

Many of us don't take inflation into consideration. I never understand why not. *Inflation is a retirement buster.* Many of you might be thinking inflation is low. Perhaps this is true now, but in light of the fact that most things in the world are cyclical, inflation will probably go up. Plus, inflation may be considerably higher for retirees, because the goods that retirees spend money on—housing, health care, travel and leisure—are all highly inflationary items.

Your personal income needs

A. Estimate the monthly income you will need at retirement:

1. Enter current monthly income	$_____
2. Multiply by 75%	$_____
3. Multiply by inflation factor (from Figure 2-3 on page 25)	$_____
= monthly retirement income needed	$_____

B. Estimate the actual retirement income you will receive:

1. Enter monthly Social Security benefit (from Figure 2-4 on page 25)	$_____
2. Multiply by inflation factor (from Figure 2-3 on page 25)	$_____
= inflation-adjusted Social Security benefit	$_____
3. Add estimated monthly company retirement benefits	$_____
4. Add anticipated monthly income from your IRA and other investments	$_____
= monthly retirement income received	$_____

C. Calculate your retirement income gap:

1. Enter monthly income needed (**A**)	$_____
2. Subtract monthly income received (**B**)	$_____
= estimated monthly retirement gap at age 65	$_____

D. Monthly investments needed to fill your retirement income gap before you reach age 65:

If your **monthly retirement income gap** is approximately:					
$500	$1,000	$2,000	$3,500	$5,000	$10,000
Age	Then set aside these **monthly payments** now:				
25	$24.57	$49.14	$98.28	$171.99	$245.70	$491.40
30	35.81	71.61	143.23	250.65	358.07	716.15
35	52.86	105.73	211.45	370.04	528.63	1,057.26
40	79.61	159.22	318.45	557.28	796.12	1,592.24
45	123.80	247.60	495.20	866.61	1,238.01	2,476.02
50	203.47	406.93	813.87	1,424.27	2,034.67	4,069.33
55	372.60	745.20	1,490.40	2,608.19	3,725.99	7,451.98
60	900.81	1,801.61	3,603.22	6,305.64	9,008.05	18,016.10

It is critical to know what will happen to your money when inflation is entered into the equation. Certainly, economic fluctuations of any sort will affect finances, but inflation is a particularly cruel adversary. Consider that if the long-term inflation rate is 6 percent, living costs will double approximately every 12 years. Another indicator of inflation's harm is purchasing power. To give you a sense of this, take a look at the impact inflation will have on your monthly retirement income. This table is based on a monthly income of $1,000 and an annual inflation rate of 6 percent.

Figure 2-5: Impact of inflation on monthly retirement income

Year	2000	2005	2010	2015	2020
Amount needed to have the purchasing power of current $1,000	$1,338	$1,791	$2,397	$3,207	$4,292
Current $1,000 will be worth	$747	$558	$417	$312	$233

Step 4: Don't forget to consider taxes

Taxes could take up to 90 percent of your dollar! It's true. Let's break it down. There are four main taxes:

1. Income taxes.
2. Capital gains taxes.
3. Estate taxes (death taxes).
4. State taxes.

Income taxes

Income taxes can eat up 30 to 40 percent of your income during retirement. It will be critical to use every applicable tool to lower income taxes. Once you retire, deductions get even lower. Here are a few suggestions:

1. **Maximize deductions.** Many wonderful ways exist to maximize deductions. For example, if you purchase a special therapeutic bed because your doctor recommended it, that might be deductible, or if you are caring for an older parent, that is also a potential deduction.

2. **Consider tax-free bonds.** In many cases, a tax-free bond or bond fund could give you more income after tax than a taxable bond. But take into consideration investment risk, maturities and several other factors. Regardless, it is a tool that should not be forgotten.

3. **Consider tax deferral.** If you have your retirement baskets properly laid out, a portion will be placed in long-term growth vehicles for the future. This is money for which you should not pay current taxes. Consider whether tax deferral would benefit you.

4. **Plan your estate in advance.** Numerous advanced estate-planning tools exist to increase deductions. Among the more popular are family limited partnerships and charitable remainder trusts.

5. **Only invest for income what you need in income.** Often, people will invest a large majority of their assets in income-producing vehicles, such as stocks that pay dividends, or bonds that pay interest. Consider only investing an amount in income-producing vehicles that you actually take the income on. If you are reinvesting the rest of the income, although you are not using it, you are still receiving income in the eyes of the IRS. Consider investing in income-producing vehicles through a tax-deferred account such as an IRA or variable annuity.

States with no state income tax

- Alaska
- Florida
- Nevada
- South Dakota
- Texas
- Washington
- Wyoming

Capital gains taxes

Although we tend not to think about it, capital gains can play a major role in our decision to sell assets such as homes and stocks.

Be very sure you understand how capital gains could affect the proceeds you receive from the sale of any of your assets. For example, consider the differences in the following scenarios:

A man and wife own a home as joint tenants. The home has significantly appreciated since they purchased it. The husband now dies and the wife decides to sell the home to be closer to her family. Will she pay capital gains taxes? Yes. In the case of joint tenants, if one tenant dies, only half of the property (the half of the deceased) is stepped up for tax purposes. Therefore, the other half of the property will show a capital gain upon sale which, in turn, will be taxed.

Now, suppose I alone own a home. The home has significantly appreciated since the time I purchased it. When I die, the new tax basis will, again, receive a step-up to the market value of the property at the time of my passing. Assuming the property is worth $200,000 when I die, and that is what my children inherit the property for, they could conceivably sell the property for $200,000 and pay no property tax.

It is important to note that most assets step-up, not just real property. Stocks and other assets are included.

1. **Section 121.** If you have lived in a home for three out of five years and are over the age of 55, you can reduce the capital gains tax you owe by requesting your Section 121 benefit, which allows you to offset $125,000 worth of gain. Note that you and your spouse are only eligible for one election between the two of you. For example, if you marry a person who has previously used his or her Section 121 benefit, then you cannot use it. Section 121 is a tremendous benefit, because it could work toward reducing your capital gains tax significantly on a personal residence. Assume you purchased a home for $50,000 and that you sell it for $100,000. You could utilize Section 121 (assuming you are not restricted from doing so) and pay no capital gains tax.

2. **Gift appreciated property.** If you plan on making gifts to other people such as children or grandchildren, why not give gifted property as opposed to cash? If you gift appreciated property, you can shift the tax burden to someone who is in a lower tax bracket.

3. **Create a charitable remainder trust.** This is an advanced estate-planning tool. As with all financial planning strategies presented in this book, consult with professionals before creating one. The concept is to create a charitable trust with a qualified charity. Deposit an asset into the trust that is highly appreciated, say a building. Sell the building and pay no capital gains taxes. Convert it to income and draw the income that is generated, or a portion of it. By doing so, you reduce the size of your estate and potential estate taxes, avoid capital gains taxes and receive deductions on your taxes for the amount of the gift.

   The downside of a charitable remainder trust is that you reduce the size of your estate for the heirs. To counter this, establish an irrevocable life insurance trust and fund it with an insurance policy owned by the trust, paid for by another entity. The theory is that the proceeds will go to your heirs directly, bypassing your estate and potential estate taxes.

4. **Take advantage of community property laws if applicable.** If you live in a community property state (Arizona, California, Idaho, Louisiana, Nevada, New Mexico, Texas, Washington or Wisconsin),

and are married, you can place your assets in community property. Unlike joint tenancy, upon the first passing of either spouse, you can sell an appreciated asset, such as a home or stock, and avoid capital gains taxes. If you keep your assets titled as joint tenants, the surviving spouse will have to pay a portion of the appreciation in estate taxes.

5. **Set up a special revocable living trust.** If you can't take advantage of the benefits of community property, you can avoid the capital gains taxes on assets held with a spouse by setting up special revocable living trusts—one for the husband, one for the wife. Some of the assets will be owned by the husband's trust and the others by the wife's trust. When either one dies, there should be a full step-up in tax basis for the assets in either trust. If an individual owner (or the sole owner of a revocable trust) dies, the property value is stepped-up for tax purposes. Whatever the property is worth upon death (or six month later if you use the alternate valuation date) is the new tax basis. This equates to no capital gains tax if the beneficiaries sell the property for the value of the property upon death.

Estate taxes (death taxes)

So you were one of the individuals who thought that just because you died, the tax collector would leave you alone. Wrong! In fact, the highest tax in the land is the death tax. After your estate has reached a value, currently $600,000, death taxes are incurred at 37 percent and quickly rise to 55 percent! Although the tax rate technically begins at $10,000, the current law allows for an individual to have an estate equal to $600,000 before the taxes begin. Assuming you have a $599,000 estate, you would not owe estate taxes. The next dollar over $600,000 is taxed at 37 percent and increases from there.

So how is your estate calculated, when you pass on, to determine your net worth for estate tax purposes? Of course the net value of all your assets, including IRAs, homes, cars and jewelry is part of your estate. One asset many people overlook as part of an estate is the proceeds (death benefit) of a life insurance policy. If you are the owner and the beneficiary of a life insurance policy, the proceeds are calculated into your gross estate when you die. One possible solution is to consider having another person or entity (such as a trust) own your life insurance. Life insurance comprises three main parts: the owner, the insured and the beneficiary. The owner of the policy does not need to be the insured. The potential downside of owning the policy is that it is considered an asset of the owner, and though the death benefit will pass to the beneficiary tax-free, it will be figured into the gross value of the owner's estate.

States with estate death taxes

- Indiana
- Kentucky
- Louisiana
- Maryland
- Massachusetts
- New York
- Ohio
- Pennsylvania
- South Dakota

Strategies to help reduce or eliminate potential estate taxes

1. **Survivor/bypass trust or revocable living trust.** Otherwise known as an A/B trust, this trust will allow a husband and wife individual $600,000 exemptions, thereby enabling the estate to be worth $1.2 million before any estate taxes are owed.

2. **Advanced estate-planning entities.** Many entities exist to help reduce the size of your estate, while discounting the value of the gift to reduce gift taxes. The more popular entities are: irrevocable trusts, family limited partnerships and personal residence trusts.

3. **Gift assets.** Every person is allowed to gift $10,000 per year, per person. You can gift to anyone you want. Theoretically, if you and a spouse have a son, for example, you could give that son $20,000 per year without owing gift taxes or filing a gift tax return. Any amount over $10,000 per person, per year, and you would either have to pay gift taxes (the same tax rate as estate taxes) or you would have to use part of your $600,000 exemption.

   The benefit of gifting is that if you are planning to give assets away when you die, you may be able to avoid death taxes by gifting the money while you are still alive.

4. **Carefully review your net worth.** If your net worth includes assets such as life insurance, consider moving those assets out of your estate. Gift the life insurance to a child or to an irrevocable trust. Be careful to follow all the rules for doing so to make certain the insurance will not be figured into your gross estate later. As with all the strategies discussed, it would be prudent to contact a professional such as a CPA, attorney or certified financial planner (CFP).

Before deciding to move, it is critical to consider the tax laws of the state you are considering. The following charts will help you compare other taxes that can be incurred depending on the state you live in.

States with no property tax relief for seniors

- Florida
- Louisiana
- Minnesota

- Oregon
- Vermont
- Wisconsin

States that tax Social Security benefits

- Colorado
- Connecticut
- Iowa
- Kansas
- Minnesota
- Missouri
- Montana
- Nebraska

- New Mexico
- North Dakota
- Utah
- Rhode Island
- West Virginia
- Vermont
- Wisconsin

Step 5: Prepare for the eventual cost of health care

I know we don't like to think about it. We would like to believe that health care is not our problem and that our families will take care of us. Unfortunately, the vast majority of us will need health care. And the burden of cost will be ours to bear.

Entitlement spending has been cut and we are living longer. Prolonged illnesses are the norm. Without planning for health care, the chance of going broke as a result of health care expenses is quite high. In fact, after the age of 65, most of us will need to spend time in a care facility or utilize home health care. The amount of aid we would get from Medicare or our HMO is slim. Medicare pays less than 2 percent of all long-term care claims.

4 ways to avoid going broke as a result of long-term care costs

1. **Don't postpone planning.** Learn what Medicare will pay, what your supplemental insurance will pay, and then go about figuring out how you will "plug the leaks." I suggest reading the two books I have written

on this issue, the *Comprehensive Guide to Social Security and Medicare* and *Safeguard Your Hard-Earned Savings.*

2. **Consider a long-term care insurance plan.** The younger you are, the more affordable a long-term care insurance plan is. However, the costs are still high, so don't worry about getting the Cadillac plan. Four years of home health care and long-term care coverage should be adequate. Make certain the insurance company is reputable and pays policyholder claims.

3. **Be careful of health maintenance organizations (HMOs).** As our entitlements are reduced, more of us are opting for lower premium HMOs. Don't be surprised if you get what you pay for. When considering an HMO, ask specific questions, such as: If your primary care doctor does not agree that you need to see a specialist, how can you bypass your primary care doctor? What treatments are not covered? Sometimes, a clause in the contract states that no experimental treatments are covered. What does "experimental" mean, exactly?

4. **Create medical documents, such as a durable power of attorney and a living will.** A durable power of attorney for health care will allow you to appoint someone to make medical decisions in the event of your incapacitation. A living will, also known as a directive to physicians, allows you to indicate whether you wish to be kept on life-support systems and whether you wish for any heroic measures to be taken to sustain your life.

## Chapter 3

Making your money work so you don't have to

Now that you've determined *how much* money you'll need, let's take a look at the possible sources of that money, as well as strategies for making the most of it. The success of your retirement requires a delicate balance, similar to a three-legged stool. If one of the legs were not there, the stool would not stand. The same can be said for retirement. There are three main components that are needed to keep your income sufficient and maintain your standard of living:

- Social Security.
- Pensions.
- Personal savings.

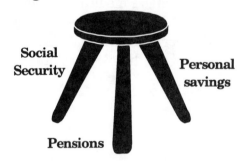

Social Security

Personal savings

Pensions

The first leg: Social Security

The first question to address is: Should you take Social Security benefits at age 62 or 65?

If you take benefits at any time prior to age 65, you will receive less than 100 percent of the benefits you would have received had you waited until the age of 65. The earliest you can take benefits is at 62, at 80 percent of what you would have received by taking benefits at age 65.

Despite the reduction in the amount you receive, it often makes sense to take benefits at age 62. If you invest the reduced amount at age 62 for those three years, you could build up a tidy sum of money. If you start drawing on that investment money at 65, the amount of income added to your normal Social Security check might equal more than the full 100 percent of benefits you might have received by waiting until age 65.

It is also important to know a few other specifics about your Social Security retirement income. First, if you earn money from a job and are under the age of 70, your Social Security income will be reduced, although there are strategies for lowering the reduction.

Furthermore, if you simply have too much income during retirement, your Social Security income will be *taxed*—up to 85 percent of your benefits! Techniques can be implemented to reduce this tax as well. I highly recommend that you read another of my books, *Comprehensive Guide to Social Security and Medicare* to learn more about your Social Security benefits.

The second leg: pensions

Recently, I heard about a lady who worked for a company for 15 years. Upon retirement, the lady eagerly awaited her pension check. With the arrival of her first month's check, she found it to be a monthly income of roughly $4. As difficult as this is to imagine, it is not uncommon.

Without delay, get a copy of the summary plan for your company's pension program, and read it carefully. Have a financial planner or the benefits manager of your personnel department review it as well. Find out how much you have in the company plan now, as well as an estimate of what will be paid out to you at retirement. By law, you can review this report once a year.

When you look over the summary, check the math. Often, an employee is short-changed, especially on the interest he or she should have earned. Be clear on how much interest you were supposed to earn and what method of calculation is used. You can then have a financial expert review your plan to ensure it is correct.

Although every pension plan is different, all are designed to insulate your employer from serious losses. In other words, when employees leave or are laid off before meeting certain minimum commitments (for example, number of years of service), it's the employee who loses out—not the company.

Another frightening possibility is that the plan may not be completely safe. Recent studies by the Pension Benefit and Guarantee Association show that many pension plans are underfunded. This could potentially cause problems as serious as a drastic reduction in your monthly check or a reduction in health benefits.

If you have a Keogh SEP, 401(k), profit-sharing program or other retirement fund, work with your financial planner or accountant to establish current values.

Regardless of the type of retirement fund you have, the two biggest considerations before benefits actually begin are: 1) What are the tax implications, and 2) What do I do with the money?

None of us wants to pay one penny more in taxes than absolutely necessary. This is especially true when a taxpayer retires and has to make decisions about allocating the funds sitting in a pension plan. It's no wonder that when clients come in, they throw their retirement plans at me as if the documents were hot potatoes. Instinctively, they know that they're holding onto the largest financial decisions they'll ever have to make.

It's a shame that after 30 to 40 years of taxing labor, we're deathly afraid of how much money we've accumulated. But the fear is justified. Every year thousands of taxpayers make strategic errors in removing and disbursing retirement funds. Don't make a rash decision on how to take your retirement benefits. Give it a lot of thought and study many months before you have to make a decision.

The pension check: Annuity or lump-sum payment?

A pension check represents both your earnings over the past decades and the compounded interest on those earnings. This income has been flourishing without any income tax impeding its growth.

Once you withdraw the funds, you must pay income tax. And the amount you pay will be affected by whether you take it all out at once or withdraw it a little at a time. You now need to decide whether to have your company make out a single check for the entire "lump sum" or to annuitize your pension benefits. If you choose the second option, you will keep your money in the company pension plan in exchange for having them mail you a check for a set amount every month, either for your lifetime, your spouse's lifetime or for a guaranteed number of years. If you are given a choice between taking a lump sum or annuitizing your pension benefits, you should be aware of the pros and cons of each.

The decision to have your pension fund annuitized or to take a lump sum can be a difficult one. There are four main factors to consider in making your decision:

1. How do you feel about managing a lump sum?

2. If you take an annuity payout, how certain are you that your company will outlive you?

3. What is a better economic benefit to you—taking a lump sum or annuitizing? In other words, if you take the lump sum and invest it, what interest rate do you need to earn to beat what you otherwise would receive from the annuity payout.

4. What are the tax ramifications in each case?

Benefits of annuitizing

The single biggest advantage of having your pension funds annuitized is that you don't have to worry about managing your money, because the company will guarantee that you'll receive a set amount every month. This is especially an advantage to those who are not competent money managers. Annuitizing could also be advantageous from a tax perspective, because you are only taxed on the interest portion of your income and not the principal.

Common annuity payout options

Maximum monthly payments. Opting for the maximum monthly allowance means you agree that upon your death, payments to your beneficiary will not continue regardless of whether you received one payment or 100 payments. By law, your spouse also has to consent to this in writing.

Lifetime payments to a beneficiary. Should you choose to name a lifetime beneficiary, one who will receive payments after your passing, your beneficiary may receive benefits in one of four ways:

1. The same monthly allowance you received for life.

2. Three-fourths of your monthly allowance for life.

3. Half of your monthly allowance for life.

4. A quarter of your monthly allowance for life.

Once the beneficiary is named, and once your retirement starts, you cannot change the beneficiary.

Guaranteed payments for certain periods. A formula is used to determine the exact amount you can receive each month based on the length of the guarantee. An advantage of this payout option is that the annuity will continue to be paid, regardless of whether you're alive. One scenario would be if a husband retires and elects a 20-year annuity. If he dies in five years, his wife will continue earning the money. If she dies in 10 years, the subsequent beneficiaries will receive the annuity income until the end of the term (in this case the 20th year).

Take an income option that best suits your needs. You might take the highest monthly check, but if you die, the income stops. If you are married, you can elect to take a slightly smaller check to ensure that when you die your spouse will still receive a check.

What is the tax on the annuity payout?

The payments you will receive from an annuity will be partially tax-free, because part of the annuity payout is considered a return of your original principal, assuming this was not pretax income. The rest is interest and the interest is taxable.

The amount you are taxed on an annuity payout is determined by three main factors: the amount the annuity earns, your life expectancy and the amount of principal the annuity represents.

Use the following example: Mrs. Smith is 75 years of age, with a life expectancy of about 12 years (144 months). She has an annuity with a current value (present value) of $10,000. The monthly payout is $105. Of that, $69.44 is considered return of principal and will be free of income tax.

Here's why: If you take Mrs. Smith's 144-month life expectancy and multiply that by the $105 monthly income that the annuity promised her, that will equal $15,120. The present value of the annuity is $10,000, which means the interest paid equals $5,120. Divide the interest of $5,120 by the life expectancy of 144 months and it will equal $35.56 per month. That represents the interest portion of the total monthly payment of $105, with the remaining $69.44 representing the principal.

Disadvantages of annuity payout

There are several possible disadvantages of annuity payout.

1. **Lack of control.** Deciding to annuitize your pension benefits is an irrevocable decision. Once you retire, you immediately start to receive checks. So, even if a better investment opportunity comes along five years after you begin receiving checks, you cannot buy into it using your pension benefits. Not having access to the principal also means you can't benefit from certain favorable tax advantages. You can't control how the assets are invested, nor can you pass the assets on to your heirs. For some people, this lack of control is a deterrent.

2. **Inflation.** Another disadvantage of annuities is inflation. Would you want to receive a pension check for the same amount 20 years from now as you are receiving today? You probably wouldn't.

3. **Low rate of return.** The income payout or annuity options that your employer gives you probably do not offer a great return on your money. At best, they will represent competitive interest rates. Chances are that you could make more money investing that retirement money.

4. **No guarantees.** If your company goes out of business, is the pension guaranteed? If the company is sold, is there a guarantee that the new company has to honor the previous company's pension?

Benefits of lump sum distribution

The biggest reason to opt for a lump sum distribution is flexibility. You can invest however and wherever you want. You now have the opportunity of investing to possibly increase your wealth, make money if inflation rises or increase your budget. Of course, these same conditions can backfire.

How to take a lump sum distribution

If you decide to take a lump sum distribution, remember one thing: *Don't take your lump sum directly*. Even if you plan on spending the money, do not instruct your employer to make the check payable to you. Rather, set up a self-directed IRA. Consult your certified financial planner with any questions on how to do this. If you take pension benefits directly, three possible taxes exist.

1. **20-percent withholding tax.** Recently, a bill was passed stating that if you do not transfer proceeds from a qualified pension plan directly to an IRA, you will incur a 20-percent withholding tax. To avoid this tax, tell your employer to transfer the assets into a *self-directed IRA.* You can then withdraw the money and avoid the withholding tax.

2. **Penalty tax.** If you are under the age of 59½ and withdraw money from an IRA, you will most likely be subject to a 10-percent premature withdrawal penalty.

3. **Income tax**. If you withdraw money from either a pension plan or an IRA, if the amount you withdraw is pre-tax money, it will be subject to income taxes in the year you take out the money. Thus, if you withdraw a big pension plan, you could face a great deal of income tax. If, however, you transfer the pension into an IRA and don't withdraw income from an IRA (until required), you will be able to continue deferring the taxes.

How to create an IRA. Creating an IRA is quite simple. You can choose a bank, brokerage firm or an independent IRA custodian that will allow you the flexibility of depositing your money in a variety of investment vehicles of your choice.

Be careful of IRA fees. I see many retirees making the mistake of opening up several IRAs because they believe they need one for each mutual fund or stock they invest in. This practice is very costly and confusing. First of all, most companies with which you have an IRA will charge you a fee. Secondly, the statements and paperwork you will receive from each company will only cause more unnecessary confusion.

Consider finding an IRA custodian that will charge one low flat fee. Make certain they do not charge exit fees or fees per asset you hold.

The third leg: personal savings

Deciding how to invest your personal savings, the third leg of the three-legged stool, is the most commonly neglected component of retirement planning. As discussed in the previous chapter, the first priority is to figure out how much you will need to retire comfortably. Once you know how much you need, you can figure out the interest rate you need to earn (the required rate of return). If you have not already figured out that number, go back to Chapter 2 and complete the worksheet on page 23.

The key to investing: a solid plan

There is no doubt in my mind that the only time anyone should invest is *after* a concrete plan is formed—after you know how much you need to make and after you know the risk level you can accept.

Begin by reviewing what we have already established. It is essential to know what interest rate you need to make on your money in order to have it grow enough with inflation, provide ample income and furnish you with a reserve should you need it later. Once you know the interest rate, or what is called your *required rate of return*, you need to earn that return with the lowest risk possible.

The best plan is a well-diversified plan. Prudent diversification will help you earn your desired return with the least amount of risk. Given that, see how you would answer the following question:

Q: Which of the following two plans would make you the most money?

Plan #1: A broadly diversified plan that invests in many types of investments, such as international, value, small cap, treasuries, bonds, real estate investment trusts and cash.

- or -

Plan #2: A traditionally diversified plan that diversifies your investments in three different accounts, including an index mutual fund based on the S&P 500, Treasury bills and cash.

A: Plan #1. Although the average investor might conclude that the second plan will make the most money, historically the first plan makes the most as a result of the further diversification. The more diversification, the less concentration you have in a given market segment, so if one market segment does poorly, you have less money allocated to it and you have less to lose. Also, further growth comes from some of the nontraditional investment vehicles.

Here's another, perhaps even more important, question.

Q: Which of the above plans is less risky?

A: Surprisingly, the answer is Plan #1 again. Because the investments are spread among areas that fluctuate at different times, this plan is actually less risky and less volatile.

The following pie chart is a sample for a properly diversified plan.

Figure 3-1: Sample asset allocation

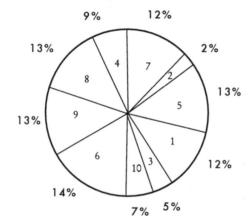

1. International Equities	5. Large Value Stocks	9. Municipal Bonds
2. Venture Capital/L.P.	6. Fixed Annuities	10. Corporate Bonds
3. Emerging Equities	7. International Bonds	
4. Large Growth Stocks	8. Real Estate	

Your investment pyramid

The image of the great pyramids has been likened to the ultimate "towers of power." With an unwavering base, they are pillars of strength that can support the weight of whatever has been thrust upon them.

A model portfolio should also have the strength of a pyramid. It should be constructed in such a way that risks and rewards are completely balanced from top to bottom. The soundest, safest investments support the hierarchy, while those that can potentially reap the greatest rewards, but also have the greatest risks, are positioned at the top. Here is what the ideal investment pyramid looks like at retirement:

Figure 3-2: Investment pyramid

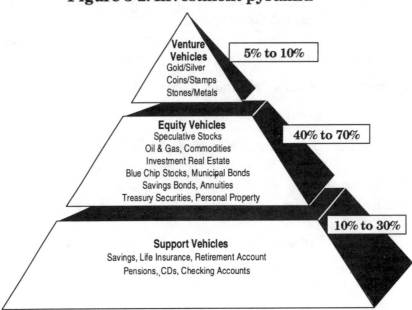

Venture Vehicles
Gold/Silver
Coins/Stamps
Stones/Metals

5% to 10%

Equity Vehicles
Speculative Stocks
Oil & Gas, Commodities
Investment Real Estate
Blue Chip Stocks, Municipal Bonds
Savings Bonds, Annuities
Treasury Securities, Personal Property

40% to 70%

10% to 30%

Support Vehicles
Savings, Life Insurance, Retirement Account
Pensions, CDs, Checking Accounts

Pyramid power at retirement

In financial terms, the investments at the bottom represent your principal. They are safe, but cannot be expected to do combat with inflation because their yields are low. The riskier investments at the top represent your capital, which can be reduced or lost altogether through faulty decisions or a downturn in the economy. Conversely, the risky investments have the potential to generate strong returns that will create growth while holding inflation and overtaxation in abeyance. You'll see, however, that those that have the greatest level of chance are squeezed in at the apex, indicating that they should be given the least amount of power.

Every portfolio needs the combined strengths of risks and rewards.

Turn the pyramid upside down

Once your investment pyramid is in place, ready to support your retirement, turn the pyramid upside down. Your "pyramid power" is now going to be called your "funnel force."

By turning your investments upside down, your risky investments will now appear at the bottom of the funnel, and will then be the first ones to be liquidated during your retirement. Your principal investments, those that are safest, are at the top and will be the last to go.

Figure 3-3: Inverted pyramid: the funnel

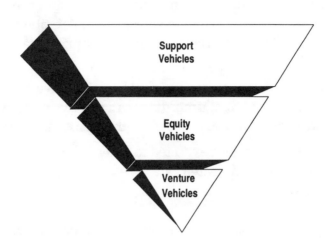

It is helpful to think of your investments sitting in a funnel because a funnel allows you to control the *flow*—in this case, the flow of funds—simply by opening and closing the valve at the bottom as needed. Ultimately, you'll be able to regulate the rate at which your investments are discharged.

What happens to the funds that come through the funnel? They will get poured into a *master account*, which is an interest-bearing checking account that allows you to monitor all your income. I'll explain in the following sections.

How to evaluate specific investments

Before actually allocating your savings to specific types of investments, it's important to have a basis for evaluating and assessing investment vehicles. We have already discussed how critical it is to measure your risks carefully and to maintain the most diversified portfolio possible. But after that, how can you be sure that you are making the right decisions?

There are numerous factors that should be considered, as well as questions that must be addressed. The following are specific aspects you should consider when selecting investments.

Yield. What are the anticipated returns and what guarantees are built in for the future? To what extent will the yield be reduced by commissions, service charges and fees? What is the annual tax liability?

Safety. Is the principal safe? What kind of market conditions will cause the values to decline? Can you bail out before the losses are substantial?

Insurance. Is either your yield or your principal guaranteed? Are they FDIC- or MBIA-insured?

Liquidity. Will you have immediate access to your money, or will you be locked in? For how long? What are the penalties for early withdrawal? How easy is it to get to your money? Are phone and wire transfers available? Will you have check-writing privileges? Are there any limitations?

Terms. How long are you committed for? Will you have any problems holding on for that amount of time? If so, can you live with the penalty for early withdrawal? Are you clear on all the terms and conditions?

Inflation. Is this investment expected to at least keep pace with inflation? What is the anticipated rate of return annually and over the lifetime of the investment?

In terms of viable investment options for retirees, combinations of the following should provide sound financial security:

- **Bank instruments.** Passbook savings, money market accounts, Certificates of Deposit.

- **Government securities.** U.S. Treasury bills (T-bills), U.S. Treasury bonds and notes, government mutual funds.

- **Equities.** Mutual funds, stocks (blue chip, growth & income, balanced).

- **Debt instruments.** Corporate bonds, bond funds.

- **Tax-advantaged investments.** Municipal bonds.

- **Insurance products.** Annuities, single pay life insurance (variable single pay).

- **Income-producing real estate investments.** Real estate limited partnerships, REITs, direct ownership.

The master account: Structuring your portfolio so you can live on your assets

We've just gone over the most important principles of investment diversification and risk tolerance, and we've reviewed the most common and desirable investment vehicles for retirees. Now it's time to look into structuring your portfolio so that you have the proper balance of investments.

There is a strategy for staying on top of your financial affairs. Let's call it the *master account;* it is the companion to your funnel force. The master account is a very simple idea, and it works—no matter how little or how much money comes in every month.

To start a master account, open an interest-bearing checking account. Use it to deposit every single check you get, whether from Social Security, tenants, pensions, CDs, annuities or the lottery. Think of this account as the "Ellis Island" for your money. Nothing gets through the gates until it's been signed in and admitted through the system. How it gets dispersed is another matter. But before anything else happens, the money has to sit in the master account.

From there, funnel money into a separate checking account that you use to pay bills, then dump the surplus into a savings account or reinvest it.

The benefits of a master account

The best reason to set up a master account is so that you'll keep track of the total amount of your income. Also, because some checks will be small, by pooling your resources, there will be a lump sum large enough to pay bills and reinvest. In effect, it will serve the same purpose as depositing a monthly paycheck.

The other important benefit is that you'll receive a monthly bank statement, which will give you an accurate reading of where your finances stand. With all of your deposits and debits listed in one place, you'll know immediately how much of a surplus you have—or that your debits are exceeding your deposits. Then it becomes your "damage control" statement, a warning to reexamine your budget and cut back.

If you don't start out with a master account, your income will be scattered. It may result in mass confusion and possibly the inability to take care of certain financial obligations.

The bottom line

The single biggest fear of retirees is running out of money. They are deeply concerned about illness, death, loneliness, separation and other emotionally charged issues as well, but these are nothing compared to the anxiety of becoming dependent on family, friends or the government for financial survival.

With the proper amount of planning, investing and budgeting, this fear can be eased. The key is to commit to knowing what you have to start with, putting the money in safe places where it can grow and provide income and monitoring it closely so that you can control the reins.

Moving 101: How to hold on to your possessions and your sanity

How can a civilization that invented microwave ovens, fax machines and computers not have a clue about how to make moving a snap? Nothing would be better than relocating without packing up a household of goods and trucking them cross-country. Unfortunately, the only way to get there is the old-fashioned way, using men and their machines. To help you fly through the ordeal with the greatest of ease, Chapter 4 offers a short course called "Moving 101." Anyone who reads this is an automatic "A" student.

In addition, call the government agency that oversees long-distance movers, the Surface Transportation Board, at 202-927-5585, for consumer information.

What does it cost to move?

Moving to the next town can be a costly proposition; moving cross-country will certainly give one pause. It's why the first question a mover is asked is "What's this gonna cost?" The trouble is that it's like asking the price of a new car. Do you want a luxury sedan or a mini-van? With which options? The questions continue until the salesperson arrives at a number—and then the negotiating begins. So it goes with moving.

The best way to get a fix on moving costs is to be aware of all the charges that can be factored into your estimate. The three most important variables include:

1. **Distance.** Movers must first determine the approximate mileage between your new and old homes by mapping out the shortest distance between point A and point B on highways that are useable for truck travel. Obviously, the longer the haul, the more costly the move.

2. **Weight.** As prices are based on every 100 pounds moved, it's best to ask at least three movers to "guess-timate" the size of your shipment. Don't be surprised by wide variations as each mover refers to its own "Table of Weights" when developing an estimate.

3. Time of year. All movers reduce their prices, but how extensively depends upon the time of year. Reserving a carrier between May 15 and September 30 (when 50 percent of all moves take place) almost guarantees that discounts will not be as deep. In fact, you can count on paying a 10-percent premium for moving during the busy season. What's more, service is often slower because of peak demand.

The following section will give you a brief overview of these services and introduce you to others that can be factored into your estimate. As you'll see, hiring a long-distance mover is much like dining at a restaurant where everything on the menu is *à la carte*. And similar to good waiters, movers like to make tempting, but costly, suggestions. The key to negotiating a fair price is being aware of the different ways they earn their keep.

Basic transportation—and more

Basic transportation includes use of the mover's truck, use of labor to move goods out of your house and load them on to the truck, driving to your destination and reassembling everything in your new home.

If your move originates and/or terminates in a high-density area, there will be additional transportation charges (ATCs). In congested locations, movers will face traffic jams, construction delays, inaccessible entrances, etc. To compensate for lost time, expect to pay up to a few dollars more per 100 pounds.

Liability insurance

By law, every interstate moving company must assume some liability against damage or loss when agreeing to move your household goods. Unfortunately, the liability they assume is at a minimum, compelling the shipper to purchase additional coverage. And even with that, the mover is protected from you almost as much as the other way around. In other words, the coverage actually limits the mover's liability if it loses or damages your shipment.

The good news is that full replacement value insurance, the maximum protection you can buy, is relatively inexpensive and worth every penny.

However, before you purchase any insurance from the mover, *check your homeowners policy*. It's possible your belongings are already covered during a move, alleviating the need for additional coverage.

If you do buy liability insurance from the mover, know your rights. By law, the mover must provide you with a copy of your policy (or a formal receipt) at the time of purchase. Without proper documentation, the moving company can be held fully liable for any claim that is a result of its negligence.

Here are the four types of available coverage:

1. Released value protection. This protection allows you to "release" your goods to the mover without making a declaration as to their value. If there is loss or damage, the mover's only obligation is to pay you up to 60 cents per pound per article. In other words, weight is the only consideration when calculating a reimbursement.

For example, if the mover breaks a seven-pound lamp, it won't matter if it was a priceless heirloom or a bargain from a local odd-lot warehouse, the maximum you would receive is $4.20. The mover does not charge for released value protection, but you know what they say about getting what you pay for.

2. Minimum declaration. Making a minimum declaration means that you believe your total shipment is valued at $1.25 per pound. If your goods weigh a total of 5,251 pounds (the average weight of an interstate move), the mover would be liable for losses or damage up to $6,563. The cost of this "added protection" varies among moving companies, but averages $5 to $7 for every $1,000 in liability.

The major difference between this protection and "released value" coverage is that the reimbursement is based on the depreciated value of the item. To settle the claim, the mover refers to a depreciation schedule for thousands of household items. Now, if the mover breaks your favorite lamp, you'll be reimbursed based on the age of the item. A three-year-old lamp that originally cost $145 might entitle you to $75. Keep in mind that all of this is contingent on proving the mover's *negligence*.

3. Lump sum declaration. If you determine that your shipment is valued at more than $1.25 per pound you can declare a specific dollar value, or a "lump sum declaration." In other words, you can declare that your 5,251-pound shipment is actually worth $10,000. The mover will charge you the same $5 to $7 per $1,000 of declared value, you'll just pay proportionately more.

4. Full value protection. Full value protection or replacement cost coverage is exactly as the name implies. You'll receive full replacement value if, because of the mover's negligence, items are damaged or lost and cannot be totally restored. The cost of replacement coverage averages $8.50 to $10 per $1,000 of valuation, but can be less if you agree to take a deductible. As with any insurance policy, the higher the deductible, the lower the premium.

Full value protection is the absolute maximum protection you can buy and the only coverage we recommend. The industry reports that 25 percent of all residential moves result in claims for losses or damages, so good liability coverage is critical.

Packing services

There are two types of services to consider. The first is *purchasing* packing materials—dishpacks, wardrobes, cartons, etc. Say what you will about movers, they have sturdier boxes than the local liquor store. For your fragile and valuable items, they are worth the money.

The second packing service is *labor*. You can opt to have the mover pack up your old residence and/or unpack your cartons at your new home.

We believe there are two very important reasons to having the movers do your packing: time and money. You can avoid weeks and possibly months of standing, bending, folding and rolling valuable breakables into newspaper when the movers are in charge.

Secondly, if the mover does the packing and there is damage, they can't blame you. Otherwise, when the boxes are marked "PBO" (packed by owner), it allows the mover to argue that damages were the result of a bad packing job (and they may be right).

The cost for packing services will vary according to your home county's current labor rates. Packing should represent approximately 10 percent of your total costs. Again, it is well worth the money!

More extras that add to the cost

In addition to all of the cost factors mentioned, there are numerous others that may be included in your estimate. Here is a brief rundown:

New York to Florida. With many more people moving south than north, some movers charge more per 100 pounds to compensate for an almost certain empty van on the return trip.

Apartment buildings. As many retirees move into high-rise condos, it's important to know that movers get added compensation for dealing with elevators, stairs and long carries (when the apartment is far from the stairs or elevators and/or the goods must be brought to a loading dock, etc.). In theory these efforts are time-consuming and tiresome, which is how moving companies justify charging more.

Storage. Unfortunately, storage can be a necessary evil even with the most advance planning. Often, people are forced to move from their home or apartment before their new home is ready for occupancy. In other instances, unexpected delays because of illness or travel arrangements prevent people from meeting the van when it arrives. If so, the mover has the right to place the entire shipment in storage. It happens more often than you think, so build storage costs, even for a few days, into your moving budget.

The average cost to store a 5,000-pound shipment for one week at a local storage warehouse can run $350 or more, depending on the part of the country (assume everything will cost more in the East). It is generally more costly to store your goods in the mover's warehouse than a local storage facility.

Expedited service. If you absolutely have to be at your new home by a certain date, the mover can speed up the amount of time it takes to make the trip. Ordering an expedited service is costly, but possible.

Exclusive use of a vehicle. If you do not want your shipment commingled with other shipments for fear of delays or problems associated with sharing space, you can request that your shipment be the only one on the van.

Guaranteed service on or between agreed dates. If you need to know the exact day the mover will show up on either end, you can arrange for guaranteed service, which provides that your shipment be picked up, transported and delivered on agreed-upon dates. If the mover fails to deliver as scheduled, you'll be entitled to compensation.

How to keep moving costs way down

If you are like most, after reading the numerous expenses incurred in a move, you are probably planning the biggest garage sale of your life! And no doubt you should. By now you've realized that you can control two of the three factors that drive costs through the roof: time of year and weight. Remember, the real expense is in *what* and *when* you move, not *where* you move.

Because you'll be paying for every 100 pounds shipped, use this proven method for moving the minimum. It calls for giving as many items as possible one of the following designations:

Sell it; donate it; toss it; give it away.

Getting estimates

Movers will provide two types of estimates: binding and nonbinding. A nonbinding estimate allows the mover to give you a best guess as to the cost of your move, but does not bind the company to that price. Ultimately, you could pay more and in some cases, less. This is because the final cost will be based on actual, not estimated, weight.

If, for example, you get an estimate but then get rid of furniture, books, etc., up until moving day, you could end up paying less. Conversely, if you told the mover not to include two beds and your lawn furniture in the estimate and later change your mind, your final bill will likely be higher than your estimate.

One would think that the problem with nonbinding estimates is that movers might "lowball" a bid to get the job. Yet a recent Interstate Commerce Commission (ICC) study found that long-distance movers overestimated prices as often as they underestimated them. Human error is most often the reason. Regardless of which type you settle on, the estimate must be put in writing in the order for service (initial commitment) and the bill of lading (final contract).

Hiring a mover

Given the number of personal circumstances that could affect your move, coupled with the different services you can opt for, it's vitally important to shop the competition. Prices will vary greatly, particularly in the off-season. It's also possible that some movers will offer discounts to seniors, veterans and members of organizations, such as AARP or Lions Club. However, and this is a big however, by no means is the cheapest quote necessarily the best quote. Make your final decision based on price as well as other important criteria. This includes:

Personal recommendations. Do you know anyone who used the mover and was pleased with the service?

Overall treatment. How were your questions and concerns addressed when you spoke with representatives of the company on the phone and in person?

Overall appearances. An industry spokesman highly recommended that you make an on-site inspection of the mover's offices and warehouse to confirm that it's a legitimate, well-run operation.

Better Business Bureau reports. It never hurts to check with your local BBB to see if there are complaints on file against the mover.

Independents vs. national carriers

Most people prefer to buy brand names because a recognized company stands behind the product. It's no different with movers. When a truck is pulling off with your valuable possessions, there's a certain comfort level in choosing an Allied or United Van Lines over Joe's Fast Moving Company. Also, if there are problems with an agent affiliated with a nationally known company, at least there's a home office to intervene.

More importantly, "common carrier" agents are under contract to meet certain performance requirements. They are not intentionally going to make mistakes or jeopardize their standing.

On the down side, common carriers may not have as much price flexibility, because they split their profits more ways than do independent movers.

As for the independents, many have excellent reputations and can provide very personalized service. In addition, they may be more affordable. Should you decide to work with a local independent mover, an on-site inspection is very important. In addition, you'll want proof that the firm is authorized by the Interstate Commerce Commission to move goods out of state. If it's not licensed, your liability coverage is null and void.

Keep in mind that neither the size of the moving company nor claims that it is "bonded," "certified" or "insured" are any guarantee of reliability. However, if you see that the mover has a CMC designation, for Certified Moving Consultant, you know that at least it passed arduous tests and complies with the highest standards set by the industry.

Tips for a smooth moving day

Here are some important suggestions for orchestrating an uneventful but speedy moving day:

- Read the bill of lading (your contract) carefully before you sign it. Keep it on your possession until your shipment is delivered, charges are paid and all claims are settled. It is your only proof that the mover is working for you.

- Make sure the bill of lading confirms the proper liability coverage you purchased when signing the order for service.

- Join the movers as they take inventory, the process of inspecting each item being shipped. Watch to see which items they designate as scratched, dented, etc. If you disagree, argue your case right there.

- If you got a nonbinding estimate and are concerned that it may be way off, you can observe the official weighing of the van by going to the scales with the mover immediately before and after the shipment has been loaded. This will confirm or deny your suspicions.

- Make sure you have worked out payment arrangements with the mover in advance. If your estimate was nonbinding, there's always a chance that the final cost will be higher. By law, you are obligated to pay the estimate plus 10 percent of the remaining balance at the time of delivery. You can usually request 15 to 30 days to pay off the balance.

- Before unloading gets into full swing, take your copy of the inventory sheets and check the condition of the items as they're pulled off the van. If you see damage, or notice something is missing, alert the mover and ask him to mark it on both your copy and the mover's copy of the inventory. This is called "taking exceptions."

Filing claims against the mover: 10 tips

1. It's not necessary to unpack and inspect all the cartons before signing the inventory sheet, but you should indicate any obvious damage to the carton's exteriors.

2. Concealed damage discovered at a later time can be reported. Leave the damaged items in the carton until the claims adjustor inspects the damage, or the claim can be denied.

3. Claims for loss and damage can legally be filed within nine months of delivery, but don't delay. The longer you wait, the easier it will be for the mover to claim the damage occurred after the move.

4. Movers must acknowledge claims within 30 days and settle them within 120 days.

5. Claim forms must be submitted with the bill of lading, so be sure to keep it in a safe place.

6. All claims must be submitted in writing, but first find out if there is a special hotline number for instructions on filing claims.

7. Don't be afraid to be overly detailed in your claim report. Settlements are often delayed because more information is needed.

8. List lost and damaged items separately, along with estimates for repairs or replacement. You may be asked to justify a replacement cost.

9. If you incurred any hotel or other living expenses caused by the mover's delays or losses, add that to the claim forms.

10. Finally, understand that the actual dollar amount you receive from the mover will be determined by the representative who does the claim inspection. In anticipation of getting the kind of adjustor who assumes your furniture was shabby to begin with, it's helpful to know that you can take your case to arbitration (at no cost to you) if you are unhappy with a settlement.

Wrapping it all up

Retiring and relocating will be one of the most highly emotional times in the lives of you and your spouse. It is a time of beginnings and endings. Of intense feelings and infinite details. It's not necessarily a time when clear thinking is an easy achievement. That's why you should be kind to yourselves by organizing a smooth, uneventful and perfectly boring move. There will be enough excitement without it!

Arkansas	1. Fayetteville
	2. Hot Springs Village
Arizona	3. Prescott
	4. Scottsdale
	5. Tucson
California	6. Palm Springs
	7. San Diego
	8. Santa Barbara
Colorado	9. Colorado Springs
	10. Ft. Collins
Florida	11. Boca Raton
	12. Daytona Beach
	13. Fort Lauderdale
	14. Fort Myers
	15. Gainesville
	16. Jacksonville
	17. Kissimmee/St. Cloud
	18. Melbourne
	19. Naples
	20. Ocala
	21. Sarasota
	22. St. Petersburg
Georgia	23. Clayton
	24. Savannah
Idaho	25. Coeur d'Alene
Indiana	26. Bloomington
Maryland	27. Annapolis
Missouri	28. Branson
	29. Columbia
Minnesota	30. Rochester
Nevada	31. Las Vegas
	32. Reno
New Mexico	33. Las Cruces
	34. Santa Fe
North Carolina	35. Asheville
	36. Raleigh
Oregon	37. Eugene
	38. Medford
South Carolina	39. Charleston
Texas	40. Austin
	41. Brownsville
	42. Kerrville
	43. San Antonio
Utah	44. Provo
	45. St. George
Vermont	46. Burlington
Virginia	47. Charlottesville
Washington	48. Bellingham
	49. Olympia
	50. Sequim

50 Fabulous P

ces to Retire in America

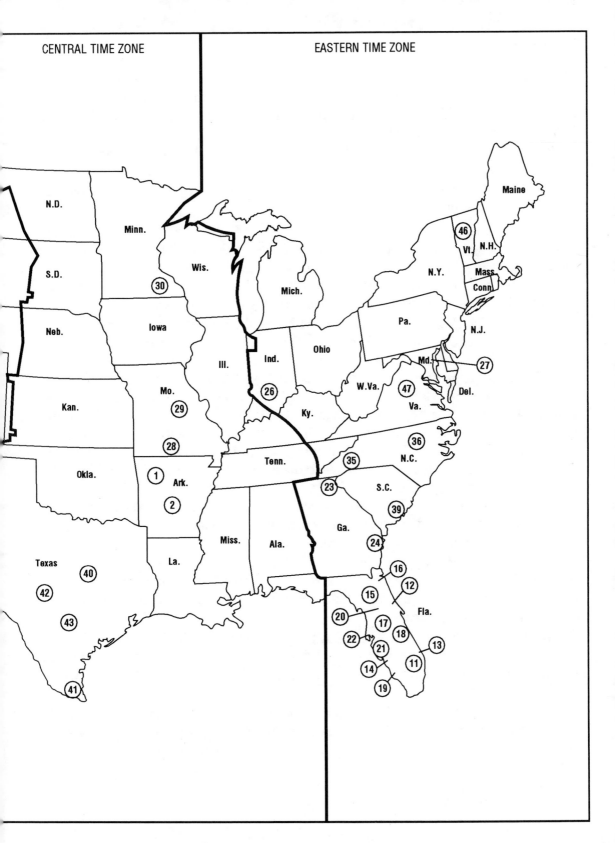

CENTRAL TIME ZONE

EASTERN TIME ZONE

N.D.

Minn.

S.D.

Wis.

Maine

46
Vt. N.H.

N.Y. Mass
Conn

Neb.

Iowa

30

Mich.

Pa.

N.J.

Kan.

Mo.
29

Ill.

Ind.
26

Ohio

W.Va.
47

Md.
27

Del.

Va.

28

Okla.

1
Ark.

Tenn.

35

23

N.C.
36

S.C.

39

2

Texas
40

La.

Miss.

Ala.

Ga.
24

42

16

12

43

15

20

17

Fla.

22

18

41

21

13

14

11

19

How to use the area profiles

Area profiles are presented in alphabetical order by state (from Arizona to Washington), then city. "Fast Facts," the handy cross-reference beginning on page 307, will help you locate them in alphabetical order by city.

The easy-to-use format of each profile allows you to read the entire summary, or quickly refer to topics of greatest interest. The following is a brief discussion of some of the terms and associations mentioned in the profiles (because of space limitations, we have explained only the most common ones here).

ACCRA: Using the latest American Chamber of Commerce Researchers Association report, we compared living-cost differences in nearly 300 urban areas. The figures reflect expenses for a household with two adults (one a salaried executive) and two children, but what's most relevant is how much more or less they spent to purchase the same products and services in that city versus another.

Climate: The Weather Channel, the 24-hour all-weather satellite network, was our exclusive source of climatological data. Everything in a community is subject to change except the weather, so be sure you're looking at areas where the climate suits you. Those with heart trouble or arteriosclerosis respond well to mild climates, while arthritics respond best to warm weather. Hay fever sufferers get relief from dry climates. **Elevation:** The higher the elevation, the thinner the air and the more difficult it can be to breathe, especially for those with heart conditions or respiratory problems. Also, for every 1,000 feet of increased altitude, the temperature is decreased by an average of 3.5°F. **Relative Humidity,** when combined with high temperatures, puts stress on the human body. If the temperature is 88 and the relative humidity is 78%, it will feel like 106. It can cause fatigue, accelerated heart rates, higher blood pressure and, in serious cases, heatstroke and sunstroke. (Consult a doctor before relocating if you have a medical condition.)

JCAHO: The Joint Commission on Accreditation of Healthcare Organizations, a private, nonprofit group, sets standards for health care facilities and evaluates their performance before rendering an accreditation. Hospitals achieving this designation offer high-quality patient care.

Median Housing Price: A median price indicates that half the houses in the market are selling for less than the median, half are selling for more. Average prices, however, are a more accurate reflection of what people are paying and generally run higher.

Utility Costs: The average monthly bills for gas and electric service are an excellent way to compare costs between locations. Actual bills, however, will vary substantially based on square footage, number of people, number of appliances, personal habits, unusually hot or cold weather, method of heating/cooling, etc.

1. Fayetteville, Arkansas

Nickname: Land of Opportunity
County: Washington
Area code: 501
Population: 51,100
County population: 128,800
% of population over 65: 11.2
Region: The Ozarks (NW Arkansas)
Closest metro area: Little Rock, 192 mi.
Median house price: $88,600
Best reasons to retire here: Clean environment, low crime, scenery, college town, affordable living, great outdoor recreation.

Fayetteville at a glance

Fayetteville is situated on the western edge of the Arkansas Ozarks, a place of great natural beauty and outdoor recreational opportunities. Four mild seasons combine with the region's spectacular topography, offering residents a multitude of outdoor activities in a breathtaking natural setting. Sport fishermen come from around the country for bass and trout, and the region is also a hunter's mecca. Rock climbing, rappelling, camping and hiking are popular. Cyclists and runners are challenged by the steep climbs and deep valleys that make up the surrounding terrain. The White River, Buffalo River, Mulberry River and other waterways provide canoeists and kayakers with year-round activity. And as home to the University of Arkansas, the cultural and educational offerings are equally impressive; seniors travel from around the country to attend the Elderhostel. (Also, check out the Senior Walk—the sidewalks of the University that bear the names of more than 100,000 graduates dating back to the class of 1876.) The Walton Arts Center is the focal point for regional arts and community activities, offering dance, drama, jazz and Broadway touring shows. As the financial and business hub of the Ozarks, Fayetteville offers the region's top medical facilities. Property taxes are low, and so is the cost of living. The employment opportunities are good, and the economy is thriving—making Fayetteville an all-around great place to be.

Possible drawbacks: Although Fayetteville retains a small-town feel, growth in the area has been explosive. Land values have increased substantially in recent years because of the influx of Fortune 500 businesses. Yet property is still very affordable compared to many other regions of the U.S.

Climate

Elevation: 1,257'	Avg. high/low:	Avg. inches		Avg. # days precip.	Avg. % humidity
		rain	snow		
Jan.	48/26	2.7	-	9	74
April	70/47	4.9	-	11	65
July	89/70	3.8	-	10	66
Oct.	75/49	3.5	-	8	66
YEAR	70/47	48.0	12	-	-
# days 32° or below: 97			# days 90° or warmer: 78		

What things cost

Overview: ACCRA's statistics indicate prices are nearly 4 percent below the national average overall, with groceries, transportation and utilities 2 to 10 percent below. Housing costs are 16 percent below the national average, but utilities are nearly 12 percent higher.

Gas company: Arkansas Western Gas Co., 501-521-5400. A $75 deposit and $10 connect fee are usually required. All-gas energy averages $120 monthly.

Electric company: Two electric companies serve the area. Southwestern Electric Power Company, 501-521-3000. Deposits, which may be waived with a letter of credit, equals two months' average service at the address. Ozarks Electric Cooperative Corporation, 501-521-2900. Applicants must pay a $20 membership fee and $20 records fee. Deposit may be required. All-electric service runs $200 to $225 monthly.

Phone company: Call Southwestern Bell, 800-990-2300. New customers must pay $50 with first month's bill. Connect fees typically run about $40. Basic service is approximately $26.

Water and sewer: 501-521-1258. Average charges are $35.

Cable company: Call TCA Cable TV, 501-521-7730.

Car registration, license: New residents must obtain a driver's license within 30 days, for $14 (renewed every four years). Exam fee: $5. Registration fees range from $17 to $30.

The tax ax

Sales tax: The State of Arkansas has a 4.5 percent sales tax, but Washington County and the city each add 1 percent for a total of 6.5 percent. Prescription drugs are exempt.

State income tax: There is a graduated income tax rising to 7 percent on taxable income above $25,000.

Retirement income: The first $6,000 of private, federal and state pensions are exempt, and Social Security income is exempt. There is a progressive schedule of death taxes based on federal taxable estate, less $60,000. State death tax is a credit against federal estate tax.

Property taxes: Taxes are based on 20 percent of assessed value. Taxes are $47.30 per $1,000 of valuation, with property assessed at 20 percent of market value. Tax on an $88,600 home is $838 a year. Residents age 62+, with an income of less than $15,000 may qualify for a homestead property tax refund up to $250. Property tax assessor, 501-444-1506.

Local real estate

Overview: The housing market in this area is quite strong in terms of both supply and demand. Taxes are on the rise, but remain very fair compared to other states. Interest rates have been at a desirable market range since 1993, bringing many buyers into the market. Many retirees are drawn to the Carly Meadows in the Beaver Lake area.

Median price for a single family home: $88,600.

Average price for a 3BR/2BA home: $72,500 for a starter home, ranging up to $300,00 for a luxury home.

Average price for a 2BR condo: New: $134,000; resale: $120,000.

Common housing styles and features: Most homes are built of brick, in traditional, southern colonial or split plans.

Rental housing market: Apartments and houses are readily available, although there is scarcity in the $1,000 to $2,000 range. With the large student population from the University of Arkansas, you may find the rental market is competitive in late spring and summer, with students seeking apartments for the fall.

Average rent for a 2BR apartment: $385 to $585 monthly.

Communities or developments most popular with retirees: Butterfield Trail Village is a life-care retirement community offering a range of housing from studio apartments to two-bedroom cottages. The Garden at Arkanshire is also popular.

Nearby areas to consider: Springdale, Bella Vista, Rogers, Beaver Lake area.

Earning a living

Business climate: Fayetteville has seen explosive growth in recent years, underscored by a jump in population of nearly 33 percent. It's estimated that nearly 1,000 people move into Northwest Arkansas each month. It's important to note that this growth has been planned and sought after, as Fayetteville's proactive economic development community has worked diligently to attract new business and industry. Major businesses include the University of Arkansas, Campbell Soup Co., Tyson Foods and Levi Strauss.

Help in starting a business: The University of Arkansas Small Business Development Center, 501-575-5148, offers training programs and seminars annually, along with free, one-on-one counseling and a resource library. The SBDC offers support to entrepreneurs concerning the Small Business Administration guaranteed loan programs. The Genesis Business Incubator, 501-575-7227, provides space and support services for new technology businesses, and it houses the active Fayetteville chapter of SCORE. Counseling for new businesses is also available through the Fayetteville Chamber of Commerce.

Job market: Jobs are available, particularly part-time work. Several temporary agencies may be able to help, as it's estimated that nearly 2 percent of the total work force in Northwest Arkansas is temporary. You'll find yourself in competition with students for low-wage part-time positions. Arkansas Employment Security Department, 501-521-5730. The unemployment rate for Arkansas is 5.6 percent; for Fayetteville, 2.4 percent.

Medical care

Health care costs in Northwest Arkansas are about 11 percent below the national average, which is another reason why Fayetteville is such a popular retirement area. Washington Regional Hospital is a fully integrated health-care system providing a wide range of services. Areas of excellence include a comprehensive cancer care program and expanded cardiology services. Washington Regional has more than 20 different service locations throughout Fayetteville and Northwest Arkansas, including Fayetteville City Hospital, a facility focusing on the elderly. The hospital offers a seniors program called 55PLUS, a membership program that offers health education services and more. Call 800-422-0322. Other area hospitals include NWA Rehabilitation Hospital, 501-444-2200, and Veterans Administration Medical Center, 501-444-5000. Physician's referral, 501-443-8598.

Crime and safety

The crime rate in this area is extremely low, even with the presence of a major university. The police attribute the nominal crime to the lack of an interstate running through town; gas station hold-ups and bank robberies are hard to pull off when there's no fast getaway. There are also many active neighborhood watch groups in the area. Washington County averages 36 crimes per 1,000 population countywide, with approximately 50 crimes per 1,000 population in Fayetteville itself. The crime rate has dropped in recent years by as much as 20 percent—at the same time that the population has grown 12 percent.

Continuing education

The Fayetteville Adult & Community Education program, 501-444-3041, offers adult classes through area public schools. Topics offered include business, trade and industry, personal enrichment and computers. Most courses run eight to 10 weeks, and they're always interested if someone would like to teach a course! The University of Arkansas Continuing Education department hosts an Elderhostel program, 800-952-1165, hosting seniors from other states and countries. Courses run for one week and are offered from March through December.

Services for seniors

The Council on Aging, 501-443-3512, serves seniors in Washington County through the Community Adult Center, which offers classes in exercise, painting and ceramics. Activities include potlucks, bowling, billiards, lectures, dances, music performances and day trips, especially to Branson to see nationally recognized musical entertainers. AARP can be contacted through the Council on Aging offices. For information on the Retired Senior Volunteer Program, call 501-521-1394.

Getting around town

Public transportation: There is limited local bus transportation on University of Arkansas transit routes and tourist trolleys. Both are free.

Roads and highways: I-40, US 71, 471 and Scenic Highway 12. US 412 connects Arkansas' northwest corner to Oklahoma.

Airport: Fayetteville Municipal Airport (Drake Field) is served by five carriers.

Let the good times roll

Recreation: The Ozark National Forest is an ideal camping spot (it's as popular as some of the hotels). Beaver Lake is a prime attraction, stretching over 500 miles of shoreline, making it the perfect spot for boating, fishing and water sports. Lake Fayetteville Park and Lake Wedington offer nature trails, picnic pavilions and swimming. Devils Den State Park and the Boston Mountains are two ideal choices for camping, hiking and fishing (great rustic cabins and campsites). The city is building a network of bicycle trails, bicycle lanes and hiking lanes, many of them long abandoned railroad corridors.

Culture: Fayetteville is an historic landmark, the site of the largest Civil War battlefield west of the Mississippi. Preserved homes and other remains from the mid-1800s dot the landscape. The Walton Arts Center offers a full season of drama, dance, music and Broadway shows, along with educational opportunities. It is also home to the Joy Pratt Markham Gallery (exhibits change every four to six weeks). The 70-piece North Arkansas Symphony presents a series of classical and pops concerts.

Annual events: Springfest in April is an old-fashioned event featuring food, crafts, parades, music and games. The Hogeye Marathon brings world-class runners to a challenging course. The June Music Festival of Arkansas offers three weeks of concerts and workshops by nationally acclaimed jazz and classical artists. The Chile Pepper Run in August is one of the region's premier running events. During October's Autumnfest, Fayetteville celebrates with three days of music, parades and special events. The Lights of Ozarks festival runs from November through January.

When the kids come: The Fayetteville Youth Center has a gym, outdoor pool, game rooms and other activities. Try whitewater tubing on the famed Buffalo River, one of four in the country identified as a national river. The Air Museum at Drake Airport is a showcase for local aviation history. The University Museum features the history of Arkansas, dinosaurs, Indian artifacts and a glass collection. Other attractions include Pivot Rock and Natural Dam, Castle at Inspiration Point, Cosmic Cavern, Onyx Cave and Blue Spring.

For more information

Chamber
Fayetteville Chamber
    of Commerce
P.O. Box 4216
Fayetteville, AR 72702
501-521-1710

Newspapers
Northwest Arkansas Times
212 N. East Ave.
Fayetteville, AR 72701
501-442-1777

*Morning News of Northwest
    Arkansas*
203 N. College
Fayetteville, AR 72701
501-444-6397

Realtor
Mary Bassett
Dykes Bassett Mix
    & Associates, Inc.
3263 N. College
Fayetteville, AR 72703
501-521-5600
Fax: 501-521-5698

2. Hot Springs Village, Arkansas

Nickname: The Other Hot Springs
County: Garland, Saline
Area code: 501
Population: 12,000
County population: 79,978
% of population over 65: 60
Region: Central Arkansas
Closest metro areas: Hot Springs, 22 mi.
Average home price: $138,000
Best reasons to retire here: Four glorious seasons, low taxes, vast array of recreational choices, private, secure community.

Hot Springs Village at a glance

Hot Springs Village is one of the most extraordinary planned communities anywhere in the nation. Situated on 30,000 acres in the heart of the Ouachita Mountains and Diamond Lakes region, there is none more beautiful or enticing. Every last detail has been thought through—from the six championship golf courses to the Coronado Natatorium and Fitness Center, from lavish lakefront homes to the magnificent grounds (25 percent of the Village will remain green). Every home faces trees, lakes or is on a fairway. Another benefit of living here is that Arkansas is one of the least expensive places to live in the country. An independent survey of 135 retirement spots showed Hot Springs lower than 85 percent of the others. Property taxes for a $100,000 home average just $700 a year. The amenities are impressive—six private, manmade lakes (including 950-acre Lake Balboa where the fish are so big, people don't have to lie about their catches), tennis, 120 clubs and organizations, shopping, a large community center, two pools and more. Outside the Village, you're in the heart of one of the most spectacular mountain and lake-filled regions in the U.S. Just 22 miles from Hot Springs, the only National Park within a city, culture and attractions can be found, as can the thermal springs that give the city its name. Residents also enjoy thoroughbred racing at Oaklawn, one of the nation's premier tracks. Sure, your friends and family may think you're crazy to come to Arkansas, but guess who'll have the last laugh?

Possible drawbacks: There seem to be three big reasons why people leave: There isn't enough hustle and bustle, they miss their families and they require a level of medical care not available here.

Climate

Elevation: 558'	Avg. high/low:	Avg. inches		Avg. # days precip.	Avg. % humidity
		rain	snow		
Jan.	53/30	4.8	-	9	75
April	73/50	5.2	-	11	67
July	93/70	4.0	-	9	68
Oct.	77/50	3.2	-	7	68
YEAR	73/49	52.0	5	-	-
# days 32° or below: 66			# days 90° or warmer: 78		

What things cost

Overview: According to ACCRA, the cost of living is nearly 8 percent below the national average. Savings are greatest in the area of housing costs, 25 percent below average. Utilities and groceries are 17 percent and 7 percent above respectively, while health care is 24 percent below.

Electric company: Contact ENTERGY, 800-330-1379. Deposits waived with letter of credit. No hook-up charge. Hot Springs Village is a total electric community. Average monthly bill: about $100.

Phone company: Southwestern Bell, 501-324-4999. Deposits: $60; waived if credit is good. Connect fee: $39.70; basic monthly rate: $19.

Water and sewer: Property Owner's Association Department of Public Works, 501-922-0200. Meter deposit: $50; no connect charge. Sewer service: $9.78 monthly.

Cable company: Resort Cable Television, Inc., 501-624-5781.

Car registration, license: New residents must obtain driver's license within 30 days. Driver's license; $14; renewed every four years. Exam fee: $5. Registration fees are $17 for cars 3,000 lbs. or less; 3,001 to 4,500 lbs., $25; 4,501 lbs., or more, $30. Department of Motor Vehicles, 501-624-4472.

The tax ax

Sales tax: The State of Arkansas has a 4.5 percent sales tax, but Garline County adds .5 percent and the city of Hot Springs adds 1.5 percent for a total of up to 6.5 percent. Drugs and medical services are exempt; food away from home is taxed at 9 percent.

State income tax: There is a graduated income tax rising to 7 percent on taxable income above $25,000. There is no deduction for federal income tax paid.

Retirement income: The first $6,000 of private, federal and state pensions are exempt, and Social Security income is exempt. There is a progressive schedule of death taxes based on federal taxable estate, less $60,000. State death tax is a credit against federal estate tax.

Property taxes: Taxes are based on 20 percent of assessed value multiplied by the tax rate. Residents age 62 and over with an income of less than $15,000 may qualify for a homestead property tax refund up to $250. There are two millage rates in Hot Springs Village, depending on the school district: .0346 or .0336. Taxes on a $100,000 home would run approximately $676 or $692. Assessor's office, 501-622-3730.

Local real estate

Overview: Homes are selling for about 96 percent of the asking price, and are on the market for an average of 131 days. Taxes have increased in both Garland and Saline counties because of reassessment. Many people purchase homes prior to retirement, because interest rates are low and resale values are rising. This enables people to purchase homes they might not be able to afford once they retire. The monthly assessment in Hot Springs Village is $26.

Median price for a single family home: $125,000.

Average price for a 3BR/2BA house: $138,370 is the average for all homes, including new construction and resales.

Average price for a 2BR condo: New and resales, $61,500 to $63,833. 3BR condominiums and townhouses sell at an average of $73,000 to $81,167.

Common housing styles and features: Most homes are one-level designs with 3BRs/2BAs, a workshop area and a two-car garage. Two-level homes are designed so the master BR/BA are on the same level as the main living area and kitchen. Guest accommodations are on the second level.

Rental housing market: Rental homes and townhouses are abundant year-round because many people invest in rental property until they are ready to move to the Village permanently. Units rent from $450 to $900 per month, depending upon location. Larger units range from $525 to $1,500 per month.

Average rent for a 2BR apartment: $450 to $600 monthly.

Earning a living

Business climate: There are 60 businesses that serve the Village, but the potential for future commercial development is questionable. Things are different in Hot Springs, where tourism is a major factor in the economy. Retirement income adds some fiscal stability to the entire region because retirees' incomes are typically fixed, and the money is spent regardless. Abundant timber, clean water and mineral resources provide the basis for industry.

Help in starting a business: The University of Arkansas at Little Rock operates Small Business Development Centers in both Hot Springs, 501-624-5448, and Little Rock, 501-324-9043. The Hot Springs office offers counseling to small-business owners, plus training and seminars covering every aspect of business management and operations. SCORE, 501-321-1700, ext. 270. Small Business Administration, 501-624-5448.

Job market: There are plenty of part-time and full-time seasonal jobs available in Hot Springs during tourist season, which is primarily the warm months from April through October. The employment base in the city is heavily weighted to services and retail and wholesale trade (combined they account for 62 percent of all employment). Unfortunately, these do tend to be at the lower end of the wage scale. The unemployment rate is 5 percent. AARP provides the Senior Community Service Employment Program, 501-321-1800, which assists persons 55 and older with limited financial resources in finding paid temporary or community work to help them sharpen job skills and receive training.

Medical care

In Hot Springs, National Park Medical Center, 501-321-1000, is a 166-bed acute care hospital. It offers a complete cardio-vascular surgery program, psychiatric services and a 24-hour emergency room. The hospital has off-site health centers in Hot Springs Village and several other areas. St. Joseph's Regional Health Center, 501-622-1000, has 317 suites and is located on a 72-acre campus. St. Joseph's has a complete cardiology program, the Heart Center, Mercy Cancer Center and a pain management clinic. St. Joseph's also operates off-site facilities. Levi Hospital, 501-624-1281, is an 89-bed facility that specializes in rehabilitation and is na-tionally known for its arthritis program, which features a therapeutic pool using the waters of Hot Springs. It also offers outpa-tient rehabilitation services in conjunction with St. Joseph's, such as physical ther-apy, hand therapy, occupational therapy and speech pathology.

Services for seniors

The Area Agency on Aging, 501-321-2811, offers information and referrals for sen-iors throughout the area. The agency can connect you with Senior Olympics, offers job counseling for older job seekers and refers services such as in-home care and independent living assistance. The Sen-ior Citizens Center, 501-624-0838, and McAuley Center near Hot Springs Vil-lage, 501-984-5594, are affiliated with St. Joseph's Health Care. Both centers offer a variety of activities and services including arts and crafts, dancing, day and overnight trips and health screen-ings. The McAuley Center also has com-puter classes.

Continuing education

Garland Community College, 501-767-9371, offers free enrollment to residents over 60 on a space-available basis. Registration is $10, and lab and materials fees are also required. Choose from topics including computers, history, painting, drawing, pho-tography, ceramics and philosophy. The Community Services department offers noncredit mini-courses that last from one day to three weeks on topics as diverse as stained glass and business law. Shepherd's Center of Hot Springs, 501-525-9001, offers personal enrichment and liberal arts courses to adults 55 and older. Classes last six to eight weeks, and there is no charge.

Crime and safety

This self-contained Village is extremely secure, with 24-hour security, plus local police and fire departments. The crime rate for Garland County is 50 incidents per 1,000 population, and for Hot Springs it's 105 incidents per 1,000 people. How-ever, as is the case with many tourist destinations, the crime rate is figured as all crimes that occur in the area as a per-centage of the *permanent* population, which greatly inflates the rate.

Getting around town

Public transportation: No local transit is available. Having a car is a must.

Roads and highways: State 70 is 15 miles south of the Village; State Road 7 is adjacent to the Village. I-30 is 30 min-utes to the east.

Airport: Little Rock Regional Airport, less than an hour away, is served by Delta, American, TWA, USAir and others.

Let the good times roll

Recreation: If you love to play golf, then welcome to the Hot Springs Village neighborhood! There are six championship golf courses in the Village that are open year-round (the Ponce de León golf course has been named among the top 100 courses in the United States), plus the ParFormance School of Golf, which teaches people to play on a 3-hole course. For $465 per person annually, property owners enjoy unlimited golf. There are six manmade lakes and two marinas for fishing, boating, water-skiing, scuba diving and sailing. Choose from 19 tennis courts with a full-time professional staff, and enjoy jogging or hiking on 14 miles of fitness trails. There are two pools, including an indoor heated one, housed in the Coronado Natatorium Fitness Center, which also features nautilus equipment, saunas, exercise classes and a professional staff. Don't forget the magnificent land beyond the village—the Ouachita Mountains, the Diamond Lakes and the natural hot springs mineral baths.

Culture: Hot Springs has a very nice arts district that is unequaled in Arkansas. Monthly Gallery Walks are held the first Thursday and Friday of each month and feature the opening of new exhibitions of national and international artists. The Ponce de León Auditorium has symphonies, ballet and other performing arts. Little Rock is less than an hour away, where you can enjoy the Arkansas Symphony Orchestra, the Ballet Arkansas and frequent Broadway productions.

Annual events: Festivals include the Racing Festival of the South (April), the Miss Arkansas Pageant and the Hot Springs Music Festival (June), Arkansas Oktoberfest and the Hot Springs Documentary Film Festival (Oct.) and Holiday in the Park (Nov.).

When the kids come: In addition to the natural surroundings, kids enjoy Magic Spring amusement park, and the Mid-America Center, which is a very special "hands-on" center. Hot Springs Mountain Tower glass elevator rides take you 1,200 feet up for a breathtaking view of Hot Springs National Park. Also check out the National Park Aquarium, Mule Line (for mule-drawn trolley rides) and Hot Springs Diamonds, which allows mining for diamonds and gems at the Crater of Diamonds State Park.

For more information

Chambers
Greater Hot Springs Chamber
   of Commerce
P.O. Box 6090
Hot Springs, AR 71902
501-321-1700

Hot Springs Village
110 Cooper Circle
Hot Springs Village, AR 71909
800-638-3181

Newspapers
The Sentinel-Record
300 Spring St.
Hot Springs, AR 71902
501-623-7711

La Villa (weekly)
121 DeSoto Center Dr.
Hot Springs Village, AR 71909
501-624-6157

Realtor
Linda Green/Sandy Newby
Big Red Realty
3850 N. Highway 7
Hot Springs, AR 71909
501-624-4448
800-643-1576
Fax: 501-623-1572

3. Prescott, Arizona

Nickname: Everybody's Home Town
County: Yavapai
Area code: 520
Population: 30,606
County population: 129,500
% of population over 65: 23.7
Region: Central Arizona
Closest metro area: Phoenix, 96 mi.
Average home price: $110,000 to $170,000
Best reasons to retire here: Gorgeous scenery and pristine environment, friendly atmosphere, great outdoor recreation.

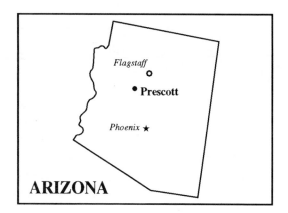

Prescott at a glance

Prescott is one of Arizona's best-kept secrets and almost everyone who moves here would like to keep it that way. The clean, pine-scented air of Prescott (pronounced "press-kit") may be among the city's rarer charms, but it's only one of the many enchantments you'll find here. Located in the heart of central Arizona, at the edge of the world's largest stand of Ponderosa pines, Prescott enjoys four mild seasons, yet it's nearly always sunny. The summers bring dry, warm desert air with cool night breezes; the winters see invigorating mountain chills and an average 32 inches of snow. And when residents speak of a "high" quality of life, they're not kidding. Prescott is a mile high in elevation, and the views don't get any better; the towering Granite Dells, which look as much like contemporary sculpture as rock formations, lie just to the north of the city. The charm of Prescott is that it's small but packed to the city limits with great services, recreation and an age-diverse population. (In fact, more than 1,200 seniors are students at the local community college.) People move here from all over the country, making it a diverse and extremely friendly community. With a backdrop of snow-covered mountains, rolling hills and Ponderosa pines as far as the eye can see, the state has lovingly coined Prescott "Arizona's Christmas City." For residents, living here is such a great gift, it's Christmas in July, too.

Possible drawbacks: Make note of the elevation. At 5,000 feet up, the thin air can cause breathing problems for some people. Those with heart conditions would be advised to check with their physicians before retiring here. Shopping is limited, as are cultural opportunities.

Climate

Elevation: 5,082'	Avg. high/low:	Avg. inches		Avg. # days precip.	Avg. % humidity
		rain	snow		
Jan.	59/26	1.4	-	5	55
April	78/40	.5	-	6	35
July	95/66	2.0	-	10	40
Oct.	80/45	1.0	-	4	40
YEAR	77/43	13.0	32	-	-
# days 32° or below: 131			# days 90° or warmer: 47		

What things cost

Overview: Prescott's ACCRA index is 4.4 percent higher than the national average, with housing nearly 16 percent above. Health care, groceries and transportation are within normal to 3 percent higher; utilities are 4 percent below.

Gas company: Call Citizens Utilities, 520-445-2210. Deposit ($70) is waived with a letter of credit. $15 connect fee. Natural gas is commonly used for hot water and cooking only. Avg. bill: $44.51/mo.

Electric company: Arizona Public Service, 520-776-3636. $25 to establish service; deposits can be waived with a letter of credit. Partial electric runs about $52/mo. All-electric averages $200.

Phone company: Contact US West, 800-244-1111. Installation: $46.50; deposit is based on credit rating. Basic service costs about $17 monthly.

Water and sewer: Contact Municipal, 520-445-3500. Deposits can be waived with a letter of credit. Service initiation fee is $8.06. Monthly bill is $30 to $70.

Cable company: Paragon Cable TV, 520-445-4511.

Car registration, license: New residents must obtain an Arizona driver's license upon establishing residency. License is a one-time purchase expiring at 60; cost is prorated by age (50 and over, $10).

After 60, licenses are renewed every five years. Cost is $12.60 for new resident registration and title fee, and an annual license tax is paid. Total fee for a 1996 Honda Accord 4-door LX (in 1996) was $468. The tax decreases 15 percent annually. Department of Motor Vehicles, 520-776-9911.

The tax ax

Sales tax: Arizona sales tax is 5 percent; Yavapai county and Prescott add to it for a total sales tax of 7.5 percent.

State income tax: Graduated from 3 percent to 5.6 percent, depending upon income bracket. No deduction for federal income tax paid.

Retirement income: Federal, state and local pensions are exempt from state income tax up to $2,500. Private pensions are not exempt. There is a $2,100 exemption for adjusted gross income for each person 65 or older.

Property taxes: In 1995, the total property tax rate for Prescott was $11.60 per $100 of assessed valuation; homes are assessed at 10 percent of market value. Sample taxes on a $100,000 home would be $1,160. Tax assessor, 520-771-3220.

Local real estate

Overview: Property taxes are reasonable here, and local government listens and responds to citizen concern for control of growth and development. Recently there has been a market correction, and asking prices have leveled off to more realistic pricing. There is wide variety of housing to choose from in the resale market. Most retirees live here permanently, although some do come here for a second-home community.

Average price for a 3BR/2BA home: $130,000 to $170,000 for a new home; resales average $110,000 to $160,000.

Average price for a 2BR condo: $85,000 to $130,000 for a new condominium; $50,000 to $70,000 for a resale.

Common housing styles and features: Southwestern-style architecture is very common in the area, with open floor plans and cathedral ceilings. Common exteriors are stucco, log, brick and rock.

Rental housing market: Prescott and surrounding areas have a lot to offer in the rental market, from apartments and townhouses to large homes. Availability varies greatly. Monthly rental for a 3BR home ranges from $600 to $1,200.

Average rent for a 2BR apartment: $536 a month. Total range is $375 to $750.

Nearby areas to consider: The Tri City area is at a lower altitude, which seems to work better for a lot of people. Prescott Valley, only 7 miles from Prescott, features lower land costs in flat to rolling terrain. Chino Valley is 12 miles from Prescott and has average lot sizes of 2 acres in flat to rolling terrain. Resale and new home prices are lower than in Prescott. It's also a great spot for people with horses.

Earning a living

Business climate: Excluding government, tourism has the greatest economic impact on the economy of Prescott and the surrounding area, and the hospitality industry runs the gamut from large hotels that service conventions to intimate bed-and-breakfasts. Private, youth and church-related camps are abundant in the area. Industry is one of the fastest-growing sectors of the economy, and Prescott is actively recruiting environmentally clean businesses. Manufacturers such as Ace Hardware, Caradon Better-Built (aluminum doors and windows) and Sturm Ruger handguns have come to the area recently. Mining is another longtime important sector of the local economy. The retirement community is a significant portion of the total population, and services are continually being developed for seniors.

Help in starting a business: Contact the Chamber of Commerce, 800-266-7534, for demographic and statistical information. Yavapai College has a very active Small Business Development Center, 520-776-2373, which offers free, one-on-one business counseling to current and prospective small business owners. The SBDC also offers many courses in small business start-up and operations.

Job market: Many jobs, particularly part-time positions, are available in the hospitality industry, as Prescott is a popular tourist and convention locale. With a growing population, real estate and construction are big contributors to employment. The unemployment rate was recently 5.5 percent. Arizona State Department of Economic Security, 520-445-5100.

Medical care

There's very good care here and Phoenix is 90 miles away. The area's major hospital is Yavapai Regional Medical Center, 520-445-2700, a 119-bed medical facility offering a 24-hour emergency room, cardiac and pulmonary rehabilitation, oncology services, adult fitness and wellness programs and more. The Department of Veterans Affairs Medical Center, 520-445-4860, has 150 beds and a VA Nursing Home Care Unit. Area residents are served by 85 physicians.

Services for seniors

Although the Adult Center of Prescott, 520-778-3000, is a recreation center for persons over 18, the majority of members are senior citizens. The center offers classes in computers, Spanish, silversmithing, oil painting, guitar, bridge and more. The center also holds dances, hosts bridge groups and offers day trips. There is a gift shop on the premises. The center has a wellness clinic that offers blood pressure checks, flu shots and other health screenings. Dues are $20 annually and class fees are low, typically $8 for an eight-week class.

Crime and safety

Violent crime is rare. The county averages 56 crimes per 1,000 population, which is quite close to the national average. Prescott's crime rate is higher, at 72 incidents per 1,000 people, but this represents total crime as a percentage of permanent population, and it does not take into account the significant tourist population.

Continuing education

For retirement-age people in the Prescott area, Yavapai Community College (YCC), 520-776-2085, offers the Yavapai Learning Institute, with "learning groups" on topics such as national affairs, 20th-century philosophy, exploring lost civilizations and play-reading. There is also a chorus. Dues are $100. YCC also has a Retirement College/Enrichment option for most courses, allowing students to take classes on a basis similar to pass/fail. Persons age 62 and over are charged a reduced fee. Topics include art, anthropology, biology, computer systems and applications, communications, creative writing, literature, gunsmithing, history, mathematics, music, philosophy, t'ai chi, psychology, sociology, Spanish and more. YCC hosts one of the West's most popular Elderhostel programs. The largest in the world, it offers many courses that involve travel to the Grand Canyon, the Hopi Mesas and other natural wonders in the area.

Getting around town

Public transportation: Prescott Transit, 520-778-7978, is a privately operated bus line that offers midday service to shopping areas and medical complexes. The service also offers Dial-A-Ride (taxi service) and Reserve-A-Ride for seniors and disabled persons that requires 24-hour reservations. The service also offers a shuttle to Phoenix four times daily.

Roads and highways: US 69, US 89, I-17, I-40.

Airport: Prescott's municipal airport (Ernest A. Love Field) offers commuter flights to Phoenix and Las Vegas.

Let the good times roll

Recreation: Prescott likes to bill itself as "The Softball Capital of the World"; players from around the world travel here to compete in summer tournaments and play on the city's 15 lighted fields. Prescott has four challenging 18-hole golf courses that are all open to the public. There are more than 900 acres of city park land for recreation; facilities include tennis courts, pools, volleyball courts, soccer fields and more. Those who relish the great outdoors will find themselves in paradise here; there are more than 20 recreation areas (for picnicking, hiking, fishing and camping) in the Prescott National Forest, located just a few miles from the city. Prescott also is nationally known as a rock-climber's mecca (it may not be your sport, but it can be exciting to watch!).

Culture: Prescott was once the territorial capital of Arizona, and the Sharlot Hall Museum occupies a site around the Territorial Governor's Mansion showcasing Arizona history, while the Smoki Museum exhibits the history of Native Americans. The Phippen Museum of Western Art sits on five acres of land and documents the history of the West through its extensive art collection. The Bead Museum on Whiskey Row features unique displays of beads and varieties of adornments from around the world. Visual arts are represented by art galleries and organizations including Yavapai Community College, the Mountain Artists Guild and the Southwest Artists Association. The Prescott Fine Arts Association presents visual arts and community theater productions. Music lovers will enjoy Yavapai College's Performance Hall, a 1,200-seat performing arts facility that hosts commercial entertainment. The Yavapai Symphony Association presents chamber music, recitals and renowned soloists.

Annual events: The Annual Phippen Art Show (late May); Territorial Days festival, with art, food and entertainment (June); Frontier Days featuring the world's oldest rodeo (it's been an annual event for more than 100 years), a golf tournament and parade (early July); the annual Banjo Blast and Bluegrass Festival (Aug.); Faire on the Square Arts and Crafts festival (Sept.). In November and December there are more than 80 events scheduled, but the Christmas Parade and Courthouse Lighting are the favorites in Arizona's "Christmas City."

When the kids come: The Grand Canyon is only 125 miles away and worth every minute of the drive. Also try the Heritage Park Zoo.

For more information

Chamber
The Prescott Chamber
  of Commerce
117 W. Goodwin St.
P.O. Box 1147
Prescott, AZ 86302
520-445-2000 or 800-266-7534

Newspaper
The Daily Courier
147 N. Corter St.
Prescott, AZ 86301
520-445-3333

Realtor
John B. Clark II
Red Arrow Real Estate
1107 E. Gurley St.
Prescott, AZ 86301
888-668-6487
Fax: 520-778-2599

4. Scottsdale, Arizona

Nickname: Arizona's Playground
County: Maricopa
Area code: 602
Population: 174,490
County: 2,355,900
% of population over 65: 12.5
Region: Central Arizona
Closest metro area: Phoenix, 20 mi.
Median house price: $142,000
Best reasons to retire here: Great climate, outstanding medical facilities, recreation (especially golf) and services.

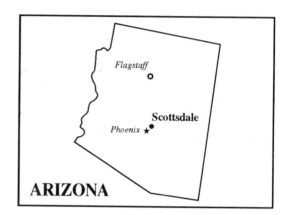

Scottsdale at a glance

The list of things to do, see and enjoy in Scottsdale is so long, you'll be overwhelmed before you even get started! No wonder, then, Scottsdale was honored with the 1993 Most Livable City Award from the U.S. Conference of Mayors. Located in the Sonoran Desert, in the shadow of the McDowell Mountains, Scottsdale represents the American West at its fabulous best, combining the history and rugged charm of the old with the comfort and ease of the new. Prices may be a bit higher here than elsewhere, but the payoff is worth it when you consider the abundance of cultural, educational, social and recreational choices. Golfers, for instance, choose from more than 48 golf courses in the immediate community and 125 in the surrounding area! The area is a regional cultural center, especially in the area of visual arts; Thursday Night Art Walks in the gallery district are quite a tradition. The heat can be a factor in activities, but hardy Scottsdale citizens have adapted by becoming a community of early risers who like to get in their outdoor recreation in the morning. If you like to dine out, Scottsdale is a treat, with fine restaurants serving diverse cuisine from cowboy-style steaks to Thai, Italian, Spanish and more. The shopping is excellent as well, and everyone is ready for Nordstrom to open in 1998 as a key element in the downtown Waterfront Development.

Possible drawbacks: Public transportation, while good in the center city, wanes in the outlying areas. Also, the climate isn't for everyone—it's advisable to make several trips at different times of the year to see how you tolerate it. After all, it's pretty darned hot, especially in the summer.

Climate

Elevation: 1,129'	Avg. high/low:	Avg. inches rain	snow	Avg. # days precip.	Avg. % humidity
Jan.	65/38	.71	-	4	40
April	84/52	.32	-	2	20
July	105/78	.75	-	4	24
Oct.	88/57	.46	-	3	26
YEAR	85/57	7.0	-	-	-
# days 32° or below: 13			# days 90° or warmer: 164		

What things cost

Overview: According to ACCRA, prices are 3 percent above average, with housing costs 7.5 percent higher. Health care is great, but costs are 15 percent higher.

Gas company: Call Southwest Gas, 602-861-1999. Service charge, $20. Deposits are waived for seniors and homeowners; renters pay $50. Information on average bills not available.

Electric company: Salt River Project (SRP), 602-236-8888. Turn-on charge is $19; deposits range from $80 to $160, but are usually waived. Arizona Public Service (APS), 602-371-7171, connection charge is $25; deposit may be required. Average electric bill is $117.

Phone company: US West, 800-244-1111. Hookup, $46.50; deposits may be required. Basic service, $16.70 to $19.70.

Water and sewer: City of Scottsdale, 602-994-2461. Start-up is $15; no deposit for homeowners. Renter deposit, two months' usage. Monthly bills are based on usage.

Cable company: TCI Cable of Scottsdale, 602-948-8488.

Car registration, license: New residents must register their car and obtain a driver's license. License cost is prorated by age (50 and over, $10). After age 60, licenses are renewed every five years. New resident registration and title fee: $12.60. Vehicle license tax is based on registration date and factory list price. Total fee for a 1996 Honda Accord 4-door LX (in 1996) was $468. The tax decreases 15 percent annually. Motor Vehicle Division, 602-255-0072.

The tax ax

Sales tax: State sales tax is 5 percent. Scottsdale adds 1.4 percent, and freeway tax of .75 totals 7.15 percent. Groceries are taxed at 1.2 percent. Drugs and medical services are exempt.

State income tax: Graduated from 3 to 5.6 percent, depending upon income. No deduction for federal income tax paid.

Retirement income: Federal, state and local pensions are exempt from state income tax up to $2,500. Private pensions are not exempt. Residents 65 and up get a $2,100 exemption for adjusted gross income.

Property taxes: In 1995, the typical tax rate here was $1.43 per $100 assessed valuation; homes are assessed at 10 percent of market value. However, property tax structures are complex, and rates vary due to special districting. For precise numbers, call the treasury office, 602-506-8511, with a parcel number.

Local real estate

Overview: Housing prices have increased from 5 to 10 percent in Scottsdale in the past two years, while property taxes remain relatively low. Retirees in this area purchase vacation homes and permanent residences, and as a group they show a marked preference for condos or new homes rather than resales. Scottsdale's planned communities have wonderful amenities, featuring everything from horse trails to championship golf courses to country clubhouses. Most developments are within a 15-minute drive of major retail centers.

Average price for a 3BR/2BA home: New homes, $95,000 to $150,000; resales average $70,000 to $150,000.

Average price for a 2BR condo: New condos, $80,000 to $125,000; resales, $50,000 to $150,000.

Common housing styles and features: Most homes are framed or block stucco with tiled roofs. Interiors may have vaulted ceilings and gourmet kitchens.

Rental housing market: Rentals range from $700 to $800 monthly for a 2BR/2BA home, although they can be $1,000 or higher. Plan well in advance if you're in need of something between October and April.

Average rent for a 2BR apartment: According to ACCRA, the average rent is $637, but our sources say desirable apartments can go from $600 to $1,200 monthly depending upon location.

Communities or developments most popular with retirees: Sun City West and Sun Lakes.

Nearby areas to consider: Mesa, Tempe.

Earning a living

Business climate: The hospitality industry employs one in four workers in Scottsdale, giving a good indication of the strength of the tourist, vacation and retirement markets. Given the ongoing population boom and amount of disposable income, prospects are good if you're thinking about working or starting a business in one of these sectors. Yet the city also has a diverse base of nontourism business, with particular strength in the service, high-tech and medical areas, and it is home to many corporate and regional headquarters.

Help in starting a business: The Scottsdale Chamber offers residents and businesses alike small business assistance including counseling, business plan development, a start-up-business guide, seminars and professional development opportunities.

Job market: For several years, Scottsdale has had an unemployment rate of approximately 3 percent. The part-time job market has traditionally been good, and with the vast number of retail and service outlets, the opportunities are likely to continue. The Plus 50 Placement Center, Inc., 602-994-4048, is a nonprofit referral agency. Neither the applicant nor the client is charged, and there are no income eligibility requirements to take advantage of the program. Scottsdale City Employment Office Job Info Line, 602-994-2395. The Job Services Office of the Arizona Department of Economic Security, 602-252-7771. The Area Agency on Aging, 602-264-4357, offers work referrals through the Age Works program.

Medical care

Medical care in Scottsdale is excellent, and there are more than 600 physicians in the area. Scottsdale Memorial Hospital Osborn, 602-481-4000, part of Scottsdale Memorial Health Systems, is a 382-bed acute-care hospital with a Level I Trauma center, magnetic resonance imaging, and a center for cardiovascular services. Scottsdale Memorial Hospital North, 602-860-3000, has 242 acute-care beds, full cardiac capabilities and a bone marrow transplant program. The two hospitals offer SAFE (Senior Adult Functional Enhancement) counseling program for older adults, assisting seniors experiencing depression or difficulty with moods. Call 602-481-4348. The Mayo Clinic Scottsdale, 602-391-8000, is a multi-specialty outpatient clinic. Patients requiring hospitalization are admitted to Scottsdale Memorial North. A new Mayo hospital is scheduled to open in 1998. Referrals are not required.

Services for seniors

Center DOAR (Developing Older Adult Resources), 602-274-5022, is a volunteer church and synagogue group that does work for seniors, including transportation, home services, caregiver respite, business assistance, insurance filing assistance and support groups. Scottsdale Civic Center Senior Center, 602-994-2375, and Elder Via Linda Senior Center, 602-391-5810, both offer recreational activities, classes and social services including counseling, free tax assistance and home-delivered meals. The Area Agency on Aging operates a Senior Helpline, 602-264-4357, that provides information and referrals.

Continuing education

A full schedule of noncredit courses, including many one-day workshops through the Senior Adult Education Program, are offered at Scottsdale Community College, 602-423-6559. Areas covered include computer training, art appreciation, cerebral aerobics, global issues, writing and more. The college also sponsors an Elderhostel, 602-423-6305. Robinson's department stores offers OASIS, Older Adult Service and Information System, 602-870-8337. Classes include computers, origami, cooking, arts and crafts, HMO seminars, exercise programs and offer travel options. There is no cost to join, but you must be at least 50. Classes are $10 plus materials.

Crime and safety

The crime index for Maricopa County is 84 per 1,000 population, with 64 per 1,000 reported in Scottsdale. Both are above the national rate of 55 incidents, but are average for an urban area. Neighborhood Watch, 602-391-5311.

Getting around town

Public transportation: Four bus lines run throughout the city, operated by Scottsdale Connection. Fares are $1.25; 60 cents for seniors 65 and over with a bus company ID.

Roads and highways: I-17 (20 min. west), I-10. No highways directly intersect the city.

Airport: Phoenix Sky Harbor International Airport is one of the nation's busiest airports and is serviced by 12 major airlines, with more than 1,000 flights arriving and departing daily.

Let the good times roll

Recreation: There are 125 golf courses in the Scottsdale area. Hikers and cyclists can enjoy touring on 40 miles of trails, and there are also trails for equestrian use. The city offers 50 public tennis courts and plenty more private ones. Cactus Park offers a 50-meter heated pool, weight room and dance studio. Naturalists enjoy Camelback Mountain Park and McDowell Mountain Regional Park. Other activities include desert jeep excursions, river rafting, hot-air ballooning and cross-country skiing.

Culture: Scottsdale is a major art center in the Southwest, with more than 100 art galleries banding together to offer Thursday Night Art Walks every week in the downtown arts district. The Scottsdale Symphony Orchestra performs here and throughout the state, and the Phoenix Symphony, one of the 35 major metropolitan symphonies in the U.S., is nearby. Arizona State University offers the Kerr Cultural Center, the Gammage Center for the performing Arts and the Lyceum Theater.

Annual events: The Fiesta Bowl Football Classic is held in Tempe on New Year's Day; in January, the Phoenix Open Golf Tournament is a PGA event that attracts the finest players. The Parada Del Sol Rodeo is in February, followed by the Scottsdale All Arabian Horse Show (the world's largest Arabian horse show). Arizona Senior Olympics, held annually in February/March, incorporate 26 sports. Also in March, enjoy the Paradise Valley Jazz Party, two days of internationally recognized musicians. In May, Cinco de Mayo celebrations take place. November brings the Indian Nations Celebration with rodeos and powwows at WestWorld; and in December enjoy the Noche de las Luminarias at the Desert Botanical Garden.

When the kids come: The Phoenix Zoo Grand Canyon National Park and Monument; Painted Desert (high desert region with spectacular scenery); Sedona, located in Red Rock Country and one of the most unique, scenic towns in the world. Also, check out the Hall of Flame Museum, America's largest fire-fighting museum, packed with lots of hands-on displays for kids. The Heard Museum helps kids to learn about Native American History.

For more information

Chamber
Scottsdale Chamber
   of Commerce
7343 Scottsdale Mall
Scottsdale, AZ 8525-4498
602-945-8481

Newspapers
Arizona Republic and Phoenix
   Gazette
120 E. Van Buren St.
Phoenix, AZ 85004-2227
602-994-3336

Scottsdale Progress Tribune
7525 E. Camelback Rd.
Scottsdale, AZ 85251-3519
602-941-2300

Realtor
Abe Stolberg
Coldwell Banker Success
   Realty
8201 N. Hayden Rd.
Scottsdale, AZ 85251
602-991-3100
800-736-2609
Fax: 602-443-5552

5. Tucson, Arizona

Nickname: The Old Pueblo
County: Pima
Area code: 520
Population: 450,000
County population: 853,000
% of population over 65: 13.7
Region: Southern Arizona
Closest metro area: Phoenix, 116 mi.
Average home price: $100,000 to $140,000
Best reasons to retire here: Mountain scenery, dry, sunny climate, abundant culture and recreation, excellent medical care.

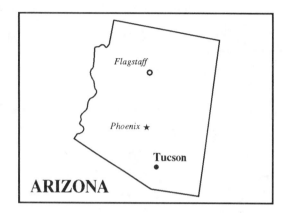

Tucson at a glance

Tucson makes a case for calling itself "home" in a way that few cities can. It's a nearly ideal urban environment of the 90s—thriving and cosmopolitan, yet it hasn't run amok with glass-and-steel skylines. Surrounded by some of the world's most majestic mountains, and true to its rich Spanish, Mexican, Native American and Anglo history, Tucson offers a unique blend of charm and contrasts: new shopping malls and crumbling adobes; two-piece suits and bike hikes at lunch. While the University of Arizona is a great source of intellect and culture, Tucson has its own identity. In fact, it's considered a "you name it, we've got it" place. After a long dry spell, the job market is as hot as the desert, and the environment is especially friendly toward small and start-up businesses, with numerous services in place. Homes are distinctly beautiful and quite affordable, especially for the West (prices range from the $80s to the $500s). The educational opportunities stimulate camaraderie, the art and cultural scene is flourishing, and the pace is uncompromisingly relaxed. Tucson residents relish their quality of life and with good reason—it's excellent.

Possible drawbacks: If you're moving from Nevada, the sweltering summer temps won't faze you. Everyone else—prepare to adjust! Even with the low humidity, July and August are great months to say *adiós*. If you have fantasies about small-town living, keep looking. Tucson is spread over 500 square miles and is just starting to experience suburban sprawl. Arizona has the highest skin cancer rate in the country. Newcomers must learn to protect themselves from the sun.

Climate

Elevation: 2,647'	Avg. high/low:	Avg. inches rain	snow	Avg. # days precip.	Avg. % humidity
Jan.	64/38	.74	-	4	50
April	81/50	.34	-	2	30
July	98/74	2.4	-	10	40
Oct.	84/56	.66	-	3	40
YEAR	82/54	11.0	1.4	-	-
# days 32° or below: 20			# days 90° or warmer: 146		

What things cost

Overview: ACCRA shows Tucson at the national average, with housing surprisingly affordable, at 5 percent below. Utilities and health care are 10 percent and 15 percent above respectively.

Gas company: Southwest Gas Corp., 800-766-9722 or 520-889-1888. Service start-up fee: $20; deposit ($50) can be waived with a letter of credit. Average monthly bill: $45.

Electric company: Tucson Electric Power Company, 520-623-7711. Connect fee: $13.50; no deposit. About $125 monthly for all-electric service; $90 for partial electric service.

Phone company: The area is served by US West, 800-244-1111. Connect fee is $46.50; deposits required based on a credit check. Basic monthly service: $21.

Water and sewer: Call Tucson Water, 520-791-3242. Water connection fee: $10; wastewater, $10. Deposit is not required.

Cable company: Call Jones Intercable, 520-744-1900, or Green Valley Cable-Vision, 520-648-0005.

Car registration, license: New residents must obtain an Arizona driver's license and registration upon establishing residency. The license is a one-time purchase expiring at 60; cost is prorated by age (50 and over, $10). After age 60, licenses are renewed every five years. New resident registration and title fee: $12.60; and an annual vehicle license tax is paid. Total fee for a 1996 Honda Accord 4-door LX (in 1996) was $468. The tax decreases 15 percent annually. Motor Vehicle Division, 520-629-9808.

The tax ax

Sales tax: Arizona sales tax is 5 percent and Tucson adds 2 percent for a total of 7 perccent. Real estate, groceries and prescription drugs are exempt.

State income tax: From 3 to 5.6 percent, depending upon income bracket. No deduction for federal income tax paid.

Retirement income: Federal, state and local pensions are exempt from state income tax up to $2,500. Private pensions are not exempt. There is a $2,100 exemption for adjusted gross income for each person 65 or older.

Property taxes: Owner-occupied housing is assessed at 10 percent of market value. A sample tax rate of $13.57 applied to each $100 of assessed value on a $100,000 home would result in property taxes of $1,357. Tax assessor, 520-740-8630.

Local real estate

Overview: Buyers are delighted by the tremendous diversity of housing styles, prices and neighborhoods and the fact that home appreciation has been flat. You can buy a house in Tucson for what a down payment goes for in Los Angeles (average monthly mortgage payment with principle and interest runs $740.)

Average price for a 3BR/2BA home: $100,00 to $140,000 covers the range for both new and resale homes. Prices can be as high as $500,000.

Median house price: $100,500.

Average price for a 2BR condo: New and resale units range from $85,000 to $110,000.

Common housing styles and features: Home design and architecture in Tucson are some of the most original *and* reasonable in the entire Southwest. Plus, dramatic mountain vistas are free with every purchase! Landscaping is desert-style with drought-resistant plants. New homes have cathedral ceilings, master suites, pools and spas, split plans and Santa Fe-style rooms (high ceilings and ceramic floors). Homes built before 1980 are concrete and brick. Post-1980 homes are frame stucco.

Rental housing market: With only a 2- to 4-percent vacancy rate year-round, housing rentals are tight. When available, they rent from $500 to $650 per month.

Average rent for a 2BR apartment: $570 monthly.

Communities or developments most popular with retirees: Saddlebrook, Sun City.

Nearby area to consider: Green Valley.

Earning a living

Business climate: In the past 10 years, the number of high-tech manufacturing and electronics companies operating in Pima County has more than doubled. In fact, Tucson is one of the fastest-growing employment centers in the U.S., growing at a projected annual rate of 3.8 percent. Small business is healthy—of the 20,000 companies that are doing business in Pima County, 98 percent are considered small, with half employing four or fewer people. Tucson is a center for science and industry in the fields of aerospace, optics, environmental technology, software development, bioindustry and teleservices.

Help in starting a business: The Chamber of Commerce has a free Business Assistance Program, whose members share expertise in areas from marketing to bookkeeping. The City of Tucson has a Business Hotline, 520-791-2519, for questions, problems with government agencies and referrals to other businesses and agencies. Tucson Economic Development, 520-791-5093, helps with retention and expansion of businesses, export and international sales assistance. Other sources of help: Pima Community College's Small Business Development Center, 520-748-4906; Business Development Finance Corporation, 520-623-3377.

Job market: The largest employers in Southern Arizona are the U.S. Army, Air Force and defense-based industries, state, county and city government, and education, especially the University of Arizona. For assistance in finding a job: Tucson/Pima County Job Club, 520-884-8280; County Dial-A-Job, 520-740-3530; Arizona Department of Employment Security, 520-791-2519.

Medical care

Medical care is some of the most advanced in the Southwest. The University Medical Center, 520-327-5461, is a teaching hospital and has been recognized as one of the nation's top hospitals. Areas of specialty include cancer treatment, cardiology, respiratory illness research and its heart transplant program. The Tucson Medical Center, 520-327-5461, emphasizes oncology, laser surgery and cardiac and diagnostic services. Carondolet St. Joseph's Hospital, 520-296-3211, is a full-service medical/surgical center. Carondolet St. Mary's Hospital, 520-622-5833, houses the Southern Arizona Burn Unit. The Veterans Affairs Medical Center, 520-792-1450, provides a full range of services to U.S. military vets. The Tucson Orthopaedic Institute, 520-694-0111, is an orthopedic medical/surgical center. Tucson also offers many nontraditional healing options, including acupressure, jin shin, shiatsu and homeopathic and naturopathic medicine. The Desert Institute of Healing Arts, 520-882-0899, is a training center in massage and shiatsu that can provide some referrals.

Services for seniors

Details about programs for seniors are available from the Senior Resource Network, 520-795-7480. The Pima Council on Aging, 520-790-7262, coordinates services and programs. Four senior centers also offer many recreational activities for seniors: Armory Park, 520-791-4865; Fred Archer Center, 520-791-4353; Eastside, 520-791-4931; and Jacobs Jesters in the Jacobs Parks YMCA, 520-881-7716.

Continuing education

The University of Arizona Extended University's SAGE (Seniors' Achievement and Growth through Education) Society, 520-624-8632, offers higher education programs in a social setting, such as brown-bag lectures with guest speakers, field trips and social events. Pima College's Senior Education Program, 520-884-6866, has noncredit liberal arts and personal enrichment classes for older adults in several Tucson-area locations.

Crime and safety

Tucson is 65 miles from the Mexican border, which means it experiences its share of drug traffic and related crime. Of greater threat to seniors are con artists and fraudulent schemes, and the Tucson police department offers awareness programs. Tucson's crime index is 123 incidents per 1,000 people, and the county rate is 101 incidents per 1,000. Both are above the national average of 55 incidents, but in line with major metropolitan areas. Residents express few fears about safety.

Getting around town

Public transportation: Sun Tran Transit, 520-792-9222, is the local intracity bus system. It ranks among the top for a city this size. Adult fare is 75 cents; seniors 65 and over pay 25 cents with ID.

Roads and highways: I-10, I-19, I-8, US 80/89, State Roads 86 and 93.

Airport: Tucson International Airport is served by 11 national and regional carriers.

Let the good times roll

Recreation: Tucson boasts more than 100 parks, 32 golf courses and more tennis courts than you can count. Swimming, jogging tracks, bike paths, roller-skating and horseback riding are widely available. Reid Park offers everything from a delightful zoo to a grand waterfall to the Therapeutics Clubhouse, a special facility for the disabled. A favorite swimming hole is the clear pool at Seven Falls in Sabino Canyon. Tucson is also the southernmost *ski* area in the continental U.S. State parks include Gates Pass, Madera Canyon, Catalina Park (a desert park), Tohono Chul Park and Mt. Lemmon in the Santa Catalinas. Spectator sports fans can watch the University of Arizona Wildcats, the Houston Astros AAA farm team (Tucson Toros), the Colorado Rockies, Arizona Diamond Backs and Chicago White Sox spring training camp. There's also greyhound racing, the Northern Telecom Open (men's pro tournament) and the Ping Welch's Championship LPGA Open.

Culture: Tucson is one of 14 U.S. cities with a professional resident theater, opera, symphony and dance company. The city also boasts a designated arts district, which includes the gallery-lined Congress Street. The Arizona Theater Company and the state's only opera company, Arizona Opera Company, are based in Tucson and earn national recognition. Don't miss the Tucson Ballet Company and the Southern Arizona Light Opera Company. Museums include the Center for Creative Photography (home of the Ansel Adams and Richard Avedon archives) and the Tucson Museum of Art.

Annual events: Fiesta de los Vaceros Rodeo (Feb.); Mariachi Conference (April); Tucson Meet Yourself (Oct.); Annual Poetry Festival and Street Fair (Dec.); NCAA football's Copper Bowl on New Year's Eve.

When the kids come: Biosphere 2, a space-age environmental project, contains several habitats where research is conducted. The Arizona-Sonora Desert Museum combines a zoo (rated as one of the 10 best in the U.S.), botanical gardens and Museum of Natural History. The Tucson Children's Museum has participatory exhibits about the human body and the environment. The Titan Missile Silo Museum, formerly part of the U.S. international defense system, is now open to the public.

For more information

Chamber
Tucson Metropolitan
  Chamber of Commerce
465 W. St. Mary's Rd.
Tucson, AZ 85701
520-792-2250

Newspapers
Arizona Daily Star
P.O. Box 26887
Tucson, AZ 85726
800-695-4492

Tucson Citizen
P.O. Box 26767
Tucson, AZ 85726
520-573-4400

Realtor
Sallie Smith, CRS
Re/Max Catalina Foothills
  Realty
5780 N. Swan, #125
Tucson, AZ 85718
800-217-8820

6. Palm Springs, California

Nickname: The Valley of Contentment
County: Riverside
Area code: 619
Population: 42,050
County population: 1,170,413
% of population over 65: 25.8
Region: South Central Ca.; Coachella Valley
Closest metro area: Los Angeles, 115 mi.
Average home price: $210,000 to $245,000
Best reasons to retire here: Country club living, dry, desert climate, world-class golf, tennis and shopping, excellent medical services.

Palm Springs at a glance

"In" places for the jet set change with the wind, but this small desert oasis has long been considered one of the world's most auspicious retreats. Whether you're stepping onto the fairway at PGA West or into a hot mineral pool with hidden rainbow jets, everything you see and do in Palm Springs comes with a first-class ticket. Situated in the heart of the low-lying Colorado desert, the mountain air is dry, and average daily temperatures are in the 70s and 80s. The winters are short and mild, and it can rain more in Florida in one day than it does here in a year. The housing market is surprisingly diversified and affordable (relative to other parts of Southern California, of course). Even though it's in the desert, Palm Springs has one of the most dependable water supplies of any area in the state. That's because of plentiful underground water sources and a well-planned system that's projected to be good for the next 40 years. One great benefit of the cool blue water is the greens—golf greens, that is. The surrounding area boasts more than 100 courses (enough to keep you busy for several lifetimes). Palm Springs also has access to outstanding medical care. The facilities, services and programs are so impressive they could be models for other cities. If you can afford it, this city is a retiree's paradise.

Possible drawbacks: The summer months are a good time to head for the highlands or anywhere where the high temperature is below 105 degrees (although the evenings can be very cool and pleasant). In Palm Springs, the living is easy, but the expenses are high. Food, restaurants, shopping, recreation, real estate and taxes are 20 to 50 percent higher than the national average.

Climate

Elevation: 482'	Avg. high/low:	Avg. inches rain	snow	Avg. # days precip.	Avg. % humidity
Jan.	70/35	.5	-	5	45
April	85/52	.5	-	3	30
July	105/70	trace	-	1	35
Oct.	90/53	.5	-	2	40
YEAR	87/54	5.0	-	-	-
# days 32° or below: 0			# days 90° or warmer: 122		

What things cost

Overview: According to ACCRA, the overall cost of living in Palm Springs is 16 percent above the national average. Housing is 20 percent above; utilities cost nearly 30 percent higher. Health care is close to 50 percent higher.

Gas company: Southern California Gas, 800-427-2200. $25 to establish service; deposits may be required pending credit evaluation. Avg. gas bill: $34 per month.

Electric company: Southern California Edison, 800-442-4950. One-time service charge: $10; deposit can be waived with letter of credit. Average electric bill: About $105 per month for partial electric service.

Phone company: Call GTE California, 800-483-4000. Installation: $46; basic service: avg. $21 per month.

Water: Call the Desert Water Agency, 619-323-4971. No deposit for residential service and no service charge. Average bill information not available.

Cable company: Continental Cablevision (Palm Desert), 619-340-2225.

Car registration, license: A California driver's license is required within 10 days of establishing residency. Fee: $12. Written and eye exams required. You must register vehicles within 20 days of residency. A smog certificate is required. There's a $300 fee if your vehicle is not certified by the manufacturer as being equipped with a state-approved emission system. Registration fee: up to $35 plus a vehicle license fee. Department of Motor Vehicles, 619-327-1521.

The tax ax

Sales tax: 7.75 percent. Drugs, groceries and medical services are exempt.

State income tax: Graduated from 1 to 11 percent, depending on income bracket. There is no deduction for federal income tax paid. There is a $4,804 standard deduction for married couples filing jointly, and a $64 credit against tax for each person filing 65 or older.

Retirement income: Federal, state and private pensions are not exempt from state income tax. Social Security income is exempt.

Property taxes: Homes are taxed at 1 percent of assessed value, although special districting can take taxes as high as 1.2 percent. Homes are appraised at 100 percent of market value, and an inflation factor raises this value annually. There is a standard homeowner's exemption of $7,000. Taxes on a $207,000 home could go as high as $2,400. Riverside County Assessor's Office, 619-778-2400.

Local real estate

Overview: Property values have stabilized and sales are increasing, finally rebounding from the deep recession of the early 90s. Asking prices had been decreasing steadily up to this point. Retirees typically purchase a home here a few years before retirement, often buying a small condominium and upgrading their residence when the main home is sold. Though housing is expensive here, the area can claim to be much more affordable than the surrounding counties of Orange, Los Angeles and San Diego.

Average price for a 3BR/2BA home: New homes start in the $110,000 range, but the mid-range is about $210,000 to $245,000. Resales can start as low as $80,000, but are more typically in the $200,000 range. Luxury homes go for $490,000 to $590,000 and up.

Average price for a 2BR condo: New, $120,000 to $145,000; resales, $80,000 to $82,000.

Common housing styles and features: Spanish tile roofs, stucco exteriors and large master bedrooms are popular.

Rental housing market: Rentals are readily available in every area of the market. Rent for a small single family home is $900 to $1,300 a month.

Average rent for a 2BR apartment: Apartments, condominiums and townhouses run $600 to $900 per month.

Communities or developments most popular with retirees: Del Webb Sun City, Desert Falls Country Club, Mesquite Country Club and Seven Lakes Country Club.

Nearby areas to consider: Palm Desert, Rancho Mirage, Indian Wells.

Earning a living

Business climate: Palm Springs is located in the center of Riverside county, which has the distinction of being California's fastest-growing county. The area has seen 79 percent growth in population in the last decade, accompanied by 38 percent growth in retail sales. Palm Springs is a major tourist and convention destination, as well as being a financial center.

Help in starting a business: The Small Business Development Center, 619-864-1311, in Palm Desert is a satellite of the regional office of Inland Empire Small Business Development Center in Riverside, about 60 miles west. The local SBDC offices offer one-on-one counseling, a library and computer lab, seminars, classes and training. Most services are free of charge, although sometimes there is a nominal charge for materials. The office serves about 600 clients annually. Every two weeks the SBDC offers a group consultation for start-up businesses. It serves the Coachella Valley. SCORE, 619-320-6682, also provides free counseling to start-up and existing businesses. The local SCORE office is housed with the area offices of the Small Business Administration. The College of the Desert in Palm Desert opens its library to the business community and maintains major databases on local business and industry trends.

Job market: With the huge retail and tourist sector, part-time and full-time jobs in these industries are readily available. Call the Employment Development Division, 619-327-8331.

Medical care

A comprehensive facility, Eisenhower Medical Center, 619-340-3911, includes Eisenhower Memorial Hospital, offering cardiology, orthopedics, cancer care, the Heart Institute, home care and a sleep disorder center. The world-renowned Betty Ford drug and alcohol recovery center is part of this facility. In Indio, JFK Memorial Hospital, 619-347-6191, has state-of-the-art diagnostic equipment, including radiology, ultrasound, fluoroscopy, CT scan and full MRI service. In addition to intensive care, coronary care, progressive care and inpatient and outpatient surgery, JFK has the latest advances in mammography technology, including a stereotactic breast biopsy, which may eliminate the need for surgical biopsy. Desert Hospital, 619-323-6511 or 800-962-3765, offers heart and cancer centers, trauma services, screenings, home health, hospice and psychiatric services.

Services for seniors

The Palm Springs Mizell Senior Center, 619-323-5684, is a full-service operation that has just about everything: fitness classes, crafts, health screenings, mature driver's classes, a writer's guild, yoga and meditation classes and more. The center also provides legal assistance, Medicare assistance and other health insurance counseling and investment seminars. There is an annual membership charge of $12, as well as a charge for some classes. Riverside County Office on Aging, 619-341-0401, can provide referrals to other area services.

Continuing education

College of the Desert, 619-346-8041, is a community college that offers for-credit classes in business, art, finance, music, nutritional care, theater arts, golf management and foreign languages. There is no audit option, but classes are only $13.25 per credit unit for California residents. California State University, San Bernardino Annex, 619-341-2883, offers classes in psychology, business, English, liberal studies and information sciences. Seniors over 60 can attend classes for $10 per semester on a space-available basis but must apply to the university. (You'll have to submit your college transcripts!) The Annex is developing a Learning in Retirement program, as well.

Crime and safety

Second-home owners with vacant houses may be susceptible, especially since budget cuts reduced Neighborhood Watch programs a number of years ago. The total crime index for Palm Springs is 93 incidents per 1,000 people, and for Riverside County, it's 73 incidents. Burglary represents a slightly higher percentage of the total rate than average. California law increases the penalty for people convicted of crimes against seniors.

Getting around town

Public transportation: Sunline system has service to Coachella Valley communities. Seniors pay a 35-cent fare.
Roads and highways: I-10, Highway 74, SR 111.
Airport: Palm Springs Regional Airport is served by major and regional carriers.

Let the good times roll

Recreation: If you love golf and tennis, you've come to the right place! There are more than 600 tennis courts in town and more than 100 public and private golf courses, featuring numerous national tournaments and invitationals. The golf courses, some of the best maintained, most challenging and prestigious places to play, include PGA West, O'Donnell Golf Club and Desert Dunes. Other popular spectator sports include professional polo matches held on 15 different fields with fieldside picknicking available. Enjoy the beauty of the desert wilderness with a trip to Mt. San Jacinto State Park, where you can take a day hike or a ride on the Palm Springs Aerial Tramway to a nearby wilderness for cross-country skiing, hiking and picknicking. It's no exaggeration to say that you can shop 'til you drop here. Palm Springs and nearby Palm Desert are famous for offering exclusive shopping, from Palm Canyon Drive to El Paseo.

Culture: The stars (both celestial and cinematic) come out at night in Palm Springs/Palm Desert for the cultural happenings. Many musical events take place at the McCallum Theater for the Performing Arts in the Bob Hope Cultural Center. The visual arts are celebrated with gallery walks along El Paseo in Palm Desert, and the Living Desert (a 1,200-acre animal park and botanical garden) hosts outdoor jazz concerts. Palm Desert has an Art in Public Places program—public buildings, schools, shopping areas and commercial centers showcase artwork for the entire community to enjoy.

Annual events: In January, it's time for the Bob Hope Chrysler Classic Golf Tournament and Nortel Palm Springs International Film Festival; February brings the California Senior Olympics and Frank Sinatra Celebrity Invitational Golf Tournament; March is time for the Newsweek Champions Cup/Evert Cup Tennis Tournament, the Nabisco Dinah Shore Golf Tournament, the La Quinta Arts Festival and the Desert Dixieland Festival; in October, the Big Bear Oktoberfest offers fun and entertainment; Fine Crafts, Wine & All That Jazz is in November; December brings the International Tamale Festival, the Festival of Gingerbread Houses and New Year's Jazz at Indian Wells.

When the kids come: The Living Desert showcases animals from the world's deserts, including zebras from Africa. Other animals includes hairy tarantulas, meerkats and various birds of prey. Then again, you could go for the real thing, and head out to the surreal desert landscape of Joshua Tree National Park.

For more information

Chamber
Palm Springs Chamber
  of Commerce
190 W. Amado Rd.
Palm Springs, CA 92262
619-325-1577

Newspaper
The Desert Sun
74-617 Highway 111
Palm Desert, CA 92261
619-341-6200

Realtor
Tim Hintz
Century 21 PS Realty
1001 N. Palm Canyon Dr.
Palm Springs, CA 92262
619-327-2121 or 619-327-1935

7. San Diego, California

Nickname: America's Finest City
County: San Diego
Area code: 619
Population: 1,149,600
County population: 2,636,300
% of population over 65: 11
Region: Southern California
Closest metro area: Los Angeles, 125 mi.
Median home price: $171,600
Best reasons to retire here: Ideal climate, excellent health care, enjoyable recreation and culture.

San Diego at a glance

When you think of San Diego, think big: The nation's sixth-largest city offers retirees the best of everything. With 12 months of glorious weather (not too hot, *never* too cold) and more than 70 golf courses, 1,200 tennis courts and 90 miles of beaches, you could easily relax for the rest of your life. But San Diego's retirees are also out taking in world-renowned attractions such as the San Diego Zoo, and great professional sports (the city is home to the Padres, the Chargers and the Hawks). San Diego also has an astonishing number of museums and cultural organizations of top-notch quality. Superb restaurants, great shopping and the friendly people add to the enjoyment. For year-round living, it doesn't get much better—the weather is almost always sunny and mild with a soft breeze. San Diego is also known for its highly rated medical facilities where more than 25 hospitals offer some of the best health and rehabilitative care in the country. The city's immense size (its population is larger than 10 states!) translates to economic power and opportunity; San Diego's GNP could be rated within the world's top 40 nations, and the economic base is very diverse. If you can think of it, chances are you can do it in San Diego.

Possible drawbacks: Unless you have deep pockets, San Diego may be a better vacation destination than a place to retire. According to ACCRA, the cost of living here is 21 percent higher than the national average. While mild climates allow people to lead healthier lifestyles, real estate, taxes and health care will take a giant bite out of a fixed income. Also, San Diego has its share of urban problems, including air quality and motor vehicle theft.

Climate

Elevation: 30'	Avg. high/low:	Avg. inches rain	snow	Avg. # days precip.	Avg. % humidity
Jan.	65/46	1.9	7	7	65
April	68/54	.8	5	6	70
July	75/64	.1	1	1	70
Oct.	74/58	.3	2	2	70
YEAR	70/55	9.5	-	-	70
# days 32° or below: 1			# days 90° or warmer: 8		

What things cost

Overview: According to ACCRA, the overall cost of living is nearly 21 percent higher than the national average, with housing 50 percent higher. All other categories are about 20 to 25 percent more expensive. The one bright spot is utilities costs, which are about 5 percent less.

Gas and electric company: San Diego Gas and Electric Company, 800-411-7343 or 619-422-4133. Turn-on charges: $14 per meter; $30 if residence has both gas and electric. Deposits waived with a credit check. Average monthly gas bill: $26. Average monthly electric bill: $75.

Phone company: Contact Pacific Bell, 800-310-2355. Connect charge is $34.75; no deposit required. Monthly service: $16.

Water and sewer: City of San Diego Water Department, 619-515-3500. No charge to begin service; no deposit.

Cable company: Cox Communications, 619-262-1122; Price Cable, 800-697-0056; Southwestern Cable TV, 619-695-3220.

Car registration, license: New residents must obtain a license within 10 days of establishing residency. License fees: $12. Written and eye exams required. New residents must register vehicles within 20 days. A smog certificate is required for registration. Registration fee is $300 for a vehicle previously registered outside of California and not equipped with a state-approved emission system. Department of Motor Vehicles, 619-565-6691.

The tax ax

Sales tax: 7 percent on retail sales; medical services, drugs and groceries exempt.

State income tax: Graduated from 1 to 11 percent depending upon income bracket. No deduction for federal income tax paid. There is a $4,804 standard deduction for married couples filing jointly; $64 credit against tax for each person filing 65 or older.

Retirement income: Federal state and private pensions are not exempt from state income tax. Social Security income is exempt.

Property taxes: Homes are taxed at 1 percent of assessed value, although special districting can take taxes as high as 1.2 percent. Homes are appraised at 100 percent of market value, and an inflation factor raises this value annually. Standard $7,000 homeowner's exemption. Taxes on a $207,000 home could go as high as $2,400. Assessment information, 619-236-3771.

Local real estate

Overview: Land is at a premium in all of California, and housing is expensive compared to almost every other area of the nation. Nonetheless, the picture has improved for buyers as a result of the economic recession of the early 90s— home values are more reasonable and property value increases are steady in most areas but not exorbitant. Many retirees opt for grand houses rather than condominiums, and planned communities are also popular.

Average price for a 3BR/2BA home: $229,000 for new and resale properties.

Median price for a single family home: $171,600.

Average price for a 2BR condo: $139,500 for new and resale condos.

Common housing styles and features: Older homes are Southern California bungalows. New home styles vary from Cape Cod to Mediterranean. Many condo developments are age-restricted and are centered around golf, tennis or boating.

Rental housing market: The area has a good supply of apartments and rental homes, but the market can be tight and/or expensive in popular retirement spots.

Average rent for a 2BR/2BA apartment: $1,162, according to ACCRA.

Communities or developments most popular with retirees: Rancho Bernardo, a planned community with excellent golfing, attracts many seniors. Homes cost from $130,000 to more than $1 million. Condos cost $80,000 at the low end, $136,000 at the middle. Other popular areas are La Jolla and Coronado.

Nearby areas to consider: Imperial Beach attracts military retirees; Alpine.

Earning a living

Business climate: In a ranking of gross national products of the world, San Diego would be 37th, just below Israel and above nations such as Venezuela, Ireland and New Zealand. (The city accounts for 1 percent of the total U.S. GNP.) San Diego is home to almost every type of business. Its major industries are agriculture, electronics, shipbuilding, industrial machinery, aerospace, oceanics, tourism and biomedical. San Diego is headquarters for Naval Base San Diego, and defense payroll and business activity pump billions of dollars into the retail and service sectors. The recession that marked the early part of the decade has ended, and the city's GNP is forecast to grow. To learn more about regional business, pick up a copy of the *San Diego Business Journal*, 619-277-6359.

Help in starting a business: The Chamber's Small Business Development Center, 619-435-9388, offers a business resource library and products such as small business seminar audiotapes, publications and workbooks. The center also offers free, one-on-one counseling to help with business plans, marketing strategies, and more. Recent seminar topics have included Business on the Internet, Building a Successful Consulting or Professional Practice and Targeting Your Market. Also try the Small Business Administration, 619-557-7250. SCORE can be reached at 619-557-7272.

Job market: The hospitality industry is a major employer in the area, with part-time jobs available throughout the retail and service industries. Call the California Employment Development Department, 619-265-0036.

Medical care

The area's research and medical service hospitals include the University of California San Diego School of Medicine, Salk, the Scripps Clinic and 28 general hospitals. Sharp Healthcare is a regional health care system including six acute-care hospitals and one specialty hospital: Sharp Memorial, 619-541-3400; Sharp Cabrillo, 619-221-3400; Sharp Chula Vista Medical Center, 619-482-5800; Grossmont Hospital, 619-465-0711; Sharp Coronado and Healthcare Center, 619-435-6251; Sharp Healthcare Murrieta, 909-677-8055; and Sharp Mary Birch Hospital for Women, 619-541-3400. Services include cardiology/cardiac surgery, diabetes center, oncology/cancer care, transplant services and senior programs. Columbia Mission Bay Memorial Hospital, 619-274-7721, is a leading provider in the beach area and Claremont. The 128-bed hospital operates the Pacific Beach Senior Health Center for outpatient senior healthcare, 619-274-3822. The nonprofit ScrippsHealth network includes six hospitals: Scripps Memorial La Jolla, 619-457-4123; Scripps East County, 619-440-1122; Scripps Memorial Encinitas, 619-753-6501; Scripps Memorial Chula Vista, 691-7000; Green Hospital of Scripps Clinic, 619-455-9100; and Mercy Hospital, 619-294-8111.

Services for seniors

Senior Social Services, 619-236-6905, is an information and referral service affiliated with 15 city-run senior centers in San Diego that offer classes and social activities. The Area Agency on Aging, 800-339-4661 (local: 619-560-2500), also offers information and referral services.

Continuing education

San Diego has an OASIS (Older Adult Service and Information System) center, 619-531-1131, at Robinson's department store in Horton Plaza. Open five days a week, OASIS offers classes, mostly free of charge, to adults 55 and older. Topics include exercise, history, conversational French, beginning Italian, art and more. San Diego State University's College of Extended Studies includes a Continuing Education Center at Rancho Bernardo, 619-487-0464, that offers wellness, liberal arts and personal enrichment classes. There is an annual membership fee of $15; course fees vary.

Crime and safety

Considering its immense size, San Diego is relatively safe. The crime index for the city is 65 incidents per 1,000 people, which drops to 58 incidents per 1,000 on the county level. For a major urban area, these numbers are very close to the national average of 55 incidents. Violent crime is rare, but motor vehicle theft is a problem (common for cities near the Mexican border). The rate is 60 percent higher than the national average. Some of the safest communities include Rancho Bernardo, San Pasquale, Miramar, La Playa, Harbor and Pomerado.

Getting around town

Public transportation: Metropolitan Transit System for bus and trolley service, 619-233-3004. Seniors pay 75 cents.
Roads and highways: I-8, I-15, I-5.
Airport: San Diego International Airport, Lindbergh Field, is served by most major airlines.

Let the good times roll

Recreation: You can start the day with a walk on the Pacific Ocean, meet friends for a sail in San Diego Bay and then head to the mountains for a picnic or to the courts for a few sets of tennis. There are more than 70 public and private golf courses in San Diego County, 1,200 tennis courts and every water sport you can think of, including great deep-sea fishing, boating and snorkeling. The San Diego Padres, the Chargers, the Hawks and the Sockers give spectator sports fans plenty to cheer about. Anza-Borrega Desert State Park has 100 miles of hiking and equestrian trails through open desert and sculpted sandstone.

Culture: The legendary San Diego Zoo in Balboa Park features more than 4,000 endangered birds, mammals and reptiles. The five art museums include the San Diego Museum of Art with collections of Italian Renaissance, Dutch and Spanish Baroque Old Masters. The Arts Center in Escondido showcases California dance, music and theater. The California Ballet Company presents a full season of professional ballet, and the San Diego Opera presents major operas at Civic Theatre. The La Jolla Playhouse is a Tony Award-winning theater, and the San Diego Repertory Theatre presents comedies, musicals and dramas from June through January.

Annual events: March brings the annual Ocean Beach Kite Festival and the San Diego Crew Classic rowing contest in Mission Bay. The spectacular Coronado Flower Show is in April, along with the Encinitas Street Fair, featuring arts, crafts, food and live music, and the Del Mar National Horse Show, an Olympic-level competition. The largest one-day street fair in California is the Spring Village Faire in Carlsbad in May. From July through September, enjoy the San Diego SummerPops outdoor concerts. In November attend the San Diego Thanksgiving Dixieland Jazz Festival, and in December it's Christmas on the Prado, a holiday event in Balboa Park.

When the kids come: The Fern Street Circus is San Diego's "new wave" circus, featuring performers age 2 to 72. The Children's Museum of San Diego is an interactive museum. At the San Diego Coaster Company, you can ride the historic Giant Dipper Roller Coaster, the Liberty Carousel and more. The Marie Hitchcock Puppet Theater features marionette shows. Also try the San Diego Zoo, Sea World of California and the San Diego Hall of Champions.

For more information

Chamber
Greater San Diego Chamber
  of Commerce
402 W. Broadway, #1000
San Diego, CA 92101
619-232-0124

Newspaper
San Diego Union Tribune
Union Tribune Publishing Co.
P.O. Box 191
San Diego, CA 92112
619-299-4141

Realtor
Bob Weurding
Century 21/All Star Realty
13161 Black Mountain Rd.,
  Suite 9
San Diego, CA 92129
619-484-1189
Fax: 619-484-9409

8. Santa Barbara, California

Nickname: The American Riviera
County: Santa Barbara
Area code: 805
Population: 89,200
County population: 391,600
% of population over 65: 12.3
Region: Southern California
Closest metro area: Los Angeles, 90 mi.
Median home price: $220,000 to $270,000
Best reasons to retire here: Gorgeous climate, topography and architecture, great recreational and cultural offerings.

Santa Barbara at a glance

Santa Barbara is known as the American Riviera, and for good reason. It has the cosmopolitan sophistication and sweeping shoreline of its European counterpart, and the casual, relaxed and culturally diverse atmosphere that makes life in Southern California so unique. One of the finest examples of California's colorful past is the Old Mission of Santa Barbara—its gorgeous setting, unique twin bell towers and beautiful facade have brought it recognition as the "Queen of Missions." Santa Barbara is situated on the only section of Pacific coastline from Alaska to Cape Horn that actually faces south, which results in a temperate climate. The area is loved by whale-watchers and mountain bikers alike, and also by those whose idea of recreation is shopping. The cultural offerings are outstanding for a city its size, from the notable collections of the Santa Barbara Museum of Art and the world-famous Brooks Institute of Photography to the Santa Barbara Dance Theatre and Contemporary Music Theatre. The area is a legendary vacation destination, attracting more than a few notable figures. In fact, Santa Barbara has another nickname, "The Western White House," Ronald Reagan's ranch and Bill Clinton's beachside retreat are here. Choose Santa Barbara as your retirement home, and you'll definitely be rubbing elbows with the rich and famous (or at least moving aside to let the police escort pass).

Possible drawbacks: With median home prices at more than $220,000 in the city (and even higher in the county), you'll need a well-stocked portfolio. There's no two ways about it, Santa Barbara is a luxury town available only at luxury prices. Also, anyone choosing to live in coastal California must accept the earthquake risk.

Climate

Elevation: 9'	Avg. high/low:	Avg. inches rain	snow	Avg. # days precip.	Avg. % humidity
Jan.	63/40	3.82	-	4	55
April	67/42	1.50	-	2	58
July	74/57	-	-	1	64
Oct.	73/51	1.23	-	2	62
YEAR	69/49	15.57	-	30	60
# days 32° or below: 9			# days 90° or warmer: 4		

What things cost

Overview: ACCRA statistics indicate the overall cost of living is only 12 percent above the national average. Still, housing costs are at least 32 percent higher than the national norm, and health care is at least 17 percent higher. Utilities are actually about 14 percent below the average.

Gas company: Southern California Gas Company, 800-427-2200. Hookup: $25. Deposits may be waived. Avg. monthly bill: $40.

Electric company: Southern California Edison Co., 800-655-4555. Hookup: $10. Deposits may be waived. Avg. monthly bill: $150, all-electric; $50 partial-electric.

Phone company: GTE California Inc., 800-483-4000. Hookup: $46; basic service: $17.25.

Water and sewer: Santa Barbara City Water Department, 805-963-1676. Connect charge: $36; no deposits.

Cable company: Cox Cable Santa Barbara, 805-683-6651.

Car registration, license: New residents must obtain a California driver's license within 10 days. Fee: $12. Written and eye exams required. Vehicles must be registered within 20 days. A smog certificate is required. A $300 fee is required for vehicles registered outside California and not certified as equipped with a state-approved emission system. Registration fees are up to $35 plus a vehicle license fee. Department of Motor Vehicles, 805-963-9741.

The tax ax

Sales tax: 7 percent on retail sales. Prescription drugs, groceries and medical services are exempt.

State income tax: Graduated from 1 to 11 percent based on income bracket. There is no deduction for federal income tax paid. Married couples filing jointly have a $4,804 standard deduction. There is a $64 credit against tax for each person filing 65 or older.

Retirement income: Federal, state and private pensions are not exempt from state income tax. Social Security income is exempt.

Property taxes: Homes are taxed at 1 percent of assessed value, although special districting can take taxes as high as 1.2 percent. Homes are appraised at 100 percent of market value, and an inflation factor raises this value annually. There is a standard homeowner's exemption of $7,000. Taxes on a $207,000 home could go as high as $2,400. Assessor's office: 805-568-2550.

Local real estate

Overview: If you aren't familiar with California real estate prices, brace yourself. The recession of the early 90s hit the state's housing market hard, but it's now stabilizing, with South Coast home sales reaching prerecession levels. There's a range of prices although the price you pay for a tiny bungalow here could buy you a palace in other parts of the country. The more affordable neighborhoods are on the west side of State Street in Santa Barbara and on the ocean side of Highway 101 in Goleta, while the highest-priced housing is in Hope Ranch and Montecito.

Average price for a 3BR/2BA home: $450,000, new; $350,000, resales. Prices can easily climb as high as $1.5 to $3 million.

Median price for a single family home: City, $277,200; county, $220,100.

Average price for a 2BR condo: New, $250,000-$300,000, although there are very few new units. Median price for a condo: $211,887.

Common housing styles and features: Spanish, Mediterranean and mission-style architecture are dominant, although California contemporary design is also popular.

Rental housing market: There is a high demand for rental properties of all types. A 3BR house can be found for $1,500 a month, but homes can rent for as high as $7,800.

Average rent for a 2BR apartment: $800 to $1,000; but $2,200 is not necessarily uncommon.

Nearby areas to consider: Ventura, Lompoc.

Earning a living

Business climate: The Santa Barbara economy is based on electronics and high-tech research, light manufacturing, education, tourism and convention services, government and finance, and retail and wholesale trade. Retail sales are strong and increasing, recovering now from the difficult recession of the early 90s. Tourism is a major industry. Hospitality businesses that cater to international travelers are seeing revenue increases. Hospitality industry sales have rebounded sharply from the recession era. *Business Digest*, 805-646-9994.

Help in starting a business: The Small Business Development Center of Ventura offers a program of one-on-one business counseling through the Santa Barbara Chamber of Commerce, 805-658-2688. At the Ventura office, clients can take advantage of training and seminars. SCORE, 805-563-9981.

Job market: County government and the University of California are the area's two largest employers. Other major employers include Raytheon, La Cumbre Plaza Shops, Delco Systems Operations, Four Seasons Biltmore and Santa Barbara Cottage Hospital. The services sector is the largest employment industry, with principal services including business, medical and health care services and education. Industries that support tourism are another major employment segment. Retail job growth is now positive, and there are increasing full-time and part-time opportunities. The unemployment rate is 6.2 percent. Employment Development Department, 805-963-0721. Santa Barbara County Job Information Line, 805-568-2820.

Medical care

Cottage Health System operates two of the area's three hospitals. Santa Barbara Cottage Hospital, 805-682-7111, is the area's major hospital and the largest facility between Los Angeles and San Francisco. The 443-bed facility has a cardiac care unit with the only cardiac electrophysiology lab between L.A. and San Francisco, as well as a new cardiac catheterization lab, respiratory care services, diagnostic radiology services, physical and occupational therapy, magnetic resonance imaging, an intensive care unit, a 24-hour emergency room and the first facility in the country solely dedicated to eye care. St. Francis Medical Center, 805-962-7661, is a 112-bed acute care hospital offering a wide range of services. Goleta Valley Cottage Hospital is a 123-bed hospital affiliated with Cottage Health System, 805-967-3411.

Services for seniors

Contact the Carrillo Recreation Center, 805-965-3813, for information on its active program of lawn bowling, ballroom dancing, classes and trips. Louise Lowry Davis Recreation Center, 805-965-6261, offers similar activities, while the Senior Activity Center, 805-963-3579, offers exercise classes, fellowship, films and creative writing. The Goleta Senior Center, 805-964-8011, has diverse programs that include tax assistance, health screenings, classes and dancing. The Senior Information & Referral Helpline, 805-682-2727, can direct you to programs and services throughout the Santa Barbara area. Central Coast Commission for the Senior Citizens/Area Agency on Aging, 805-965-3288. RSVP, 805-963-0474.

Continuing education

University of California Santa Barbara, 805-893-4200, offers continuing education classes that can be taken on a credit or noncredit basis. Topics include decorative arts, stress management, computer classes (from basic instruction to sophisticated applications), interior design, art classes, psychology and more. Enrollment is open, and classes range in length from one-day seminars to 12 weeks. Students register quarterly, and costs range from $95 to $345 and more.

Crime and safety

Crime in Santa Barbara has dropped significantly in recent years. Property crimes decreased from 52 to 45 incidents per 1,000 people between 1993 and 1994 (the most recent year for uniform reporting). County wide, the crime rate is approximately 44 incidents per 1,000 people, while Santa Barbara reported 55 occurrences per 1,000 population—the same as the national average.

Getting around town

Public transportation: Santa Barbara Metropolitan Transit District (MTD), 805-683-3702. Adult fares are $1, seniors 62 and over pay 50 cents.

Roads and highways: US 101, State Roads 144, 154, 192, 217, 225.

Airports: Los Angeles International is the closest major airport. Santa Barbara Municipal has Santa Barbara Airbus, which offers nonstop flights seven times daily to LAX. American Eagle, USAir Express, United Express and Skywest (the Delta Connection) also serve the airport.

Let the good times roll

Recreation: Thanks to the excellent climate, there's no shortage of recreational and sports activities to enjoy. There are six golf courses in the area and plenty of public tennis courts (although use permits are required; get them at the courts). Cycling, swimming, sailing, water-skiing and windsurfing are popular year-round, and there are dozens of foothill trails for day hikes in the Santa Ynez Mountains. Santa Barbara offers great spectator polo at the Santa Barbara Polo Club on Sundays from April through November. The area is also a gardener's paradise, and there are five gardens open to the public, including the Santa Barbara Botanic Garden and the Mission Rose Garden. Just north of Santa Barbara is the Santa Ynez valley, where more than 20 vineyards prosper.

Culture: The Santa Barbara Museum of Art is one of the nation's finest regional museums, featuring works of important American artists including John Singer Sargent, Georgia O'Keeffe, Edward Hopper and Thomas Eakins as well as works of the European Impressionists. The Lobero Theater is home to the Contemporary Music Theatre, Santa Barbara Grand Opera Association, Santa Barbara Dance Theater, the Santa Barbara Chamber Orchestra and the Gilbert and Sullivan Company of Santa Barbara.

Annual events: Whale watching is ongoing from January through April; March brings the Santa Barbara International Film Festival and the International Orchid Show (one of the most prestigious horticultural events in the world). In June, enjoy the wonderful Summer Solstice Parade. In August, sports lovers gear up for the Pacific Coast Open Polo Tournament and Santa Barbara Triathlon. In September, it's time for the Santa Barbara International Jazz Festival and Santa Barbara Golf Open LPGA Tournament. In December, residents enjoy the Christmas Parade.

When the kids come: The Santa Barbara Zoological Gardens is a favorite attraction, with more than 700 animals living in natural habitats. The Museum of Natural History fascinates kids with a bee colony and Chumash Indian village dioramas. The museum also operates the "Sea Center" which is home to many examples of marine biology. On windy days, fly a kite at Shoreline Park.

For more information

Chamber
Santa Barbara Chamber
of Commerce
504 State St.
Santa Barbara, CA 93101
805-965-3023

Newspapers
Santa Barbara News Press (daily)
P.O. Box 1359
Santa Barbara, CA 93101
805-564-5200

The Independent (weekly)
1221 State St., #200
Santa Barbara, CA 93101
805-965-5205

Realtor
Lois Landau/Emilie McMinn
Coldwell Banker Premier
Properties
1111 Coast Village Rd.
Santa Barbara, CA 93108
805-969-7810
Fax: 805-565-3128

9. Colorado Springs, Colorado

Nickname: America's Choice City
County: El Paso
Area code: 719
Population: 312,856
County population: 465,885
% of population over 65: 8
Region: Pikes Peak/Rocky Mountain area
(central Colorado)
Closest metro area: Denver, 70 mi.
Average home price: $125,000 to $154,000
Best reasons to retire here: Ideal climate,
stunning scenery, a thriving arts community.

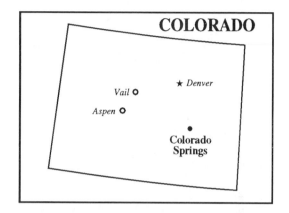

Colorado Springs at a glance

Colorado Springs lies at the foot of Pikes Peak, which inspired the words to "America the Beautiful"—a bit of historical trivia that tells you exactly why this area is such an appealing place to retire. At one time, the Ute, Sioux, Shoshone, Cheyenne and Arapaho peoples gathered to worship at the mineral springs near Pikes Peak, further evidence that this area has inspired awe in all who have seen it for hundreds (if not thousands) of years. Modern Colorado Springs is a major tourist attraction; the Pikes Peak region hosts 5.4 million visitors annually, generating $740 million in revenue and employing 13,000 people. The city is also an important military post (Fort Carson) that boasts a healthy, clean environment, excellent recreational opportunities, respected colleges, responsive government and a tradition of community spirit. Add on good neighborhoods and excellent health care and you've got a great place to retire. The U.S. Olympic Complex is here—home to 11 of the national governing bodies of Olympic sports, and site of numerous Olympic trials and other sporting events. Also, thanks to the philanthropy of the El Pomar Foundation, construction is going forward on the 8,000-seat convention/sports venue of the Colorado Springs World Arena. Completion is expected in late 1997 or early 1998. Finally, when you think Colorado Springs, think parks. With almost 7,400 acres of park and open space in its municipal inventory, and hundreds of thousands of acres of state and national parkland and forests nearby, it's the ultimate place for nature enthusiasts.

Possible drawbacks: The cost of living is on the rise. Also, be sure to make note of the altitude. If you have heart, circulatory or lung problems, check with your doctor.

Climate

Elevation: 6,311'	Avg. high/low:	Avg. inches		Avg. # days precip.	Avg. % humidity
		rain	snow		
Jan.	41/16	-	4.6	5	60
April	59/33	0.98	7.1	7	55
July	84/57	3.1	-	14	55
Oct.	64/37	0.71	3.1	5	50
YEAR	61/35	13.0	41	-	-
# days 32° or below: 161			# days 90° or warmer: 19		

What things cost

Overview: According to ACCRA, the overall cost of living in Colorado Springs is about 2 percent higher than the national average, with housing 16 percent above and health care 22 percent above. Utilities are 14 percent below.

Gas, electric, water and sewer: Colorado Springs Department of Utilities, 719-636-5401, provides all basic utilities services within the city limits. If meters are already in service, no startup charge. Deposits are usually not required. Avg. utilities bill: $110-$140 (gas, electricity, water and sewer are billed together within the city limits).

Additional natural gas company: People's Natural Gas, 719-392-3491.

Additional electric companies: Intermountain Rural Electric Association, 719-687-9277; Mountain View Electric Association, 719-495-2283.

Phone company: The area is served by US West, 800-244-1111 or 719-636-6200. Hook-up: $35; deposits waived with a credit check. Basic service: $19/mo.

Cable company: Contact Cablevision, 719-633-6616.

Car registration, license: New residents must obtain a driver's license within 30 days. A written exam is required. License fee: $15. Driver's license, 719-598-2929. Colorado plates required within 45 days of residency. Fees vary based on car. Emissions test required. Registration information, 719-520-6240.

The tax ax

Sales tax: 3 percent; county 1 percent and city 2.1 percent for a total of 6.1 percent. Drugs, groceries and medical services are exempt.

State income tax: A flat tax rate of 5 percent of federal taxable income. Pensions and Social Security income subject to federal tax are not exempt.

Retirement income: The first $20,000 in taxable pensions and Social Security is exempt for each taxpayer 55 and older. Standard deduction from adjusted gross income for married couples filing jointly when the partners are both over age 65.

Property taxes: Homes are assessed at 10.36 percent of market value, and this percentage of value is multiplied by the millage rate, which is complex and varied in Colorado Springs. As a rule of thumb, property taxes are about 1 percent of assessed value. Taxes on a $100,000 home would be about $1,000. Tax assessor, 719-520-6600.

Local real estate

Overview: Colorado Springs currently has an active and balanced buyer/seller market with a vacancy rate of about 10 percent. New construction availability is fair with a typical lot costing $43,000. Condominiums and townhouses, though available, aren't much in demand.

Average price for a 3BR/2BA home: New, $154,000; resales, $125,000.

Median price for a single family home: $114,700.

Average price for a 2BR condo: From $60,000 to $90,000, but prices in the southwest and north are higher, from $100,000 to $500,000 The overall average is $127,000 for a new unit and $98,000 for a resale.

Common housing styles and features: Front porches, full basements, patios and decks, and solar heating are among the amenities common to homes in Colorado Springs. Open construction styles that take advantage of sunshine are popular. Exteriors are made mostly of natural materials such as stucco, stone, wood or brick. Most homes do not have or need air conditioning.

Rental housing market: Rentals are available, but a 5-percent vacancy rate can make them hard to find. The average rental price for a 3BR home is in the $900 to $1,100 range. There aren't many 2BR homes available. A 1BR/1BA apartment rents for $475 per month; a 2BR/2BA for $710; and a 3BR for about $829. Apartments at a recreational community with clubhouse and pool start at $845 per month.

Nearby areas to consider: Monument, Tri-Lakes, Woodland Park.

Earning a living

Business climate: Colorado Springs was fortunate to escape the military budget-cutting of the mid-90s, and Ft. Carson remains largely intact, which is vital to the community since it is the largest employer. The city is focused on diversifying, but today more than half the city's economic output is dependent upon the military. Several high-tech companies recently relocated or expanded here, including Rockwell Semiconductor Systems. The city also is national headquarters for many nonprofit organizations, including Junior Achievement, the National Olympic Committee and Focus on the Family. Tourism is a major industry, pumping $740 million annually into the economy and employing 13,000 people. Pick up the *Colorado Springs Business Journal*, 719-634-5985.

Help in starting a business: Call the Small Business Development Center, 719-592-1894, for free business assistance and training programs.

Job market: Major employers in El Paso County include Fort Carson, MCI Communications, Hewlett Packard Co., Penrose-St. Francis Healthcare Systems, Focus on the Family, Digital Equipment Corp. and the famous Broadmoor Hotel. The unemployment rate is about 4 percent. For assistance in finding a job, try 40 Plus, 719-472-6220, a club of professionals helping peers with job searches. The membership program includes four days of training on current job search and interviewing techniques, and members can make use of a fully equipped professional office. The state agency is Rocky Mountain Service Employment and Redevelopment, 719-578-5444.

Medical care

Colorado Springs has five major hospitals, including the facilities of Penrose-St. Francis Healthcare System—Penrose Hospital, Penrose Community Hospital and St. Francis Health Center. Penrose Hospital, 719-776-5000, offers a comprehensive cancer care center, heart center, and cardiovascular, gastrointestinal and pulmonary laboratories. St. Francis Health Center, 719-776-8800, emphasizes outpatient surgery, and Penrose Community Hospital, 719-776-3000, specializes in family services, rehabilitation and diagnosis of breast cancer. Memorial Hospital, 719-475-5000, has a reputation for offering the latest technology and state-of-art medical, critical and surgical care. Centers of excellence include cancer and heart disease. Rehabilitation Hospital of Colorado Springs, 719-630-8000, provides comprehensive services for people recovering from catastrophic illness or injury.

Services for seniors

The Senior Center, 719-578-6808, offers a full range of activities and services. The center also works with Pikes Peak Community College to present classes in organ, piano, French, creative writing, literature and computers. Health screenings and services are available, including massage therapy. Three publications in the area are just for seniors: *The Beacon* (formerly *Senior Beacon*), 719-570-9424; *Senior Times*, 719-481-2321; and *Prime Times* (targeted to military retirees), 729-634-8113. The Pikes Peak Area Agency on Aging offers a Senior Information and Referral line, 719-471-2096.

Continuing education

The University of Colorado at Colorado Springs Continuing Education department, 719-262-3364, offers a variety of continuing education classes on topics such as travel (recent seminars have covered areas such as the Caribbean, Peru and Alaska), as well as writing and computer classes. Pikes Peak Community College, 719-576-7711, is an open enrollment campus offering a broad curriculum in disciplines from anthropology to word processing. Classes offered at the Senior Center are available to residents at greatly reduced tuition rates.

Crime and safety

Senior Victim Assistance Team of the Colorado Springs Police Department, 719-444-7438, is made up of trained volunteers who assist with paperwork, trauma counseling and other support services. The metropolitan area is covered by city, county and state law enforcement agencies. The crime rate is based on the 1994 FBI crime index (serious crimes per 1,000 population), of 55. A rate of 36 is well below that of most major metropolitan areas.

Getting around town

Public transportation: City of Colorado Springs Transit, 719-475-9733. Bus fares are 75 cents for adults and 35 cents for those 60 and up with any ID card.

Roads and highways: I-25, US 24 and 85/87, State Highways 83, 94 and 115.

Airport: Colorado Springs Airport, only 10 minutes away, is served by 11 airlines.

Let the good times roll

Recreation: With 250 sunny days a year and a typically mild climate, Colorado Springs offers year-round fun for golfers (with 11 public and semiprivate courses), tennis players, runners, hikers and bikers. These "warm-weather" sports hardly preclude the possibility of winter athletics, as some of the nation's most spectacular downhill skiing (Vail, Aspen, Breckenridge) is only a few hours away. There are 100 parks in the city, and 22 state parks and 17 national parks and forests are also nearby. Spectator sports fans enjoy professional teams in nearby Denver, including the Colorado Rockies (baseball), the Denver Broncos (football), the Nuggets (NBA basketball) and the Avalanche (hockey). Closer to home, the Sky Sox, the Rockies' minor league team, play at Sox Stadium. The Airforce Academy has football, baseball, basketball and hockey teams.

Culture: The nationally known Colorado Springs Symphony offers concerts of classical masterworks and pops selections in the Pikes Peak Center, a world-class facility. The Star Bar Players bring repertory theater to the area, while the Fine Arts Center Repertory Theater presents Broadway productions. The Colorado Springs Dance Theatre hosts a winter series of nationally recognized ballet, jazz and modern dance companies. The Fine Arts Center features collections of Native American and Hispanic art, as well as 19th- and 20th-century Western art. The Gallery of Contemporary Art at the University of Colorado at Colorado Springs sponsors traveling exhibitions.

Annual events: Imagination Celebration (March and April); The St. Patrick's Day Parade (March); Classic Colorado Championship Chili Cook-Off (June); the Fabulous Fourth (July); the Great Pikes Peak Cowboy Poetry Gathering (Aug.); *The Nutcracker* by the Colorado Springs Symphony, Tulsa Ballet Company and 100 local children (Nov.); Festival of Lights Celebration and Holiday Parade (Dec.).

When the kids come: Ghost Town depicts a general store, saloon and Victorian home, while Rock Ledge Ranch provides a living history of an early Colorado Springs ranch. The Flying W is a working cattle ranch with various museum buildings, rides, gift shops, cowboy-style "grub" and live country music. The Colorado Springs Children's Museum is recommended for children ages 2 to 12. Pikes Peak Cog Railway takes visitors on a trip to the 14,110 ft. summit. Manitou Cliff Dwellings, 5 miles west of Colorado Springs, is an outdoor museum portraying the lives of Native Americans.

For more information:

Chamber
The Chamber—Colorado
  Springs
2 N. Cascade Ave.,
  Suite 110
Colorado Springs, CO 80903
719-635-1571

Newspaper
*Colorado Springs Gazette
  Telegraph*
30 S. Prospect St.
Colorado Springs, CO 80901
719-632-5511

Realtor
Vicki Rusinak, Relocation Dir.
Rusinak Real Estate, Inc.
7820 N. Academy Blvd.
Colorado Springs, CO 80920
719-594-0100 or 800-481-3485
Fax: 719-593-9137

10. Ft. Collins, Colorado

Nickname: Poster City, USA
County: Larimer
Area code: 970
Population: 93,600; county 194,200
% of population over 65: 9.6
Region: Rocky Mountains
Closest metro areas: Cheyenne, Wyoming, 45 mi.; Denver, 66 mi.
Average home price: $146,000 to $187,000
Best reasons to retire here: Beautiful scenery, outstanding recreation and education, dry mountain climate.

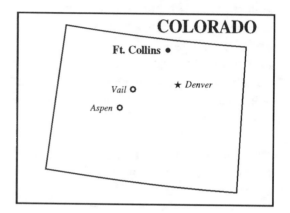

Ft. Collins at a glance

If ever there was a user-friendly city, Ft. Collins is it! Cars and commerce do not dominate life here—it's as though city leaders sat down and said, "What can we do to maintain a high quality of life?" For one thing, they made sure that every residential area was within walking distance to a beautiful park as well as shopping. All that planning worked. Ft. Collins has often been ranked as one the nation's most livable cities, and it's easy to understand why. For a city this size, the amount of recreational and cultural opportunities is remarkable. Hiking, biking, mountain climbing and fabulous cross-country skiing are just the start of outdoor living. Thanks to Colorado State University and a very culturally minded community, the performing arts, galleries and musical events are (literally) everyday occurrences. In fact, there's so much to do in Ft. Collins you'll wonder why you bought a home, because, after all, you'll hardly ever be there! The surrounding terrain, with its majestic vertical cliffs, waterfalls and sparkling blue lakes, provides daily doses of inspiration. This is a semi-arid region, with only 10 inches of rainfall a year (but 56 inches of snow!) In fact, dry air dominates in all four seasons. And while Canadian air masses make the winters cold, the snow melts in a few days. The sun shines close to 300 days a year. If you want to live in a city that's as inviting as a picture postcard, try Ft. Collins.

Possible drawbacks: There is a dearth of doctors willing to accept Medicare without supplemental insurance in this town. Medical care, though good, currently requires supplemental private insurance or travel. Poudre Valley Hospital has plans to address this issue in the near future.

Climate

Elevation: 5,033'	Avg. high/low:	Avg. inches		Avg. # days precip.	Avg. % humidity
		rain	snow		
Jan.	41/16	-	7	6	59
April	58/32	1.0	9	10	58
July	86/57	1.8	-	10	49
Oct.	65/35	.7	4	5	55
YEAR	62/35	10.0	56	-	-
# days 32° or below: 169			# days 90° or warmer: 22		

What things cost

Overview: According to ACCRA, the cost of living in Ft. Collins is nearly 10 percent above the national average, with housing at 29 percent above the norm. Groceries and health care are 10 and 13 percent above, while utilities are 30 percent less.

Gas company: Public Service Company, 970-225-4010. Hook-up charges: $8 or $28, depending whether a transfer or new hook-up. No deposit. Gas heat/appliances average $60 monthly.

Electric company: City of Ft. Collins Electrical Utilities, 970-221-6785. Hook-up: $10.67, no deposit. Public Service Company (outside city limits), 970-225-4010. All-electric homes average $110 monthly; partial electric service, $50.

Phone company: Contact US West, 800-244-1111. Hook-up: $35; deposit required pending credit check. Basic monthly service: $18.50.

Water and sewer: The City of Ft. Collins Water and Wastewater Utilities, 970-221-6681. At the time of this writing, the city was switching to metered service. No deposit or service charge unless the water is off, in which case it's $15. Average monthly rate is $50.

Cable company: Columbine CableVision, 970-493-7400.

Car registration, license: Driver's license required within 30 days of residency. License fee: $15. For information, call 970-223-3648. Residents must display Colorado plates on vehicles within 45 days of residency. Fees are based on the automobiles weight, age and taxable value. Emissions test required.

The tax ax

Sales tax: 3 percent. Ft. Collins adds an additional 3 percent. Drugs, groceries and medical services are exempt.

State income tax: Flat 5 percent of federal taxable income. No local income tax assessed. Pensions and Social Security income subject to federal tax are not exempt.

Retirement income: First $20,000 in taxable pensions and Social Security exempt for taxpayers 55 and older. Standard deduction for married couples filing jointly when both are over age 65.

Property taxes: Ft. Collins property owners pay a millage rate of about .08754 per $1,000 of assessed value; homes are assessed at 10.36 percent of market value. Taxes on a $175,000 home would run about $1,590. Taxes typically run .8 to 1 percent of the market price of the property. Larimer County Tax Assessor, 970-498-7050.

Local real estate

Overview: Prices have stabilized in recent years, with sales prices averaging about 97 percent of asking prices. Still, buying a home is about 30 percent more expensive here than the national average. Property taxes are currently stable and are not expected to rise. Most retirees relocate to the area permanently; Ft. Collins is not a major second-home market. There are many new developments, including golf communities, that are targeted to senior citizens, but these are not exclusively for persons over a certain age.

Average price for a 3BR/2BA home: New homes average about $187,000, while resales average $146,000.

Average price for a 2BR condo: New units average $110,000 and resales average $93,000.

Common housing styles and features: Condominiums and townhouses are popular, as are patio homes, which feature maintenance-free yards that are cared for by development management or the homeowner's association. Many builders in this area are building specifically to suit the needs of seniors.

Rental housing market: A great number of new apartment complexes have been built in recent years, so finding an apartment is relatively easy. However, demand is high because of area growth and the presence of Colorado State University. Single family homes for rent are scarce.

Average rent for a 2BR apartment: $600 to $800 monthly.

Nearby areas to consider: Loveland, Windsor.

Earning a living

Business climate: The economy is growing, with nearly a 6-percent jump in employment recently. Most new employment has come from construction. Ft. Collins is home to a diverse mix of business, industry and services, and the area's major sectors include education (Colorado State University and Front Range Community College), retail and manufacturing. A local major manufacturer is Symbios Logic (formerly Microelectronics Products Division), which develops, designs, manufactures and markets semiconductors, and is the world leader in SCSI chip technology and sales. Another major employer is Anheuser-Busch. Also, Ft. Collins has been fertile ground for microbreweries; there are now five in town.

Help in starting a business: The One-Stop Shop, Small Business and International Development Center, 970-226-0881, is a source for business relocation information, counseling, research, training and support services. It is sponsored by the Chamber of Commerce, the City of Ft. Collins, Colorado State University, Front Range Community College, Ft. Collins Incorporated and SCORE. The Small Business Hotline of the Office of Regulatory Reform, 800-333-7798, offers a Colorado business start-up kit.

Job market: Major employers include Colorado State University, Anheuser-Busch, Hewlett-Packard, Kodak Colorado, Symbios Logic and Wal-Mart. The Senior Employment Service Program, 303-223-2470, ext. 218, is a nonprofit job search information service offering information, referrals and counseling for people 55 and over.

Medical care

Poudre Valley Hospital, 970-495-7000, is a 235-bed regional medical center with a Regional Heart Center for medical/surgical management of heart disease and the cardiovascular system, a Regional Neurosciences Center for management of stroke and injury, an oncology unit, a Regional Wound Care Center and a Breast Diagnostic Center. The hospital is served by 243 staff physicians; 84 percent are board-certified. The medical staff represent 35 specialties, including allergy, cardiology, endocrinology, gastroenterology, oncology, hematology, radiology and more. The hospital, one of the most active surgery centers in the state, will soon open a clinic to serve people on Medicare and Medicaid without additional insurance, and the uninsured. HealthSouth, 970-493-0161, is a rehabilitation center offering physical therapy, hand, foot and ankle therapy and general orthopedic care. The Ask-A-Nurse-Alliance, 800-505-6877, offers 24-hour health information as well as doctor and dentist referral.

Services for seniors

Ft. Collins Senior Center, 970-221-6644, is an activity center emphasizing athletics, day trips, special events and education. The center offers a four-lane lap pool, spa, gym, classrooms, kitchen and multipurpose room. Classes include arts and crafts, aquatics, dance (line and ballroom), yoga, t'ai chi and computers. The center offers many day trips to regional gambling centers, museums and more. The center also has health screenings and services, including massage therapy and flu shots.

Continuing education

Colorado State University, 970-498-5288, offers a Learning in Retirement Institute for those 55 and older. Three programs are offered per year, each with six unique sessions meeting once a week. Front Range Community College, 970-226-2500, has day, evening and weekend classes that are open to seniors. Noncredit topics include personal computer training, stress management, self-esteem, photography, music and more. Seniors can also enroll in any credit class.

Crime and safety

The Ft. Collins police department is proactive, offering a variety of crime prevention programs and services, including home security surveys, fraud prevention seminars and Neighborhood Watch programs. The effort seems to be worth it, because Ft. Collins is a very safe place to live. The city reported a total crime index of 45 incidents per 1,000 people, and Larimer County reported 37 incidents per 1,000.

Getting around town

Public transportation: Buses are operated in the city by Ft. Collins Transport, 970-221-6620. Adult fares are 85 cents; seniors ride for 40 cents. It is a pass-oriented system, and seniors 60 and older can purchase a pass for $17 a year.

Roads and highways: I-25, US 87.

Airports: Denver International Airport (one hour and 15 minutes away), serves travelers with domestic and international flights. Ft. Collins-Loveland Municipal Airport offers commuter flights to Denver International.

Let the good times roll

Recreation: The area has the traditional sports in abundance (seven golf courses in town, and a total of 19 courses in the region). But it also has an extensive recreational trail system that accesses most of the city without contacting major motor traffic, and 75 miles of bike trails to boot. There are 36 public parks, and Rocky Mountain National Park is a one-hour drive away. Closer to town you'll find the Arapaho and Roosevelt National Forests, which encompass the Arapaho National Recreation Area, the Cache la Poudre Wild and Scenic River and eight wilderness areas. Horsetooth Reservoir offers fishing, water-skiing, swimming, rock climbing, camping and hiking. Whitewater rafting is very popular.

Culture: Everything starts with the Lincoln Center, which has four exhibition galleries and two theaters, and hosts 1,700 events a year. Lincoln Center houses Ft. Collins Children's Theatre, Dance Connection, Larimer Chorale, Opera Ft. Collins and the Front Range Chamber Players. The world-class Ft. Collins Symphony Orchestra performs at Lincoln Center, as does the Openstage Theatre, a company that presents a full season of classic and contemporary plays. Canyon Concert Ballet puts on several productions each year at the center. Colorado State University has the Curfman and Hatton Galleries, which showcase artworks by internationally known artists, as well as faculty and students.

Annual events: The Ft. Collins Bluegrass Festival is a three-day event with live music and great food (Feb.). April brings the Poudre Valley Art Show. The Colorado Brewers' Festival features samples from more than 100 breweries (June). Skookum Day features demonstrations of blacksmithing, branding, milking, weaving and other frontier crafts (July). New West Fest is a festival of arts, crafts, food and live music (Aug.), and the city hosts the three-day Ft. Collins Hot Air Balloon Festival (Sept.).

When the kids come: The Discovery Science Museum has hands-on experiments and displays for kids of all ages that focus on science and technology. Swetsville Zoo is not a zoo for animals—it features more than 100 artworks, including dinosaurs, flowers, animals and windmills constructed from scrap metal.

For more information

Chamber
Ft. Collins Area
  Chamber of Commerce
225 S. Meldrum
Ft. Collins, CO 80522
970-482-3746

Newspaper
Fort Collins Coloradoan
P.O. Box 1577
Ft. Collins, CO 80522
970-493-6397

Realtor
Doug Dodds
Coldwell Banker Everitt
  & Williams
2900 S. College Ave.
Ft. Collins, CO 80525
970-223-6500
800-276-2365
Fax: 970-223-6809

11. Boca Raton, Florida

Nickname: The City for All Seasons
County: Palm Beach
Area code: 407
Population: 68,272 (incorporated area)
County population: 863,518
% of population over 65: 24.9
Region: Southeast Florida
Closest metro area: Ft. Lauderdale, 44 mi.
Average home price: $135,000 to $160,000
Best reasons to retire here: Exclusive communities, low crime rate, great recreation and culture, waterfront living.

Boca Raton at a glance

Retiring to Boca Raton is like having your cake and eating it, too. You'll find yourself in a city with distinctive architectural character and lush landscaped surroundings. Living in Boca Raton is about living the good life—golf, tennis, exclusive country clubs, boutiques, fine dining and countless cultural amenities. It's also about enjoying weather so glorious (how does a balmy 75 degrees in January sound?) it would make anyone's day. Boca Raton is attractive to retirees, as nearly 25 percent of the population is over age 65. But it's is also home to many movers and shakers—in fact, *The Wall Street Journal* recently ranked it the number-one Florida city in which executives want to live. Boca Raton has many extraordinary communities and clubs, including the famed Bocaire Country Club and the Boca Raton Resort and Club. There are plenty of awe-inspiring homes to look at in this beautiful city, but even the smaller, less costly townhouses, condominiums and homes are as pretty as a picture. There are also many miles of beautiful public beaches to go with the carefully planned residential communities. And in spite of its rather exclusive image, Boca Raton is still a city of newcomers—60 percent of South Florida residents have moved here in the past 30 years.

Possible drawbacks: If you plan to summer where you winter, make sure you can stand the heat. The high temperatures and humidity in this part of Florida can be taxing. Boca is expensive because it can afford to be (the average household income is above $46,000). Retirement is supposed to be a time when your expenses decrease along with your income, but depending on where you move from, you may have the opposite experience in Boca.

Climate

Elevation: 19'	Avg. high/low:	Avg. inches		Avg. # days precip.	Avg. % humidity
		rain	snow		
Jan.	75/56	2.6	-	7	78
April	83/65	3.5	-	7	72
July	90/74	6.5	-	15	79
Oct.	84/70	8.7	-	13	80
YEAR	83/66	62.0	-	-	-
# days 32° or below: 3			# days 90° or warmer: 92		

What things cost

Overview: According to ACCRA, the composite cost of living index for Boca Raton is slightly more than 5 percent above the national average. Utilities and health care are each more than 10 percent higher than average, and housing is about 5 percent more than the norm. Groceries are 3 percent below the average.

Gas company: Florida Public Utilities Co., 407-278-2636. Few consumers have access to natural gas in Boca Raton.

Electric company: Florida Power & Light, 407-395-8700. The standard deposit is $240. There is a one-time $16 set-up charge. ACCRA found the average monthly cost for an all-electric home was $119.59.

Phone company: In Boca Raton, Bell South, 407-780-2355, or 800-753-0710 outside. There is a $40 connection fee, and a deposit of $75 or more may be required. Basic service costs about $14.79 monthly.

Water and sewer:. A deposit of $80 or more is required. Residential sewer charges are $10.34 for the first bathroom and $5.17 for each one thereafter. Public Utilities Department; 407-393-7750.

Cable company: Comcast Cablevision of Boca Raton, 407-391-7556; West Boca Cablevision, 407-848-1600 (in Palm Beach County, call 800-930-2225).

Car registration, license: New residents must obtain a Florida license within 30 days of establishing residency. Driver's license, $20; renewal, $15. (Renew every six years for safe drivers, four years otherwise.) No restrictions on seniors. Title fees: new car, $31.25; used, $33.25. Initial (one-time) registration fee: $100. Registration fees: up to $45, depending upon weight of car.

The tax ax

Sales tax: State sales tax is 6 percent, with exemptions on groceries, medical services and prescription drugs.

State income tax: None.

Retirement income: Florida ranks high among popular retirement states because the overall tax burden is modest. There's no income tax and no death or estate taxes on an estate of up to $600,000.

Property taxes: The 1995 millage rate was $21.4003 per $1,000 of assessed value. Florida offers a $25,000 homestead exemption to those whose primary residence is in Florida. Sample taxes on a $100,000 home would be $1,605. Tax appraiser's office, 407-276-1250.

Local real estate

Overview: Boca Raton enjoys stable property taxes, although housing prices have increased about 5 percent in recent years. Many retirees live in Boca part-time and maintain second homes in other parts of the country. This is especially true for those who buy in country club developments.

Median price for a single family home: $134,082.

Average price for a 3BR/2BA house: $160,000 new or $135,000 for a resale. These figures don't tell the whole story. Boca Raton is upscale, and the sky's the limit on size and amenities.

Average price for a 2BR condo: $85,000 new or $78,000 for a resale.

Common housing styles and features: Mediterranean and California contemporary styles are popular. Stucco walls, great rooms, tiled floors and private pools are common. The interiors are awesome expanses of bright white and light. Florida's native flora creates beautiful gardens and distinctive landscapes.

Median rent for a 2BR apartment: $632 a month.

Rental housing market: The rental market fluctuates seasonally, but anything under $700 goes immediately. An average rent for a 2BR home would be $950, with condos going for $750. Average 2BR apartment rents run $650 to $900, although rents can be much higher.

Communities or developments most popular with retirees: Century Village, Whisper Walk, Palm Springs, Delray Pines, Broken Sound and Stonebridge.

Nearby areas to consider: Delray, Boynton Beach, Palm Beach Gardens, Jupiter.

Earning a living

Business climate: Boca Raton is a high-powered business center; an amazing array of companies are located or headquartered here, including IBM, McDonald's Corporation, Sony Professional Products, Levitz Furniture Corporation, Federal Express, Core International, Scott Paper Company and Siemens. At the same time, it is a very active retail market, but be warned—business owners need to be prepared to pay higher than average commercial rents. It's an extremely competitive and expensive market to do business in, so it's not a great place for anyone to start a business with anything less than a full-time commitment. The good news is, median household income in Boca Raton is $46,099, making it a lucrative consumer market.

Help in starting a business: The Palm Beach Development Board grants monies from its Job Growth Incentive Fund to relocating or expanding companies in Palm Beach County. Contact the Greater Boca Raton Chamber of Commerce for information on necessary operating licenses, taxes and other assistance, 407-395-4433.

Job market: Growth in employment through the year 2005 is expected to be nearly 39 percent, with healthy gains projected in all economic sectors. The Job Service of Florida, 407-737-4925 (Delray), offers job-seeking assistance to Florida residents. The Senior Aides Employment Program, 407-355-4787 (West Palm Beach), provides referrals for part-time employment for seniors (over 55) in the nonprofit and business sectors. The recent unemployment rate for this area was 5.8 percent.

Medical care

Boca residents used to travel to take advantage of top medical treatment, but now there are many choices close to home. Boca Raton Community Hospital, 407-395-7100, is a 394-bed facility staffed by 450 physicians. Services include the Lynn Regional Cancer Center, cardiac and MRI services, rehabilitation and pain management programs. West Boca Medical Center, 407-488-8000, is a 185-bed, acute-care facility with more than 540 affiliated physicians in 45 specialties. Delray Community Hospital, 407-498-4440, is a major provider of specialized services for cardiac patients, but also offers a full range of medical, surgical and emergency services. It is a 211-bed acute care facility with 400 staff physicians. North Broward Medical Center, 954-786-6400, is a 419-bed hospital with a special focus on mature adults, and treatment centers in cancer, neurology, diabetes, arthritis and rehabilitation.

Services for seniors

The Elder Helpline is an information and referral agency that connects seniors with services, including legal counseling, meals, transportation and information for job seekers. Call 930-5040 *if you're in the county.* (The 930 exchange is available to people in Palm Beach County only.) Outside the area, call 407-547-8677. The Mae Volen Senior Center, 407-395-8920, offers 25 different services to low-income residents, and it's also an excellent resource for learning about transportation, health screenings and other needs. To contact the local chapter of AARP, call 407-368-8252.

Continuing education

Florida Atlantic University offers the Lifelong Learning Society, 407-367-3136. Membership fees are $30 annually, and eight-week courses are about $45. There are 6,500 to 7,500 people enrolled in this program. Classes include art, music, history and philosophy. Lynn University offers the Institute for Learning in Retirement, 407-994-2085 or 407-994-0770. The Institute has personal enrichment and liberal arts courses for persons 55 and over. Fees vary.

Crime and safety

Boca's crime index was 50.3 incidents per 1,000 population which is very safe among Florida cities. Palm Beach County is higher, with 88.4 crimes per 1,000 population (although in line with the rest of Florida). The Boca Raton Police Department encourages citizen involvement through the Citizens Police Academy, held three times annually.

Getting around town

Public transportation: CoTran bus fares are $1 for adults, 50 cents for seniors 60 and over. Door-to-door service is available from Dial-A-Ride, 407-930-8747.

Roads and highways: I-95, Florida Turnpike, Sawgrass Expressway, A1A, US 1 and US 441.

Airports: Palm Beach International airport is serviced by 20 carriers. Other airports are Fort Lauderdale/Hollywood and Miami International.

Ports: Port Everglades in Fort Lauderdale/Hollywood, the Port of Palm Beach and Port of Miami-Dodge Island.

Let the good times roll

Recreation: Year-round outdoor living is the appeal of Boca. There are 27 public parks with tennis courts, boat docks, swimming pools and more. There are 25 golf courses in town, and if you tire of these, there are 145 courses to be played in the county! Nature-lovers enjoy Red Reef Park and Okeeheelee Nature Center. The Atlantic Ocean, Intracoastal waterway and many lakes and canals provide boating, swimming and water sport activities. Coral reefs offshore attract scuba divers, and Boca is great for anglers and fly fishermen. For major league sports fans, the newly named Pro Player Stadium (formerly known as Joe Robbie Stadium), and home of the Miami Dolphins and the Marlins, is 40 minutes away. Shopping is superb in Boca; there are more than two dozen centers, including the Town Center Mall, with six major department stores and 176 specialty shops.

Culture: The Florida Symphonic Pops is south Florida's premier Pops orchestra, while the Florida Philharmonic Orchestra performs classic, pops and family concerts. Caldwell Theatre Company is known for cutting-edge productions, and the Royal Poinciana Playhouse in Palm Beach is a longtime favorite for Broadway shows. Boca Ballet Theatre Company presents a summer ballet in Boca, and Ballet Florida performs classical and modern dance. The largest cultural organization in the city is the Boca Raton Museum of Art. The International Museum of Cartoon Art, a unique institution, opened in 1996.

Annual events: The South Florida Fair in January features rides, food, games and entertainment. Artigras in February showcases works by artists and craftsmen in Palm Beach Gardens. The Delray Beach Tennis Winter Championships features top women pros; "Meet Me Downtown" arts and crafts festival in Boca Raton (March) and Wine and All That Jazz (July) are two extremely big events, along with Boca Festival Days in August.

When the kids come: The Children's Science Explorium is a fun, hands-on science center. You can also try the Dreher Park Zoo in West Palm Beach, or Lion Country Safari, a "cageless" zoo with 1,300 animals. Finally, the Sports Immortals Museum has the largest collection of sports memorabilia in the world.

For more information

Chamber
Greater Boca Raton Chamber
of Commerce
1800 N. Dixie Highway
Boca Raton, FL 33432-1892
407-395-4433

Newspaper
The News
33 SE 3rd St.
Boca Raton, FL 33432
407-368-9400

Realtor
Linda Reedy
ERA Trend Setter Realty
9900-A SW 18 St.
Boca Raton, FL 33428
954-783-2921
Fax: 954-783-0699

12. Daytona Beach, Florida

Nickname: The World's Most Famous Beach
County: Volusia
Area code: 904
Population: 62,855
County population: 396,631
% of population over 65: 23.1
Region: East Central Coastal Florida
Closest metro area: Orlando, 54 mi.
Average home price: $95,000 to $115,000
Best reasons to retire here: Casual lifestyle on the ocean, proximity to popular attractions, very affordable housing and living costs.

Daytona Beach at a glance

Daytona Beach claims to be "The World's Most Famous Beach," and given the nearly half a million visitors who flock to it in the spring, the claim seems to fit. Yet there are plenty of retirees who think Daytona Beach is more than a nice place to visit—it's a great place to *live*. Daytona is for the young at heart, with excellent restaurants, shopping and outdoor recreation. Residents also look forward to the world-famous Daytona 500 NASCAR Race and other annual racing events. More importantly, living costs are low, the housing market is diversified and affordable, the temperatures vary by season (but it's still a warm place to retire) and there's an abundance of cultural opportunities and continuing education programs. Seniors especially love the Elderhostel program of Stetson University in nearby Deland. Native Daytonans mention sun, sand and speed as the area's prime attributes, and it's true that the easy-going lifestyle that revolves around special events, activities and endless sunshine explains the phenomenal appeal. Daytona Beach is actually only one of seven cities nestled in the Halifax area of Volusia County. The other municipalities that make up the area are Daytona Beach Shores, Holly Hill, Ponce Inlet, Port Orange, Ormond Beach and South Daytona. Unincorporated communities include Allendale, Ormond by the Sea and Wilbur by the Sea.

Possible drawbacks: While some residents swear by Daytona, others swear *at* it. Every spring the crowds come; and with every summer comes the intense heat. Daytona is a poor choice for someone uninterested in the sun-and-fun lifestyle. You also need to tolerate the excesses of youth—spring break can get rowdy along the beach.

Climate

Elevation: 40'	Avg. high/low:	Avg. inches		Avg. # days precip.	Avg. % humidity
		rain	snow		
Jan.	69/48	2.1	-	7	78
April	80/59	2.4	-	6	72
July	90/72	6.7	-	14	80
Oct.	81/65	5.5	-	10	80
YEAR	80/61	50.0	-	-	77
# days 32° or below: 6			# days 90° or warmer: 63		

What things cost

Overview: According to the Florida Price Level Index, prices in Volusia County are 2 percent below the average for Florida.

Gas company: People's Gas System, 904-253-5635. Deposits average $85 and connection fee is $25. Average bills are $35 monthly. Few residents have access to natural gas.

Electric company: Florida Power & Light Co., 904-252-1541. Deposits range from $25 to $240. $16 charge to establish account. Average electric bill: information not available.

Phone company: The area is served by Bell South, 800-753-2909. In Daytona, call 904-780-2355. Connection fee is $40. A deposit, if required, averages from $60 to $90. Basic service is $14.15 monthly.

Water and sewer: Call the appropriate city hall. Daytona Beach, 904-258-3130, has a standard deposit of $144. Other city halls include Daytona Beach Shores, Holly Hill, Ormond Beach, Port Orange and South Daytona.

Cable company: TCI Cablevision (Daytona Beach, DB Shores, Port Orange and Ponce Inlet), 904-760-9950. CableVision (Ormond Beach), 904-677-1232. Cablevision Ind. (Holly Hill), 904-767-6811. Tomoka Cable (unincorporated areas), 904-677-4262.

Car registration, license: New residents must obtain a Florida license within 30 days of establishing residency. Driver's license, $20; renewal, $15. (Renew every six years for safe drivers, four years otherwise.) No restrictions on seniors. Title fees: new car, $31.25; used, $33.25. Initial (one-time) registration fee: $100. Registration fees: up to $45, depending upon weight of car.

The tax ax

Sales tax: Florida has a 6-percent state sales tax with exemptions for food (except restaurant meals), medical services and prescription drugs.

State income tax: None.

Retirement income: Florida takes a relatively small tax bite from retirees. There are no income taxes and no death taxes on an estate of up to $600,000.

Property taxes: Millage rates in Volusia County range from $22.81029 to $27.75415 per $1,000 of assessed value. Florida offers a $25,000 homestead exemption to permanent residents whose primary residence is in Florida. Taxes on a $100,000 home range from $1,710 to $2,082. Appraiser's office, 904-254-4601.

Local real estate

Overview: Asking prices in the Daytona area have been increasing steadily, but are still far less than many other areas of Florida. Buyers typically get excellent value for the money invested in a home. Property taxes have been stable in recent years. Many retirees in the area have followed a progression from vacationing in the area, to purchasing a second home, to becoming a permanent resident.

Median price for a single family home: $69,6000.

Average price for a 3BR/2BA home: $115,000 new; $95,000 for a resale. Comparable homes in Orlando or Miami would run about 30 percent more.

Average price for a 2BR condo: $145,000 for a new oceanfront property; $73,000 for resale inland, or $115,000 for an oceanfront resale.

Common housing styles and features: Split plans with private master bedrooms, screened "Florida rooms" and screened-in swimming pools are popular.

Rental housing market: A 3BR house averages $750 a month. In season, a furnished condo on the ocean can run $1,200 to $1,400 a month.

Average rent for a 2BR apartment: $425 to $475 per month.

Nearby areas to consider: Ormond-by-the-Sea is a beautiful township, also on the beach side of the Daytona Peninsula. (It's the northernmost point in Volusia County.) It offers affordable small houses and condominiums no more than three blocks from the ocean.

Earning a living

Business climate: Services and wholesale and retail trade account for almost half of all employment, with government making up another 19 percent. The manufacturing base in Daytona is somewhat weak. Small businesses are having a rough go of it unless they cater to tourists or are in durable medical goods and health care services. Competition is heavy.

Help in starting a business: Stetson College at Deland offers regular seminars for persons interested in developing new small businesses. The seminars are offered through the Deland and Holly Hill Chambers of Commerce. Topics covered include how to start a business, how to write a business plan, bookkeeping and tax preparation and marketing. Cost is $30 per seminar or $100 for the series of four. Call the chambers for more information. SCORE, 904-255-6889, in Daytona Beach, is a group of retired business executives who provide consulting and counseling to small businesses and entrepreneurs at no charge. The Volusia County Business Development Corporation, 904-274-3800, is an excellent source of information on economics of area. This nonprofit, county-wide development group is dedicated to attracting new employers and aiding existing industry.

Job market: Wages in the area tend to be low; the per-capita income is approximately $15,648. The unemployment rate was recently 6.4 percent. For job search assistance, call the Job Service of Florida, 904-254-3780. There is no charge to the individual or business using this service.

Medical care

Daytona Medical Center, 904-239-5050, is a 214-bed general acute care hospital with Same Day Surgery, angiography and digital vascular imaging, ultrasound, cardiac catheterization, respiratory therapy, nuclear medicine and respiratory therapy. Memorial Hospital-Ormond Beach, 904-676-6000, is a community hospital with more than 200 physicians. Memorial Heart Institute is Volusia county's only comprehensive cardiovascular center performing open heart surgery. Halifax Medical Center, 904-254-4000, is the largest medical facility on Florida's east coast. It has the only Level II Trauma Center between Jacksonville and Palm Beach and is a nationally recognized regional Oncology Center. Halifax also has the Women's Health Place, a Pain Management Center and Rehabilitation Center. Its Passport Club, 904-254-4020, for people 50 and over, offers advantages including restaurant and some pharmaceutical discounts. It also offers a speaker's bureau, newsletter and travel assistance.

Services for seniors

The Council on Aging of Volusia County operates an Elder Helpline, 904-253-4700, for the area. It also runs the Senior Employment Referral Service, which employs people 55 and older, matching those who want to supplement their income with people who need services. The Senior Citizens Law Unit, 904-255-6573, is part of Central Florida Legal Services. It assists seniors in a broad range of legal matters, including consumer law, contract law and family law. Income plays a role if litigation is required.

Continuing education

Stetson College at Deland offers a popular Elderhostel program for persons age 55 and over. Elderhostel, 904-822-7500, operates 20 weeks a year, offering a series of three "mini courses" on a variety of subjects. Participants stay on campus for the week, although there is space for commuters. Cost is $335 per session, or $145 for commuters. Topics include religious history and issues, creative writing, philosophy and ethics, Shakespeare and much more. Daytona Beach Community College, 904-255-8131, ext. 3646, has tuition waivers for resident seniors 60 and older on a space available basis.

Crime and safety

Daytona has a fairly high crime rate, at 133 per 1,000 population. The county-wide rate drops to 61.2 per 1,000 persons. There are 22 active Neighborhood Watch Programs in the city, and the Beach Patrol has more than 1,000 volunteers, including hundreds of seniors.

Getting around town

Public transportation: VOTRAN is Volusia County's public transportation system providing service on scheduled routes seven days a week. Call 904-756-7496. Seniors with VOTRAN ID cards or Medicare can ride for 35 cents. VOTRAN Gold service is for those requiring personal assistance.

Roads and highways: I-95, I-4, A1A, Rt. 1.

Airport: Daytona Beach International Airport is served by ComAir, Continental, Delta, Gulfstream Airlines, USAir and USAir Express.

Let the good times roll

Recreation: Volusia County has 20 public and semi-private golf courses, including the LPGA International. There are also 60 parks with beaches, camping, fishing and boating, and three canoe trails. Daytona Beach has 25 marinas and has some of the best ocean fishing. Marlin are found in the Gulf Stream. Sailfish, Dolphin and king mackerel are caught on trolled baits. Surf fishing offers pompano, flounder and Jack Crevalle. For spectator sports fans—the Daytona Cubs play home games in Jackie Robinson Ballpark.

Culture: The Museum of Arts and Sciences showcases collections of American and decorative arts, and arts of Cuba. Also at the museum are natural and earth sciences exhibits and the area's only planetarium. The Southeast Museum of Photography is one of the largest museums devoted exclusively to photography in the U.S. The Symphony Society of Daytona Beach offers performances featuring world-renowned musicians. Every other year, Daytona Beach serves as the summer home of the London Symphony Orchestra. The Theater Center, Inc. is a nonprofit community theater group that sponsors the St. Johns River Players and the Storybook Children's Theater. Seaside Music Theater, Florida's only professional repertory company, has five major productions annually. The Casements in Ormond Beach is the one-time home of John D. Rockefeller Jr., now an historical site and cultural center.

Annual events: The biggest event of the year, the Daytona 500 NASCAR Winston Cup, caps off a week of races in February known as Speed Week. April brings the Magnolia Street Festival with parades, entertainment, crafts and more. In May catch the Sprint Titleholders Championship Golf Tournament at LPGA International; July is the Jazz Matazz Jazz Festival at The Casements. October brings the Ormond Senior Games.

When the kids come: Try the action at Go-Kart City. Dunn Toys & Hobbies bills itself as "the South's Largest Toy Store." Orlando is less than an hour away, featuring Disney World, EPCOT Center, Universal Studios and more.

For more information

Chamber
The Chamber
Daytona Beach/Halifax Area
126 E. Orange Ave.
  (City Island)
P.O. Box 2474
Daytona Beach, FL 32115
904-255-0981

Newspapers
Daytona Beach News-Journal
901 6th St.
Holly Hill, FL 32117
904-252-1511

Orlando Sentinel
Daytona Beach Office
125 E. International
  Speedway Blvd.
Daytona Beach, FL 32118
904-252-2549

Realtor
Rachel McGrath/Ed Rancourt
ReMax All Pro Realty
2701 S. Ridgewood Ave.,
  Suite 10C
S. Daytona, FL 32119
904-788-2600
800-791-7108
Fax: 904-788-3288

13. Fort Lauderdale, Florida

Nickname: The Venice of America
County: Broward
Area code: 954
Population: 147,678
County population: 1.3 million
% of population over 65: 20.8
Region: Southeast Gold Coast
Closest metro area: Miami, 26 mi.
Median house price: $105,900
Best reasons to retire here: Recreation and culture, great medical care, waterfront living at almost every income level, solid economy.

Fort Lauderdale at a glance

Even for Florida, where everything seems special, Fort Lauderdale has a unique feeling. It's beautiful, cosmopolitan, and it's a city on the water everywhere you look—whether it's the Atlantic Ocean, the New River, the Intracoastal waterway, or the many canals that connect the city. In fact, with more than 300 miles of waterways in the city, you can travel a good part of Fort Lauderdale by boat—a feature that has earned it the nickname "The Venice of America." Fort Lauderdale and 27 other municipalities that are considered part of the greater Fort Lauderdale area take up about one-third of Broward County, with the remainder of the county dedicated to a Seminole reservation and Everglades wetlands. Once associated with spring break (350,000 college students flocked here in the days of yore), it's not "party central" anymore. The city is now a retreat for European travelers. Hotels fly the flags of Germany, England, France and more alongside the U.S. flag. Las Olas Boulevard is once again alive with sophisticated boutiques and fine restaurants. Seniors find that Fort Lauderdale offers the excitement of a big city with many features of a much smaller town. There are great cultural and recreational opportunities, and the shopping is superb.

Possible drawbacks: Added together, the 28 municipalities of the greater Fort Lauderdale area are a *big* city. Broward County is also in the center of a three-county area (including Palm Beach and Dade counties) where 31 percent of all Florida residents live. In addition, the city hosts more than 5 million visitors and tourists annually, so you can expect long lines, traffic and higher prices.

Climate

Elevation: 16'	Avg. high/low:	Avg. inches rain	snow	Avg. # days precip.	Avg. % humidity
Jan.	77/57	2.15	-	-	59
April	83/66	3.44	-	-	57
July	90/75	6.04	-	-	66
Oct.	85/70	7.66	-	-	65
YEAR	84/67	60.83	-	-	62
# days 32° or below: 0			# days 90° or warmer: 76		

What things cost

Overview: According to the Florida Price Level Index, Broward County is the fourth most expensive of any Florida county. Food prices were reported at nearly 7 percent above the Florida average, with housing 3 percent above and health care 4 percent above.

Gas company: People's Gas, 954-525-6451. Deposits average double the monthly billing for a property. Deposits can be waived based on credit history. Connect charges range from $10 to $25 monthly. $25 to $35 average monthly bill, depending on usage.

Electric company: Florida Power & Light, 954-797-5000, requires a deposit of up to $240 on most homes with air conditioners. There is a $16 service charge to connect. Average bill for a single family home is approximately $120.

Phone company: Bell South (Broward County), 954-780-2355, or 800-753-0710 outside. A deposit of $85 to $100 (possibly higher) required for most customers. Basic service is $14.15 monthly.

Water and sewer: Utilities Department, 954-938-6856. A $55 deposit is required within the city corporate limits. Sanitation for a single family home runs $27.59 a month, but water and sewer rates are based on consumption.

Cable company: Selkirk Communications, 954-527-6600.

Car registration, license: New residents must obtain a Florida license within 30 days of establishing residency. Driver's license, $20; renewal, $15. (Renew every six years for safe drivers; four years otherwise.) No restrictions on seniors. Title fees: new car, $31.25; used, $33.25. Initial (one-time) registration fee, $100. Registration fees: up to $45, depending upon weight of car.

The tax ax

Sales tax: 6 percent except on groceries, prescription drugs and medical services.

State income tax: None.

Retirement income: No inheritance or duplicate estate taxes on an estate amount of up to $600,000.

Property taxes: Florida property taxes are based on millage rates, and the state offers a $25,000 homestead exemption for Florida residents whose primary residence is in the state. Millage rates are figured on the assessed value, which should be 100 percent of the market value. Millage rates in Broward County range from 22.8152 to 29.2084. Tax assessor's office, 954-357-6830.

Local real estate

With Fort Lauderdale's 28 municipalities, the housing market is diverse. It's a buyers' market, with housing in price ranges to suit every budget. Because of concern about crime, gated communities are increasingly common. With 50 golf courses in the county, many people choose to own a home on the fairway. It's also easy to own a home on the water, with more than 300 miles of inland canals in the area.

Median price for a single family home: $105,900.

Average price for a single family home: New, $156,129; resale, $111,789. Most new construction (and vacant land) is in the southwestern part of Broward County, near the Everglades.

Average price for a 2BR condo: New, $92,473; resale, $60,984. Like nearby Boca Raton, average prices in Fort Lauderdale are misleading, as you'll find some of the most luxurious housing in Florida in this area, with prices topping out at more than $1 million on the coast.

Common housing styles and features: Ocean access and waterfront homes are available from $150,000 and up.

Rental housing market: Renters have a variety of options, although the most affordable rentals—those that start at $600 a month—are in the west.

Average rent: $425 to $775 per month for a 2BR apartment; $555 to $1,290 on the beach. Rents can go as high as $8,000 for a beach house.

Nearby areas to consider: Boca Raton, Deerfield, Lighthouse Point, Highland Beach, Pompano Beach, Coconut Creek, Parkland.

Earning a living

Business climate: Progress has its price. Fort Lauderdale has changed its image and moved upscale in the tourist market, taking rents along with it. Like neighboring Boca Raton, parts of town are becoming expensive places to do business. Tourism pumps $3 billion into Broward's economy annually, so there's money to be made in retail and services catering to tourists, if you commit yourself. In fact, 96 percent of all Broward's businesses have 50 employees or less, testifying to the strength of the small business climate. On the corporate side, there are more than 100 Fortune 500 firms with facilities in this region, including Blockbuster Entertainment Division/Viacom, Kemper National Services, American Express TRS and Motorola. Broward County is also home to a growing number of Latin American headquarters for companies such as Microsoft and Outboard Marine Corp.

Help in starting a business: Try the City of Fort Lauderdale Economic Development Department at 954-468-1515 or the Broward Economic Development Council at 954-524-3113. The local offices of SCORE can be reached at 305-356-7263.

Job market: The retail and service sectors account for more than 50 percent of all employment in Broward County. The average annual pay was recently calculated at $25,391, but in retail trade the total was only $15,700. The boating industry is also a major employer in the area, pumping more than $2.2 million into the economy every year. The Job Service of Florida can be reached at 954-730-2600. Call 954-563-8991 for the Senior Aides Employment Program.

Medical care

There is one physician to every 395 citizens of Broward County, and there are 20 acute care hospitals that provide a full range of inpatient and outpatient services. JCAHO-accredited Broward General Medical Center is a 744-bed facility that is part of the North Broward Hospital District (which also includes North Broward Medical Center, Imperial Point Medical Center and Coral Springs Medical Center). These tax-assisted hospitals offer a variety of programs for seniors, including STAR (Seniors Together Achieve Rewards), a free membership program for people 55 and older that offers free screenings and health programs for seniors. To reach Broward General, call 954-355-4400. Florida Medical Center, also JCAHO-accredited, is a 459-bed facility specializing in open heart surgery, and it has a bone marrow stem cell center, one of only three in the nation. It offers free monthly lectures and support groups for seniors. Call 954-735-6000, ext. 4032.

Services for seniors

The Elder Helpline, 954-484-4357, is a great resource for information on services and activities for seniors. The Federation of Senior Citizens, 954-749-3802, aids and assists seniors with daily needs, including referrals for doctors, hospitals, attorneys and meals. The Holiday Park Social Center, 954-761-5383, has an incredible range of programs for seniors, including day and overnight trips, dancing, golf classes, cookouts and more. Cost for the programs (except trips), is nominal. They also sponsor the South Florida Senior Games.

Continuing education

Nova Southeastern University has the Institute for Retired Professionals, which offers life enrichment, wellness and liberal arts courses. Call 954-475-7036 for information. Broward Community College, 954-494-4004, is preparing a new senior program. The Adult Community Education Department of the Broward County School Board, 954-765-6000, offers yoga, stress reduction, painting and more. Florida Atlantic University, 954-351-4180, offers seminars, workshops and short courses for personal development, and offers the Institute for Learning in Retirement at its Boca Raton campus.

Crime and safety

Fort Lauderdale has a crime rate of 186 incidents per 1,000 population, the highest rate of any city we looked at in Florida. Broward County had 92.6 crimes per 1,000 population.

Getting around town

Public transportation: Broward County Transit, 954-357-8400, has a 50 percent senior discount and provides service to 65 percent of the county.

Roads and highways: I-95, Florida's Turnpike, I-595, I-75 (also called Port Everglades Expressway), Sawgrass Expressway, A1A.

Airport: Fort Lauderdale/Hollywood International Airport is served by 37 airlines, with an average of 350 flights a day.

Port: Port Everglades is the world's second largest cruise port, with 10 passenger terminals.

Let the good times roll

Recreation: Boating is big; residents own more than 42,000 boats and snowbirds bring in another 10,000. The Atlantic Ocean also offers snorkeling, swimming or diving to investigate sunken ships and 69 miles of coral reefs. Fishing catches include bass, sailfish, dolphin, mackerel, bluefish, amberjack, black-fin tuna and swordfish. There are more than 50 golf courses and 500 tennis courts, 100 nightclubs and 2,500 restaurants. The Baltimore Orioles are here for spring training, and the Florida Marlins and Miami Dolphins play at the newly named Pro Player Stadium (formerly known as Joe Robbie Stadium) in Miramar. There's also the Miami Heat pro basketball team and the Florida Panthers of the National Hockey League. For nature lovers, Sawgrass Recreation Park is close to the protected Everglades, and there are dozens of state parks on beaches that feature horseback riding, picnicking, camping and fishing.

Culture: A 1.5-mile linear park known as Riverwalk parallels the New River downtown, linking the downtown arts and science district with the historical district and Las Olas Boulevard. It's the home of the Museum of Art and, nearby, the Museum of Discovery and Science. The Broadway-caliber Broward Center for the Performing Arts is here, as is the Miami City Ballet and Fort Lauderdale Ballet Classique. The Philharmonic Orchestra of Florida, Sinfonia Virtuosi and Chorus of Florida, and Florida's Singing Sons Boychoir are major musical institutions, while opera lovers enjoy the Opera Guild and Gold Coast Opera. If theater is your love, try the Parker Playhouse or Sunrise Musical Theater.

Annual events: Jan./Feb. brings the Las Olas Art Fair; the Seminole Tribe Fair, Taste of Fort Lauderdale and the Florida Renaissance Festival. In March it's the PGA's Honda Golf Classic, the Fort Lauderdale Festival of the Arts and Las Olas Arts Festival. In October, check out the Five Star Pro Rodeo and Senior Games swimming competition. November brings the International Boat Show, with the Winterfest Boat Parade in December.

When the kids come: Butterfly World in Coconut Creek features thousands of the world's butterflies. Flamingo Gardens is a 60-acre wildlife haven for flamingos, peacocks and birds of prey. Seminole Native Indian Village is an authentic tribal settlement.

For more information

Chamber
Greater Fort Lauderdale
   Chamber of Commerce
512 NE Third Ave.
Fort Lauderdale, FL 33301
954-462-6000
Fax: 954-527-8766

Newspapers
Sun-Sentinel
200 East Las Olas Blvd.
Ft. Lauderdale, FL 33301
954-356-4000

Palm Beach Post: 407-820-4290

Boca Raton News: 407-395-8300

Miami Herald: 954-527-8440

Realtor
Linda Reedy
ERA Trend Setter Realty
9900A SW 18th St.
Boca Raton, FL 33428
954-783-2921
Fax: 954-783-0699

14. Fort Myers, Florida

Nickname: The City of Palms
County: Lee
Area code: 941
Population: 45,495
County population: 369,072
% of population over 65: 24.9
Region: Southwest Florida
Closest metro area: Naples, 30 mi.
Median home price: $77,700
Best reasons to retire here: Gorgeous beaches and barrier islands, diversified real estate, subtropical climate, casual living.

Fort Myers at a glance

Fort Myers has a history of attracting inventive and entrepreneuring souls to the Gulf for respite: The great American inventor Thomas Alva Edison spent his winters in Fort Myers, right next door to his friend, automobile magnate Henry Ford. (The homes of both men are now museums open to the public.) Edison is reported to have said, "There's only one Fort Myers, and 90 million people are going to find out about it." He was right. During snowbird season, there are so many Ohio license plates, it's easy to be temporarily confused as to where you are. The secret is definitely out of the bag. Fort Myers and its barrier islands (Captiva and Sanibel) along with the resort town of Cape Coral offer beauty, charm, sophistication and upscale living. Regardless of where and how you live, everyone has a love affair with the soft, quartz sand beaches. In fact, newcomers often ask, "Are the beaches always so beautiful?" The answer? Only 99 percent of the time. The towering Royal Palms first brought here by Edison complement the Spanish Mediterranean architecture that predominates in the area. Modern Fort Myers is a city with a three-part economic base: tourism, construction and retirement/income dollars. As the local Chamber of Commerce points out, the economic contribution of retirees is stable, and tends to offer insulation against other economic factors.

Possible drawbacks: The high humidity, increasing housing costs and population boom have cut some retirement plans short in the area. Traffic can be horrendous in January, February and March, when snowbirds are in full force, and you'll encounter crowds in Fort Myers Beach and on Sanibel Island. Land prices soared in the early part of the decade due to scarcity. And the raccoons do more than beg in city parks—they bite.

Climate

Elevation: 13'	Avg. high/low:	Avg. inches rain	snow	Avg. # days precip.	Avg. % humidity
Jan.	75/52	1.6	-	5	81
April	85/62	2.0	-	5	72
July	91/72	8.9	-	15	80
Oct.	85/68	4.4	-	8	82
YEAR	84/64	54.0	-	-	-
# days 32° or below: 3			# days 90° or warmer: 123		

What things cost

Overview: According to ACCRA, Fort Myers is slightly below the national average in overall living costs. Housing is nearly 7 percent below average, while utilities cost almost 10 percent more. Groceries and health care are average.

Gas company: No natural gas.

Electric company: Florida Power & Light, 941-694-0183. Deposits are from $25 to $240, based on the history of the property. There is a connect charge of $16. According to ACCRA, the average electric bill is $119.74.

Phone company: Sprint/United Telephone-Florida, 800-699-0728. There is a nonrefundable $50 connection fee. Deposits are based on previous history, and they are often waived. Basic service runs about $17.42 monthly.

Water and sewer: Contact the City of Fort Myers, 941-332-6855. Inside Fort Myers limits, a deposit of about $105 is required for service on water, sewer and trash removal. Monthly charges for full service average between $50 and $70.

Cable company: Contact Jones Intercable, 941-334-8055, or Colony Cablevision, 941-463-6145.

Car registration, license: New residents must obtain a Florida license within 30 days of establishing residency. Driver's license, $20; renewal, $15. (Renew every six years for safe drivers, four years otherwise.) No restrictions on seniors. Title fees: new car, $31.25; used, $33.25. One-time, initial registration fee, $100. Registration fees: under 2,500 lbs., $26.60; 2,500-3,499 lbs., $34.60; 3,500 lbs. and over, $44.60.

The tax ax

Sales tax: 6 percent state sales tax. Exempt are groceries, prescription drugs and medical services.

State income tax: None.

Retirement income: Florida ranks high among popular retirement states because the overal tax burden reamins modest. There's no income tax, no death or estate taxes on an estate of up to $600,000, and property taxes are lower than many other areas of the country.

Property taxes: The millage rate for Fort Myers is approximately $21.4237 per $1,000 of assessed value. Florida offers a homestead exemption of $25,000 for Florida residents whose primary residence is in the state. Taxes on a $100,000 home run approximately $1,606. Call the Lee County Tax Collector's Office, 941-339-6000.

Local real estate

Overview: Fort Myers offers a large market of upper-priced homes (in the $200,000 to $600,000 range), and there are many golf course communities with prices from $90,000 to $300,000. Taxes along waterfront properties (including canals, the river and the Gulf of Mexico) have increased substantially in recent years, although Fort Myers still can claim to have some of Florida's best land values and opportunities for buying waterfront homes. Retirees tend to prefer new, gated communities with activities.

Median price for a single family home: $77,700.

Average price for a 3BR/2BA home: Average prices are in a wide range, from $80,000 to $175,000. Resale range is from $70,000 to $150,000.

Average price for a 2BR condo: $90,000 to $350,000 in golf course communities; in the mid-$70s to $120,000 in other communities.

Common housing styles and features: Open, spacious and casual floor plans are preferred, and pools and spas are often included. Ceilings tend to be high.

Rental housing market: There are abundant choices in the rental market, with average rents of $450 to $550. Seasonal rentals in furnished units range from $1,200 to $3,000 per month.

Median rent for a 2BR apartment: $608 monthly.

Communities or developments most popular with retirees: Lexington, Gulf Harbor, Country Creek.

Nearby areas to consider: Cape Coral, Lehigh Acres.

Earning a living

Business climate: Fort Myers and Lee County anticipate tremendous population and economic growth through the 1990s, with production and agriculture becoming increasingly important to the area's economy. Retirees' income also plays an important role (nearly 25 percent of the population is over 65). Especially during tough economic times, the steady income of retirees helps provide stability and some insulation from recession, as the dollars are fixed, guaranteed and spent.

Help in starting a business: Edison Community College's Small Business Development Center, 941-489-9200, offers classes and free counseling services that include management assistance to new and existing small businesses, contracting with the government and energy conservation assistance information. The Horizon Council, 941-338-3161, is a public/private partnership in Lee County dedicated to retaining existing business and encouraging new business development. It publishes a regular newsletter and has Data on Disk, a computer disk you can order with facts, demographics and other statistics about the Lee County business climate.

Job market: The most recent unemployment rate reported for the area was 5.3 percent. The service and retail sectors account for 55 percent of all employment in Lee County. Major employers include Lee Memorial Hospital, Publix Super Markets, the Mariner Group (resorts and real estate), Southwest Florida Regional Medical Center and county and city government. The Job Service of Florida, 941-278-7140, offers job search assistance to all Florida residents.

Medical care

Lee Memorial Hospital offers highly specialized services including the Diabetic Treatment Center and Neuroscience and Stroke Centers. The Older Adult Share Club, 941-334-5949, entitles seniors to participate in hospital-sponsored wellness programs and social activities. Its second campus is Lee Memorial HealthPark Medical Center, 941-433-7799. Southwest Florida Regional Medical Center, 941-939-1147, is a 400-bed acute care hospital that is home to the Heart Institute, the Chest Pain Unit and the only kidney transplant program in southwest Florida. Columbia Gulf Coast Hospital, 941-768-5000, offers deep discounts to seniors. It features a plan that entitles Medicare patients to waive their deductible and out-of-pocket expenses for inpatient care. For those with commercial insurance, substantial discounts are offered on inpatient and outpatient care. It also has a Senior Health Center. Cape Coral Hospital, 941-574-2323, has all private rooms and free transportation to and from day surgery and radiology treatments.

Services for seniors

The City of Fort Myers Senior Center, 941-332-1288, offers a variety of activities for a small fee. The Dr. Ella Piper Center, 941-332-5346, provides services to seniors of all income levels and physical abilities. Lake Kennedy Senior Center in Cape Coral, 941-574-0575, across the river from Fort Myers, has 1,500 members and offers day and overnight trips. Membership costs $9, plus additional fees for individual programs. To reach the Elder Helpline, call 941-433-3900.

Continuing education

Edison Community College offers a variety of programs of interest to seniors. Lifelong Learning Courses, 941-732-3707, cost $3 to $5 per contact hour and cover topics such as computers, health, civics, finance and art. Edison also offers general interest noncredit courses in creative writing, business, languages, personal development and more. In addition, the college hosts an Elderhostel that has a commuter option. The Lee County School District offers adult courses through the area's high schools, including photography, ceramics, quilting and computers. Costs range from $10 to $35 per class. Call 941-334-7172.

Crime and safety

Fort Myers had one of the lowest crime rates of any community we researched in Florida, with about 70 crimes per 1,000. Additionally, Lee County's crime statistics were quite low, at about 58 crimes per 1,000 population. The biggest headaches are break-ins (attributed to transients) and drug abuse in certain sections of town. For the most part, the area is quite safe.

Getting around town

Public transportation: Lee County Transit (which covers 75 percent of the county) offers half-price fares to disabled citizens or seniors with Medicare cards. Monthly passes, $18, regular price, $33.

Roads and highways: I-75 (merges with Alligator Alley), US 41, State Road 31, Highway 80.

Airport: Southwest Florida Regional Airport is served by 11 airlines and offers 397 flights per week.

Let the good times roll

Recreation: The area's expansive shoreline offers water recreation year-round. Between the Gulf of Mexico, the Caloosahatchee River and Pine Island Sound, there's swimming, boating and everything to do with the sea. If you like shelling, Sanibel Island—the world's "Seashell Capital"—is nearby (don't forget to bring a bag to collect sand dollars). Back on shore are some lovely parks and nature walks including Lake Park (great paddleboating) and Everglades Wonder Garden (exotic and native wildlife). In winter/spring the Minnesota Twins and the Boston Red Sox are in town, and there's also the Sun Sox, a senior league. There are more than 25 public and private golf courses in the area.

Culture: Downtown is home to Arcade Theatre, which presents children's programs, plays and movies. The Barbara B. Mann Performing Arts Hall brings entertainment from Broadway shows to ballet, and it's also home to the Southwest Florida Symphony Orchestra & Chorus. The Edison and Ford Winter Estates are restored, side-by-side museums now open to the public for tours, including Edison's laboratory and botanical garden. The Lee County Alliance of Arts brings numerous events to town.

Annual events: In January, 300 artisans come to town for the Lee Sidewalk Arts & Crafts Show; in February, Fort Myers celebrates the Edison Festival of Light, with more than 40 events, culminating in Florida's largest nighttime boat parade. March is time for the Annual Sanibel Shell Fair, the Annual All Florida Championship Rodeo and the Seniors Festival, featuring games, concerts and a two-day expo; the Indian Pow-Wow in April brings together people of more than 100 Native American nations. In May, fishermen enjoy the Annual Tarpon Tides Tournament. In October, there's Oktoberfest and Jazz on the Green. And in December, try the Christmas Boat-a-Long in Cape Coral.

When the kids come: The Imaginarium is a new attraction featuring a walk-through brain, a surround-sound theater, an aquaculture tank and more. Sun Splash Family Waterpark in Cape Coral has more than two dozen wet and dry attractions. Kart World offers miniature golf, bumper boats, go carts and more. Kissimmee Billie Swamp Safari in Clewiston is on the 2,000-acre Seminole reservation and features ecotours, airboat rides and reptile shows.

For more information

Chamber
Greater Fort Myers Chamber
  of Commerce
P.O. Box 9289
Fort Myers, FL 33902
941-332-3624

Newspaper
Fort Myers News-Press
2442 Anderson Ave.
Fort Myers, FL 33902
941-335-0200

Realtor
Lois A. Tous, GRI
Priscilla Murphy Realty, Inc.
13831 Vector Ave., Suite 105
Fort Myers, FL 33907
941-482-5112
800-447-5112
Fax: 941-482-7653

15. Gainesville, Florida

Nicknames: The Tree City, University City
County: Alachua
Area code: 352
Population: 90,753
County population: 191,000
% of population over 65: 9
Region: North Central Florida
Closest metro area: Jacksonville, 78 mi.
Average home price: $80,000 to $90,000
Best reasons to retire here: University offers culture and education, reasonable cost of living, excellent medical facilities.

Gainesville at a glance

Gainesville is a charming college town with beautiful old homes and tree-lined streets. It is located in Alachua County, a 965-square-mile area, 65 percent of which is a wilderness of forests, lakes and wetlands. In its early history, Gainesville was a citrus capital, but a series of freezes ended that economic venture. A new direction was set in 1906, when the University of Florida was established in town. Now one the nation's 10 largest universities, the University of Florida brings significant educational and cultural opportunities to Gainesville residents, offers excellent health care and is the major employer in the city. Over and over again, Gainesville ranks at the very top in surveys of best places to live in America. Its small-town charm, beauty and security mixed with the sophistication of its intellectual and cultural climate makes it desirable. There is a consensus that seniors are a welcome part of the mix in this diverse and lively college town. Another special aspect of Gainesville is the change of seasons; the fall foliage is beautiful, and though the heat of a summer day can be torrid, things cool off quite nicely at night. Add affordable living costs and abundant recreational opportunities, and you've got a winner.

Possible drawbacks: The hardest thing to find in Gainesville is something negative to say about the town. However, the student population is quite large—38,000 during the regular school year—and they make their presence known. If the excesses of youthful enthusiasm get on your nerves, you may need to avoid the campus area. Also, if you're interested in part-time work, you will compete with students for jobs.

Climate

Elevation: 165'	Avg. high/low:	Avg. inches		Avg. # days precip.	Avg. % humidity
		rain	snow		
Jan.	71/46	2.5	-	7	78
April	81/57	3.2	-	7	70
July	92/73	7.0	-	18	78
Oct.	83/62	4.3	-	8	77
YEAR	81/59	51.0	-	-	-
# days 32° or below: 18			# days 90° or warmer: 91		

What things cost

Overview: The overall cost of living in Gainesville is about 3 percent below the national average. Grocery costs are slightly below the national average, and utilities are slightly above. Housing costs are almost 7 percent below average, and healthcare is about 5 percent below.

Gas and electric: Gainesville Regional Utilities, 352-334-3434. The average monthly bill for gas is $25, although costs can peak at $60 to $85 in winter months. The average monthly bill for an all-electric residence is between $45 to $90, with severe months (Aug., Jan.) ranging from $75 to $190. There is a $10 service charge and a 10 percent county utility tax. Other monthly charges include: water waste, $11 to $14; storm water runoff, $5; water, $6 to $12; and refuse, which runs $13.50 to $19.

Phone company: Call Southern Bell, 352-780-2355. A deposit, averaging $75, may be required to begin service. Basic service averages $13.30 monthly.

Cable company: Cox Cable University City, 352-377-2123.

Car registration, license: New residents must obtain a Florida license within 30 days of establishing residency. Driver's license, $20; renewal, $15. (Renew every six years for safe drivers, four years otherwise.) No licensing restrictions on seniors. Title fees: new car, $31.25; used, $33.25. Initial (one-time) registration fee, $100. Registration fees: under 2,499 lbs., $24.60; 2,500-3,499 lbs., $34.60; 3,500 lbs. and over, $44.60.

The tax ax

Sales tax: 6 percent, with food and prescription drugs exempt.

State income tax: There is no state income tax in Florida.

Retirement income: Florida ranks high among the popular retirement states because the tax bite remains modest. There are no income taxes or death taxes on an estate valued at up to $600,000, and property taxes are low.

Property taxes: Florida offers a $25,000 homestead exemption for permanent residents whose first home is in Florida. Millage rates are calculated on the appraised value of the home, which should be the same as the market value. Millage rates in the Gainesville area range from $26.7902 to $29.7442. Taxes on a $100,000 home with a homestead exemption, for example, would be approximately $2,009 at the low end to $2,230.82 at the highest rate.

Local real estate

Overview: Prices are on the rise in this area, although housing costs are still very affordable compared to other parts of the country and especially to coastal regions of Florida. In this area, retirees tend to gravitate toward social, recreational and golf course communities when purchasing a home.

Median price for a single family home: $89,900.

Average price of a 3BR/2BA home: New homes average $90,000, and resales average $80,000.

Average price for a 2BR condo: New condos: $75,000; resales: $70,000.

Common housing styles and features: Single family homes are mostly one-story, with one-car garage or carport. Old homes are all-electric, while newer homes have gas utilities.

Rental housing market: There are many options at every level, including apartments, condominiums and homes. During the academic year, the market tightens considerably.

Average rent for a 2BR apartment: Apartments range from $300 to $700 per month, although ACCRA reported an average rent of $634.

Communities or developments most popular with retirees: Meadowbrook Golf Community, Turkey Creek Forest (for homes under $100,000) and Haile Plantation, a 1,600-acre master-planned community near the University of Florida that has won residential environmental awards from the Florida Association of Realtors.

Nearby areas to consider: Melrose, Keystone.

Earning a living

Business climate: Gainesville's economy is diverse and vital, with the retail, service and health care sectors being especially strong. Unemployment recently hit 4.2 percent, a level many communities would envy. The University of Florida is a major factor in the local economy, and the health care industry is the second-most important employment sector.

Help in starting a business: The Chamber of Commerce offers a variety of information and programs for new small-business owners. It publishes a free pamphlet on business assistance services, including information on free advisory programs and groups. The guide also has information on getting business loans. The chamber also works with the Gainesville Innovation Network (GAIN) in providing assistance. GAIN has volunteers that nurture fledgling businesses by providing expertise and assisting in the search for financing. For details, call 352-334-7100. The local SCORE chapter can be reached at 352-375-8278. Also, you may wish to contact the University of Florida's Small Business Development Center at 352-377-5621. The SBDC offers free, confidential, one-on-one counseling to business owners at all stages of business development.

Job market: The job market is good if you're seeking a job in the university, insurance, medical or environmental areas. However, if you're searching for part-time opportunities, especially in retail, you'll be competing with students. The Jobs and Benefits Office, 352-955-2245, can offer assistance to senior job-seekers of all income levels.

Medical care

Alachua County is home to four hospitals and 1,200 physicians, surgeons and dentists, which is the largest per capita count in Florida (1 doctor/dentist for every 75 citizens). The hospitals are Alachua General, 352-372-4321, a full-service center with a 24-hour, emergency medical department. North Florida Regional Medical Center, 352-333-4000, is a 267-bed facility with 300 physicians on staff. Its 60-acre campus contains the Cancer Center for comprehensive cancer care and the Achievement Center for comprehensive physical rehabilitation and fitness. Shands Hospital, 352-395-0111, is a 558-bed facility on the campus of the University of Florida. It is the leading referral center for Florida and the whole of the Southeast. Veterans Administration Hospital, 352-376-1611, has 473 beds to serve eligible patients and it is the site of the VA's geriatric research.

Services for seniors

RSVP (Retired and Senior Volunteer Program) offers a free *Retirement Living Guide*. RSVP Gainesville has 600 volunteers who contribute 27,000 hours to the community through 75 different volunteer stations, including all four area hospitals, arts agencies, the Alachua County Library District, the Gainesville Police Department, social programs for children, families and seniors and many other organizations. The Center for Aging Resources maintains the toll-free Elder Helpline, offering telephone assistance for older persons and their caregivers and providing practical information about any problems. Contact them at 800-262-2243 or 352-629-7407.

Continuing education

The University of Florida is the nation's 10th largest, the oldest university in Florida and the largest university in the South. It is also among the nation's top 25 research universities. It allows seniors who have been state residents for at least one year to audit courses free of charge pending available space. With 17 schools and colleges, there's a lot to choose from.

Crime and safety

There were 116 crimes per 1,000 people in Gainesville in 1994. The crime index for Alachua County was 100 incidents per 1,000 people. Both the city and county rates are higher than the national rate of 55 incidents per 1,000, and are near the mid-range of Florida cities we researched. Local law enforcement uses various techniques to educate seniors and protect them from crime. The Alachua County Sheriff's Office participates in the Meals on Wheels program, with deputies delivering meals and educating seniors on home frauds. The sheriff's office also works with other organizations in specific areas to conduct gun safety programs and home security analyses.

Getting around town

Public transportation: Regional Transit System, 352-334-2600.

Roads and highways: I-75, US 301, 441 and Rt. 26.

Airports: Gainesville Regional Airport is served by four national and regional carriers. Jacksonville International Airport (78 miles away) is a hub for 10 major airlines and six regional carriers.

Let the good times roll

Recreation: Nature lovers will be awed by the many beautiful sites in Alachua County. These include Bivens Arm Nature Park (57 acres of oak hammock and marsh), Morningside Nature Center (a living history farm), Devil's Millhopper State Geological Site (a spectacular, 500-ft. wide, 120-ft. deep sinkhole filled with rare plants), Kanahapa Botanical Gardens (62 acres of woodlands, meadows, vineries and gardens) and Paynes Prairie State Preserve (a 20,000-acre wildlife sanctuary). Fishing is popular in the area's six freshwater lakes. There are seven golf courses, including public and private links, and tennis courts are numerous. Athletic events at the University of Florida are popular with local residents of all ages. Gainesville has been ranked among the nation's top 10 bicycling communities, featuring 60 miles of roadways with bicycle lanes. If you prefer to ride horses you can visit Canterbury, an equestrian showplace.

Culture: Through the University of Florida's new, 1,800-seat Center for the Performing Arts, the Gainesville community is treated to dance performances, theater and orchestral concerts featuring world-renowned performers. The University also features the Samuel P. Harn Museum of Art, where works of art from around the world are displayed. Gainesville's Hippodrome State Theater is one of only four state-supported theaters in Florida, bringing the community a continuing series of plays featuring renowned artists.

Annual events: February brings the Hoggetowne Medieval Faire, attracting more than 20,000 people. The Gatornationals are held in March, with the fastest dragsters competing for $1 million. April brings the Spring Art Festival, featuring wares by 300 artists and craftsmen. In October, it's the Celebration of the Autumn Moon, with a one-mile path of luminarias, live music and entertainment.

When the kids come: Morningside Nature Center (an 1880s working farm where kids can do chores and feed the animals) is very popular. Tubing is a favorite pastime at the area's many natural springs, and Gainesville is only a short drive (45 miles) from Silver Springs, one of Florida's oldest and biggest attractions.

For more information

Chamber
Gainesville Area Chamber
  of Commerce
300 East University Ave.
P.O. Box 1187
Gainesville, FL 32602-1187
352-334-7100

Newspaper
Gainesville Sun
2700 SW 13th St.
Gainesville, FL 32608
352-378-1411
800-443-9493

Realtor
Meredith McConnell
Bosshardt Realty Services, Inc.
5542 NW 43 St.
Gainesville, FL 32653
352-371-6100
800-284-6110
Fax: 352-378-2737

16. Jacksonville, Florida

Nickname: Florida's First Coast
County: Duval
Area code: 904
Population: 714,300
County population: 981,600
% of population over 65: 11
Region: Northeastern Florida
Closest metro area: Daytona Beach, 92 mi.
Average home price: $90,000 to $150,000
Best reasons to retire here: Mild climate, reasonable cost of living, excellent housing prices, and lots of outdoor activities.

Jacksonville at a glance

Jacksonville is a city of surprises and delights. It is the largest city in square miles in the continental United States, but its many distinct neighborhoods and municipalities give it a small-town friendliness (what a delight)! The Jacksonville area is known as the "First Coast" because it was near here that Spanish explorer Ponce de León first set foot on Florida soil. The first European to see what many generations of Americans regard as paradise, he named the land "La Florida"—the Flower. Today, Jacksonville is still a major point of entry into Florida for visitors, with more than 3.8 million traveling through Jacksonville International Airport annually. For retirees, the First Coast area still lives up to de León's favorable first impressions, offering a mild climate and abundant recreational, cultural and educational opportunities. Jacksonville is sited near, around and by the water—depending upon which body of water you're talking about—the St. Johns River, the Atlantic Intracoastal waterway, the Atlantic Ocean or one of the numerous rivers and lakes. It's the home of major sports and sporting events (the NFL Jacksonville Jaguars, the Players Championship and the Association of Tennis Professionals Classic). And when it comes to real estate, you'll find a true buyer's market, with prices averaging 18 percent below the national average.

Possible drawbacks: The winters are wonderful here, but the summers can be scorchers. Also, as the gateway to Florida, Jacksonville is easily accessible from highways and interstates—which means traffic can be heavy (crossing the Buckman Bridge is said to take ages, even on a good day).

Climate

Elevation: 26'	Avg. high/low:	Avg. inches		Avg. # days precip.	Avg. % humidity
		rain	snow		
Jan.	67/43	2.72	-	10	56
April	79/55	2.77	-	8	50
July	91/72	5.60	-	11	56
Oct.	80/59	2.90	-	3	50
YEAR	79/57	51.32	trace	105	55
# days 32° or below: 16			# days 90° or warmer: 83		

What things cost

Overview: According to ACCRA, Jacksonville's over-all cost of living is 5 percent below the national average, but housing costs were a whopping 20 percent below.

Gas company: People's Gas, 904-739-1211. Deposits are required and run $40 and up. Turn-on charge is $25. Natural gas is not commonly used.

Electric company: The Jacksonville Electric Authority (JEA) services most of Duval County. A deposit of $20 to $125 is required depending upon property usage records. Average monthly cost for an all-electric home is $113. St. Johns and Nassau counties are served by Florida Power and Light, 800-226-6543.

Phone company: Southern Bell Telephone, 800-753-2909. Cost to establish service is $40. A deposit of $50 to $80 may be required. Basic service averages $16 per month.

Water and sewer: The majority of services are arranged through JEA offices under Establishing Electrical Service, 904-632-5200. Some residences have private utilities. Call to determine relevant service. Water and sewage bills run about $35 per month.

Cable company: Call Continental Cablevision, 904-731-7700.

Car registration, license: New residents must obtain a Florida license within 30 days of establishing residency. Driver's license, $20; renewal, $15. (Renew every six years for safe drivers, otherwise four years.) Title fees: a new car is $31.25; used, $33.25. Initial (one-time) registration fee: $100. Registration fees: up to $45, depending upon weight of car.

The tax ax

Sales tax: The state of Florida's retail sales tax is 6 percent, and Duval County adds a 5-cent option tax.

State income tax: There is no personal income tax in Florida.

Retirement income: There are no income, death or estate taxes on an estate valued at up to $600,000.

Property taxes: There are six districts in Duval with millage rates ranging from 21.2286 to 23.6612. Millage rates are applied to the appraised value of the home, which should be 100 percent of market value. Florida has a $25,000 homestead exemption. Sample taxes on a $150,000 home would range from $2,654 to $2,958. Duval County Tax Collector's Office, 904-630-2000.

Local real estate

Overview: A buyer's market for some time, many folks are astonished by how much they can afford. Of countless developments to choose from, plenty are designed around golf. There are more than 25 retirement communities and/or facilities in the Jacksonville area. There has been slow but steady appreciation in market values in recent years, with minor property tax increases.

Median price for a single family home: $83,100.

Average price for a single family home: Jacksonville's sheer size makes this a tough one to pinpoint. The more affordable range, which would likely be a standard suburban housing area, includes homes in the $90,000 to $150,000 range, while homes in waterfront communities may range from $150,000 to $300,000 and up.

Average price for a 2BR condo: Condos in standard suburban areas are available in a range from $35,000 to $60,000; the jump to waterfront units is steep— ranging from $200,00 to $300,000.

Rental housing market: Average rent for a 2BR apartment is $525 to $550. Apartments are from $350 to $1,000, while homes can vary from $500 to $2,000 depending upon size and location.

Communities or developments most popular with retirees: Orange Park Golf and Country Club, Jacksonville Golf and Country Club, The Champions Club at Julington Creek, Deerwood, Sawgrass, Plantations and many more.

Nearby areas to consider: Orange Park, Fleming Island, Ponte Vedra, St. Augustine.

Earning a living

Business climate: Jacksonville is a busy seaport city with a diverse economic structure, and it has seen tremendous economic growth since the mid-1980s. There is no shortage of labor, but job growth has been steady, and unemployment is typically below the national average. It is one of the South's financial capitals, with nearly 10 percent of the Duval County work force employed in the finance, real estate or insurance industries. Another important factor in the local economy is the military spending. The retail market has rebounded considerably since the early 1990s, with firms like Barnes & Noble launching multistore expansions. However, much of this activity is taking place in suburban areas and not in the downtown market.

Help in starting a business: Chamber of Commerce Business Services Center, 904-924-1100, presents programs during the year targeted at developing businesses. Small Business Referral Network, 904-646-2489, is a free service to small business owners. It offers a resource directory and can connect you with accountants, attorneys, bankers, insurance agents, business consultants and more. Service Corps of Retired Executives can be reached at 904-443-1911.

Job market: The rate of job growth in Jacksonville and environs has been about 12,000 jobs per year since 1980, or about 25 percent over a little more than a decade. Major employers include AT&T American Transtech, Barnett Bank, Blue Cross and Blue Shield, CSX Transportation, Lamborghini, PGA Tour, ATP Tour and Merrill Lynch Credit Corporation. Jobs and Benefits Center, 904-798-4780.

Medical care

First Coast residents enjoy easy access to health care, with more than 2,300 physicians practicing in the area and 20 hospitals that provide services from emergency care to diagnostic evaluation and transplant services. Major area hospitals include: Baptist Medical Center/Wolfson Children's Hospital, 904-393-2000; Memorial Hospital, 904-858-7600; St. Luke's Hospital, 904-296-3700; St. Vincent's Medical Center, 904-387-7300; and University Medical Center, 904-549-5000, which has one of four Level I trauma centers in the state of Florida and operates minor emergency clinics located throughout the area. The Mayo Clinic of Jacksonville, 904-953-2000, was the first Mayo Clinic to be established outside Rochester, Minnesota. Mayo Clinic patients requiring hospital care are referred to St. Luke's.

Services for seniors

The Jacksonville Senior Services Program, 904-630-0928, offers everything from field trips and events to counseling and meals. It operates 25 senior and community centers throughout the city open 8:30 a.m. to 3 p.m. daily. Other services include the Elder Helpline, at 904-789-9503, and St. Vincent's Senior Access Line, 904-387-7354. Both of these are information and referral sources for persons age 55 or older in the Jacksonville area. There are more than a dozen chapters of AARP in the Jacksonville area. Call the Elder Helpline or St. Vincent's Senior Access Line for area coordinator listings.

Continuing education

Florida Community College (FCC) at 904-633-8390, offers reasonably priced ($11 to $20 per 10-week session) noncredit courses through its GOLD (Golden Opportunities for Lifelong Development) program. Classes are held in sewing, cooking, weight management, nutrition and computers. FCC also offers a Widowed Persons Program, with advice on dealing with loss, including money management issues. According to program organizers, the group also has served as a networking and support group for persons adjusting to life alone.

Crime and safety

Jacksonville's crime index is 97 incidents per 1,000 population and Duval County is nearly the same, which is higher than the national average, but in line for populous Florida. The Office of the Sheriff-Jacksonville Police is the law enforcement agency for the consolidated area of Jacksonville/Duval County. The Crime Prevention Division offers free programs on flimflam and crime games, personal safety and more. Community Affairs Division, Crime Prevention, 904-630-2160.

Getting around town

Public transportation: Free bus service is provided to seniors 60 and older by the Jacksonville Transportation Authority.

Roads and highways: I-10, I-95, I-295.

Airport: Jacksonville International Airport was recently recognized as one of the nation's fastest-growing airports. It is a hub for 10 major airlines and six regional carriers.

Let the good times roll

Recreation: In 1994, Jacksonville was selected as the 30th National Football League franchise, and the Jacksonville Jaguars were born. The team played its first season in 1995, kicking it off in the renovated, 80,000-seat Jacksonville Municipal Stadium (formerly the Gator Bowl). There are 19 public boat ramps and numerous marinas in Duval County. The area offers great freshwater fishing and saltwater fish include snapper, grouper, dolphin, marlin and kingfish. If golf is your sport, Jacksonville is your spot. The First Coast area is home to the PGA Tour world headquarters, World Golf Village and the Golf Hall of Fame. It's also the home of the Players Championship at Sawgrass. There are 17 public courses, seven semi-private clubs, 16 private courses and six resort courses. The Association of Tennis Professionals (ATP Tour) is in St. Johns County, hosting the ATP Tour Classic each October. The Bausch and Lomb Women's Association Championship and the DuPont All American Championships are also held in the area annually.

Culture: The Cummer Museum of Art and Gardens, Jacksonville Art Museum, and the Alexander Brest Museum and Gallery at Jacksonville University feature permanent collections and traveling exhibitions of art. Visit the Museum of Science and History and learn about the ecology of the St. John's River, or look at the stars in the Alexander Brest Planetarium. Residents also enjoy the Jacksonville Symphony Orchestra. The annual Jacksonville Jazz Festival is the largest free jazz festival in the world with more than 130,000 visitors flocking to hear the sounds of legendary greats. Community theater groups include the Alhambra Dinner Theatre and Case Theatre Company.

Annual events: The annual River Run, designated as the USA 15K National Championship, is in March. The Players Championship is in April, and a Taste of Jacksonville, a weekend of entertainment is in May. The Fourth of July brings an all-day festival in Metropolitan Park, culminating with "Skyblast." The Jacksonville Jazz Festival is held in October.

When the kids come: Disney World and Universal Studios are in Orlando, 146 miles away. Closer to home, there's Jacksonville Zoological Gardens, featuring more than 600 animals. Also, visit the Museum of Science and History, Science PODS (Personally Operated Discovery Stations) and Kidspace for the very youngest visitors.

For more information

Chamber
Jacksonville Chamber
  of Commerce
3 Independent Dr.
Jacksonville, FL 32202
904-366-6600

Newspaper
Florida Times-Union
One Riverside Ave.
Jacksonville, FL 32202
904-359-4255

Realtor
W. Wane Weir
Re/Max on Park Avenue
2233 Park Ave., Suite 500
Orange Park, FL 32073
904-269-8100
Fax: 904-269-8108

17. Kissimmee/St. Cloud, Florida

Nickname: Heaven's Place
County: Osceola
Area code: 407
Population: 32,759 Kissimmee;
14,900 St. Cloud
County population: 126,675
% of population over 65: 14.6
Region: Central Florida
Closest metro area: Orlando, 11 mi.
Average home price: $85,000 to $88,000
Best reasons to retire here: Climate, year-round recreation, major attractions nearby.

Kissimmee/St. Cloud at a glance

This part of Central Florida is an area originally inhabited by the Caloosa people, who enjoyed a land of natural beauty, with abundant lakes, mild, sunny days and cool nights. They called it "Heaven's Place," and many of today's retirees agree. While Kissimmee/St. Cloud offers easy access to the coastal beaches, this Central Florida area features excellent fishing and boating, an economy that is prosperous and growing, and a low cost of living. Historically, the area has been favored by seniors—St. Cloud actually began as a retirement settlement for Civil War veterans. Osceola is now one of Florida's fastest-growing counties, having seen a 132 percent increase in population between the 1980 and 1990 censuses, yet it is still largely undeveloped and agricultural. Citrus groves cover the county's fertile lands, and it is also prime cattle country. There are more than 100,000 acres of recreational waters in Osceola County, all set in a warm climate that allows for year-round enjoyment. The Kissimmee Chain of Lakes attracts boating and fishing enthusiasts from around the world, and area wildlife is abundant—you'll find white-tailed deer, songbirds, wading birds, ospreys, turkey and bobcats here, in proximity to the excitement of Orlando. Shopping can be a dream come true in this area, running the gamut from boutiques to outlet centers with terrific prices.

Possible drawbacks: The newer parts of Kissimmee cater to the tourists who flock to Orlando attractions, and it's nothing but miles of hotels, restaurants and tourist attractions. Tourism has become a major force in the economy, but wages tend to be very low as a result. Proximity to the world's largest tourist attractions is a factor every prospective resident needs to consider.

Climate

Elevation: 90'	Avg. high/low:	Avg. inches		Avg. # days precip.	Avg. % humidity
		rain	snow		
Jan.	71/50	2.15	-	6	57
April	82/61	1.80	-	5	46
July	90/73	7.25	-	18	59
Oct.	83/66	2.42	-	9	56
YEAR	81/61	48.11	-	115	55
# days 32° or below: 2			# days 90° or warmer: 105		

What things cost

Overview: Detailed cost of living information for Kissimmee/St. Cloud is not available, but the Florida Price Level Index indicates that Osceola is the 19th most expensive of Florida's 67 counties. Food costs are almost 6 percent higher than the Florida average. Nearby Orlando's ACCRA composite index is about 2 percent below the national average, with housing nearly 9 percent below the norm. Utilities cost about 10 percent more than the national average.

Gas company: None.

Electric, water and sewer services: Contact the Kissimmee Utility Authority, 407-933-7777, provides electric, water and sewer services in the Kissimmee and a surrounding 85-square mile area. Deposits may be waived. The City of St. Cloud, 407-957-7373, provides all three services to its residents and surrounding 200-square mile area. Deposit and service charge required for connection. Average electric bill is $100 monthly.

Phone company: Sprint United Telephone of Florida, 407-339-1811 (Osceola County). Deposits may be waived. Basic service costs are $15 monthly.

Cable company: Time-Warner Cable, 407-847-8001 (Kissimmee); Cablevision of Central Florida, 407-892-8466 (St. Cloud).

Car registration, license: New residents must obtain a Florida license within 30 days of establishing residency. Driver's license, $20; renewal, $15. (Renewal every six years for safe drivers, four years otherwise.) No special restrictions on seniors. Title fees: new car, $31.25; used, $33.25. Initial (one-time) registration fee, $100. Registration fees: up to $45, depending upon weight of car.

The tax ax

Sales tax: 6 percent. Groceries, prescription drugs and medical services are exempt. Osceola County collects an extra 1 percent of sales for special projects. There is also a tourist tax of 4 percent on housing rentals of six months or less.

State income tax: None.

Retirement income: Florida has no income taxes and no death taxes on an estate valued at up to $600,000.

Property taxes: Kissimmee millage rates are $21.8198 per $1,000 of assessed value; St. Cloud millage rates are $21.4535 per $1,000 of assessed value. Assessed value should be 100 percent of market value, though due to complex regulations, it may be slightly less. Taxes on a $100,000 home in Kissimmee would run $1,636; in St. Cloud, $1,609. Osceola County Property Appraiser, 407-847-1350.

Local real estate

Overview: In spite of explosive growth in recent years, Osceola County is only about 5 percent developed, which is surprising given the proximity to Orlando and the sheer volume of tourist business in the area. Resales of existing single family homes have historically shown better-than-average appreciation.

Average price for a 3BR/2BA home: $88,000 for a new home; $85,211 for a resale.

Average price for a 2BR condo: New condominiums average about $70,000, while resales average about $58,000.

Common housing styles and features: There is a great variety to choose from in terms of architectural style, from colonial to contemporary, provincial to Californian. "Florida look" housing typifies the area, featuring spacious, open floor plans and stucco exteriors. Construction costs are reasonable, and lots on the water are still available.

Rental housing market: The rental market in this area is somewhat seasonal, so it's best to make rental arrangements as far in advance as possible. You'll pay a premium price from December through March.

Median rent for a 2BR apartment: $450 to $550 monthly.

Communities or developments most popular with retirees: Good Samaritan Retirement Village is home to 2,000 residents age 62 and older, with accommodations ranging from garden-type patio apartments to mobile home sites.

Nearby areas to consider: Buenaventura Lakes and Poinciana are two of the fastest-growing communities.

Earning a living

Business climate: The arrival of Walt Disney World and its many attractions in Orlando has had an enormous impact on the area business community for more than three decades, adding international tourism, manufacturing and service-related industries to the county's agricultural economic base. Some five million visitors spend more than $2 billion annually in Osceola County. The retail market is still growing, but it's extremely competitive. Nonetheless, growth is expected: a whopping 32-percent increase is projected for the area through the year 2000. Cattle ranching remains a cornerstone of the local economy, as does citrus growing. (Central Florida accounts for 25 percent of Florida's total citrus production, and recent trade agreements have made the future of citrus export even more lucrative.)

Help in starting a business: The University of Central Florida (in Orlando) houses a Small Business Development Center, which offers a variety of seminars and free, one-on-one counseling. For more information, call 407-823-5554. You can reach the local chapter of SCORE at 407-648-6476.

Job market: Osceola is the third-fastest growing county in Florida. Employment growth is keeping pace with business development, but because most jobs are in the tourist industry, wages have a tendency to be very low. Job Service of Florida, 407-897-2880, is a statewide government network that assists any and all Florida residents who are seeking employment.

Medical care

Osceola County's primary care hospitals are Florida Hospital-Kissimmee, Osceola Regional Hospital and St. Cloud Hospital. They have a total of 373 hospital beds, and 150 physicians serve area residents. JCAHO Columbia Medical Center Osceola announced plans in 1994 to build a new, state-of-the-art hospital to meet the growing needs of the county. The hospital has emergency services, a cardiac catheterization lab, CT scanning, an oncology unit, nuclear medicine and radiological services and treatment. It is operated under Columbia Health Care, Inc., 407-846-2266. Florida Hospital-Kissimmee, 407-846-2266, is owned and operated by the Seventh Day Adventist Church and serves as a community hospital for greater Orlando and referral hospital for Central Florida and much of the southeastern U.S. Orlando Regional Healthcare System, 407-892-2135, provides services at St. Cloud Hospital, including same-day surgery, cancer treatment and physical therapy.

Services for seniors

Osceola County Senior Citizen Center/ Council on Aging, 407-846-8532, provides a variety of services for older persons including homemaker services, legal counsel or referral and transportation services. The center also offers social and educational activities, including dancing, art classes, bridge, Tai Chi and much more. The Elder Helpline can be reached through the offices of Senior Resource Alliance, 407-623-1380. The Elder Helpline provides information and assistance referrals to appropriate agencies.

Continuing education

The University of Central Florida in Orlando has a Learning Institute for Elders, 407-249-4778. It offers life enrichment and liberal arts courses in four- to 12-week terms for an annual fee of $125. There is no outside study required and no tests. Florida residents age 60 and over can also register for regular classes free of charge on a space-available basis. The college is located about an hour from Kissimmee.

Crime and safety

Recent statistics for Kissimmee indicate a high index of 120 incidents per 1,000 population, but note this is a total crime incidence reported against permanent residents only (excluding the tourist population). St. Cloud fares much better at approximately 65 incidents per 1,000, and Osceola County averages about 80 incidents per 1,000 residents.

Getting around town

Public transportation: Lynx public transportation provides bus service in Osceola, Orange and Seminole counties. Service is regular, although somewhat limited. Seniors 65 and over pay 25 cents per ride or can purchase a monthly pass for $12.

Roads and highways: The Florida Turnpike, Florida Greenway and I-4 link Osceola County with major Florida cities. US 441/17-92 carries traffic north/south, while US 192 provides east/west access.

Airport: Orlando International Airport is 15 miles northeast of Kissimmee and has 20 scheduled carriers, including eight international airlines.

Let the good times roll

Recreation: Boating and fishing are very popular in this area. The Kissimmee Chain of Lakes attracts people from all over the world, and Lake Tohopekaliga is the site of many fishing tournaments. The Kissimmee Waterway, a 50-mile long chain of lakes, connects Lake Tohopekaliga with Lake Okeechobee, and in turn, with the Atlantic Ocean and the Gulf of Mexico. Hunting is available throughout Osceola County's 838,000 acres. It includes a vast area of prairie, the Osceola Plain, where songbirds, wading birds, ospreys and sandhill cranes are often seen. If you like major league sports, the Houston Astros arrive for spring training in Osceola County. Basketball fans can see the Orlando Magic play. There are six public and private golf courses in the area for those who enjoy the links, and there are also numerous tennis courts.

Culture: The Osceola Center for the Arts is the site of year-round activity, with its theater and exhibition space. The Osceola Players present Broadway musicals, light opera and drama on center stage. The players also sponsor visiting groups such as the Orlando Opera Company, the Orlando and Florida symphonies and the Southern Ballet.

Annual events: The Silver Spurs Rodeo in February is the largest east of the Mississippi. The Kissimmee Bluegrass Festival in March is a four-day event featuring bluegrass and gospel music, crafts and barbecues. St. Cloud's Spring Fling in March features three days of outdoor activities, with high-speed power boat races, competitive bass fishing, antique car displays and an arts and crafts show. Kissimmee JazzFest is in April. Balloonfest brings balloonists from all over Florida to enjoy a beautiful September weekend. The Florida State Air Fair in October brings two days of aerobatics, wing-walking and displays. Christmas Boat Parade is during the second week of December.

When the kids come: Kids definitely think it's Heaven's Place, too! Disney World, EPCOT Center, Universal Studios Florida and Sea World of Florida are all within easy reach.

For more information

Chambers

Kissimmee/Osceola County
  Chamber of Commerce
1425 E. Irlo Ave.
Memorial Highway
Kissimmee, FL 34744
407-847-3174

Greater Osceola County/St.
  Cloud Chamber of Commerce
1200 New York Ave.
St. Cloud, FL 34769
407-892-3671

Newspapers

Orlando Sentinel
804 W. Emmett St.
Kissimmee, FL 34741
Orlando, FL 32801
407-931-5930

The News-Gazette (weekly)
108 Church St.
Kissimmee, FL 34741
407-846-7600

Realtor

Rajia N. Ackley
Ackley Realty Inc.
22 W. Monument Ave.
Kissimmee, FL 34741-5192
407-846-4040
Fax: 407-846-3407

18. Melbourne, Florida

Nickname: The Space Coast
County: Brevard
Area code: 407
Population: 65,583
County population: 435,752
% of population over 65: 16.5
Region: East central Florida
Closest metro area: Orlando, 67 mi.
Median home price: $78,200
Best reasons to retire here: Well-managed, small city, low living costs, casual lifestyle on the Atlantic coast.

Melbourne at a glance

Keep your eye on the sky, because when you're in Melbourne, you are on the Space Coast. Shuttle launches underscore the rocketing pace of growth in this high-tech city, which also happens to be a low-key place to live and retire. The cost of living in Melbourne is average, housing is affordable (even near and on the beach), and the population is educated and age diverse. Newcomer-bashing is a favorite local activity, but in reality, only one in four current residents were born in Brevard County. The local economy is fueled by the government and government-related business, which makes the town's fortunes somewhat susceptible to budget-cutting. Patrick Air Force Base has an important economic impact on the area and also draws a great number of military retirees. From watching baseball spring training to watching the sea turtles nest and hatch, there is plenty to do in the Melbourne area. It's a surfer's paradise, but even if surfing is not your sport, you can always enjoy it as a spectator. There's also natural beauty to take in, including the Merritt Island National Wildlife Refuge. Fishing, boating, golf and tennis are also popular. Close enough for an overnight sail to the Bahamas, Port Canaveral, which serves the area, is North America's second largest multi-day cruise port. In fact, Disney Cruise Lines' recently announced that Port Canaveral would be home base to one or two megaships.

Possible drawbacks: People who leave are generally those who come from big cities and miss the razzle-dazzle. Melbourne is still small to some people. Also, much of the city lacks curb appeal. It doesn't come close to the civic beauty of Boca Raton; in fact, there are many areas in need of repair. However, development is beginning to address the aesthetic issue.

Climate

Elevation: 33'	Avg. high/low:	Avg. inches rain	snow	Avg. # days precip.	Avg. % humidity
Jan.	73/55	2.1	-	6	80
April	82/60	3.5	-	7	72
July	90/73	7.0	-	16	80
Oct.	85/69	7.0	-	13	82
YEAR	82/64	56.0	-	-	-
# days 32° or below: 3			# days 90° or warmer: 78		

What things cost

Overview: According to the Florida Price Level Index, Brevard County prices are about 1 percent above the Florida average, the excess a result of grocery prices, which are 9 percent higher.

Gas company: The City Gas Co. of Florida, 800-993-7546 or 407-632-1734. A $30 meter deposit is required, along with a $20 turn-on fee. Gas heat is rare. Average gas bill: $34 monthly; appliances run $12 to $14.

Electric company: Florida Power & Light, 407-631-2000, requires a $240 deposit and a one-time service charge of $16. Average electric bill: $75 to $150 monthly, depending upon air conditioning usage.

Phone company: The area is served by Bell South, 800-753-2909. Connection charge is $40. Basic monthly charges are about $13. A deposit of $65 or more may be required.

Water and sewer: Water, sewer and deposit rates vary in Brevard County. Melbourne supplies water to most South Brevard residents. Call 407-727-2900. The city requires a $120 deposit for its mainland customers and $103 for those on the beach.

Cable company: TimeWarner Cable, 407-254-3300.

Car registration, license: New residents must obtain a Florida license within 30 days of establishing residency. Driver's license: $20; renewal, $15. (Renew every six years for safe drivers, four years otherwise.) No restrictions on seniors. Title fees: new car, $31.25; used, $33.25. Initial registration fee $100 (one-time fee). Registration fees: up to $45, depending upon weight of car.

The tax ax

Sales tax: 6 percent. Prescription drugs, medical services and food are exempt, except prepared and restaurant foods.

State income tax: None.

Retirement income: Florida takes a small tax bite from retirees. There are no income taxes and no death taxes on an estate of up to $600,000.

Property taxes: Millage rates in Melbourne are 19.548 per $1,000 at 100 percent of assessed value. Assessed value should be 100 percent of market value. Florida offers a $25,000 homestead exemption for Florida residents whose primary home is in the state. Taxes on a $100,000 home would come to approximately $1,466. Property appraiser's office, 407-264-6700.

Local real estate

Overview: Brevard County ranked first in the south and 10th in the nation as one of the most affordable places to buy a home, according to a recent survey by the National Association of Home Builders. For first-time home buyers and retirees, both existing and new 3BR/2BA homes can be found in the $60,000 to $80,000 range (beach-side areas generally 20 percent more). On the mainland, Palm Bay is the fastest-growing city within the county. Cypress Creek offers country living amidst lakes and beautiful pines.

Median price for a single family home: $78,200.

Average price for a 3BR/2BA home: New homes on the mainland average $120,00; barrier island homes average $200,000. Resales on the mainland average $80,000; barrier island resales average $118,000.

Average price for a 2BR condo: $184,750 on barrier island only (no new construction on the mainland); resales range from $40,000 to $250,000.

Common housing styles and features: Most homes feature split plans. Large, screened-in patios are popular. One-story ranch styles with a garage or carport and central air conditioning are also common. There are no basements.

Rental housing market: Renters can find homes, condos or apartments available for $450 a month and up. A 3BR/2BA pool home averages $750 to $1,000 monthly.

Average rent for a 2BR apartment: $450 to $500 per month.

Nearby areas to consider: Palm Bay, Indiatlantic Beach, Melbourne Beach.

Earning a living

Business climate: The economy of Brevard County and Melbourne is heavily affected by government funds for military and space operations, but it is diverse nonetheless. Manufacturing in the area is strong, accounting for 26 percent of the economic base, compared to a national average of 13 percent. Tourism is the second strongest segment. Brevard County ranks 10th among all Florida counties in the number of small business establishments, and eighth in small-business employment.

Help in starting a business: The Economic Development Commission of East central Florida, 407-242-1800, assists businesses and industries with relocation or expansion, providing statistical and demographic information, site selection assistance, community tours and more. Also try the Small Business Development Center, 407-254-0305, ext. 2760, or the Space Coast Development Commission in Titusville, 407-269-3221. SCORE, 407-254-2288, provides assistance in all aspects of business ownership, including legal and tax issues, financial planning and marketing.

Job market: Brevard County is one of the nation's fastest-growing areas. Despite recent layoffs in defense and aerospace industries, the unemployment rate dipped below 5 percent for the first time since 1990. High-tech and aerospace employers include Lockheed Space Operations, Martin Marietta, Rockwell International and Johnson Controls World Services. Other major employers are Holmes Regional Medical Center, Brevard Community College, city and county government and Sea Ray Boats. Call Job Service of Florida, 407-984-4830.

Medical care

HealthFirst is a new health care conglomerate in Melbourne that unites Holmes Regional Medical Center with its affiliates Palm Bay Medical Center and Cape Canaveral Hospital. The Pro-Health and Fitness Center is a wellness program of HealthFirst. The membership facility offers a pool, water aerobics, seminars on nutrition, and screenings for cholesterol and prostate cancer, blood pressure, etc. Call 407-676-7149. Wuesthoff Hospital, 407-636-2211, ext. 1500, offers a program called Senior Works that gives discounts on food service, travel, vaccinations and the gift shop, and members can attend quarterly meetings on topics such as investing, health and wellness programs. Parish Medical Center, 407-268-6111, has a sleep disorder program and pain management program.

Services for seniors

The South Brevard Senior Association, 407-723-5983, operates a recreation center that offers art classes, *mah-jongg*, cards, bingo, dances and dance classes. The center also has a library, travel desk for planning trips, a geriatric center, and it offers legal aid. There are several AARP chapters in the area—start with AARP Melbourne, 407-259-8320. Brevard Elderlearning, 407-783-8539, is an affiliate of the Elderhostel Institute and has monthly meetings that provide activities and learning opportunities for seniors. Elder Helpline, 407-631-2747, is an information and referral service for everything of interest to seniors.

Continuing education

Continuing education courses for seniors on topics ranging from computers to quilting are offered at Brevard Community College, 407-632-1111. Winter Park Vocational School, 407-647-6366, has SeniorNet, which is a club for senior citizens who enroll in computer classes. The school also offers sewing and cooking classes. Rollins College, 407-646-2604, offers continuing education, although the focus of the program is professional development, not personal enrichment.

Crime and safety

The city of Melbourne had a total crime index of 94.21 per 1,000 population, which is a moderate to high rate compared to other Florida cities. Programs on crime prevention include Neighborhood Watch, home security surveys and lectures on personal safety and residential security.

Getting around town

Public transportation: Buses operate throughout Brevard County. For information, call Space Coast Area Transportation (SCAT), 407-633-1878. Trips for the disabled and disadvantaged can be reserved. Reservations for residential service can be made. Bus routes change daily depending upon reservation and destination information.

Roads and highways: I-95, US 1, 192, A1A and Beeline Expressway.

Airport: Melbourne International is served by three major airlines: Continental, Delta and USAir. It is also served by regional carriers, in addition to frequent charter and air freight flights.

Let the good times roll

Recreation: The Florida Marlins play at Space Coast Stadium for spring training, and then the Class A Brevard Manatees take over. Surfing is a hot sport in Melbourne; two-time world champion Kelly Slater hails from the area. There are major annual events in the sport, including Easter Surfing Festival and National Kidney Foundation Labor Day Surfing Festival. Scuba diving is also extremely popular here. The Melbourne area (including Palm Bay, Titusville and Cocoa Beach) boasts 16 public and semi-private golf courses, 33 boat ramps, 28 marinas and fishing camps, and 10 beautiful beaches, including three recently designated as among Florida's 10 best. Nature lovers will enjoy the Merritt Island Wildlife Refuge, which is home to more threatened and endangered species than any other refuge in the U.S.

Culture: The Brevard Cultural Alliance operates a special events hotline, 407-773-ARTS. The Brevard Museum of Art offers exhibitions and art classes, along with children's exhibits in physical sciences. Other area museums are the Brevard Museum of History and Natural Science in Cocoa and the Liberty Bell Museum in Melbourne. Music interests include the Brevard Symphony Orchestra and the Florida Space Coast Philharmonic. Theater is thriving in Brevard County; local and national performers in music, dance and theater (including Broadway shows) are booked into the recently renovated Maxwell C. King Center at Brevard Community College. The Melbourne Civic Theater is a community theater group that does four productions a year, and the Phoenix Production Company is a semiprofessional company offering sophisticated theater productions.

Annual events: Annual Bluegrass Festival (March), Easter Surfing Festival (March or April), Indian River Festival (April), Melbourne Art Festival (April), Octoberfest (October), Annual Native American Festival (December) and Holiday Boat Parade (December).

When the kids come: Orlando is less than an hour away, so Disney World, EPCOT Center, MGM, Universal Studios Florida and Sea World of Florida are within easy reach. And don't miss the opportunity to go to Spaceport USA at the Kennedy Space Center.

For more information

Chamber
Melbourne Palm Bay Area
 Chamber of Commerce
1005 E. Strawbridge Ave.
Melbourne, FL 32901
407-724-5400

Newspapers
Florida Today
P.O. Box 419000
Melbourne, FL 32941-9000
407-259-5000

Orlando Sentinel
737 Apollo Blvd.
Melbourne, FL 32901
407-453-5500

Realtor
Donna L. Buchanan
Melbourne Realty, Inc.
212 W. New Haven Ave.
Melbourne, FL 32901
407-723-3421
800-749-3421
Fax: 407-984-0544

19. Naples, Florida

Nickname: None
County: Collier
Area code: 941
Population: 21,167
County population: 197,400
% of population over 65: 23
Region: Southwest Florida
Closest metro area: Fort Myers, 30 mi.
Average home price: $160,000 to $200,000
Best reasons to retire here: Great golf, year-round warmth and sunshine, waterfront living, a low crime rate.

Naples at a glance

The focus of this community seems to be living the good life—golfing and sunning on the beaches. Dining out is something of an art in Naples, and shopping can be a social event. Naples is rife with ultra-luxurious homes and communities. Some say this city is the Palm Beach of Florida's west coast, but residents beg to differ. Naples is a haven for Midwestern entrepreneurs, executives and conservatives with old money. Known as a quiet and sophisticated town, Naples has long been an exclusive community where limousines are common. It has a reputation of being accessible only to the very wealthy. While this has been true for many years, residents said things are definitely changing. There's evidence that more and more middle-income families and seniors are moving to the area, and housing and amenities are being developed for their needs. In fact, Collier County grew at the astonishing rate of 76.9 percent between 1980 and 1990, a sign that change is coming. Perhaps the rest of the world is discovering that Naples sits just south of an imaginary line that marks the beginning of Florida's subtropical climate. The winters are delightfully warm and the summers, though hot, are cooler than expected. There's another side to the community that may suit adventurers—its proximity to the Everglades, the only surviving subtropical ecosystem in the continental U.S.

Possible drawbacks: Some people find that it's too quiet in Naples. Without a steady circle of friends to invent activities and functions, there's little to do (especially at night). Also, there is no public transportation, and real estate prices are some of the highest in the state. As with all of Florida, the summers can be brutal, although Naples fares better than many other Florida cities.

Climate

Elevation: 13'	Avg. high/low:	Avg. inches		Avg. # days precip.	Avg. % humidity
		rain	snow		
Jan.	75/52	1.6	-	5	81
April	85/62	2.0	-	5	72
July	91/74	8.9	-	18	80
Oct.	85/68	4.2	-	8	82
YEAR	84/64	54.0	-	-	-
# days 32° or below: 3			# days 90° or warmer: 123		

What things cost

Overview: The Florida Price Level Index indicates that the cost of living in Collier County is about 3 percent more expensive than the Florida norm. Food costs run about 9 percent more than average, housing about 3 percent more and health, recreation and personal services are about 1 percent more.

Electric company: Florida Power & Light, 941-262-1322. Average electric bill: $16. Set-up charge for new account; $240 maximum deposit for new customers (two months' projected bills for specific address). The system-wide average bill is $75.69, although you can expect to pay as much as $175 a month.

Phone company: United Telephone Systems, 800-335-3111. Basic service costs $13.02 per month. Installation starts at $50 and a deposit may be required.

Water and sewer service: There is no deposit or charge required for connecting to water, sewer and trash services in the city of Naples. The bimonthly bill averages $100 to $150. Call the City of Naples, 941-434-4717; Collier County, 941-434-5080; or Golden Gate, 941-455-1583.

Cable company: Colony Cablevision of Florida, Naples, 941-793-3577; Naples Cablevision, Golden Gate, 941-598-1104.

Car registration, license: New residents must obtain a Florida license within 30 days of establishing residency. Driver's license, $20; renewal, $15. (Renewal every six years for safe drivers with no traffic offenses in previous three years.) There are no special restrictions on seniors. Title fees: new car, $31.25; used, $33.25. Initial registration fee, $100 (one-time fee). Registration fees: up to $45, depending upon weight of car.

The tax ax

A 6-percent tax is levied by Florida; exempt are food, medicine and professional services. In addition, Collier County levies a 2-percent tourist tax.

State income tax: No personal income tax in the state of Florida.

Retirement income: No income taxes, no death taxes on an estate of up to $600,000, and low property taxes.

Property taxes: Collier County has 269 different millage rates; the average rate is about $15 per $1,000 of assessed value, which should be 100 percent of market value. Most millage rates range from $13.3207 to $16.65. Sample taxes on a $180,000 home would run from $2,065 to $2,581. Contact the property appraiser's office, 941-774-8141.

Local real estate

Overview: Real estate, like most things in Naples, tends to be pricier than most other Florida locations. The private golf communities are especially prestigious, with championship courses and breathtaking homes. Selling prices for homes in Naples are generally 94 to 97 percent of asking prices. The oceanfront property is spectacular, and compared to Florida's east coast, you don't have to spend a million to buy something palatial (a mere 3/4 of a million will do the job).

Average price of a 3BR/2BA home: New homes and resales start at $160,000, and $200,000 is considered average.

Average price for a 2BR condo: New condos average $175,000; resales average $190,000.

Common housing styles and features: The architecture in Naples is modern, mostly 1-story (although 2-story homes are cropping up) with distinctive interiors and fabulous landscape design. The most popular home plans in the area are split with a master bedroom on one side and guest bedrooms on the other.

Rental housing market: Since Naples is such a popular vacation and winter community, rentals can be difficult to obtain on short notice. (Although if you're thinking of renting out your own home while you're "up north," it's nice to know that most rentals are already spoken for one year in advance).

Average rent for a 2BR apartment: Can range from $700 to $1,800 monthly, depending upon location.

Nearby areas to consider: Bonita Springs, Pelican Bay.

Earning a living

Business climate: For at least the past 10 years, Florida has experienced tremendous economic and population growth. According to the Chamber of Commerce, Naples has surpassed the overall Florida boom. Naples is one of the fastest-growing metropolitan areas in the United States, with an affluent population and solid business resources. Services, agriculture and retail dominate, but employers run the gamut from education to health care to tourism. It is a highly educated community, with more than half the residents having attended college.

Help in starting a business: Contact the Economic Development Council of Collier County at 941-263-8989. It offers information packets on starting a business in Collier County that include up-to-date statistics on diskette. The Chamber of Commerce also has a New Business Assistance Committee.

Job market: Job Service of Florida assists all citizens who are seeking employment regardless of income level. Call 941-434-5006. The Senior Community Service Employment Program (SCSEP) is a government-funded program sponsored locally by AARP. The programs serves low-income seniors (the guidelines are strict), but it also acts as an advocate for senior employment throughout Collier County. The program has witnessed a resurgence of opportunities for seniors in recent years. Call 941-435-9188 in Naples. There are usually plenty of part-time opportunities during the tourist season (hotels, restaurants and boutiques hire extra employees). But frankly, most of the retirees who settle here aren't looking for employment opportunities.

Medical care

The Naples area is fortunate to have high-quality health care facilities that are convenient for most residents. Everyone we spoke to agreed that the facilities are very modern, the nursing staffs are caring and the area physicians are of top caliber. Naples Community Hospital, located in southwest Naples, is a 400-bed facility staffed by 283 physicians. The hospital is not a single building; it encompasses a wellness center, a health resource center, exercise facilities and a day surgery facility. Areas of excellence include the International Spine Institute of Florida, centers for management of cancer and chronic pain, and a $10 million heart surgery center scheduled to open in late 1996. Plans for the near future include the addition of a skilled nursing bed unit and a seniors' center that will combine medical services for seniors in one location. North Collier Hospital is a 50-bed acute-care satellite facility of Naples Community Hospital. Everyone says it looks more like a hotel than a hospital, with its luxurious ambiance and bright skylights. A major addition to its emergency room was recently completed.

Services for seniors

The Collier County Council on Aging for Active Seniors publishes an excellent, comprehensive directory listing services available to older persons. It's free of charge; call 941-774-8443. The local AARP chapter can be reached at 941-775-2763. The Elder Helpline, operated in every Florida county, is an information and referral resource on services and activities. In Collier County, call 941-774-8443.

Continuing education

Edison Community College, 941-732-3707, offers lifelong learning courses; costs are $3 to $5 per contact hour, and topics include computers, health-related subjects, civics, finance and art. Collier County Public Schools, 941-643-2700, offers adult and community education courses, including art and computer classes, foreign languages, fishing, investing, sign language and a variety of writing courses. Classes last three to seven weeks and range in cost from $7 to $50.

Crime and safety

Most of Collier County is served by the Collier County Sheriff's Department, which offers crime prevention programs and uses community-oriented policing. The crime rate in Naples and Collier County is relatively low. In 1994, Naples had 76.6 crimes per 1,000 population, while Collier County had 54 incidents per 1,000. The Sheriff's department points out that the crimes reported are totals for the year, but population figures don't reflect the dramatic influx of seasonal residents. The beaches are under the jurisdiction of Naples Police and Emergency Services.

Getting around town

Public transportation: None.

Roads and highways: US 41, also known as Tamiami Trail. I-75 connects Naples to cities on both Florida coasts.

Airports: Southwest Florida International in Fort Myers is served by most major airlines. Naples Municipal Airport is served by American Eagle, Cape Air, GP Express, Gulfstream, United Express and USAir.

Let the good times roll

Recreation: Golf is a way of life in Naples. There are more than 45 golf courses in Collier County, more per capita than anywhere else in the world. The Senior PGA Tour and the LPGA play here. There's plenty of tennis as well, with the Naples Bath & Tennis Club, the World Tennis Center and city parks. There are only seven miles of beaches in Naples, but they're made of gorgeous sugar sand (quartz), and are renowned for shelling, sailing, fishing and boating. Nature lovers enjoy a variety of ecosystems in nearby national and state preserves and parks, including the Everglades and the Ten Thousand Islands, an area south of Naples where mangrove trees, with their large, "walking" root systems, have created 10,000 "islands" along the shore. You can really go overboard with backwater fishing here, too, or stay right in town at the Naples Pier (1,000 feet out into the Gulf). If it can be done outdoors, it can be done in Naples—in style!

Culture: The Philharmonic Center for the Arts features a concert hall, Pavilion theater, four art galleries and two sculpture gardens, and it's home to the Naples Philharmonic Orchestra and the Miami City Ballet. From October through March, the Naples Concert Band offers free Sunday concerts at Cambier Park, while in the summer, residents enjoy Jazz on the Gulf at the Naples Beach Hotel and Golf Club. Theater groups include the Naples Players, Pelican Theater Company, the Once-in-a-While Park Players and Marco's Broadway Baby Grand. The Naples Art Association, Art League of Marco Island and Naples Artcrafters host exhibitions by area artists, while two dozen commercial galleries showcase national and international artists.

Annual events: The IntelliNet Challenge Senior PGA golf tour event is held in February. Swamp Buggy Races, popular events featuring vehicles used for traveling swamplands, are held in February, May and October. The Taste of Collier and Great Dock Canoe Races are in May, and in December there's the Avenue of Lights Parade and Walk and the Naples Bay Boat Parade.

When the kids come: If the children are old enough, the most fascinating place to go is Everglades National Park. There's also Caribbean Gardens, Home of Jungle Larry's Zoological Park, featuring rare and endangered animals. Sun Splash Family Waterpark in Coral Gables is open March through October, offering rides and water fun.

For more information

Chamber
The Naples Area Chamber
of Commerce
3620 Tamiami Trail N.
Naples, FL 33940
941-262-6141

Newspaper
Naples Daily News
1075 Central Ave.
Naples, FL 33940
941-262-3161

Realtor
Jeannie Cordin
Coldwell Banker McFadden
& Sprowls
3701 Tamiami Trail N.
Naples, FL 33940
941-261-1551
Fax: 941-262-5867

20. Ocala, Florida

Nickname: The Kingdom of the Sun
County: Marion
Area code: 352
Population: 60,000
County population: 216,000
% of population over 65: 22.7
Region: North Central Florida
Closest metro area: Gainesville, 35 mi.
Median house price: $61,400
Best reasons to retire here: Relatively low cost of living, affordable housing, mild climate, plenty of outdoor recreation.

Ocala at a glance

The Chamber of Commerce claims that "Ocala has it all," and they just might be right! In 1995, Ocala/Marion County was named one of the Top 10 All-America Cities by the National Civic League. Modern Ocala began as an agricultural community because of its rich soil and abundant, clean waters (the city is situated over Florida's largest aquifer). Today, thoroughbred horses are among the most important products raised on this gently rolling terrain. In fact, Marion County is considered by equine experts to be one of four places in the world that has ideal conditions for breeding world-class horses, and there are more than 400 horse farms in the area to prove it! People are attracted to the rural setting, the tall oak trees and beautiful land that surrounds Ocala, and to the mild climate that offers a change of seasons. It's also nearly an ideal place for retirees, with its affordable housing, lower-than-average cost of living and mild climate. The pace here is relaxed. Ocala is a quiet town with its own distinct charm; Victorian architecture lines the blocks just east of historic downtown. There's plenty to do if you like the outdoors, including golf, tennis, boating and canoeing. There are also more than 200 spring-fed lakes and rivers in the area (surrounded by 430,000 acres of national forests), which offer great fishing, water recreation, hiking and camping. Ocala is close to many major cities and attractions, but you don't have to put up with the tourists in your own backyard!

Possible drawbacks: The crime rate is surprisingly high for a small community, although the trouble is not violent. Shopping is somewhat limited in the area, and there's no public transportation.

Climate

Elevation: 90'	Avg. high/low:	Avg. inches		Avg. # days precip.	Avg. % humidity
		rain	snow		
Jan.	71/46	2.91	-	7	56
April	84/58	3.05	-	6	47
July	92/71	8.49	-	19	60
Oct.	84/61	2.81	-	9	55
YEAR	83/59	53.86	-	120	56
# days 32° or below: 12			# days 90° or warmer: 120		

What things cost

Overview: Ocala is not a city that national organizations routinely analyze for its cost of living. Available statistics are somewhat dated, but they are consistent on one point: Ocala is affordable, especially the cost of housing. The closest city of similar size is Gainesville, 35 miles away; Gainesville has an overall cost of living index about 3 percent below the national average.

Gas company: West Florida Natural Gas Co., 352-622-0111, charges a $20 connection fee and $55 deposit that can be waived with good credit. Bills average $14 a month for one appliance; up to $200 a month for gas heat and pool heater.

Water, sewer and electric: The City of Ocala Utility Services, 352-629-8411, charges a deposit of $125 that can be waived with a letter of credit. There is an $18 charge to connect. Depending upon the size of the home, costs can range from $150 to $300 a month.

Phone company: Sprint, 352-351-4151. Deposits are based on individual usage. Basic service is $15.

Cable company: Cox Communications, 352-237-1111.

Car registration, license: New residents must obtain a Florida license within 30 days of establishing residency. A driver's license is $20; renewal, $15. (Renew every six years for safe drivers, four years otherwise.) No restrictions on seniors. Title fees: new, $31.25; used, $33.25. Initial (one-time) registration fee, $100. Registration fees: up to $45 depending upon wieght of car.

The tax ax

Sales tax: 6 percent, with exemptions on groceries, medical services and prescription drugs.

State income tax: None.

Retirement income: Florida ranks high among the popular retirement states for taking the smallest bite from retirees' incomes. There's no income tax, no death taxes on an estate valued at up to $600,000, and no state tax on Social Security.

Property taxes: Florida offers a $25,000 homestead exemption for permanent residents whose principal home is in Florida. To estimate annual taxes, deduct $25,000 from the appraised value (which should be equal to the market value), multiply the balance times the millage rate and divide by $1,000. Millage rates range from $20.7181 to $22.8018. For more detail, call the county property appraiser's office at 352-368-8300.

Local real estate

Overview: Asking prices in Ocala tend to be quite close to selling prices, and property taxes are low. Ocala also has a great array of housing choices, from condominiums and homes to farms in horse country. Many prospective buyers feel that purchasing a resale home or condominium in a retirement or country club community is the best buy. Most important, there is a sense of community wherever you go, which may be why so many retirees relocate here permanently, instead of purchasing second homes in the area.

Median price for a single family home: $61,400, according to the National Association for Realtors.

Average price for a 3BR/2BA home: New homes average $109,00; resales average $91,000.

Average price for a 2BR condo: New condominiums average $59,000; resales average $50,000.

Rental housing market: There is very limited availability, especially because rentals tend to go quickly once they become available.

Average rent for a 2BR apartment: Approximately $500 to $700 per month.

Communities or developments most popular with retirees: The area has many condominium communities that feature country club amenities. Ocala rates for this type of construction are quite affordable, ranging from $59,000 to $105,000. The most popular developments are Top of the World, Spruce Creek and Oak Run.

Nearby areas to consider: Summerfield, Belleview, Dunnellon.

Earning a living

Business climate: Ocala's economy is based on manufacturing, agriculture, construction, real estate, tourism and the wholesale, retail and service industries.

Help in starting a business: If you're entering a business such as health care, manufacturing, wholesaling or transportation, the Economic Development Council, 352-377-5621, is the place to call. The Manufacturing/Technology Center can help small manufacturers with technical and production problems. The Small Business Development Center of the University of Florida, 352-377-5621, is located 35 miles away in Gainesville. It is a national outreach program of the Small Business Administration designed to assist persons going into business or already in business. The SBDC offers free, confidential, one-on-one counseling to small-business owners in all phases of operation, from start-up to established businesses looking to expand. If you want to start a retail or service sector business, call the Ocala Chamber of Commerce; its small business program is one of several networking opportunities available there.

Job market:. In 1995, Marion County crossed a 20-year low in its unemployment rate, reflecting its diverse and stable economy. The retail and service sectors are healthy, and both have shown employment growth in recent years. The most recent county unemployment rate available (February 1996) was 5.1 percent. The Job Service of Florida offers assistance to job seekers of all ages and income levels throughout Florida. In Marion County, call 904-732-1272.

Medical care

Columbia Ocala Regional Medical Center, 352-732-2700, is noted for its cardiac care facilities and oncology unit. The center offers home health care services and physical rehabilitation centers. Programs for seniors include the national program Senior Friends, 352-368-1338, offering free health and blood pressure screenings, senior aerobics and water aerobics at discounted prices, discounts on health seminars, a mall walking program and more. Munroe Regional Medical Center is a 323-bed acute care facility with 221 physicians on staff, with a Heart Center, Sleep Laboratory and wellness programs. It is part of the Munroe Regional Health System, which offers home health care services, a Lifetime Fitness and Rehabilitation Center, and a membership program offering discounted health services, free health-related screenings, seminars and programs, medical transportation and more. Annual fee: $8. Call 352-351-7560.

Services for seniors

Together with its affiliate 8th Avenue Senior Center, 352-629-8545, the Multipurpose Senior Center, 352-629-8351, offers dances and dancing lessons, cards, shuffleboard, computer classes and more for free or a nominal charge. Marion County Senior Services, 352-629-8661, offers assistance to disabled seniors including counseling, meals and transportation. The Elder Helpline, 352-629-7407, is an information and referral service available in every Florida county, that assists seniors in locating services and information about all areas of interest, from health care and legal assistance to recreation and social opportunities.

Continuing education

Central Florida Community College offers Senior Institute, an organization for seniors to promote continued education, learning opportunities and social opportunities. Membership costs $125 a year (additional charges for materials or specific events), or $50 per term. Topics may include current affairs, creative writing, astronomy, art, music, history, philosophy, yoga and more. Institute members are eligible to use the college library, tennis courts, swimming pool, attend plays and concerts. Call 352-854-2322.

Crime and safety

Many people we spoke with said that they moved to Ocala from urban areas to escape the high crime rates. Nonetheless, Ocala's own crime rate is high, at approximately 150 incidents per 1,000 population. (The Marion County rate drops to 63 incidents per 1,000.) The most common incidents are larcenies (67 percent), including gas drive-offs and bicycle theft.

Getting around town

Public transportation: Ocala does not have public transportation, but Senior Services Transportation, 352-622-2450, will provide transportation to doctor and dental appointments, with 48 hours notice. It also provides scheduled trips to assist seniors in running routine errands.
Roads and highways: I-75, US 27, State Road 40.
Airports: Local air service is available through the Ocala Municipal Airport. Gainesville (40 miles north) provides major airline service. The Orlando airport is 75 miles south.

Let the good times roll

Recreation: Ocala is great for outdoor lovers. Boating and camping around the area's 200 lakes and springs is popular, as are tubing, canoeing and kayaking. The 430,000-acre Ocala National Forest is beautiful for camping and riding, and in designated areas, hunting for quail, deer, duck and dove is permitted. Marion County is great for freshwater fishing, and saltwater fishing is close by in either the Atlantic Ocean (70 miles away) or the Gulf of Mexico (40 miles away). There are more than 4,500 horse farms in and around Ocala, and riding is a popular recreational activity in the area. There are also 12 public and four private golf courses in Marion County, and several parks have public tennis courts, including the Fort King Tennis Center. Marion County is also where you'll find Silver Springs, one of Florida's oldest tourist attractions, and home of the glass bottom boat. More than 550 million gallons of sparkling water flow each day from Silver Springs, the largest artesian spring formation in the world.

Culture: The Appleton Museum of Art features a 6,000-work collection of European painting and sculpture, as well as preColumbian, South American, Native American, West African and Asian art. Theater and performing arts groups abound, including the Ocala Civic Theatre, the Marion Performing Ballet, Ocala Dance Theatre, and the Central Florida Symphony. Silver Springs provides a variety of concerts throughout the year.

Annual events: Major events include the Live Oak International Draft Horse Show (Feb.); Taste of Ocala, the Annual Brick City Festival and the Spring Bluegrass Festival (March); God and Country Day, put on by the Ocala Jaycees on July 4; and the Florida Horse and Agriculture Festival in October. There are also rodeos throughout the year.

When the kids come: Silver Springs now has Wild Waters, featuring seven flumes and a giant wave pool. There is a Jeep Safari where visitors are taken into the Florida jungle to drive through a pit of wild alligators. Discovery Science Center is a hands-on place with educational events and activities. Orlando is a little more than an hour away with all it has to offer: Disney World, MGM Studios, EPCOT Center, Universal Studios, Sea World and more.

For more information

Chamber
Ocala/Marion County
 Chamber of Commerce
110 E. Silver Springs Blvd.
Ocala, FL 34478
352-629-8051

Newspaper
Ocala Star-Banner
2121 SW 19th Avenue Rd.
Ocala, FL 34474
352-867-4010

Realtor
Elizabeth Holder
Re/Max Premier Realty
2300 South Pine Ave.
Ocala, FL 34471
352-732-3222
800-476-5055
Fax: 352-732-3229

21. Sarasota, Florida

Nickname: The Culture Coast
County: Sarasota
Area code: 941
Population: 52,694
County population: 296,453
% of population over 65: 32
Region: Florida West Coast
Closest metro area: Tampa, 50 mi.
Average home price: $121,000
Best reasons to retire here: Gorgeous Gulf Coast city, cultural offerings, good services for seniors, outdoor recreational activities.

Sarasota at a glance

There is no place like Sarasota for a comfortable, action-packed and intellectually stimulating retirement. Everything you could ask for in outdoor recreation (except, we note without regret, snow sports), culture and high quality of life is within a 15-minute drive at most. Perhaps Sarasota's greatest distinction among other choices in Florida is the city's cultural offerings. Patrons of the arts revel in the theater, symphony, opera, dance and enjoy world-class displays of visual arts as well, along with several international film festivals of a quality reserved for much larger cities. The housing market varies from luxury homes to condominium developments, old-fashioned tree-lined streets to golf course communities. (Sarasota has a nice mix of wealthy and middle-class residents, all of whom take advantage of the beauty and ambiance.) And, of course, Sarasota's beaches pack plenty of appeal, with 35 miles of powdery white sand, 150 miles of waterfront and six beautiful barrier islands on the azure waters of the Gulf of Mexico. The downtown waterfront has glistening high-rises and gourmet dining establishments. In this city's favor is its friendly attitude toward senior residents—there's an abundance of services and special continuing education opportunities, including the popular Lifetime Learning Institute.

Possible drawbacks: Leadfoots beware, every day is Sunday for Sarasota drivers. Snowbird season brings a lot of traffic—and traffic is something this town doesn't need more of. The summer's heat and humidity is sweltering—you may need to head for cooler climates from June through September. The cost of living in Sarasota is almost exactly on the national average, but that's higher than most Florida locales.

Climate

Elevation: 25'	Avg. high/low:	Avg. inches		Avg. # days precip.	Avg. % humidity
		rain	snow		
Jan.	71/60	2.3	-	6	80
April	82/72	2.1	-	5	72
July	90/82	8.4	-	16	80
Oct.	84/75	2.5	-	7	79
YEAR	82/72	49.0	-	-	-
# days 32° or below: 6			# days 90° or warmer: 85		

What things cost

Overview: Recent ACCRA statistics showed the composite index for Sarasota was 99.9, with most categories within 1 percent of the national averages, except utilities and health care, which were 6 and 9 percent higher respectively.

Gas company: Call 941-366-4277 for People's Gas. The turn-on charge is $25. Deposits are waived with a letter of credit; otherwise they run twice the monthly bill for the property, ranging between $30 and $300. Few customers have gas appliances in this area.

Electric company: Florida Power & Light, 941-379-1424. When required, residential deposits average $240. The connection charge is $16. Bills can range from $100 to $200 monthly depending upon the size of the home. ACCRA's average was about $114.

Phone company: GTE, 800-483-3200. The service order charge is $55, but there are no deposits. Monthly charges average $15 to $16.

Water and sewer: City of Sarasota, 941-954-4196. Deposits for a single family home are approximately $148. There is no connection charge. Bills average $54 monthly.

Cable company: Comcast Cablevision, 941-371-6700.

Car registration, license: New residents must obtain Florida license within 30 days of establishing residency. Driver's license, $20; renewal, $15. (Renew at six years if safe driver, four years otherwise.) Title fees: new car, $31.25; used, $33.25. Initial (one-time) registration fee, $100. Registration fees: up to $45, depending upon weight of car.

The tax ax

Sales tax: 6 percent except on groceries, medical services and prescription drugs. Sarasota adds 1 percent sales tax.

State income tax: None.

Retirement income: Florida is among the best of the popular retirement states for taking the smallest tax bite from its retirees. There are no income or death taxes on an estate valued at up to $600,000, and property taxes tend to be low.

Property taxes: $20.9652 millage rate in the city of Sarasota. Millage rates are applied to the appraised value of the home, which should be 100 percent of market value. Florida has a $25,000 homestead exemption. Sample taxes on a $150,000 home would be $2,621. Tax collector's office, 941-951-5620.

Local real estate

Overview: Housing prices have seen steady appreciation in recent years, with higher than average appreciation for waterfront and golf course properties. Condominiums have seen less appreciation, and some have depreciated. Retirees are purchasing permanent homes and second vacation homes in equal numbers in this area. Some of the best buys in the market are resale homes. Communities of keen interest include Longboat Key, Lido Key, Siesta Key, Venice.

Median price for a single family home: $104,500.

Average price for a 3BR/2BA home: According to the Sarasota Board of Realtors, the average price is $121,000, but prices for new homes can go as high as $500,000. Resales average $179,000.

Average price for a 2BR condo: According to the Sarasota Board of Realtors: $108,000. There is an enormous range of units available, from $30,000 to $500,000.

Common housing styles and features: The majority of area homes are one-story ranch types with stucco exteriors. More expensive homes have tile roofs, and most homes offer screened lanais.

Rental housing market: According to ACCRA, the average rent is approximately $626. However, rent prices are largely determined by location, and units can go as high as several thousand per month. Seasonal rentals can be difficult to find in winter, so plan ahead.

Average rent for a 2BR apartment: $626 monthly.

Nearby areas to consider: Venice or Bradenton.

Earning a living

Business climate: In the past, Sarasota experienced seasonal fluctuations in its economy—a result of the city's heavy dependence on the tourist and retirement markets. The Chamber of Commerce formed the Committee of 100 to seek high-wage jobs for Sarasota, resulting in 33 percent expansion of the labor market in 14 years. Sarasota, now home to a large financial business community, was recently ranked fourth in the nation for job growth by the United States Bureau of Labor Statistics.

Help in starting a business: The University of South Florida's Small Business Development Center, 800-SEE-SBDC, is a good place to start. New and current business owners first participate in a STEPS seminar (the cost is $25) that covers everything about the basics of starting a business, including feasibility analysis. Once you have taken the seminar, you are eligible for free, one-on-one counseling, use of the resource center and additional workshops and seminars. Subsequent services are free of charge. The local office of SCORE can be reached at 941-955-1029. The Sarasota Business Center of Sarasota County Technical Institute, 941-361-6309 or 941-361-6310, offers affordable office and retail space, utilities, use of computers, fax machines and management assistance.

Job market: Part-time employment is plentiful in the retail sector. The unemployment rate is about 5.2 percent. Job Service of Florida, call 941-361-6100. For Sarasota County, call 941-951-5495.

Medical care

There are 773 physicians in the Sarasota vicinity, and six hospitals, including Doctors Hospital of Sarasota/Columbia HCA. This facility has a mature adult counseling program—intensive mental health services for persons 55 and older experiencing grief, depression, anxiety or other problems. The hospital also has a new intensive care unit, cardiopulmonary care services and a Senior Friends program, 941-342-1007, with a mail-in prescription service, Emergency Alert Response System and free health screenings. Sarasota Memorial Hospital, 941-917-9000, has nearly 1,000 beds and is one the nation's largest public hospitals. Its Senior Care program offers Medicare and insurance claims assistance, health education, discounts at local and national businesses and the Lifeline medical emergency link. Special areas include an advanced surgery center and cardiac, imaging and rehabilitative services. Venice Hospital, 941-485-7711, and Englewood Community Hospital, 941-475-6571, serve residents in southern Sarasota County. Englewood is a Columbia/HCA facility with 100 beds, while Venice has about 350 beds.

Services for seniors

The nonprofit and nonsectarian Senior Friendship Centers provide information and referral services via the Elder Helpline, 941-955-2122. The centers, including the Friendship Center in Sarasota and the Kathleen K. Caitlin Center in Venice, offer a variety of social activities, along with transportation services, case management, in-home services, a monthly newsletter and more.

Continuing education

The Sarasota Institute of Lifetime Learning is a 25-year-old, all-volunteer organization that presents a lecture series each winter. The series attracts 200 to 600 listeners on Tuesdays, Wednesdays and Thursdays to hear locally and nationally recognized speakers. Topics include international affairs, social issues, music, art and more. Schedules for the January through March series may be obtained through public libraries. Manatee Community College, 941-755-1511, ext. 4334, offers noncredit courses through the Open Campus program. Topics include golf instruction, writing, fashion, language and more. Costs are $16 to $54. Computer skills classes are about $115.

Crime and safety

Sarasota's crime index for 1994 was 115 incidents per 1,000 population, although the county index dropped to 58 crimes per 1,000. Both are higher than the national average of 55 crimes per 1,000. Bike patrols downtown and street beats in neighborhoods are taking aim at bringing the rate down.

Getting around town

Public transportation: Sarasota County Area Transit, 941-316-1007. Fare is 25 cents for all riders. Service is countywide.

Roads and highways: I-75, US 41 (Tamiami Trail), US 301.

Airport: Sarasota Bradenton International Airport serves 1.7 million visitors annually via 10 major airlines.

Port: The Port of Manatee is Florida's fourth-largest deep water port. It is a 30-minute drive from downtown Sarasota.

Let the good times roll

Recreation: The Sarasota area offers water recreation galore, whether it's enjoying one of 10 public beaches, sailing, snorkeling, boating or fishing. There are 48 golf courses in or near the area. Nearby Oscar Scherer State Recreation Area is 1,385 acres of pine and scrub woodland with streams for canoeing, nature trails, campgrounds and bicycle paths. Myakka River State Park is one of the best fishing parks in Florida. Reefs are prime fishing spots; there are several natural reefs in the area, and Sarasota has an excellent artificial reef program. A unique feature is the Marie Selby Gardens, featuring a collection of 6,000 orchids and 20,000 plants.

Culture: Sarasota's reputation as Florida's Cultural Capital began with circus magnate John Ringling. He collected art and built the John and Mable Ringling Museum of Art to house his collection. His adjacent mansion exhibits Ringling Brothers and Barnum & Bailey circus memorabilia. The Van Wezel Performing Arts hall offers performances by the Florida West Coast Symphony, as well as touring Broadway shows and famous entertainers. Florida Studio Theatre produces a summer season and a nine-month season of contemporary works as well. Sarasota Ballet of Florida and Ballet Eddy Toussaint USA provide everything from classical ballets to modern dance, while the Sarasota Opera Company has become one of the area's most successful arts organizations. The Asolo Theatre Company is a superb regional theater, and Florida Studio Theatre offers professional contemporary plays and musicals.

Annual events: The annual Sarasota Circus Festival and Parade, January; Sarasota Festival of the Arts, February; Sarasota Jazz Festival, April; the Sarasota Music Festival in June presents chamber music concerts. Offshore Grand Prix, July; Taste of Sarasota, October; Sarasota French Film festival (the only one of its kind in the U.S.), November. Also in November is the Cine-World Film Festival.

When the kids come: Mote Museum Aquarium has 200 varieties of fish and invertebrates, with a 300,000-gallon shark tank and a marine life touch tank. Sarasota Jungle Gardens has 10 tropical acres with winding trails, beautiful gardens, a petting zoo and butterfly museum. The Gulf Coast World of Science features science and nature hands-on exhibits for children of all ages.

For more information

Chamber
Sarasota Chamber
 of Commerce
1819 Main St.,
 Suite 240
Sarasota, FL 34236
941-955-8187

Newspaper
Sarasota Herald-Tribune
P.O. Box 308
Sarasota, FL 34230-0308
941-365-5060

Realtor
Juanita S. Bryan
American Dream Realty
Paradise Shopping Plaza
3800 S. Tamiami Trail
Sarasota, FL 32349
941-951-1246
800-330-1246

22. St. Petersburg, Florida

Nickname: The Suncoast
County: Pinellas
Area code: 813
Population: 240,318
County population: 855,763
% of population over 65: 26
Region: Central Florida, West Coast
Closest metro area: Tampa, 10 mi.
Median home price: $78,300
Best reasons to retire here: Year-round sunshine, outdoor recreation, affordable living, "the world's biggest day camp for seniors."

St. Petersburg at a glance

St. Petersburg has long attracted retirees, thanks in large part to its excellent recreational offerings and sunny weather. The city boasts 361 days of sunshine annually, earning it the name "The Suncoast." The tropical climate is cooled by sea breezes, and afternoon thunderstorms are predictable from June through September. The storms can be spectacular, though—the Tampa Bay area averages 90 days of lightning a year. The city is located on the Pinellas peninsula, which has water on three sides. On the western side of the peninsula facing the Gulf of Mexico you'll find Clearwater. The eastern and southern sides face Tampa Bay, where you'll find St. Petersburg and (across the bay on the mainland) Tampa. St. Petersburg, affectionately known as St. Pete, is the largest municipality in the area. If you envision an active retirement lifestyle, this city is for you. From professional sports events to high-quality cultural offerings, from golf and tennis to the 300 miles of shoreline dotted with marinas, parks and preserves, you can keep busy 365 days a year. It's a city that caters to and cares for its senior population, yet the median age is 38.6, which surprises some who think of the area strictly as a retirement mecca. St. Petersburg's economy is thriving, supporting an age-diverse population.

Possible drawbacks: St. Petersburg is such a great place to be that everyone wants to be there. This has made the city a crowded place to live. It has also led to some big-city problems, including homelessness and drug-related crime. Still, it is ranked in the middle of all Florida cities for its crime rate, though its population is the largest.

Climate

Elevation: 25'	Avg. high/low:	Avg. inches rain	snow	Avg. # days precip.	Avg. % humidity
Jan.	71/60	2.3	-	6	80
April	82/72	2.1	-	5	72
July	90/82	8.4	-	16	80
Oct.	84/75	2.5	-	7	79
YEAR	82/72	49.0	-	-	-
# days 32° or below: 6			# days 90° or warmer: 85		

What things cost

Overview: ACCRA statistics show cost of living about 3.5 percent below the national average. Housing is nearly 8 percent below, utilities are 5 percent above and health care is 6 percent above.

Gas company: Contact People's Gas, 813-895-3621. The deposit is based on an average monthly bill of $20 to $200 depending upon usage. $35 to $75 average monthly bill, depending upon heating.

Electric company: Florida Power Corporation requires a deposit of $180, although it may be waived. Connection charges range from $5.50 to $15. Call 800-999-7989 outside Florida. Average electric bill ranges from $90 to $113.

Phone company: General Telephone Company, 800-483-4200. Charges are $55 to connect, but no deposit is required. Basic service is $16 per month.

Water and sewer: City of St. Petersburg, 813-893-7341. Most deposits are $104 for water, sewer and trash removal. Cost of services is $31 plus the water used. Most two-person households pay in the $45 to $50 range.

Cable company: Paragon Cable, south Pinellas, 813-579-8400; Vision Cable of Pinellas, north Pinellas, 813-797-9900; TCI Cablevision, Pinellas, 813-736-1436; Time Warner Cable, Tierre Verde and Isla del Sol, 813-864-1551.

Car registration, license: New residents must obtain Florida license within 30 days. Driver's license, $20; renewal $15. (Renew every six years for safe drivers; four years otherwise.) No restrictions on seniors. Title fees: new car, $31.25; used, $33.25. Initial (one-time) registration fee, $100. Registration fees: between $26.60 to $44.60.

The tax ax

Sales tax: 6 percent state tax plus 1 percent county tax. Groceries, prescription medications and medical services are exempt.

State income tax: None.

Retirement income: Florida ranks high among popular retirement states because the overall tax bite remains modest. There are no income taxes, no death taxes on an estate valued at up to $600,000, and property taxes are generally low.

Property taxes: $26.5003 millage (city, county, schools all in one) on assessed value, which should be 100 percent of market value. There is a $25,000 homestead exemption for Florida residents whose primary residence is in Florida. Tax appraiser's office, 813-582-7652.

Local real estate

Overview: Housing prices have been stable in recent years, except for waterfront and beach properties, which appreciate every year. Most retirees are looking for smaller homes or condominiums, and resales are popular. St. Petersburg is located on a peninsula, and there is very little land available. Most new construction is north of Clearwater, with developments ranging from a few acres of townhomes or single family homes to thousands of acres of single family homes, townhomes and/or condominiums with community amenities.

Median price for a single family home: $78,300.

Average price for a 3BR/2BA home: New, $90,000 to $140,000 and up; resales, $70,000 to $120,000.

Average price for a 2BR condo: New, $90,000 and up; $50,000 to $100,000 for a resale.

Common housing styles and features: Virtually all homes are ranch style without basements; most have tiled roofs, Florida rooms and lanais.

Average rent for a 2BR apartment: $400 to $600 monthly.

Rental housing market: Rentals are available in virtually every type of community in the area, either annually, or seasonally. Seasonal rentals are substantially higher.

Communities or developments most popular with retirees: Mainlands of Tamarac and Five Towns.

Nearby areas to consider: The entire Tampa Bay area, including Pinellas and Hillsboro counties.

Earning a living

Business climate: The principle industries are high-tech manufacturing and tourism. St. Petersburg/Tampa Bay is frequently cited as a top area to locate a business, and has a strong economy. Tampa Bay is now home to operations, affiliates and subsidiaries of more than 187 of the Fortune 500 firms. Recent arrivals in the area include Time Warner, Bausch & Lomb, Salomon Bros. and Xerox. Major employers include GTE, the Home Shopping Network, Essilor of America (manufacturer of prescription eyeglass lenses), Times Publishing Co. and Tribune Co., and the area's many medical facilities/hospitals. Major industries include tourism, citrus, food production, electronic manufacturing, aerospace, computers, electronics and pharmaceuticals. Buying power in Pinellas County is significant; the county is ranked sixth in Florida, ahead of Broward.

Help in starting a business: The Small Business Development Center at the University of South Florida Tampa, 813-974-4274, offers seminars, plus free one-on-one counseling, workshops and computer resources. The City's Economic Development Office, 813-893-7700, is a funding agency and retention program for existing small businesses. The St. Petersburg Certified Development Corp., 813-895-2504, provides small business loans and informal technical assistance.

Job market: The unemployment rate in the area is 6.2 percent. Municipal job openings, 813-893-7033. Job Service of Florida, 813-893-2255 (St. Petersburg) or 813-570-3000 (suburban). Detailed lists of major employers can be obtained through the Chamber of Commerce.

Medical care

Pinellas County has 23 hospitals with more than 6,500 beds. Some of the major facilities are listed here. Bayfront Medical Center, 813-823-1234, is the largest community teaching hospital in St. Pete, with a major trauma center and Bayflite Medical Emergency helicopter. St. Anthony's Hospital, 813-825-1067, is a major medical center providing cardiology and vascular medicines, comprehensive cancer care and a center for radiation treatment. Palms of Pasadena Hospital, 813-381-1000, has centers of excellence in orthopedic and joint replacement surgery, cardiology, cardiac catheterization, general and vascular surgery, geriatrics and cancer treatment. Physician's referral with Pinellas County Medical Society, 813-541-1159. In addition to health care facilities, the county is gaining an international reputation in the fields of biotechnology, opthalmics, pharmaceuticals, medical equipment and health care.

Services for seniors

Acting as a bridge between the community and older citizens, the St. Petersburg Office on Aging, 813-893-7102, monitors services and programs. Its Sunshine Center provides social, recreational and educational programs including seminars, entertainment, painting and more. Neighborly Senior Services, 813-573-9444, offers 27 services to 14,000 seniors including in-home care, transportation, adult day care and meals. The Senior Helpline, 813-576-1533, provides information on finding doctors and nursing homes, transportation services, dining facilities and home-delivered meals.

Continuing education

Through the University of South Florida, the Division of Senior Programs, 813-974-2403, has three components. SeniorNet courses are designed for computer novices and taught by seniors. Annual costs are $35 to $40, plus course fees. The tuition waiver program allows residents 60 and over to take credit courses free on a space-available basis. The Learning in Retirement Institute offers study groups. Membership fees are $20; study groups cost $25 to $40.

Crime and safety

The crime rates for St. Petersburg and Pinellas County are average among Florida cities, although the city has the largest population of any Florida location we researched. In St. Pete, 99.5 crimes were reported per 1,000 population; 69.5 incidents per 1,000 countywide.

Getting around town

Public transportation: Pinellas Suncoast Transit Authority, 813-530-9911, offers seniors discounts on bus fare. Dial-A-Ride-Transit, 813-531-0415, is door-to-door transportation for the mobility-impaired.

Roads and highways: I-275, I-4, US 19.

Airports: Tampa International is served by 20 airlines and services more than 9.5 million passengers annually. St. Petersburg/Clearwater Airport is a full-service facility for corporate jets and private aircraft.

Ports: The Port of Manatee and the Port of Tampa are two deep-water ports. A third, the Port of St. Petersburg, is primarily a passenger cruise-ship facility.

Let the good times roll

Recreation: There are more than 40 golf courses in Pinellas County. If you enjoy nature, there are 102 city parks in St. Petersburg, on 2,400 acres, including a 7-mile preserved waterfront and a 47-mile hiking/biking trail—the longest urban linear trail in the U.S. Baseball spring training brings four teams to the area, including the Baltimore Orioles and St. Louis Cardinals to St. Petersburg, the Philadelphia Phillies in Clearwater and the Toronto Blue Jays in Dunedin. The NFL's Tampa Bay Buccaneers play at Tampa Stadium, and the National Hockey League Tampa Bay Lightning play in the Thunderdome. Powerboating is popular here—more world speed records have been set on St. Petersburg's Lake Maggiore than any other race site. Fishing is fantastic, with abundant kingfish, king mackeral, marlin, grouper and tuna.

Culture: There are so many excellent theater, music and visual arts groups that it's impossible to mention them all. The Florida Orchestra is Tampa Bay's professional orchestra. American Stage is an equity theater that presents the best in contemporary and classical theater. Visual arts centers include The Salvador Dali Museum, which has the world's most comprehensive collection of works by the surrealist painter. The Museum of Fine Arts showcases European, American, preColumbian and East Asian works.

Annual events: The city hosts more than 400 events a year, including the college football Hall of Fame Bowl in January, the International Folk Fair (food fests, song and dance) and the Major League Legends of Baseball Game in March, Taste of Pinellas in June and the St. Petersburg Boat Show in November. Other major events include the Kahlua Cup International Yacht Races at Clearwater Yacht Club in November; the mixed team JCPenney Classic (December) at Innisbrook and the LPGA tournament (February) are the annual golf tournaments in the area.

When the kids come: Busch Gardens (Tampa) and Disney World/EPCOT Center (90 minutes away). The Clearwater Marine Science Center Aquarium Museum is a multipurpose aquarium.

For more information

Chamber
The St. Petersburg Area
 Chamber of Commerce
100 Second Ave. N.,
 Suite 150
P.O. Box 1371
St. Petersburg, FL 33731
813-821-4069

Newspapers
St. Petersburg Times
490 First Ave. S.
St. Petersburg, FL 33701
813-893-1111

Tampa Tribune
202 S. Parker St.
Tampa, FL 33606
813-272-7500

Realtor
Catherine McClain
Marie Powell Associates, Inc.,
 Realtors
3325 66th St. N.
St. Petersburg, FL 33710
813-381-245
800-FLA-REAL
Fax: 813-343-5642

23. Clayton, Georgia

Nickname: Where Spring Spends the Summer
County: Rabun
Area code: 706
Population: 1,613
County population: 11,648
% of population over 65: 34
Region: Blue Ridge mountains (NE Georgia)
Closest metro area: Atlanta, 115 mi.
Average home price: $80,000 to $125,000
Best reasons to retire here: Scenic, year-round recreation, safe, affordable.

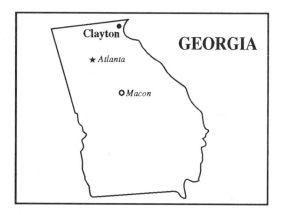

Clayton at a glance

Clayton and surrounding Rabun County are, in a word, awesome. Once you lay eyes on the beautiful peaks of the Blue Ridge mountains, the sparkling waterfalls, crystal-clear Lake Burton and get a taste of four gentle seasons, it will be hard to justify city living. Maybe that's why this small town is predicted to have 70 to 80 percent growth in the population of retirees by 2010. This community has proven to be a haven for senior citizens who want to escape the noise, hustle, bustle and grind for friendly, relaxed and gorgeous surroundings. For the outdoor enthusiast, there's plenty to do, including hiking, canoeing, fishing, whitewater rafting, kayaking, skiing (this is the home of Sky Valley, the southernmost ski resort in the U.S.) and, of course, tennis and golf (golfers can count on 253 playable days). And Clayton is a friendly place. Many seniors have coffee clubs, for which restaurant owners give the group a key to their restaurant. Club members open the restaurant, make their own coffee, clean up and go on their way. The housing market offers a wide selection of styles and prices, and the health care is surprisingly good for such a small community. Crime is something you only read about in the paper (and it happens somewhere else). But the icing on the cake is Rabun County's mountain climate—cool evenings, warm sunny days in spring and summer, and winters that are rarely frigid. As one happy resident put it, "Those looking for a Mayberry or Brigadoon seem to find it here."

Possible drawbacks: This is small-town living with its predictable shortcomings: limited culture and education (the nearest college is 35 miles away), limited job opportunities and limited shopping. If you thrive on cosmopolitan comforts, you should look elsewhere.

Climate

Elevation: 1,925'	Avg. high/low:	Avg. inches rain	snow	Avg. # days precip.	Avg. % humidity
Jan.	51/32	5.6	3	14	70
April	69/44	5.5	trace	12	60
July	84/64	7.5	-	14	74
Oct.	69/46	4.8	-	8	70
YEAR	68/46	67.0	10	-	-
# days 32° or below: 82			# days 90° or warmer: 20		

What things cost

Overview: The Chamber of Commerce reports that the cost of living in Rabun County is slightly below the national average, but no organization officially tracks living costs here, so this cannot be verified.

Gas company: There is no natural gas; propane gas is available through Ferrellgas, 706-782-4239, Tugalogas, 706-782-4543, and other local services. Gas heating averages $70 monthly.

Electric company: Georgia Power Corp., 706-782-4236. Deposit is not required after credit check. Connect fee: $18. Average bill for all-electric: $100 monthly; $30 to $40 for partial electric.

Phone company: Alltel, 706-782-5001. Deposit ($100) may be waived. Installation: $43; basic monthly service: $25-$30.

Water and sewer: City of Clayton, 706-782-4512. Deposit and connect fee total $37. Homeowners pay a $10 service charge. Bills average $35.

Cable company: Northland Cable, 706-782-4249; Mountain View Enterprises, Inc., 706-782-7635.

Car registration, license: Driver's license, $15 (four years). A vision test is required. There are no special requirements for seniors. Registration fee: $20; title fee: $18. New residents must register within 30 days. License tags cost $20 annually, but there is also a property tax ranging from $4 to $500 depending upon make and year of car.

The tax ax

Sales tax: 4-percent sales tax on retail goods; 6-percent on food. The county exercises an additional 1 percent Special Project Fund tax and Local Option tax.

State income tax: Adjustments are necessary on taxable income, with tax rates ranging from 1 percent to a maximum of 6 percent. There is no deduction for federal income tax paid.

Retirement income: Retirement income exclusion of up to $10,000 for 62 or older. Retirement income includes federal, state and private pensions, unearned income and the first $4,000 of earned income.

Property taxes: County property taxes are determined by millage rates and 40 percent of assessed fair market value. The combined county and school millage rate is approximately $15.24 per $1,000 of assessed value. Additional tax for incorporated Clayton is $6.50. Taxes on a $100,000 home would be about $820. Tax assessor's office, 706-782-5068.

Local real estate

Overview: Increases in the cost of building materials have pushed up the price of new homes in recent years, but taxes have remained modest. Most retirees in this area are escaping crowded urban areas, and they tend to relocate permanently. Most move to areas outside of Clayton, not into the town itself. Many choose housing in the country club area, small cabins in the woods or homes on the lake (these are the most expensive, starting at $200,000 and climbing to prices as high as $1 million). County land is at a premium since the federal government or Georgia Power owns 75 percent of it.

Average price for a 3BR/2BA home: New homes average $125,000; resales average $90,000 to $100,000.

Average price for a 2BR condo: $110,000 for new condos; resales average $75,000 to $95,000. Few retirees here are interested in buying condos.

Common housing styles and features: Natural cedar or pine homes and log cabins are popular, but housing of all types is available. Most homes are built on sloping, mountainside lots, so they almost all have a back porch or deck to enjoy the view. Most homes also have basements.

Rental housing market: The rental market is *very* tight, and you may need the help of a realtor. Apartment rentals are $400 to $650 per month; homes are $475 to $700 for a nice 2BR unit.

Nearby areas to consider: Habersham County, Union County.

Earning a living

Business climate: Textile manufacturing is by far the largest single sector of the Rabun County economy, but tourism, health care and retirement market services play a very important part. Because tourism and the retirement sector are projected to grow substantially through the year 2010, hospitality services to these consumers are a growth market, which is good news for entrepreneurs and small businesses. The retail sector has room for expansion, but business owners need to be prepared for seasonal fluctuations, as this sector depends on tourist traffic.

Help in starting a business: Call the Rabun County Chamber of Commerce, Georgia Mountains Area Planning and Development Commission at 404-536-3431, or the Rabun County Economic Development Authority at 706-782-4812. North Georgia Technical Institute (Clarksville, 706-754-7700) is the area's centerpiece for job training, administering the Quick Start program to prepare new or expanding businesses for the first day of operation.

Job market: Unemployment is consistently low in the county, but few retirees work. According to the Chamber of Commerce, there are ample opportunities to work, but retirees volunteer a great deal more. Wages in the area are low, and per capita income is nearly 32 percent below the national average. Major employers are Fruit of the Loom, Don'L and Sara Lee Knit Products—all textile manufacturers. Health care is also an important employer.

Medical care

There are two hospitals in Clayton: Ridgecrest Hospital, 706-782-4297, and Rabun County Memorial Hospital, 706-782-4233. This JCAHO-accredited hospital offers state-of-the-art facilities for acute care, a 24-hour emergency room and intensive and coronary care. The hospital also provides radiology, mammography, physical therapy, respiratory therapy, inpatient and outpatient surgery, geriatric care and a psychiatrist who specializes in assisting older adults. Rabun County Memorial Hospital is an acute care medical/surgical hospital that provides cardiac monitoring, physical and respiratory therapy, radiology, ultrasound and a 24-hour emergency room. This Medicare-certified hospital is a member of the American and Georgia Hospital Associations but was not, at the time of this writing, JCAHO-accredited.

Services for seniors

The Chamber of Commerce Silver Eagles is a special retirees' organization that acts as a networking and social activities center. The group is active and growing. Many members are former corporate presidents, executives and business owners. Membership is now at about 200 couples and singles. AARP is also very active. Many seniors volunteer for Habitat for Humanity, Sharing and Caring and Heart Board of Directors. According to the Chamber of Commerce, there are more than 60 civic organizations in Rabun County, and seniors are involved in all of them.

Continuing education

There are no community colleges in town, but seniors can attend classes at several colleges and universities in the area. These include Piedmont College in Demorest (33 miles) and Clemson University in Clemson, S.C. (45 miles). In addition, Talullah Falls School, a private college prep school, offers adult classes in liberal arts topics, crafts, paintings, exercise and more. Many are free; others are inexpensive. Call 706-754-3171.

Crime and safety

Rabun County is easily the safest area we researched. Residents often leave their homes unlocked and the keys in their cars. Clayton's crime index is 10 incidents per 1,000 population, and the countywide index is 24 incidents per 1,000. Both are far lower than the national average of 55 incidents per 1,000 population. Violent crime is practically unheard of.

Getting around town

Public transportation: There is none, so a car is a necessity.

Roads and highways: US 441 and 23 (north-south); US 76 (east-west); I-85 in Commerce, Ga. (55 miles away); I-40 in Clyde, Ga. (65 miles away).

Airports: Atlanta, Athens, Greenville and Asheville have commercial air service. Atlanta International Airport (115 miles away) is served by most major airlines; Greenville/Spartanburg airport (83 miles away) is served by 10 carriers.

Let the good times roll

Recreation: Popular activities are fishing, camping, whitewater rafting and hiking in the beautiful Blue Ridge mountains, especially in Black Rock Mountain State Park. There are RV campgrounds, tent sites, picnic areas, a beautiful lake and two back country trails. Tallulah Gorge State Park is a new park created through a partnership with Georgia Power Company, featuring one of the most spectacular gorges in the eastern United States. Moccasin Creek State Park on the shores of Lake Burton is another great place for camping and fishing. Other campgrounds include Rabun Beach, Tallulah River and Tate Branch. Sky Valley is one of the southernmost ski resorts in the United States. It also offers golf, tennis, hunting, rock climbing and horseback riding. Rabun County Country Club has a 9-hole public golf course. The U.S. Forest Service owns 63 percent of all property in Rabun County, guaranteeing that the area will stay scenic and beautiful for years to come.

Culture: Rabun County, a favorite place for artists, is the home of The Hambridge Center for the Creative Arts and Sciences. Although it is primarily an artist' program not open to the public, it does offer public workshops and seminars. Residents enjoy the Highlands Playhouse, which is only 22 miles away. Many people drive to Atlanta to take advantage of big-city cultural offerings such as the Atlanta Ballet, the Emory Museum of Art and Archeology and the High Museum of Art, which offer excellent programs throughout the year. The Atlanta Symphony Orchestra is another cultural draw, as are the numerous theaters in Atlanta.

Annual events: Clayton's Arts & Crafts festivals are well-known in these parts: the Cabbage Festival in September features a craft show and cabbage cook-off in Dillard; the Rabun County Homemakers' Festival in Dillard (August) has crafts shows at the Farmer's Market; the Hay Day festivals feature costume parties, sidewalk sales and other festivities several times a year.

When the kids come: Aside from visiting the wonderful state parks and lakes for fun, people travel to Atlanta to see the Atlanta Zoo, Fernbank Science Center and Planetarium, Carter Center Library, Atlanta Botanical gardens and the Japanese Rose Gardens.

For more information

Chamber
Rabun County Chamber
    of Commerce
P.O. Box 750 QL
US Hwy. 441 N.
Clayton, GA 30523
706-782-4812

Newspaper
The Clayton Tribune (weekly)
P.O. Box 425
Clayton, GA 30525
706-782-3312

Realtor
Jackie West
Coldwell Banker Hal West Realty
US Hwy. 441 S.
Clayton, GA 30525
706-782-2222
Fax: 706-782-4504

24. Savannah, Georgia

Nickname: Hostess City of the South
County: Chatham
Area code: 912
Population: 150,000
County population: 270,000
% of population over 65: 25
Region: Southeast
Closest metro area: Charleston, S.C., 105 mi.
Average home price: $120,000 to $150,000
Best reasons to retire here: Beautiful settings, relaxed, great cultural offerings, casual living near the water.

Savannah at a glance

Savannah has been cited by many international publications as the most beautiful city in North America, and it's a distinction the city richly deserves. Founded in 1733 by Englishman James Edward Oglethorpe, Savannah was America's first planned city, laid out as a system of 24 blocks with many public squares. Today, Savannah's Historic District is its crown jewel. The nation's largest registered urban historic landmark district offers visitors a walk back in time. More than 2,400 historically or architecturally significant homes line the 22 blocks that remain of the original plan. Savannah also offers visitors and newcomers alike a real taste of the South and Southern hospitality. The city is green year-round and famous for its spectacular private gardens. There are restaurants that appeal to every taste and pocketbook, but the area is most famous for delicious, spicy Low Country cooking, with its okra and seafood gumbos, oyster and crab stews, she-crab soup, roasted oysters, jambalya, fried shrimp and more. The city is also a very diverse one, welcoming people from all backgrounds. (You might be surprised to learn that the nation's second-largest St. Patrick's Day Parade occurs here, capping off a week of celebrations.) Retiring to Savannah offers a mild climate with a distinct change of seasons, moderate property and income taxes, a broad selection of housing choices, many recreational opportunities and gracious Southern living that's unsurpassed.

Possible drawbacks: The wonderfully mild Savannah winters are offset by torrid heat and humidity in summer. Other than that, Savannah is pretty darned nice!

Climate

Elevation: 46'	Avg. high/low:	Avg. inches rain	snow	Avg. # days precip.	Avg. % humidity
Jan.	61/39	2.92	-	T	55
April	78/54	2.93	-	-	47
July	91/71	7.87	-	-	60
Oct.	78/56	2.81	-	-	53
YEAR	77/55	51.15	-	T	54
# days 32° or below: 36			# days 90° or warmer: 57		

What things cost

Overview: According to ACCRA, overall living costs in Savannah are about 6 percent below the national average, with housing costs nearly 9 percent below and transportation costs 16 percent below.

Gas company: Georgia Natural Gas Co., 800-427-5463. There is a $25 charge to connect and a deposit of $75 that is waived with good credit. Avg. bill: Many areas do not have gas. In winter, heating bills average $100 a month. Appliances only: approximately $30 a month.

Electric company: Savannah Electric and Power Company, 912-232-2152. The deposit ($150) is waived with a letter of credit, and the connect fee is $10. Average electric bill: All-electric averages from $180 to $250. Partial electric service averages about $78.

Phone company: The area is served by BellSouth, 912-780-2355 (800-356-3094 if calling out of state). The connect cost is $42.50. Deposits may be waived. Basic service is approximately $21.

Water: City of Savannah, 912-651-6460. A $60 deposit required if you rent your home. The bimonthly charge for water, sewer and trash removal in Savannah is $54 plus water used. Averages about $120 every two months for total service.

Cable company: Cablevision of Savannah, 912-354-7531.

Car registration, license: Driver's license, $15, issued for four years. No special licensing restrictions for seniors. The registration fee is $20 and title fee is $18. License tags cost $20 annually, but there is also an annual property tax ranging from $4 to $500 depending upon the make and year of the automobile.

The tax ax

Sales tax: 4 percent on all retail goods. Savannah levies an additional 2 percent on everything except drugs and medical services. Food is taxed at 6 percent in Georgia.

State income tax: Tax rates range from 1 percent 6 percent depending upon income bracket. There is no deduction for federal income tax paid.

Retirement income: There is a retirement income exclusion of up to $10,000 for people 62 or older. Retirement income consists of federal, state and private pensions, unearned income and the first $4,000 of earned income.

Property taxes: County property taxes determined by tax rates and 40 percent of market value. Millage rates are 32.11 in incorporated Savannah and 35.87 in unincorporated areas. Board of Assessors of Chatham County, 912-652-7272.

Local real estate

Overview: Property values in Savannah are trending upward, so it is considered a very good area for investment. Property taxes are higher than most Southern cities, but average if you're relocating from the Northeast. Most retirees relocate to the area permanently, although many residents of Skidway Island are snowbirds. The selection of condominiums in Savannah is limited.

Median price for a single family home: $62,700.

Average price for a 3BR/2BA home: $150,000 new; $120,000 resale.

Average price for a 2BR condo: New condos average $120,000 to $140,000; resales average $110,000 to $130,000.

Common housing styles and features: In the downtown area there are many beautiful, historical homes. Homes in this area have consistently shown a strong return on investment. Suburban areas offer a wide array of choices from small ranch-style homes to traditional antebellum estates.

Rental housing market: Rentals are hard to find in this area, and very high in price. Most people opt to purchase a home in lieu of paying pricey rents. Avg. rent: $600 and up in a good area.

Communities or developments most popular with retirees: Southbridge and Skidway Island. Features include golf, tennis, swimming and other amenities. Savannah Quarters is a large resort development with home prices starting at $120,000.

Nearby areas to consider: Rincon or Richmond Hill.

Earning a living

Business climate: Savannah is an unusual place in the American economic scene, because it still derives 40 percent of its economic base from manufacturing, with an additional 20 percent each in the port and military. The service sector accounts for only 10 percent of the economy, and tourism the final 10 percent. Tourism is the fastest-growing segment of the local economy, which bodes well for small businesses in retail and tourist areas.

Help in starting a business: The Small Business Assistance Corporation, 912-232-4700, offers financing through the Small Business Administration and has a valuable resource guide of agencies that can assist new business development. Savannah Economic Development Authority, 912-233-9606, provides confidential assistance for businesses wanting to establish, locate or expand in Savannah. Business Outreach Services of the University of Georgia, 912-356-2755, offers consulting, continuing education and more. The Business Outreach Service will help prospective business owners develop and update their business plans, analyze their financial records, identify sources of capital and more. SCORE can be reached at 912-652-4335. This organization offers free business assistance in the form of counseling.

Job market: Savannah has enjoyed 8 percent growth in employment in the first four years of the 90s, with the majority of new jobs coming in retail, business, medical and personal services. The area is considered vulnerable to unemployment because of the high percentage of jobs in blue-collar and military sectors.

Medical care

Savannah has three major hospitals served by more than 600 physicians. Candler Hospital, 912-692-6000, Georgia's first hospital, is now a 335-bed facility with specialized services including the Advanced Surgery Center, Diabetes Center, Gastrointestinal Center and Savannah Regional Heart Center. Effingham Hospital (Springfield, 912-754-6451), is an acute medical/surgical hospital with 45 beds and a 105-bed nursing home, affiliated with Candler Health Systems, Inc. Serving patients in 35 counties in Georgia and South Carolina, Memorial Medical Center, 912-350-8000, is a two-state licensed medical center. It is a regional referral center for cancer care and the Heart Institute. St. Joseph's Hospital, 912-925-4100, is a 305-bed hospital that was rated one of the best in the U.S. by JCAHO. It offers a HeartCare Center, the Center for Orthopedic Excellence, the CancerCare Center, the Center for Digestive Diseases and the Diabetes Unit.

Services for seniors

The Coastal Senior, 912-233-3622, is a monthly publication that caters to seniors with active lifestyles. It is available free of charge at stores, libraries and senior centers. Senior Citizens Inc. is a community and service organization that acts as a proponent for seniors. It operates three of the city's 13 Golden Age Centers, which provide day programs including classes, special events, seasonal activities and meals. The Elder Rights Project of Georgia Legal Services, 912-651-2180, can provide answers to legal questions about seniors' rights. RSVP, 912-234-7556.

Continuing education

Armstrong State College, 912-927-5257, has 75 academic degree programs, and seniors over 62 can take classes for free. The Coastal Georgia Center for Continuing Education, 912-651-2550, offers short courses, seminars, lectures and more. Classes are offered in three locations and cover a wide range of subjects—including computer training, creative arts, gardening, health, yoga, business, languages and "The Fine Art of Writing Church News."

Crime and safety

In 1994, Chatham County had approximately 75 crimes per 1,000 population. Savannah police reported a rate of approximately 86 crimes per 1,000, somewhat higher than the national average of 55 per 1,000 population.

Getting around town

Public transportation: Chatham Area Transit, 912-233-5767. Seniors ride for half-price with Chatham County senior ID. Service is extensive, and it is possible to live without a car.

Roads and highways: I-16, I-95 and State Highways 17 and 80.

Airport: Savannah International Airport is served by three major carriers. Midway Connection provides nonstop service from Raleigh/Durham to Savannah, and Savannah to Hilton Head Island. Jet Express offers service between Savannah and Chicago, Washington and New York City.

Port: The Port of Savannah is the largest foreign commerce port in the area.

Let the good times roll

Recreation: Savannah has nine private golf courses and two public links. The city also boasts eight large parks offering camping, fishing, boating, tennis, golf and other sports, in addition to picnicking, hiking and more. If you like spectator sports, Savannah is home of the minor league Savannah Sand Gnats, a farm team for the Los Angeles Dodgers. The NFL's Jacksonville Jaguars draws a crowd from Savannah whenever they play in the Gator Bowl.

Culture: Savannah Theatre Company puts on children's productions in the oldest continually operating theater site in the country. During the summer, jazz, big band and Dixieland fill downtown Johnson Square with sound. The Savannah Symphony Orchestra plays a regular season of concerts at Savannah Civic Center's Johnny Mercer Theatre, then goes outdoors for the summer to the Telfair Museum (Savannah's premier art museum, opened in 1885). Others include the Regency-style house museum Owens-Thomas House, the King-Tisdell Cottage museum, dedicated to preserving aspects of African-American history, and the birthplace of Juliette Gordon Low, the Girl Scouts of America founder.

Annual events: In March, enjoy the annual Savannah Tour of Homes and Gardens. St. Patrick's Day is the biggest event in Savannah, which hosts the second-largest parade in the U.S., with more than 250,000 people coming to celebrate. Arts on the River Weekend each May is a multi-art festival; Forsyth festival in September presents performances from local and regional artists, including the Savannah Jazz Orchestra, Center Stage Dance Company and Ballet South. Savannah Maritime Festival in August celebrates Savannah's rich nautical history, with cultural and sporting events, dances and arts and crafts fairs. Octoberfest on the River features entertainment, arts and crafts.

When the kids come: Tybee Island is a great place for picnicking, fishing, sailing and swimming, and has a traditional, down-home flavor. River Street Train Museum features a guided tour of antique toy train displays, a large, operating train layout, memorabilia and more. The University of Georgia Marine Extension Service Aquarium is a public aquarium located on Skidway Island, featuring 50 species of local fish and invertebrates.

For more information

Chamber
Savannah Area Chamber
  of Commerce
292 W. Oglethorpe Ave.
Savannah, GA 31401
912-944-0444

Newspaper
Savannah News-Press
111 W. Bay St.
Savannah, GA 31401
912-236-9511

Realtor
Betty Stevenson
Re/Max Advantage Realty
1111 King George Blvd.
Savannah, GA 31419
912-920-7750
800-232-5243
Fax: 912-920-7753

25. Coeur d'Alene, Idaho

Nickname: City by the Lake
County: Kootenai
Area code: 208
Population: 26,611
County population: 77,450
% of population over 65: 18
Region: Northern Idaho
Closest metro area: Spokane, Wa., 32 mi.
Median home price: $100,840
Best reasons to retire here: Pristine lake country, fabulous skiing, year-round recreation, affordable housing, quality health care.

Coeur d'Alene at a glance

Picture yourself living in a region of rolling wheat fields, green forests, snow-capped mountains and more than 75 crystal-clear lakes, and you've got Coeur d'Alene. Also known as the "City With a Heart," it has stolen more than a few hearts. But enjoying the spectacular natural setting is only the beginning of the beauty of retiring here. This Idaho lake city is alive with activity and sparkles with energy. Located on the shores of the beautiful lake from which it takes its name, water sports and recreation are available in town and all along the 109 miles of shoreline. Life can become a wonderful vacation of golfing, fishing, canoeing and sailing—and that's just in warm weather. Cross-country skiing and snowmobiling are waiting for you at other times of the year. Because of its natural beauty, recreational opportunities and amenities, Coeur d'Alene has become a popular convention and visitor destination. This significantly boosts the economy and has prompted growth, but Coeur d'Alene is still far from overrun. The cost of living is within reach, especially in the area of real estate.

Possible drawbacks: If you don't like snow, this is not the place for you. During most winters there is not more than 6 inches of snow accumulated at any time, but Coeur d'Alene has had up to 4 feet at once. If you are looking for real estate outside of Coeur d'Alene, determine if year-round access is available. Many areas just outside of Coeur d'Alene get much more snow than the city. Also, public transportation is extremely limited, so a car is a necessity. You can spend a lot of time in that car, too, because services and educational and business opportunities may require you to travel to reach them.

Climate

Elevation: 2,333'	Avg. high/low:	Avg. inches		Avg. # days precip.	Avg. % humidity
		rain	snow		
Jan.	33/19	1.3	21	17	82
April	60/32	1.4	1	11	59
July	85/50	.8	-	5	46
Oct.	58/32	2.9	.6	9	71
YEAR	58/34	20.0	58	-	-
# days 32° or below: 140			# days 90° or warmer: 10		

What things cost

Overview: No recent comparative data on Coeur d'Alene's cost of living is available, but housing and utilities costs are in line with or below many other retirement areas we researched.

Gas and electric company: Call the Washington Water Power Company, 208-664-0421. No deposits or turn-on charges are required, but there is a minimum monthly charge of $3.28 for natural gas. Avg. gas bill: $50 monthly, including heat and appliances. If appliances only, the average bill is about $15.

Electric company: Kootenai Electric Cooperative, 208-765-1200. There is no charge to turn on service and no deposits are required. Some homes that are more than 20 years old are all-electric, but most new developments have natural gas heat and appliances. An average bill for an all-electric home is $100 to $150, while partial electric averages $25 a month.

Phone company: Call GTE Northwest, 800-483-4100. Connection charge is $30; deposits are usually not required. Basic service rates vary from $16.20 to $25, depending upon the calling area desired.

Water and sewer: City Utilities Water Department, 208-769-2227. No hook-up charge. Average bimonthly bill is $40.

Cable company: Century Communications, 208-667-5521.

Car registration, license: You must obtain license and registration within 90 days of establishing residency. Driver's license, $20.50. Written exam and eye test are required for new residents. Registration fees, based on vehicle age, range from $20 to $49.

The tax ax

Sales tax: 5 percent; drugs and medical services are exempt.

State income tax: Graduated from 2 to 8.2 percent, depending upon income. No deduction for federal income tax paid.

Retirement income: Federal, state and private pensions are not exempt; Social Security benefits are. There's a standard $7,600 deduction for married couples filing jointly when both are over 65.

Property taxes: County average is 1.7 percent, but a homeowner's exemption of up to 50 percent for primary residences (with a $50,000 limit) usually put this amount at about 1 percent of the house's sale value. Property is assessed at 100 percent of market value. Tax assessor's office, 208-769-4400.

Local real estate

Overview: Asking and sale prices have been steady recently, as have local property taxes. With owner-occupied houses, the rule of thumb is that taxes are approximately 1 percent of the sale value of the home. The Coeur d'Alene market, though relatively small, offers a wide variety of housing choices, from condominiums with country club-style amenities, to gated developments, to over-55 communities, to manufactured home parks. Most retirees who come here are relocating permanently; it is not a big second home market.

Median price for a single family home: $100,840.

Average price for a 3BR/2BA home: New homes average between $85,000 to $135,000, while resales average $90,000 to $175,000. The vast majority of the housing in this area was built in the 1950s.

Average price for a 2BR condo: New, $79,000 to $89,000; resale, $75,000 to $85,000.

Unique housing features: Most new homes are built to Northwest energy code standards, so heating is efficient.

Rental housing market: There is more rental housing available today than there has been for some time. Average rent for a 2BR home is $500 to $700 a month; 2BR condominiums rent in the neighborhood of $650. Apartments are typically in the $450 to $550 range.

Nearby areas to consider: Shoshone County, 30 to 50 miles east of Coeur d'Alene, or Benewah County, 35 to 50 miles south of Coeur d'Alene.

Earning a living

Business climate: The resort industry and associated retailing are major employers in the area, and business is booming. The population of Kootenai county is trending toward 30 percent growth in a mere five years, so opportunities in the service industry are available. Lumber and agriculture, longtime mainstays of the economy, have decreased in importance but still provide significant business activity. Major employers include Hagadone Hospitality, Kootenai Medical Center, Coeur d'Alene School District, North Idaho College, GTE and Century Publishing. Small business is big here; the Chamber boasts 1,050 member firms in a community of less than 30,000 people.

Help in starting a business: The Panhandle Area Council, 208-772-0584, provides free counseling services, accounting assistance, on-the-job training and more. The Council also offers small business loans and community grants. The Small Business Development Center at Idaho College, 208-769-3285, offers business training, assistance with business plan development, marketing, personnel and all the steps necessary to start or grow a small business. The center has a library and research assistance via the Internet. Also, try the Silver Valley Economic Corporation, 208-752-5511.

Job market: Job Service, 208-769-1558, is a federal employment security agency whose services are free and available to everyone. The service matches job seekers with employer needs, and veterans receive special priority and job training. It also uses the Internet to post job listings. The number of the 24-hour Job Service Hotline is 208-769-1550.

Medical care

Although Coeur d'Alene is a small community, high-quality health care is available. The 187-bed Kootenai Medical Center, 208-666-2000, is an award-winning regional health care facility that offers a new specialized emergency room center, critical care units and excellent rehabilitation and oncology departments. The hospital provides many wellness programs, including free health screenings. The North Idaho Immediate Care Center, 208-667-9110, offers general medical and minor emergency services; it's open seven days a week. North Idaho Cancer Center is known throughout the Northwest for its excellent programs and professional staff. Pine Crest Hospital and Counseling Center, 800-221-5008, is an acute care center with separate units for children, adolescents and adults. The Counseling Center offers a free initial consultation to those seeking help with chemical dependency or anger management.

Services for seniors

Lake City Senior Center, 208-667-4628, organizes activities such as bridge, cribbage, china painting and dance classes. The center also offers income tax and banking assistance, a legal aid ombudsman and a monthly newsletter. The local chapter of AARP meets there, as well as a club called the Rambling Rovers, a travel group. The center works with the office of Aging and Adult Services, area hospitals and other agencies. Additional senior centers are located in nearby Post Falls, Rathdrum and Spirit Lake. To contact the Area Agency on Aging, call 208-667-3179. Information and referral services are available at 800-642-9099.

Continuing education

North Idaho College is set on a wooded 44-acre campus and enrolls 6,000 students in noncredit and special interest classes, including arts and literature, health, language, nutrition, personal growth, regional topics and financial planning for seniors. It also hosts an Elderhostel program, 208-769-3444, which has a limited number of commuter spaces available. Ten programs are offered annually at two sites, including the magnificent Schweitzer Mountain Resort, and costs are around $360.

Crime and safety

Coeur d'Alene reported a crime index of about 90 incidents per 1,000 population in 1994, although the rate was 55 per 1,000 for all of Kootenai county, which is the national average. Bear in mind that crime indexes reflect total crime reported, while the population figures do not include seasonal influxes of tourists, vacationers and conventioneers.

Getting around town

Public transportation: The Northern Idaho Community Express (NICE), 208-664-9769, offers door-to-door transportation around North Idaho.

Roads and highways: I-90 serves Coeur d'Alene and connects it with Spokane, Washington, just 32 miles away. State Highway 95 is the connection to the north and south.

Airports: Spokane International is about 45 minutes to the west and is served by seven national and regional carriers. The Coeur d'Alene airport at Hayden Lake serves private aircraft.

Let the good times roll

Recreation: All sorts of water activities are available on Lake Coeur d'Alene and nearby lakes, rivers and streams. Fishing is especially impressive, with more than one-third of the state's record catches coming from this region, including Chinook salmon, Gerrad rainbow trout and bull trout that tip the scales at 30 pounds. The St. Joe and Coeur d'Alene Rivers have Class II and III rapids and stretches for the experts, plus calm areas ideal for canoeists and rafters. There are 11 public, semiprivate and private golf courses, including the Coeur d'Alene Resort Golf Course, recently selected by *Golf Digest* as the most beautiful resort golf course in the U.S. (The course, which has the world's only floating green, is open to the public.) Hikers, bikers and runners enjoy the views along the paved Centennial Trail. The skiing is spectacular, especially at Silver Mountain (36 miles south). Horseback riding is popular in the summertime, and nature lovers enjoy watching the eagles arrive at Wolf Lodge Bay in November.

Culture: The Carrousel Players, a professional theater company, specializes in Broadway musicals. The Lake City Playhouse, offering contemporary and classic productions, is the only equity theater troupe in the Inland Northwest. The Silver Mountain Ski & Summer Resort presents a concert series in July and August that features a variety of well-known entertainers. Other nationally recognized entertainers and musicians visit the area's three colleges. Historical museums and sites include the Museum of North Idaho, the Wallace District Mining Museum and Fort Sherman Powder House.

Annual events: The Fred Murphy Pioneer Parade is a popular attraction in May; Art on the Green, a three-day festival in August, brings local, regional and national artists together for an arts and crafts festival with music, theater, dance and food. Octoberfest happens in nearby Post Falls in early October; and the Festival of Lights Parade kicks off the holiday season in November.

When the kids come: Aside from the many outdoor activities enjoyed by all ages, kids love Silverwood, an amusement park that features an enchanted Victorian Village along with roller coasters, raft rides, an antique aircraft museum and carnival events.

For more information

Chamber
Coeur d'Alene Chamber
   of Commerce
1621 North Third St.,
   Suite 100
Coeur d'Alene, ID 83814
208-664-3194

Newspaper
The Idaho Spokesman-Review
608 NW Boulevard
Coeur d'Alene, ID 83814
208-765-7100

Realtor
Roger Atge
Re/Max Preferred Realty
Harbor Plaza, Suite 103
Coeur d'Alene, ID 83814
208-664-1190
800-662-1190
Fax: 208-765-8637

26. Bloomington, Indiana

Nickname: The Break Away Town
County: Monroe
Area code: 812
Population: 60,633
County population: 108,978
% of population over 65: 8.5
Region: Southern Indiana
Closest metro area: Indianapolis, 50 mi.
Average home price: $120,000 to $150,000
Best reasons to retire here: Great cultural and recreational facilities, affordable lifestyles, lush rural setting.

Bloomington at a glance

Bloomington may be a small place, but there's more culture, recreation and sports packed into this town than you'll find in many major metropolitan areas. This little southern Indiana city is situated in a lake-filled region of rolling hills, national forests and a pleasant, temperate climate, adding to the enjoyment of those who are hikers, bikers, fishermen, sailors and campers. Culture enthusiasts are only minutes away from a world of operas, symphonies, ballets—some of the most captivating performances in the Midwest. Even the architecture is inspiring, with the Indiana University Art Museum designed by I.M. Pei, and the world-class Musical Arts Center, featuring a sculpture by artist Alexander Calder. And then there's the "Hoosier Hysteria" you've heard so much about. Residents cherish their Big Ten football and (especially) basketball teams, cramming into Memorial Stadium and Assembly Hall in hopes of another great season. Real estate opportunities in Bloomington and surrounding Brown County are a wonderful assortment of small, large, contemporary, colonial, suburban country, wooded, lake-view and golf community homes, condominiums and apartments. Housing in this area is also very affordable (at 4 percent below the national average), and the overall cost of living is below average, as well.

Possible drawbacks: The summer humidity can be quite uncomfortable, but hurry back for the fall foliage—it's gorgeous. Traffic in town can be a nightmare, especially during the football and basketball seasons. Medical care is limited, with only one hospital in the area. Although Bloomington Hospital is quite good, you may have to travel to Indianapolis to visit specialists or for particular problems or treatments.

Climate

Elevation: 851'	Avg. high/low:	Avg. inches		Avg. # days precip.	Avg. % humidity
		rain	snow		
Jan.	41/24	3.0	-	12	75
April	64/42	3.7	-	13	65
July	88/64	3.5	-	9	67
Oct.	69/44	2.5	-	8	71
YEAR	62/43	40.0	17	-	-
# days 32° or below: 113			# days 90° or warmer: 27		

What things cost

Overview: According to ACCRA, the cost of living in Bloomington is slightly more than 3 percent below the national average, with groceries and utility costs higher than average. Savings result from housing costs at 4 percent below average, and health care costs at 7 percent below.

Gas company: Indiana Gas Company, 800-777-2060 (after hours: 800-284-4295). Average bill is $51 monthly (higher in winter). Natural gas is frequently used for home heating. New customers must pay a $70 deposit but no connection fee.

Electric company: Call PSI Energy, 812-336-6371.

Average electric bill: Partial electric service average $68 monthly. No deposits or hook-up fees.

Phone company: Contact Ameritech, 812-556-3510. Connection fee: $47; basic service: $18. No deposits required.

Water and sewer: City of Bloomington Utilities, 812-339-1444. The charge to connect is $18; no deposit. Rates for water and sewer are based on usage. Average bills are $25, but could go up to $33.

Cable company: TCI, 812-332-9486; Triax, 800-874-2924.

Car registration, license: New residents must obtain a license and register vehicles within 60 days. Driver's license costs $6; eye test and written exam required. Driving test may be waived. Licenses renewed every four years; every three years over age 75. Plate fee is $12.75; excise tax of $12 to $532 is due on cars, motorcycles and trucks of 11,000 lbs. or less. Monroe County adds a surtax of 10 percent based on state excise tax.

The tax ax

Sales tax: 5 percent; groceries, prescription drugs and most services are exempt.

State income tax: Indiana's state income tax is 3.4 percent of gross income, and Monroe County adds an option income tax of 1 percent of gross income.

Retirement income: There is a $1,000 personal exemption and an additional $1,000 per person for those 65 and older. Federal pensions are exempt up to $2,000.

Property taxes: Rates vary for each $100 of assessed valuation (based on 1/3 true cash value). There is a $2,000 homestead exemption, plus a variable homestead credit off net tax due. The formula for computing property taxes is made additionally complex by accounting for discounted reproduction cost and depreciation. Bloomington millage rate is 9.29 per $100 of assessed value. Tax assessor's office, 812-349-2501.

Local real estate

Overview: Traditionally, Bloomington and Brown County have been big second-home markets. Retirees come looking for ranch-style homes with acreage and wooded surroundings or new condo/golf communities. Homes start at $150,000, but many are in the $200,000 to $300,000 range (particularly in the exclusive parts of Brown County). Condos cost much less.

Average price for a 3BR/2BA home: $120,000 to $150,000 covers the range for new and resale homes.

Median price for a single family home: $96,000.

Average price for a 2BR condo: $110,000.

Common housing styles and features: 3BR, 1 to 2 baths, garages, basements.

Rental housing market: With faculty and students constantly moving in and out, there's always plenty of activity in the rental market, but rental housing can be quite scarce at some times of the year, such as the beginning of autumn.

Communities or developments most popular with retirees: Look at Lake of the Four Seasons and The Pointe for golf communities. Meadowood is strictly a retirement development.

Average rent for a 2BR apartment: $400 to $800 a month. Houses: $500 to $1,500 a month.

Nearby areas to consider: Nashville, Brown County, 20 minutes from the center of town, offers privacy, exclusivity and countrified living, with some homes costing up to a half-million dollars. Nashville (pop. 500) is a quaint village in the center of Brown County.

Earning a living

Business climate: Bloomington is a competitive market with a highly educated work force. But the retail potential is excellent, with many businesses trying to cater to the Indiana University student population, which pumps approximately $48 million annually into the local economy.

Help in starting a business: Bloomington's Small Business Development Center, 812-339-8937, offers a free guide to starting a business and conducting market research. It has business orientation sessions twice monthly, and new business owners can meet with SBDC counselors and SCORE counselors and executives. The center has a New Business Incubator facility where new small businesses rent space and share fax and copy machines, voice mail, conference rooms and more.

Job market: Competition for jobs is stiff. Bloomington's unemployment rate is 2.9 percent, compared to national figures of 5.3 percent. While this low rate might sound promising, it actually reflects the fact that residents accept work without much regard to pay because the good-paying jobs are so hard to find; wages in Bloomington are the lowest of 11 metropolitan areas in Indiana. There is stiff competition for even part-time retail and service jobs, due to the large student population. The largest employers are in the manufacturing, education and medical sectors, including General Electric, Cook Inc., Thomson Consumer Electronics, Indiana University and Bloomington Hospital. Call Indiana Workforce Development, 812-331-6002, for more information on the labor market.

Medical care

Bloomington Hospital, 812-330-5252, is the only full-service, accredited hospital in the area, with 214 physicians on staff. It is a regional referral center serving nine counties in south central Indiana. It offers comprehensive cancer care, an outpatient Radiology Oncology Center and complete heart services: open-heart surgery, coronary angioplasty and a four-phase cardiac rehabilitation program. It also has a Diabetes Foot Clinic, a 24-hour emergency department, a sleep disorders center and a Seniority Plus program, 812-336-9300, for persons age 55 and over. Services include Lifeline, a 24-hour emergency response system that links you to the hospital by a wireless button for a small monthly fee. You also receive a directory of senior services in Bloomington, free insurance claims assistance, free health seminars, a newsletter, free and discounted health screenings, discounted exercise classes, assistance with living wills and more. In addition, Indianapolis offers several top-notch major medical facilities within an hour's drive, including Indiana University Medical Center.

Services for seniors

The Bloomington Area Agency on Aging, 812-334-3383, is an excellent source for referrals on seniors services, including legal services, prescription assistance and seasonal help, such as lawn mowing. Aside from providing valuable services, it publishes several directories with listings and coupons. Many of the national senior organizations have local chapters, including RSVP, 812-334-3383, and SCORE, 812-336-6381.

Continuing education

Indiana University, 812-855-5108, does not have a continuing education program for seniors, although classes are open to any resident on a nondegree basis. The noncredit program offers classes in humanities and the arts, music, gardening, business, computers and more, without enrolling in the University. IU runs a very popular mini-university each June where more than 100 professors lecture on various topics.

Crime and safety

There are 67 crimes per 1,000 people in Monroe County, which is higher than the national average of 55 per 1,000. Nonetheless, residents perceive Bloomington as a very safe community. Violent crime is rare, and when it does occur, it is rarely random (domestic problems are the source of many violent crimes). Burglaries and thefts are more prevalent, but mostly when the campus empties.

Getting around town

Public transportation: Bloomington Transit, 812-336-RIDE. Fare is 75 cents; 35 cents for seniors. A car is a necessity for residential areas, as well as for Brown County.

Roads and highways: State highways 37, 45, 46, 48 and 446 run through or near town. Bloomington is 45 miles west of I-65 and 45 miles south of the junctions of I-65, I-69, I-70 and I-74.

Airports: Monroe Airport offers direct flights to and from Chicago and Indianapolis. Indianapolis International Airport (45 minutes away) is served by eight national and several regional carriers.

Let the good times roll

Recreation: Four local golf courses, a yacht club, an indoor tennis club and two 40-acre sports parks (Winslow and Twin Lakes) are just a few of the recreational features the Bloomington area boasts. Lake Monroe and Lake Lemon are the places to head to for fishing, boating, hunting, picnicking, swimming and hiking. Lake Lemon is also great for bird watching; Griffy Lake has wonderful trails for wildlife observation or just plain fun. The Pointe Golf and Tennis Club on Lake Monroe is a beautiful facility. Brown County and Nashville offer great boutique and craft shopping, and they are very popular destinations on autumn weekends, when folks flock to the area to take in the spectacular fall color.

Culture: It may seem unlikely that such a small town would be a cultural capital of the Midwest, but Bloomington is deserving of such recognition. As home to one of the finest music schools in the world (the IU School of Music), concertgoers are the first to enjoy up-and-coming opera stars, musicians and stage performers who often achieve international recognition. The MAC (Musical Arts Center) has the longest-running opera season in the western hemisphere, and the Fine Arts Auditorium features top entertainers. The museums are equally deserving of attention; the Fine Arts Museum features a collection of more than 25,000 works of art.

Annual events: The Little 500 Bike Race, held in April, is legendary. Crappiethon USA is a fishing tournament in May where fish are tagged for prizes; the Bloomington Renaissance Festival occurs in June; Taste of Bloomington is in July; in September, the 4H Monroe County fair is held, and so are the Senior Games of Indiana, when more than 500 people age 55 and older compete in more than 20 team and individual sports. The 10K Marathon is in November and the Canopy of Lights and Madrigal dinners are featured in December.

When the kids come: Aside from the multitude of campus activities and sights, kids love the Cyclotron (light shows) and Kirkwood Observatory (observe the night sky) at IU. Lake Lemon, Lake Monroe and Hoosier National Forest provide outdoor recreation, and there are movie theaters and minigolf courses in the area. Fifty miles away in Indianapolis, check out the world's largest Children's Museum and the Indianapolis Zoo. And of course, there's the world-famous Indianapolis Motor Speedway where the Indy 500 is run.

For more information

Chamber
The Greater Bloomington
   Chamber of Commerce
P.O. Box 1302
Bloomington, IN 47402
812-336-6381

Newspaper
The Herald-Times
1900 S. Walnut St.
P.O. Box 909
Bloomington, IN 47402
812-332-4401

Realtor
Mike Peek
Century 21 Peek & Association
1409 N. College
Bloomington, IN 47404
812-336-7713

27. Annapolis, Maryland

Nickname: The Sailing Capital of the World
County: Anne Arundel
Area code: 410
Population: 34,070
County population: 447,700
% of population over 65: 9.5
Region: Chesapeake Bay
Closest metro area: Baltimore, 24 mi.
Average home price: $201,000 to $229,000
Best reasons to retire here: Water recreation, culture, small-town charm with major cities nearby.

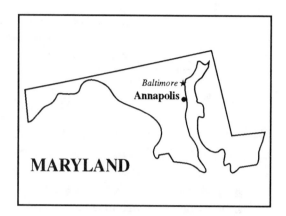

Annapolis at a glance

The greatest appeal of Annapolis lies to the east—the Chesapeake Bay and life on the water. There are more than 400 miles of waterfront to explore and enjoy in Anne Arundel County, and all of the county is within one-half hour of the bay and its tributaries. It's considered the sailing capital of the U.S., and the city has an international yachting flavor, although boaters of all kinds love the area. Many retirees who live here are Naval Academy graduates who enjoy the facilities of the Navy. The city also has small-town charm, combined with proximity to the big city benefits of Washington, D.C., and Baltimore. (It's a popular weekend retreat and second home community for residents of these cities.) Rich in history, Annapolis served briefly as the capital of the United States. It is the capital of Maryland and the home of the third oldest institution of higher learning in the United States—St. John's. It also boasts more surviving colonial buildings than any other city in the country. Annapolis residents relish living face-to-face with so much history; life and business have gone on in the city's Historic District for more than 300 years.

Possible drawbacks: Although better described geographically as part of the mid-Atlantic region, you'll find the cost of living here is pretty much East Coast, which is high. Taxes are also higher here than in many other popular retirement locations. The weather is temperate, but some may find the winters too cold and the summers too humid. The local economy is dependent on government, which makes it vulnerable to economic downturns and government downsizing.

Climate

Elevation: 57'	Avg. high/low:	Avg. inches rain	snow	Avg. # days precip.	Avg. % humidity
Jan.	42/25	2.91	5	10	58
April	65/42	3.07	0.1	11	49
July	87/67	4.07	0	9	53
Oct.	68/46	3.12	0	7	54
YEAR	65/45	40.46	18	112	54
# days 32° or below: 100			# days 90° or warmer: 31		

What things cost

Overview: There are no current cost of living statistics for Annapolis, but nearby Baltimore is about 2 percent below the national average. Utilities, groceries and transportation costs are above the norm, but housing and health care are below.

Gas and electric company: Baltimore Gas & Electric Co., 800-685-0123. There is a one-time service charge of $20. Deposits are required pending credit history, and begin at $25. Homes with gas heat average $130 monthly, partial gas (appliances only) averages $40, while the average is $150 a month for all electric units and $50 monthly for partial electric units.

Phone company: The area is served by Bell Atlantic, 410-224-1900. The connection fee is $48. Deposits and advance payments may be required, based on credit history. Basic service is $19.42 monthly for unlimited local calls.

Water and sewer: City of Annapolis, 410-263-7953. There's no charge to connect to service or transfer billing, and fees are based entirely upon usage. Costs average $32.50 a month.

Cable company: Jones Intercable, Inc., 410-987-8600; North Arundel Cable-TV, 410-987-5811; TCI Cablevision of Annapolis, 410-268-7551.

Car registration, license: Driver's license, $36; renewal, $20. Licenses valid for five years. Applicants must pass a written and vision test. New residents must register within 30 days. Two-year registration fees: passenger vehicles of 3,700 lbs. or less, $54; over 3,700 lbs., $81, plus an $8 surcharge. Excise tax is 5 percent of retail value; minimum excise tax is $100.

The tax ax

Sales tax: 5 percent excluding groceries and prescription drugs.

State income tax: A graduated tax rate peaking at 5 percent of taxable income in excess of $3,000. There is a $1,200 exemption per person from adjusted gross income, and an additional $1,000 per person 65 and older. This county has a personal income surtax of 50 percent of the state individual income tax liability.

Retirement income: There is a federal, state and private pension income exclusion of up to $13,100 for persons 65 or older.

Property taxes: Anne Arundel county's property tax rate is $2.50 per $100 of assessed value. In Annapolis, you pay $3.23 per $100 of assessed value. The assessed value is calculated at approximately 40 percent of cash value. Property tax assistance, 410-222-1144.

Local real estate

Overview: Home prices have dropped about 5 percent in recent years, although taxes have increased about 2 percent. (Maryland's economy is dependent upon government, and downsizing has affected the housing market, driving prices downward.) Land in Annapolis is scarce, so resales typically command good prices. Waterfront properties are popular and plentiful, although they are expensive. The market is tilted toward buyers, nonetheless, the retirement housing market has been upbeat. Home settings are varied, from waterfront to golf course communities, from historic houses to modern condominiums and townhouses.

Average price for a 3BR/2BA home: New homes average $201,000. Resales average more—$229,000—because they are often on the more desirable lots.

Average price for a 2BR condo: New condos go for $129,400, while resales average $112,300.

Rental housing market: Rentals tend to go very quickly, as the supply does not begin to meet the demand. Proximity to water is a major factor in rental housing pricing.

Average rent for a 2BR apartment: $900 to $1,000 monthly.

Common housing styles and features: Annapolis has many historic neighborhoods with both colonial and Victorian style architecture, as well as waterfront homes and communities.

Communities or developments most popular with retirees: Heritage Harbour, South River Condominium.

Nearby areas to consider: Severna, Edgewater, Crofton.

Earning a living

Business climate: The county's economy is grounded in high-tech communications, distribution and computer support services. Growing industries include environment-related technology, regional data centers and life sciences. Retail and service industries account for more than 50 percent of available employment. Major area employers include US Air, Westinghouse Electrical Systems and Davco Food/Wendy's. Government is also a major factor in the economy, accounting for 18 percent of all employment. Average household income is 20 percent above the national average, and 47 percent of all households in the county have incomes over $50,000.

Help in starting a business: The Anne Arundel Economic Development Corporation has a Small Business Development Center that offers free, one-on-one counseling and location assistance. It also has an Incentive Fund—a direct loan and loan guarantee program that can provide financial assistance, 410-222-7410. Try the Annapolis Economic Development Corporation, 410-263-7940, and the Annapolis Chamber of Commerce, which is very active. For demographic information, call the Department of Planning and Code Enforcement of Anne Arundel County at 410-222-7432. SCORE local offices can be reached at 410-266-9553.

Job market: The county unemployment rate is 4.7 percent. According to the Maryland Department of Economic and Employment Development, the average weekly wage in Anne Arundel County is $515. Maryland State Employment/Job Service, 410-974-7920. Community Action Senior Aide Program, 410-626-1913.

Medical care

The county's major medical center is Anne Arundel Medical Center, 410-267-1000, a 291-bed hospital with 400 physicians on staff. It has acute care services and a fully equipped emergency room. Special programs for seniors include 55+ Services, including Ask-A-Nurse-Advantage, a 24-hour health information line with assistance of a registered nurse available. The program also includes special exercise classes, nutritional counseling, Lifeline personal emergency response and more. North Arundel Hospital, 410-787-4000, is a community hospital with an Immediate Care Center for treatment of major and minor injuries. It offers free health screenings throughout the year, including stroke assessment and cancer screenings, daily blood pressure checks and quarterly cholesterol screenings. Physician referral: Anne Arundel County Medical Society, 410-544-0312.

Services for seniors

The one-stop center for information on services and benefits is the Maryland Office on Aging, 800-243-3425. Also contact the Anne Arundel County Department on Aging, 800-492-2499, which offers information services, a discount card honored by many county businesses and a comprehensive directory of services for seniors. American Association of Retired Persons, 800-424-3410. Senior Law Project, 410-263-8330, provides legal consultations and/or referrals, and representation in some cases. The Charles Ballard Senior Health Center, 410-647-4449, provides health guidance in a recreational and social environment. Low-impact aerobics are a specialty.

Continuing education

With much to offer, Anne Arundel Community College, 410-541-2325, has 49 associate programs and 26 certificate programs, plus a large-scale noncredit continuing education program, with more than 900 sections, some geared specifically for senior adults. Senior offerings include painting, physical education, computers, languages, history, literature, travel programs and more. St. John's College, 410-626-2881, offers continuing education in liberal and fine arts, including travel programs.

Crime and safety

Annapolis had a recent crime index of approximately 81 incidents per 1,000 population, but Anne Arundel County's index was 46 incidents per 1,000—lower than the national average of 55. The Anne Arundel County Sheriff's Office, 410-222-1189, has information on consumer issues pertaining to seniors, and has Triad, an alliance of agencies which address problems affecting seniors.

Getting around town

Public transportation: Service is provided by Annapolis Transit. Bus service is 75 cents, but seniors with ADPT ID cards ride for 35 cents middays and evenings. Door-to-door transit is available with 24 hours notice.

Roads and highways: US 50/301, Rt. 295 (Baltimore/Washington Parkway), I-95, I-97.

Airport: Baltimore Washington International Airport is served by 30 carriers and 650 daily flights.

Port: Port of Baltimore.

Let the good times roll

Recreation: Anne Arundel County is best known for boating and water activities including fishing, crabbing, skiing, sailing and swimming. Two state parks and 70 county parks offer a variety of recreational pursuits. Golf lovers can take advantage of 11 private and semiprivate golf courses. Spectator sportsmen love Navy Football, basketball and lacrosse games. Sandy Point State Park, on Chesapeake Bay, offers swimming, fishing, crabbing, boating, windsurfing, hiking, picnicking and camping. The Arundel Olympic Swim Center is a public, indoor 50-by-25 meter swimming pool and adjacent wading pool that also features a poolside spa.

Culture: Cultural groups that make Annapolis such an extraordinary place to live include the Annapolis Opera, Summer Garden Theatre and the Colonial Players, which presents five theater-in-the-round productions annually and periodically offers adult acting and directing workshops. Maryland Hall for the Creative Arts is a nonprofit community arts center for visual, performing and creative arts, and is the home of the Annapolis Symphony Orchestra, the Ballet Theatre of Annapolis and the Annapolis Chorale. Local and national performers appear at Maryland Hall, the Naval Academy, St. John's College and Anne Arundel Community College.

Annual events: The Annapolis Waterfront Arts Festival is in May, and the famed Naval Academy Graduation occurs in late May. Also look for the Fourth of July Celebration at City Dock; the Anne Arundel County Fair in September; the Maryland Renaissance Festival from August through October; and the Kunte Kinte Heritage Festival in September. The Anne Arundel Scottish Highland Games are in October; and the Candlelight Pub Crawl in December is another popular event. Ring in the New Year with First Night Annapolis.

When the kids come: Ghost Tours of Annapolis, 410-974-1646, offers candlelit walking tours through historic Annapolis to hear tales of 300 years of spirits (April to November). The National Aquarium in Baltimore features more than 5,000 creatures in naturalistic exhibits. And, of course, Annapolis is very near to Washington, D.C., and the various museums of the Smithsonian Institution, as well as monuments to our national heritage.

For more information

Chamber
Greater Annapolis
  Chamber of Commerce
One Annapolis St.
Annapolis, MD 21401
410-268-7676

Newspapers
The Capital Gazette
2000 Capital Dr., Box 911
Annapolis, MD 21401
410-268-5000

The Washington Post
P.O. Box 1534
Annapolis, MD 21404
800-477-4679

Realtor
Miriam Stem
Home Port Properties
2901 Riva Trace Pkwy.
Annapolis, MD 21401
410-266-8378
Fax: 401-841-5456

28. Branson, Missouri

Nickname: None
County: Taney
Area code: 417
Population: 4,454
County population: 25,561
% of population over 65: 21
Region: Southwestern Missouri
Closest metro area: Springfield, 35 mi.
Median house price: $89,979
Best reasons to retire here: Hunting, fishing, great live music entertainment, low cost of living, excellent health care nearby.

Branson at a glance

Since the beginning of the 1990s, Branson has become synonymous with live entertainment, especially country music. The neon-lit city now claims to have more live entertainment theaters than anywhere in the United States, and list of the performers is dazzling: Mel Tillis, Andy Williams, Glen Campbell, Anita Bryant, the Lennon Sisters, Wayne Newton and more. But long before it was an attraction for music lovers, this part of the country appealed to retirees, and nature was (and still is) the star attraction. The Ozark Mountains offer spectacular views of unspoiled woods and lakes. Wildflowers are abundant, as are wild creatures, including deer, foxes, coyotes, bobcats and more. It has been a popular tourist area for decades, thanks to Bull Shoals Lake and the creation of manmade Table Rock Lake and Lake Taneycomo. A small tourist industry was built around these lakes, followed by amusement parks and live music venues. In 1983, country performer Roy Clark built a theater in Branson. What followed was an avalanche of tourists, publicity and more musical venues. Fishing, biking, hiking and hunting are primary activities around Table Rock Lake and Lake Taneycomo, famous for its trophy trout. Bull Shoals Lake is relatively undeveloped, with rugged shores and spectacular fishing. And, if you're willing to make the short drive to Springfield, you'll also find great continuing education opportunities.

Possible drawbacks: The influx of tourists—nearly six million annually—creates traffic jams along the main route through this linear town. The city publishes a brochure of back routes to try to alleviate the problem. Unemployment in winter months, when tourism is minimal, can be up around 20 percent.

Climate

Elevation: 1,500'	Avg. high/low:	Avg. inches		Avg. # days precip.	Avg. % humidity
		rain	snow		
Jan.	47/21	1.61	3	8	60
April	70/44	4.20	0.2	11	55
July	87/62	3.49	-	8	56
Oct.	72/44	3.64	-	7	54
YEAR	69/43	41.47	14	107	57
# days 32° or below: 115			# days 90° or warmer: 35		

What things cost

Overview: No comparative data is available on the city of Branson, but the ACCRA composite index for nearby Springfield is 7.5 percent below the national average. Utilities prices in the Branson area are reported particularly low.

Gas company: Natural gas service not available.

Electric company: Call Empire District Electric Co., 417-334-3174. If you can provide proof of past good credit via a letter from another utility, deposits are not required. For co-op power: White River Valley Electric, 417-334-6531. Typical monthly electric bills are $100.

Phone company: GTE, 800-483-3400. Deposits (determined by a credit check) are rarely required. Hook-up charges are $20.60, and basic monthly rate is $13.50.

Water and sewer: City of Branson Water Department, 417-334-3345, requires a $25 deposit from homeowners and $50 from renters. There is no charge to initiate service. An average monthly bill is $25.

Cable company: Rural Missouri Cable TV, 417-334-7897.

Car registration, license: Within 30 days of establishing residency, drivers must obtain a Missouri license, renewable every three years. Written and vision tests are required without valid license from another state. License is $7.50; $5 for test. Registration fees are based upon vehicle horsepower. License Bureau, 417-334-2496.

The tax ax

Sales tax: State sales tax in Missouri is 4 percent, and Branson levies additional sales taxes. Most purchases are taxed at a rate of 7.225 percent. Drugs and medical services are exempt.

State income tax: Graduated from 1.5 percent to 6 percent.

Retirement income: Federal, state and private pensions are not exempt from Missouri income tax, but there is an exemption of up to $6,000 for government pensions for married couples with modified Missouri adjusted gross income under $32,000. Social Security benefits subject to federal tax are not exempt. There is a $7,600 standard deduction from adjusted gross income for married couples filing jointly when both are age 65 or older.

Property taxes: City, county, school and state property taxes totaled $3.81 per $100 of assessed value, and homes are assessed at 19 percent of market value. Sample taxes on a $100,000 home would be about $724. County assessor, 417-546-4751.

Local real estate

Overview: Property taxes in the area are low, but they are increasing with the growth of the area and higher demand for services. Asking prices have been decreasing recently because there have been plenty of desirable properties on the market. The trend is leveling off, however. Retirees in this area tend to relocate permanently; it is not a big second home market.

Median house price: $89,979.

Average price for a 3BR/2BA home: New homes, $75,000 to $150,000; resales, $80,000 to $125,000.

Average price for a 2BR condo: New units, $65,000 to $95,000; resales, $85,000 to $100,000.

Unique housing features: Older homes are mostly one-story, but newer homes are more varied in design and frequently feature walk-out basements. Native stone makes for many handsome exteriors.

Rental housing market: Home rentals are in short supply, but condos and apartments are available, largely due to a recent construction surge in response to short supplies of rental units.

Average rent for a 2BR apartment: $450 to $600.

Communities or developments most popular with retirees: Lakewood Estates and Taneycomo Terrace offer lakefront properties, fishing, pools and social activities geared for seniors. However, Branson retirees tend to be a rather active lot, and so they are incorporated into many neighborhoods throughout the community.

Nearby areas to consider: Ozark, Nixa, Forsyth, Kimberling City.

Earning a living

Business climate: Branson and its surrounding areas have seen tremendous growth in the past decade in the tourist and retirement markets, meaning there are plenty of job opportunities in the service sector. Part-time jobs are readily available in Branson, although the pay may be low. For a closer look at the business community, look for the *Branson Business Journal,* 417-546-2520.

Help in starting a business: Springfield has Southwest Missouri State University, which operates a Center for Economic Development, 417-836-5667. Within the center is a Small Business Development Center, 417-836-5685, offering confidential, individual consultations on business plans, marketing strategies, financial analysis and more. The SBDC also has a WIN program (Wal-Mart Innovation Network), which assists inventors and innovators by evaluating consumer product ideas. About 20 percent of ideas are recommended by WIN to economic development partners for further assistance in development, licensing or commercialization. The Springfield chapter of SCORE can be reached at 417-846-7670. SCORE volunteers share their expertise with small-business owners.

Job market: Branson has become a major national tourist attraction, with over 5.8 million visitors in 1994. There are many job offerings in support of the tourist business, including part-time positions. The Missouri Division of Employment Security has information on job openings through its Job Service, 417-895-6899. The unemployment rate is 4.2 percent.

Medical care

Skaggs Hospital, 417-335-7000, a 99-bed facility, is currently undergoing expansion to serve the growing Branson community. It offers an emergency room, Level III Trauma Center and a critical/intensive care unit as well a Community Wellness Center. Transportation to scheduled medical appointments is offered to seniors free (call 417-335-RIDE). St. John's Regional Health Center, a 1,016-bed facility in Springfield, is one of the top 100 hospitals in the U.S., with below-average patient costs. The Professionals, 800-909-TEAM, is a free service of St. John's in which RNs answer health questions. Springfield also has Springfield Columbia North, 417-882-4700, as well as Columbia South, 417-837-4000, with intensive care, geriatric mental health care, physical rehabilitation facilities, chemotherapy and the Senior Friends program, 417-882-4700, ext. 535. Also in Springfield are Cox Medical Center North and South, a community hospital system with more than 800 beds, intensive and coronary care units, oncology and more.

Services for seniors

The Taney County Council on Aging, 417-546-6100, serves as an information and referral center for seniors in the area. The Council on Aging is housed at the Senior Friendship Site in Forsyth, which offers a homeworkers program and transportation service. The Branson Senior Center, 417-335-4801, affiliated with the Council on Aging, offers quilting, bridge, china painting, line and square dancing, social programs—and complimentary tickets to some of Branson's spectacular entertainment.

Continuing education

The College of the Ozarks in Point Lookout, 417-334-6411, a four-year liberal arts college, allows nondegree students to enroll in regular classes. It also hosts an Elderhostel, 417-334-6411, ext. 4486. Southwest Missouri State University in Springfield, 417-836-6660, offers noncredit classes and programs and, for older adults, an "Alumni Camp" that is not limited to college alumni. Drury College in Springfield, 417-873-7207, has an open admission policy for all its classes, and seniors 55 and older receive 10 percent discount on for-credit enrollment and can audit classes for $25.

Crime and safety

The most recent crime index was 59 incidents per 1,000 population in the area. Branson itself reported a rate of about 230 incidents per 1,000 population, but it's critical to note that these figures include total crime reported reflected as a percentage of the *permanent* population, listed as a mere 4,400 people. Given the millions of tourists annually, it's actually a very safe place to be.

Getting around town

Public transportation: None.

Roads and highways: Missouri Highway 165; 76 Country Boulevard; Shepherd of the Hills Expressway. Major roadway upgrades are ongoing to facilitate the explosive growth of tourist traffic.

Airport: Springfield-Branson Regional Airport is served by six national and regional carriers with links to major hubs in surrounding states.

Let the good times roll

Recreation: The Branson/Lakes area is great for those who love the outdoor life. Six golf courses in the area are playable nearly year-round, thanks to the moderate climate. Tennis and other popular sports are readily available. But the real recreational appeal of the area is the fishing at the area's three major lakes: Lake Taneycomo (rainbow trout), Bull Shoals (record-size striped bass) and Table Rock Lake (famous for bass and crappie). Sailing, skiing, swimming, scuba diving and parasailing are other popular water sport activities, and houseboats, pontoons, fishing and ski boats are available at area marinas. Spelunking is a major activity—after all, Missouri is known as the "cave state." Hunting, particularly for deer and turkey, is also popular. There's also plenty of shopping at both boutiques and outlet malls throughout the region, and lots of amusement parks.

Culture: Americans first became acquainted with the Ozarks in 1907, when Harold Bell Wright's Novel *The Shepherd of the Hills* was published and became a national bestseller. Today the Shepherd of the Hills Homestead and Outdoor Theater is the home of the nation's largest outdoor historical drama, reenacting Wright's novel nightly. Silver Dollar City preserves the everyday work and trade of the 1880s through the work of master crafters. Thomas Hart Benton's "Departure of the Joads" is displayed at the Ralph Foster Museum on the campus of College of the Ozarks, along with art and artifacts of the Ozark region. There are many galleries in the area, as well as crafts shops, particularly potters' shops. To get involved with the local arts scene, call the Branson Arts Council, 417-336-4255.

Annual events: From March to May is the Annual White Bass Round-Up; April brings the Annual Fine Arts Invitational Show in Forsyth; the Branson Blues Festival is in May; in August look for the Old-time Fiddle Contest; September brings the Autumn Daze Craft Festival and Sidewalk Sale in Branson; Veterans Day parades and festivities are in early November; and in December, enjoy the annual Adoration Parade in Branson.

When the kids come: Branson is a family town, and most of the attractions, including many of the shows, are good for kids. Cosmic Cavern in Berryville offers tours through one of the area's prettiest caverns; Mutton Hollow Entertainment Park features specialty shops, native crafts and fair rides; Silver Dollar City is a major amusement park.

For more information

Chamber
Branson/Lakes Area
  Chamber of Commerce
P.O. Box 1897
Branson, MO 65615
417-334-4136

Newspaper
Branson Daily News
114 N. Commercial St.
Branson, MO 65616-2404
417-334-3161

Realtor
Leon O'Brian
Branson Realty, Inc.
1440-D State Highway 248
Branson, MO 65616
417-334-3466 or 800-766-0922
Fax: 417-334-3470

29. Columbia, Missouri

Nickname: An Easy Place to Call Home
County: Boone
Area code: 573
Population: 74,072
County population: 121,479
% of population over 65: 8.4
Region: Central Midwest; central Missouri
Closest metro areas: St. Louis, 127 mi.;
Kansas City, 129 mi.; Springfield, Ill., 168 mi.
Average home price: $100,000 to $125,000
Best reasons to retire here: Rural setting,
big-city culture, excellent health care.

Columbia at a glance

Columbia may seem like an unlikely place to discover gold, but in the midst of the "Show-Me" state, you'll find one of the most enticing and unpretentious places to live in the United States—a fact that has been repeatedly noted by national experts. This clean and green city has some of the best health care services available (more doctors per capita than anyplace in the U.S. except Rochester, Minn., home of the Mayo Clinic), and abundant cultural opportunities thanks to three major colleges/universities that call Columbia home: The University of Missouri-Columbia, Stephens College and Columbia College. There's plenty to do outdoors, from golf and tennis to hiking, camping, mountain biking and even hot-air ballooning. You'll find several state parks, recreation areas and forests, where the hiking is beautiful, especially during the spectacular and colorful fall season. The city is located in Boone County, named for Daniel Boone, who explored the area. Boone's pioneering spirit is still alive today in Columbia's business environment, thanks to the highly educated work force and low tax structure. Services for seniors are excellent, particularly at the Columbia Senior Center, which offers a wide variety of recreational activities in a new facility. All in all, Columbia is a great place to spend your golden years. (And Columbia couldn't be happier to have you—call 800-652-9028 to request a free video from the Chamber of Commerce's Retirement Coordinator.

Possible drawbacks: Columbia provides health care to the entirety of central Missouri, so although there are many doctors in the area, it's not always easy to get in. Also, air service to the area is limited, so you choose between a two-hour drive to the closest major airports or take an expensive shuttle.

Climate

Elevation: 758'	Avg. high/low:	Avg. inches		Avg. # days precip.	Avg. % humidity
		rain	snow		
Jan.	38/21	1.0	6	6	67
April	65/45	3.7	1	11	55
July	87/67	3.9	-	8	54
Oct.	69/47	3.4	-	9	56
YEAR	64/45	35.0	23	106	60
# days 32° or below: 108			# days 90° or warmer: 37		

What things cost

Overview: According to ACCRA, the overall cost of living is 7 percent below the national average. The biggest savings are in housing and utilities costs.

Gas company: Union Electric-Columbia Gas Division, 800-552-7583. Deposits, if required, are usually double the average bill for the property. No connect charges. Natural gas for heating is used in 78 percent of homes in Columbia. Avg. bill: $140 monthly. Partial gas averages $60.

Electric company: There are two major providers in the area: City of Columbia, 573-874-7380, and Boone Electric Cooperative, 573-449-4181. Avg. bill: $50 monthly, while all-electric homes average $80 to $150 monthly.

Phone company: GTE, 800-483-4400. Deposits, based on credit history, are $50 and up. There is a $20.60 connect charge, and basic service costs $12.15 per month.

Water and sewer: City of Columbia, 573-874-7380. Water service averages $7.50 monthly. Sewer averages $5.84 monthly. Solid waste rates are $8.65 monthly. Deposits run $10 to $75, depending upon the number of services the city supplies to the residence.

Cable company: TCI Cablevision of Missouri, Inc., 573-443-1535 and Capital Cable, 573-875-8875.

Car license, registration: Within 30 days of establishing residency, drivers must obtain a driver's license, renewable every three years. No written or vision tests if you have a valid license from another state. $7.50 for license, $5 for test. Registration fees based upon vehicle horsepower. Call the License Bureau, 573-882-9593, for more information.

The tax ax

Sales tax: 6.975 percent in Columbia.

State income tax: Graduated from 1.5 to 6 percent depending upon income bracket.

Retirement income: Federal, state and private pensions not exempt from Missouri income tax, but there is an exemption of up to $6,000 for government pensions for married couples with modified Missouri adjusted gross income under $32,000. Social Security benefits subject to federal tax are not exempt. There is a $7,600 standard deduction from adjusted gross income for married couples filing jointly when both are 65 or older.

Property taxes: Rates range from $5.65 to $6.08 per $100 of assessed valuation, assessed at 19 percent of fair market value. For example: $100,000 x 19% = 19,000/$100 = $190, $190 x $5.65 = $1073.50 taxes owed.

Local real estate

Overview: The real estate market here is strong. Homes appreciated 8 percent in a two-year period in the early 90s. More recently, appreciation has been 4 to 6 percent annually with taxes near 1.125 percent per $1,000 value. There are many housing options available, from traditional neighborhoods to golf communities, from condominiums to farms and estates. Out-of-town buyers are often astonished at how far their housing dollars go, with housing prices about 18 percent below the national average. Most retirees relocate here permanently; this is not a strong second home market.

Median price for a single family home: Northeast Columbia $81,000; northwest Columbia, $67,200; southeast Columbia $70,900; southwest Columbia $125,500.

Average price for a 3BR/2BA home: For a new ranch home with an unfinished basement: $125,000. The average resale price is about $100,000.

Average price for a 2BR condo: There is currently no new condominium construction. Resales average $45,000 to $65,000 depending upon location and amenities. For $100,000 and up, you'll find a spacious 2BR/2BA condominium on a golf course.

Rental housing market: There is great variety available in this market, from apartments to duplexes to homes. Duplexes average $400 monthly; homes average $500.

Average rent for a 2BR apartment: $250 to $400 monthly.

Nearby areas to consider: Ashland, Fulton, Jefferson City, Booneville.

Earning a living

Business climate: Columbia has a diverse economic structure in spite of the fact that it's known as a college town. It is ranked among the 25 best cities for small business by *Entrepreneur* magazine because of educational and medical strengths. The city's low tax rates are also very attractive. The health and insurance industries are very important in the area, and several Fortune 500 companies have offices in Columbia, including Dana Corporation, 3M and Quaker Oats. The retail sector has been exceptionally strong in Columbia in recent years, with 65 percent growth in sales in the first five years of the 1990s.

Help in starting a business: The Small Business Development Center, affiliated with the University of Missouri School of Business, offers free, one-on-one counseling to people trying to start a business, as well as to existing businesses. Call 573-882-7096. The local chapter of SCORE can be contacted through the Columbia Chamber of Commerce. The chamber also offers the "Pocket Guide to Planning and Starting a Business in Boone County." Also, call the Small Business Assistance First Stop Shop, located in the Department of Economic Development in Jefferson City, 800-523-1434.

Job market: The work force in Columbia is highly educated, and more than 20 percent of all workers are employed in a health-related field. Top employers in the area are the University of Missouri, University of Missouri Health Sciences Center and Boone Hospital Center. You can reach the Division of Employment Security at 573-882-8821. Several employment agencies may also be able to help.

Medical care

Columbia has seven major hospitals and 700 physicians. Boone Hospital Center, 573-875-4545, is a 344-bed regional referral center that excels in cardiology , oncology and more. It offers WELLAWARE, a group of resources, programs and people focusing on wellness and prevention. Columbia Regional Hospital, 573-875-9000, is a 301-bed, full-service hospital with state-of-the-art diagnostic and medical treatment. Oncology, opthamology, neurology and internal medicine are areas of excellence, and there is strong emphasis on senior health care. Harry S. Truman Memorial Veterans' Hospital, 573-443-2511, is a 346-bed VA teaching hospital and regional referral center for cardiology and cardiac surgery. University Hospitals and Clinics, 573-882-4141, is a 400-bed tertiary referral center with a Level I Trauma Center.

Services for seniors

The Columbia Senior Center is a focal point for community activities. The new facility offers classes, dances, other activities and meals. Most activities are free and the meals, served daily, are reasonably priced. The center, 573-874-2050, is open seven days a week and is available for day and evening programs. Many groups, including AARP and RSVP, hold their meetings here. The Boone County Council on Aging, 573-443-1111, is a resource and referral agency for senior services. It houses the Columbia offices of RSVP. *The Senior Times* is a free monthly publication that provides a directory of senior services. It is available through its offices, 573-499-1830, or the Chamber of Commerce.

Continuing education

Even though this is a college town, the area universities and colleges do not offer much in the way of noncredit continuing education. Fortunately, the Department of Parks and Recreation offers a full schedule of adult classes in personal enrichment, self-improvement, art, music, gardening and more. Call the Recreation Hotline at 573-874-7663 for more information. Also, the Columbia Career Center (affiliated with Columbia Public Schools, 573-886-2610), offers a variety of classes for adults, including home economics, cooking, computers, languages, music and much more. The University of Missouri-Columbia, 573-882-7403, offers a few noncredit courses for personal enrichment, although its primary focus is continuing professional education. Columbia College courses are open to all, although they are all credit courses.

Crime and safety

The crime rate in Boone County is below the national average, with 50 crimes reported per 1,000 population. Crime in Columbia was slightly higher, at 61 incidents per 1,000 population. Violent crime is rare.

Getting around town

Public transportation: Columbia Area Transit System, 573-874-7282. Basic fare is 50 cents; seniors pay 25 cents. No bus service on Sundays.

Roads and highways: I-70 and US 63.

Airport: Columbia Regional Airport provides hourly shuttles to the St. Louis and Kansas City airports and is served by two regional carriers.

Let the good times roll

Recreation: Columbia has three public golf courses and three private clubs. When the weather turns cold, you can turn to Columbia Indoor Golf—a virtual reality golf experience. Horseshoe tournaments, archery, softball and aquacise are available through Columbia's Parks and Recreation Department. Joggers, bikers and hikers enjoy the MKT Nature and Fitness Trail, a 4.7-mile urban walkway to a densely wooded passageway. The city maintains 47 parks with 1,850 acres for picnicking, boating, fishing and more. Camping is popular in Cedar Creek State Forest and Three Creeks State Forest. In fact, Columbia is blessed in its proximity to gorgeous natural areas, such as Grindstone Nature Area, Rock Bridge State Park and Finger Lakes State Park.

Culture: The MU Museum of Art and Archeology houses a collection of 13,000 works of art and artifacts from prehistoric cultures to the present. The Museum of Anthropology has Midwestern archeology and artifacts. Columbia Art League has exhibitions by regional and national artists, and several university galleries display contemporary art. Columbia Entertainment Company and Maplewood Barn Theatre feature community talent. Missouri Symphony Society presents orchestral performances featuring nationally known artists. Hearnes Center hosts everything from rock 'n' roll to country music super stars to special celebrity performances.

Annual events: Taste of Mid-Missouri, March; Moo Day parade, April (people act silly in public for no apparent reason); Memorial Weekend Salute to Veterans Air Show and Parade in May; Summer Art Festival, June; Show-Me State Games, July; Boone County Heritage Festival, September; Holiday Parade and Downtown Lighting, November.

When the kids come: Nature areas that attract adults appeal to kids, too—especially the MKT Nature and Fitness Trail and Finger Lakes State Park. Also, Arrow Rock (45 minutes west) is an historic frontier community on the Santa Fe Trail offering a glimpse of life 100 years ago. Lake of the Ozarks is less than two hours away, an area offering natural attractions as well as Big Surf Waterpark. St. Louis is two hours away with Six Flags, the St. Louis Zoo and the St. Louis Children's Museum.

For more information

Chamber
Columbia Chamber
of Commerce
Thomas G. Walton Bldg.
300 S. Providence Rd.
P.O. Box 1016
Columbia, MO 65205-1016
573-874-1132

Newspapers
Columbia Missourian
P.O. Box 917
Columbia, MO 65205
573-882-5700

Columbia Daily Tribune
P.O. Box 798
Columbia, MO 65205
573-449-3811

Realtor
Vicky Miserez
RE/MAX Boone Realty
33 E. Broadway
Columbia, MO 65203
573-876-2811
800-475-2811
Fax: 573-445-3703

30. Rochester, Minnesota

Nickname: The Best Small City in America
County: Olmsted
Area code: 507
Population: 76,060
County population: 113,237
% of population over 65: 10
Region: Southeastern Minnesota
Closest metro area: Minneapolis, 76 mi.
Average home price: $125,000 to $150,000
Best reasons to retire here: High-quality medical care and senior services, low cost of living, low crime rate.

Rochester at a glance

The peaceful charm of the Zumbra River valley has attracted many different people to the Rochester area through the years, from the old-time pioneers to today's retirees and modern corporate nomads. They come here seeking a high quality of life—Rochester is consistently cited as one the best places in the country for *anyone* to live, based on its clean environment, excellent health care (it's the home of the Mayo Clinic), strong economy, low cost of living, extremely low crime rate and diverse recreational and cultural offerings. Living in Rochester also means experiencing the city's commitment to community and more traditional values. However, that commitment does not stand in the way of innovation: Rochester boasts medical and computer facilities that are among the most advanced in the world. As a result, the city tends to attract a highly educated population, which in turn lends a cosmopolitanism to this small town that some might find surprising. Rochester is also near beautiful recreational areas, such as the historic Bluff Country (just a few miles south and east of town) with its scenic hills, steep, valleys, forests and meadows. In warm weather there's plenty of golf, fishing, tennis and hiking, and there's great cross-country skiing in winter (travel to Northern Minnesota for excellent downhill skiing). Though the recreation and entertainment options are more low-key than in other popular retiree areas, there's more than enough to do here, and a nearly ideal city to support your golden years ambitions.

Possible drawbacks: It is cold, cold, cold up here, so it's best to embrace it and find something to do outside during the long winter, or be ready to fly south to one of those Florida cities covered earlier in the book!

Climate

Elevation: 988'	Avg. high/low:	Avg. inches		Avg. # days precip.	Avg. % humidity
		rain	snow		
Jan.	22/4	.65	8	9	73
April	55/34	2.36	2	12	70
July	81/60	3.74	0	10	63
Oct.	60/39	1.82	1	8	59
YEAR	54/34	27.47	45	117	65
# days 32° or below: 163			# days 90° or warmer: 6		

What things cost

Overview: According to ACCRA statistics indicate the overall cost of living is about 2.5 percent below the national average, with housing nearly 10 percent below the norm, and some of the nation's best health care at about 2.5 percent below the national average.

Gas company: People's Natural Gas/ EnergyOne, 800-252-1166 or 507-288-6721. There is no deposit or hook-up charge unless the gas is off, in which case the charge is $50 and an inspection is also required. Forced-air gas heat homes average about $85 monthly. Most residences have gas heat.

Electric, water and sewer company: Rochester Public Utilities, 507-280-1500. There is no start-up charge, nor a charge for service calls. Deposits are waived pending a credit check or letter of credit from another utility. Deposits range from $30 to $300. Most area homes have gas heat. Partial electric service: $75 monthly. Water and sewer: About $30 monthly.

Phone company: The area is served by US West, 800-244-1111. Hook-up: $18.75; no deposit. Typical monthly charge: $22.

Cable company: TCI of Southern Minnesota, 507-289-1611.

Car registration, license: New residents are required to obtain a Minnesota driver's license within 60 days of residency. Fees range from $18.50 to $37.50 depending upon vehicle class. Department of Public Safety, 507-285-7412. Registration, 507-282-4711.

The tax ax

Sales tax: State sales tax is 6.5 percent.

State income tax: Graduated from 6 percent to 8.5 percent depending upon income bracket. There is no deduction for federal income tax paid. Social Security benefits subject to federal income tax are not exempt, nor are federal, state or private pensions.

Retirement income: There is a $7,600 standard deduction for married couples over 65 filing jointly. There is also a deduction for disabled or over 65 with adjusted gross incomes of less than $28,000 for an individual and $35,000 for a couple.

Property taxes: The tax rate in Rochester totals 129.480 percent, and the rate is applied to a percentage of the market value of the home. (1 percent of the first $72,000 of assessed value, and 2 percent of any value in excess of $72,000). Annual taxes on a $150,000 home would be approximately $2,960. Property tax assessor, 507-285-8124.

Local real estate

Overview: After being a seller's market for several years, the real estate market has stabilized, although a recent slowdown in new construction may reverse the trend in the future. Selling prices are within 95 to 97 percent of asking prices, and taxes also are stable. The Rochester market has a great diversity of size, style and location, including new subdivisions, resales, rural acreage and modern townhouse units. This is not a second-home market; retirees who relocate here tend to stay.

Average price for a 3BR/2BA home: $150,000 for a new home; resales are about $125,000.

Average price for a 2BR condo: The total range for a resale condominium is $45,000 to $250,000. There has been little or no new construction of condominiums recently.

Common housing styles and features: Most homes have finished basements. Ranches and multi-level homes are popular; and many homes are available on wooded lots.

Communities or developments most popular with retirees: Highpoint and Five Oaks condominiums, Waterford, Wood Haven, Oak Cliff.

Rental housing market: A wide range of units is available, from short-term efficiencies for Mayo Clinic patients ($350 monthly) to long-term apartment and home rentals ($550 to $1,200 monthly).

Average rent for a 2BR apartment: $566 monthly.

Nearby areas to consider: Look into Lake City, Pine Island, Byron, Stewartville, Lanesboro.

Earning a living

Business climate: Rochester is often named by business publications as a top place for entrepreneurs, because of its high-tech infrastructure, highly educated work force and position as a leading community in the medical and electronics fields. Agribusiness and agriculture are also important, as more than half of Olmsted County is farmland. Common crops are soybeans, corn and peas, and dairy farming is also significant. Seneca Food Corp., which has a division in Rochester, recently acquired the Green Giant line of vegetables and will enhance production at its Rochester plant.

Help in starting a business: The Rochester Area Economic Development, Inc., (RAEDI), 507-288-0208, administers a Seed/Venture Fund that focuses on expansion and formation of businesses, as well as offering financing and incentives to firms relocating or expanding in the area. The Small Business Development Center at Rochester Community College, 507-285-7536, serves small businesses, as well.

Job market: The Mayo Clinic employs 16,000 people. Medical field employment accounts for nearly 30 percent of all available jobs. Wholesale and retail trade constitute 21 percent; manufacturing and construction account for 18 percent. IBM Rochester has 5,100 workers at its production plant. The hospitality industry is also important, with more than 300,000 people coming to the Mayo Clinic annually. Rochester's unemployment rate is about 2.4 percent, low enough to indicate that some residents work for low wages because jobs are scarce. Department of Economic Security Job Service, 507-285-7315.

Medical care

Rochester is home to the Mayo Clinic, 507-284-2511, known worldwide for its quality care. Rochester Methodist Hospital, 507-266-7890, is a Mayo Foundation Hospital staffed by Mayo Clinic doctors. The acute-care facility offers newly developed programs in oncology/hematology and bone marrow transplants. St. Mary's Hospital, 507-285-8485, is one of the largest private, nonprofit hospitals in the world. Medical services encompass some of the most advanced techniques and technologies, including computer-assisted neurosurgery, magnetic resonance imaging and kidney stone and gallstone dissolution without surgery. St. Mary's is staffed by Mayo Clinic physicians and has eight intensive care units. Olmsted Community Hospital, 507-285-8468, also in Rochester, is a 47-bed hospital staffed by Olmsted Medical Group physicians.

Services for seniors

Located in a landmark armory building downtown, Senior Citizens Services, Inc., 507-285-1404, offers everything from information and referral to operation of several senior dining sites. Classes are offered in exercise, knitting, personal finance, square and round dancing and more. Services include massage therapy, free blood pressure and hearing screenings, insurance and benefits counseling. Southeastern Minnesota Area Agency on Aging, 507-288-6944, is a funding oversight agency as well as a provider of direct services. The Senior Linkage Line, 800-333-2433, is an information and referral service that covers the state. AARP, 507-289-7415.

Continuing education

Seniors can audit classes on a space-available basis at the University of Minnesota Rochester Center, 800-947-0117 or 507-280-2838. Subjects include art history, creative writing, English literature, and computer applications from basics to creating Web pages. Rochester Community College, 507-280-3157, has the Elder Institute with classes in computers, history, arts, music, t'ai chi and more. Rochester Public Schools, 507-285-8350, offers community education classes to seniors 62 and older at half price.

Crime and safety

The crime indexes for both Rochester and Olmsted County are among the lowest of any community we researched, and crime has been decreasing since 1991. Rochester reported a crime rate of 44 incidents per 1,000 population, and Olmsted County's rate was only 34 incidents per 1,000. Olmsted County also has a SALT (Seniors And Lawmen Together) program, 507-285-8500, offering a Vacation Check program in which volunteers conduct outside searches of homes while owners are away.

Getting around town

Public transportation: Rochester City Bus Lines, 507-288-4353. From 8:15 a.m. to 2:45 p.m. seniors pay half-fare, 50 cents.
Road and highways: I-90, I-35, US 14, 52 and 63, State Highways 30, 40 and 296.
Airport: Rochester Municipal Airport is served by two major airlines, American (connecting to Chicago) and Northwest (to Minneapolis).

Let the good times roll

Recreation: For a long time, Olmsted County's Parks and Recreation Department has operated sports programs in 64 parks. Chester Woods Park opened recently, immediately doubling the size of the system with its 188-acre reservoir with a swimming beach, boating and fishing piers. The Douglas Trail has bicycle and bridle paths used in the winter by snowmobilers and cross-country skiers. There are six public and semi-private golf courses in the area, one indoor and two outdoor pools, 30 miles of hiking/biking trails and 23 tennis courts. The Rochester Olmsted Recreation Center offers indoor swimming, two ice rinks and a gym. If you like spectator sports, travel to nearby Minneapolis/St. Paul and take in the Minnesota Twins (baseball), the Minnesota Vikings (football) or the Minnesota Timberwolves, an NBA expansion team. In Rochester, enjoy the Rochester Honkers (named after the city's gigantic Canadian goose population), a franchise of the new Northwoods Collegiate Baseball league. The Mustangs, a Junior A hockey team, has had many of its members go on to play college hockey.

Culture: Rochester Art Center features prints, paintings, drawings and exhibits by regional and national artists. Rochester Civic Music consists of various ensemble groups, including the Rochester Symphony Chamber Orchestra, the Rochester City Band and the Rochester Symphony Orchestra and Chorale. The organization presents six concerts a year, three in a classical series and three in a pops series. In the summer, Civic Music sponsors Down by the Riverside, a series of free concerts in Mayo Park. Rochester Civic Theater has a Main Stage Company and a Young People's Theater. Rochester Repertory Theater Company presents classical and contemporary works.

Annual events: Rochester World Festival, celebrating cultures of the world (April); the Olmsted County Free Fair, with a midway, grandstand shows, livestock shows and the largest county draft horse show in the nation (July); the Greek Festival with food, music and dancing (August); Festival of Trees at Mayo Civic Center, with displays of trees and holiday food (November); Yulefest, a Christmas music celebration by the Rochester Symphony Orchestra, Chorale and Ballet Company (December).

When the kids come: Try Whitewater State Park, with its limestone cliffs, hardwood forests and many miles of trails. In Minneapolis/St. Paul, check out the Science Museum of Minnesota.

For more information:

Chamber
Rochester Chamber
  of Commerce
220 S. Broadway, Suite 100
Rochester, MN 55904
507-288-1122

Newspaper
Rochester Post Bulletin (daily)
18 First Ave. SE
Rochester, MN 55904
507-285-7600

Realtor
Marilyn D. Stewart, CRB, CRS
Edina Realty-Rochester
1301 Salem Rd. SW
Rochester, MN 55902
507-288-7665 or 800-872-1522
Fax: 507-288-7706, ext. 130

31. Las Vegas, Nevada

Nickname: Entertainment Capital of the World
County: Clark
Area code: 702
Population: 352,821
County population: 985,827
% of population over 65: 15.7
Region: Southern Nevada
Closest metro areas: Los Angeles, 285 mi.; Phoenix, 180 mi.
Average home price: $119,000 to $121,000
Best reasons to retire here: Night life, good tax structure, affordable housing, dry climate.

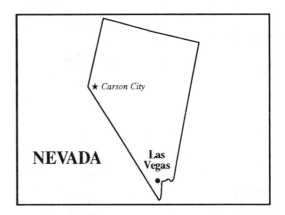

Las Vegas at a glance

If nothing else about this city appeals to you, you'll love the fact that Nevada residents pay *no* income tax, no inheritance or estate taxes (property taxes are favorable, too), and if you're in business, the tax bite is barely a nibble. The real estate market is as vast as the desert. Every imaginable type of dwelling and price range is here, with new golf communities and condo developments in the southwest section. The varying desert climate is a surprise to many. The temperature can drop into the 30s on a January night, only to be followed by a day of sunshine and temperatures in the 60s. (Newcomers often think its a fluke. It's not!) Fall and spring bring constant sunshine and comfortable temperatures in the 60s and 70s. With more than 320 days of sun and low humidity, the outdoor life is unbeatable. Recreation at the nearby national and state parks offers everything from skiing to hiking and canoeing, and golf and tennis are playable all year. There's also a high level of cultural activity, particularly in the area of dance, with the Las Vegas Civic Ballet, Opus Dance Ensemble of Las Vegas, Theatre Ballet of Las Vegas and Nevada Dance Theatre UNLV performing regularly. Services for seniors, as well as health care, are in abundance and the area referral and networking sources are excellent. It's easy to get help. Those we spoke to said, "You may think you know Las Vegas—but you don't really know it until you live here."

Possible drawbacks: It gets so hot in July and August, you'll start daydreaming about Alaskan cruises (temperatures regularly top 105 degrees). There will be days when you wished that gambling was legal but tourists were not. This is a big city and it has its share of traffic, crime and red tape.

Climate

Elevation: 2,180'	Avg. high/low:	Avg. inches		Avg. # days precip.	Avg. % humidity
		rain	snow		
Jan.	56/33	.31	-	3	45
April	78/50	.27	-	2	28
July	104/75	.44	-	3	18
Oct.	81/53	.22	-	2	27
YEAR	79/52	3.8	1.7	-	-
# days 32° or below: 39			# days 90° or warmer: 140		

What things cost

Overview: ACCRA statistics show that the cost of living is 1 percent above the national average. Transportation and health care are each more than 15 percent above average, while housing and groceries are 3 to 5 percent above. Utilities costs, however, are 26 percent below.

Gas company: Southwest Gas Corp., 702-365-1555. $25 connect charge. Deposit (if required): $50. Average bill is $10 to $40 monthly.

Electric company: Nevada Power Company, 702-367-5000. $15 connect fee; deposit not required for people older than 62. Average monthly bill: $73 for partial electric; $155 for all-electric.

Phone company: Sprint, 800-877-7077 or 702-244-7400. Installation: $36.60; deposit $50, pending credit check. Basic service: $11 for unlimited local calls.

Water: Las Vegas Valley Water District, 702-870-2011. No connect charge. No deposit for homeowners with good credit. Average monthly bill: $40.

Sewer: Call Clark County Sanitation, 702-458-1180 or 800-782-4324. Costs are a flat $187.72 per year; $204.89 if you have a swimming pool. Condos/townhouses are $101 per year.

Cable company: Prime Cable of Las Vegas, 702-383-4000.

Car registration, license: New residents must obtain a Nevada driver's license within 30 days of establishing residency. Driver's license, $20.50; persons over 65 pay $15.50. Written exam and eye test required. New residents must register vehicles within 45 days. Registration: $33; requires a smog inspection. There is an annual privilege tax based on 35 percent of the manufacturer's original suggested retail price. Tax is paid at $4 per $100 valuation, and depreciates with vehicle age. Department of Motor Vehicles, 702-486-4368.

The tax ax

Sales tax: 7 percent, with drugs and groceries exempt.

State income tax: Nevada has no state income tax.

Property taxes: Homes are assessed every 5 years at 35 percent of appraised value and taxed at a rate that varies from $2.1682 to $3.0568 per $100 of value. Appraised values are typically lower than market value because the method used in assessment accounts for depreciation and replacement value of the home. Sample taxes on a home appraised at $135,000 would be $1,205 to $1,449. Assessor's office, 702-455-3882.

Local real estate

Overview: New homes are currently outselling resales by nearly four to one—there is something new available to fit almost any budget. Most retirees moving to this area are relocating permanently, although some purchase second homes.

Median price for a single family home: $115,000.

Average price for a 3BR/2BA home: New homes average $119,000; resales, $121,000. New homes are selling at prices lower than resales due to a large inventory.

Average price for a 2BR condo: New units average $80,000; resales, $83,000.

Common housing styles and features: Most homes are single-story frame construction designs with stucco exteriors, tile roofs and contemporary layouts. Everything is air-conditioned!

Rental housing market: Homes and apartments are readily available. Home rentals in newer areas of town are $850 to $950 per month. Average 2BR apartment rent: $585 to $610 monthly according to the Chamber; our sources estimate that $650 to $800 is more like it.

Communities or developments most popular with retirees: SunCity Summerlin is one of the most successful retirement developments in the country. A second development, Sun City Green Valley Ranch, is under construction.

Nearby areas to consider: Henderson, halfway between Las Vegas and Lake Mead, is a community of young and old, with scores of new, planned communities and developments. Boulder City is a clean, green oasis situated near Lake Mead and Hoover Dam. It's the only city in Nevada that prohibits gambling.

Earning a living

Business climate: Southern Nevadans have a very optimistic view of their economy. In a recent survey, almost 92 percent said they think the economy will either grow or stay the same. And residents have good reason to feel so optimistic; virtually every major business indicator shows the business environment is improving. Growth is occurring in almost every sector. In 1994, 39 regional/national companies relocated or expanded here, including 24 manufacturing firms. California firms represent the vast number of businesses relocating to Nevada.

Help in starting a business: The Small Business Development Center, 702-261-3908, offers counseling, seminars and classes. It also has a resource center and computer access for clients. The Nevada Development Authority, 702-791-0000, assists industrial and manufacturing businesses that are expanding or relocating here. Small Business Administration, 702-388-6611.

Job market: There are many jobs, both full and part-time, in the tourism and gaming industries. Las Vegas is home to 11 of the world's top 13 hotels and has more hotel and motel rooms than any other city in the nation. With more than 28 million visitors annually, tourism is the area's number one industry, and there are many jobs available, although they are not necessarily high-paying. High-tech research, manufacturing, retail and wholesale trade and medical make up other major employment sectors. AARP Community Service Employment Program, 702-648-3356. The unemployment rate is 6.1 percent.

Medical care

Desert Springs Hospital, 702-733-8000, is a 225-bed hospital with 800 physicians on staff. The full-service facility provides cardiac care, orthopedic care and a pain management center. Columbia Sunrise Hospital Medical Center, 702-731-8800, is a 688-bed hospital with more than 1,200 physicians. It offers a full range of adult medical/surgical services, including a Level III Trauma Center, sleep disorders center and a new surgical complex. University Medical Center, 702-383-2000, has 560 beds and more than 900 physicians. The cardiac care unit has open heart surgery, angioplasty and other special procedures. Its oncology program offers 24-hour individualized treatment. It has a Level II trauma center (the only one in Southern Nevada). Valley Hospital Medical Center, 702-388-4000, has 398 beds and more than 1,000 physicians. The hospital has the most advanced cardiac catheterization lab in the area, and a Flight for Life flying emergency room. Two hospitals under construction are Summerlin Medical Center in nearby Summerlin, and Columbia Mountain View Hospital & Medical Center.

Services for seniors

Las Vegas Senior Complex, 702-229-6454, offers classes in Western line dancing, crocheting and knitting, aerobics, clogging and more, for $3 per session. The center also has billiards, a gym and swimming pool, and it hosts trips. There is no charge to belong, although a $2 donation is requested. Medicare Information Counseling & Assistance, 702-486-4602, offers referrals for assistance in dealing with medical insurance problems.

Continuing education

UNLV offers the Center for Lifelong Learning (known as EXCELL), a member-directed, member-governed organization for sharing knowledge and generating interpersonal and group dialogues. Call 702-895-4469. Study groups cost $35 per semester, which allows you to take one or several courses. The college also offers an Elderhostel that has a commuter option when space is available. General-interest courses offered through UNLV continuing education include computer courses, writing, estate-planning, yoga for seniors, marketing and publishing.

Crime and safety

Gangs are an unwanted import from California. Nevertheless, the area is safe. The crime index for Las Vegas and Clark County is 77 incidents per 1,000 people, which is higher than the national average, but lower than most metropolitan areas, especially considering that the city hosts 28 million tourists annually.(Crime incidence is calculated in relation to the permanent population.)

Getting around town

Public transportation: Citizens Area Transit (CAT), 702-228-7433. Seniors 62 and over ride anywhere for 50 cents. In Las Vegas itself, eight trolleys provide two loops in the highly trafficked areas.

Roads and highways: I-15 runs north-south through Las Vegas; US 93, 95 and 466.

Airport: McCarran International Airport. So many tourists come to Las Vegas that this airport is well-served and often has attractive price packages.

Let the good times roll

Recreation: If you think that gambling is the only thing to do here, you don't know Vegas. Death Valley National Park is world-renowned for its stark beauty. Lake Mead, the largest man-made lake in the Western Hemisphere (formed by Hoover Dam), has 500 miles of shoreline and six marinas, and you can enjoy dinner cruises, watersports, beaches and tours. Floyd R. Lamb State Park, only 20 minutes from downtown, has four stocked ponds, picnicking, hiking paths and more. Want to get away from the desert? Toiyabe National Forest, one of Nevada's most scenic alpine regions, is only 40 minutes away. You can ski or enjoy camping, hiking and horseback riding. Golfers will find 27 courses in Las Vegas or the surrounding areas. If you enjoy watching sports, the Las Vegas Stars AAA baseball team are the farm club for the San Diego Padres. Vegas is the boxing capital of the world, with most major titles contested here. College sports fans know the success of the UNLV Runnin' Rebels; pro teams include the Las Vegas Thunder (International Hockey League Southwest Division), Las Vegas Sting (Arena Football League) and the Dust Devils (Continental Indoor Soccer League.)

Culture: The "Entertainment Capital of the World" boasts its own kind of culture: 365 days of round-the-clock nightclub acts featuring comedians, singers, dancers and more. For more highbrow tastes, the performing arts include the Las Vegas Civic Ballet, Opus Dance Ensemble of Las Vegas, Nevada Dance Theatre UNLV, Nevada Symphony Orchestra, Actors Repertory Theatre, Las Vegas Little Theatre and Nevada Opera Theatre. Museum-goers can enjoy everything from the Las Vegas Museum of Art to pop culture sites like the Liberace Museum.

Annual events: Hell Dorado Days in May features a parade and rodeo competitions. In the fall, Art in the Park attracts about 100,000 to Boulder City for fine arts displays and crafts. Celebration of the Arts, in early fall at Summerlin Library, features arts and crafts and attracts thousands. Shakespeare in the Park is a three-day festival in September. In October it's time for the Las Vegas Balloon Classic; and December brings Winter Wonderland, a day at the county's Sunset Park with games, entertainment, ice carvings and craft workshops.

When the kids come: Try Virtual World or Cyber Station family fun centers; Sky's the Limit rock climbing and hiking, Zoological-Botanical Park ("The Children's Zoo") or the MGM Grand Adventures theme park.

For more information

Chamber
Las Vegas Area Chamber of
  Commerce
711 E. Desert Inn Rd.
Las Vegas, NV 89109
702-735-1616

Newspaper
Las Vegas Sun
121 S. Martin Luther King Blvd.
Las Vegas, NV 89106
702-385-3111

Realtor
Judy Roscoe/ReMax Absolute
  Realtors
8544 W. Lake Mead Blvd.
Las Vegas, NV 89128
702-378-5036 or 800-730-3491
Fax: 702-732-8308

32. Reno, Nevada

Nickname: The Biggest Little City in the World
County: Washoe
Area code: 702
Population: 150,620
County population: 294,290
% of population over 65: 11
Region: Southwest
Closest metro area: Sacramento, 140 mi.
Average home price: $100,000 to 140,000
Best reasons to retire here: Low taxes, great outdoor recreation, entertainment and events, fabulous scenery.

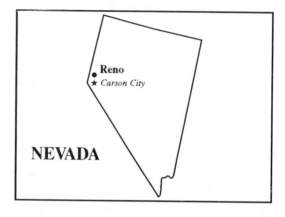

Reno at a glance

In your search for great places to retire, you may want to take a gamble on Reno. Gaming and golf have long made this a vacation destination, but more and more people are choosing to call it home, thanks to its beautiful natural surroundings, strong economy, great neighborhoods, mild climate and low taxes. The bonuses, of course, are the sparkling alpine lakes and tantalizing views of the Sierra Nevadas. You can choose to do almost anything here from hang gliding to horseback riding, but most people enjoy the spectacular skiing (there are 25 exceptional ski resorts within 90 minutes). Culture, entertainment and special events are year-round fixtures (Reno has its own ballet, opera and philharmonic orchestra). The Reno/Sparks/Lake Tahoe area has also been dealt a great economic hand—business growth is strong, and the decade has seen dozens of companies relocate here, including Porsche Motors and Ralston Purina. Reno's location makes it a perfect distribution hub to other western cities, and it is emerging as a warehousing and small business center. Of course, with more than 7 million tourists a year being lured to the tables and slopes, the area's $2.5 billion visitor industry is the real winner. The economic opportunities for entrepreneurial types, together with the beautiful environment, endless recreation and sympathetic tax environment make Reno a great choice for active retirees. Perhaps that makes Reno the 1990s answer to "How the West Was Won."

Possible drawbacks: Life in the desert means getting accustomed to driving long stretches of road at high speeds in order to get anywhere. Although the taxes are low, the overall cost of living is on the high side, with real estate taking a sizable bite out of the budget.

Climate

Elevation: 4,500'	Avg. high/low:	Avg. inches		Avg. # days precip.	Avg. % humidity
		rain	snow		
Jan.	45/18	.6	6.2	4	54
April	64/30	.3	1.5	3	34
July	91/47	.3	-	3	21
Oct.	70/31	.4	.3	3	30
YEAR	67/32	4.6	25.9	39	36
# days 32° or below: 187			# days 90° or warmer: 47		

What things cost

Overview: ACCRA statistics indicate that the cost of living in Reno is 12 percent higher than the national average, with housing coming in at more than 25 percent more and health care nearly 16 percent more. Utilities are the only category that offer any savings, at 3 percent less than the norm.

Electric, water and gas company: Sierra Pacific Power Co., 702-689-4444. Deposits of $50 and up can be waived with a letter of credit. The service establishment charge is $15. Electric bills average $65 to $85 in winter and can go as high as $130 in summer. Gas bills average $45 a month. Water bills average $29 a month.

Phone company: Call Nevada Bell, 702-702-333-4811. Installation is $45, and a deposit may be required pending the result of a credit check. Basic monthly rate is about $14.

Cable company: Contact TCI Reno, 702-850-8555; Continental Cablevision of Reno, 702-851-3110.

Car registration, license: A Nevada driver's license must be obtained within 30 days of establishing residency. New residents must register vehicles within 45 days. Licenses are $20.50; but for persons over 65, they're only $15.50. A written exam and an eye test are required. Car registration requires a smog inspection and costs about $33. There is an annual privilege tax based on 35 percent of the manufacturer's original suggested retail price. Tax is paid at $4 per $100 valuation, and depreciates with vehicle age. Call the Department of Motor Vehicles, 702-688-2368.

The tax ax

Sales tax: In Nevada, it's not so much the "tax ax" as it is the "tax lacks." State sales tax is 2 percent, and Reno adds 5 percent for a total sales tax of 7 percent, with drugs and groceries exempt.

State income tax: Nevada has no state income tax.

Property taxes: Homes are assessed every 5 years at 35 percent of appraised value and taxed at $3.1542 per $100 assessed value. Example: A $100,000 home, assessed at $35,000, would result in $1,104 annual taxes. Appraised values are typically lower than market value because the method used in assessment accounts for depreciation and replacement value of the home. There is a senior citizens rebate of up to $500 for homeowners 62 and older with gross incomes of less than $19,100.

Local real estate

Overview: The market is well-balanced between buyers and sellers and has shown steady growth in recent years. Resale inventory is up 5 to 10 percent over the past few years; residents are trading up or custom-building. Resales priced right sell very quickly. With low property taxes and many new manufacturers relocating, activity is brisk.

Average price for a 3BR/2BA home: $100,000 to $140,000 covers the range for both new homes and resales. $200,000 buys a 2000 sq. ft home with a 2-car garage and 90' x 100' lot.

Median price for a single family home: $137,100.

Common housing styles and features: Ranches are the most popular style, usually with wood or vinyl siding. Cathedral ceilings and master suites are becoming more common. Many houses have great rooms—a combination living, dining and family room.

Average price for a 2BR condo: New and resale units: $86,000 to $110,000.

Rental housing market: Single family homes are scarce and very expensive—available at a minimum of $800 per month. There are plenty of apartments available, ranging from $450 to $650 per month. There is also good availability for condominium rentals, starting at $450 and up for a 2BR.

Nearby areas to consider: Carson City, 30 miles south of Reno, is the capital of Nevada and smaller than Reno, with nice residential areas. Fernley is a very small (pop. 5,000), quaint town about 30 miles east.

Earning a living

Business climate: *Entrepreneur* magazine recently rated Reno as the nation's best small city for small business, because of its affordable land and access to Western cities, lack of state income or corporate tax, and an influx of businesses from California. Recently relocated companies include Citation/Caliber Medical (medical instruments), Fullerton Design/Zip Nut (aerospace fasteners) and Transkrit Corp. (business forms printer). The rate of unionization in Nevada is a mere 5 percent, not quite one-third of the national rate. Thanks to its prime geographic location, Reno is emerging as a warehousing, manufacturing and distribution center. Tourism is also an important industry: Gaming and recreation have driven the economy for the past 30 years, and they continue to do so. These sectors employ more than 21 percent of the county's 145,000-strong work force. Businesses that service hotels and casinos are profitable.

Help in starting a business: Help is available from the Small Business Development Center, 702-623-1064, which offers seminars on a variety of small business management topics and free, confidential counseling to owners of existing and prospective small businesses.

Job market: Reno's top 10 employers are all either government or gaming related, including the State of Nevada, Harrah's and the Reno Hilton. Retail, trade and services account for more than 60 percent of employment. The unemployment rate is 5.5 percent and has been decreasing in recent years. Nevada Employment Security Division, 702-688-2300.

Medical care

The Reno area has eight medical facilities with a total of 1,594 beds, offering a full range of health care services. Medical services are provided by more than 620 physicians/surgeons. Northern Nevada Medical Center, 702-331-7000, is a comprehensive medical center specializing in diabetes and inpatient rehabilitation services. St. Mary's Regional Medical Center, 702-323-2041, is an acute-care facility offering comprehensive medical care and specializing in cardiac surgery, home care and rehabilitation. Washoe Medical Center, 702-328-4100, specializes in rehabilitation, psychiatric care, trauma unit, renal dialysis, and it has a special Women's and Family Center. Washoe Medical Center also offers a variety of wellness programs, and a clinic specializing in senior health care. There is also the Veterans Administration Medical Center, with a nursing home care unit, psychiatric unit, alcohol drug treatment and medical/surgical facilities.

Services for seniors

The Reno Senior Center, 702-328-2575, is a hub for senior activities in Reno, offering a full schedule of classes and activities that include art, ceramics, clogging and line dancing, bridge, poker, billiards and much more. The center also has a public library as part of its site, and it provides a variety of services to seniors, including legal assistance (for wills, homesteads, etc.), as well as Medicare and Medicaid assistance. The Division for Aging Services of Reno can be reached at 702-688-2964. Call RSVP at 702-784-1807.

Continuing education

The University of Nevada Reno offers Eldercollege, 702-784-8053, a peer learning program that is a membership organization. For $35 per semester ($65 per couple), members participate in liberal arts, life enrichment and technical courses. The Eldercollege is located in downtown Reno, and some courses are offered at the Senior Center.

Crime and safety

As a convention and entertainment center, Reno attracts millions of visitors annually. Residential and retail burglaries are kept under control by a network of Neighborhood Watch Groups. A private security staff is employed by several of the larger businesses, assisting the police department in preventive safety programs. The police force (290 members) started using community-oriented policing in 1987, asking that the community give input and help identify problems. Representatives from departments from around the country have come to see how this program works. Reno's total crime index is 72 incidents per 1,000 population, and the county rate is 60 crimes per 1,000. Both are higher than the national average.

Getting around town

Public transportation: Call Citifare, 702-348-7433. It offers 23 bus routes throughout Reno. Fare is $1 for adults; 50 cents for seniors with Citifare ID card.

Roads and highways: I-80 and US 395. US 50 and 95 are within 50 miles.

Airport: Reno/Tahoe International Airport is served by 10 national and regional carriers.

Let the good times roll

Recreation: Reno has plenty of outdoor recreation, including golf (25 courses), tennis, horseback riding, cross-country skiing, downhill skiing, ice-skating and snowmobiling. The nation's largest concentration of ski resorts is located within 90 minutes of downtown Reno. Pyramid Lake and a number of other streams and lakes offer fishing, boating, water-skiing, hiking, camping and swimming. Within an easy day's drive are a wealth of federal parks and forests, including Sheldon National Wildlife Refuge, Fallon National Wildlife Refuge, Humboldt National Forest and Toiyabe National Forest. Over the border in California, you'll find Eldorado and Tahoe National Forests, Lassen Volcanic National Park, Desolation Valley Wilderness and Yosemite National Park. Although there are no major league pro teams, the University of Nevada Wolfpack play all college sports. Other teams include the Reno Rattlers (pro soccer), Reno Renegade (pro hockey) and Reno Diamonds (baseball).

Culture: Reno has the Philharmonic Orchestra; Reno Chamber Orchestra; Nevada Opera Association; the Nevada Festival Ballet and the Reno Little Theater. Community groups include the Washoe County Community Concert Association and the Sierra Nevada Chorale. The Nevada Museum of Art is Nevada's largest art museum. The Nevada State Museum has natural history exhibits. Of course, with gaming central to the area's economy, the entertainment industry is big, with many cabaret lounges and nightclubs.

Annual events: Cinco De Mayo's Fiesta Nevada Celebration and the Reno West Coast Wine Competition (May); Reno Rodeo, featuring world-class athletes (June); the Reno Basque Festival celebrates the Basque heritage with food, dancing, weightlifting and carrying and the "Irintzi"—the competition for the longest, loudest yell (Aug.); the Great Reno Balloon Race brings 150 of the nation's top hot air balloonists to compete (Sept.); the Italian festival (Oct.); the New Year is time for Buck N' Ball—a rodeo with live bands and dancing.

When the kids come: Children will enjoy the Fleischmann Planetarium; the Children's Museum; Great Basin Adventure, a children's theme park; Liberty Belle's Slot Machine Collection; the National Automobile Museum; Wild Waters theme park; and the Sierra Safari Zoo.

For more information

Chamber
Greater Reno-Sparks
  Chamber of Commerce
P.O. Box 3499
Reno, NV 89505
702-686-3030

Newspapers
Reno Gazette-Journal
955 Kuenzli Lane
Reno, NV 89502
702-788-6200

Sparks Tribune
1002 C St.
Sparks, NV 89431
702-358-8061

Realtor
Lornie B. Wagner
Coldwell Banker Plummer
  & Associates
290 E. Moana Lane, Suite 1
Reno, NV 89502
702-689-8228

33. Las Cruces, New Mexico

Nickname: The City of Crosses
County: Dona Ana
Area code: 505
Population: 67,000
County population: 145,000
% of population over 65: 8.7
Region: South Central New Mexico
Closest metro area: El Paso, Texas, 45 mi.
Average home price: $87,000 to $120,000
Best reasons to retire here: Low taxes, temperate climate, recreation, healthy environment and a slow pace.

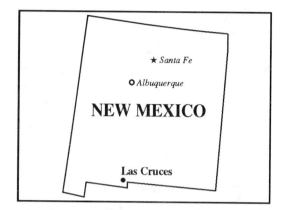

Las Cruces at a glance

Las Cruces is the second-largest city in New Mexico, and one with a rich and colorful history. More than 400 years ago Spanish conquistadors came here in search of the seven Cities of Gold. These explorers brought the holy cross with them, symbolizing their faith in the land, and Las Cruces, the "City of Crosses" was born. The area's historic mix of Hispanic, Indian and American Western culture gives Las Cruces its unique Southwestern style, and the landscape is nothing short of awesome, with the Organ mountains to the east, the Chihuahuan desert surrounding, and the nearby Rio Grande cutting a green and fertile path through it all. Although the city has developed into a small metropolitan area, it has the feel of a great hometown, and many retirees are adding their spirit to the city's ambience. Why do they move here? How about for great entertainment, a diverse assortment of arts, recreation and cultural attractions, good medical services, beautiful weather, year-round golf, wonderful shopping, dining on the spicy regional cuisine (Las Cruces' climate is ideal for growing chiles) and the spectacular environment? And if that's not enough, what about an affordable cost of living that doesn't come at the expense of a great lifestyle. Taxes are low, but services are surprisingly abundant. Was there something else you needed?

Possible drawbacks: Some feel that a small-town, small-mind mentality prevails, stifling economic development and efficient planning for the future. This is the land of *mañana*. The pace is slow; if you're a fast-moving type, it could be culture shock. Watch out for severe dust storms in the spring. Strong winds gust over the fields, picking up dirt along with momentum. But overall, the climate and lifestyle are wonderful.

Climate

Elevation: 3,896'	Avg. high/low:	Avg. inches		Avg. # days precip.	Avg. % humidity
		rain	snow		
Jan.	57/30	.3	-	4	50
April	79/49	.2	-	2	30
July	95/70	1.5	-	8	48
Oct.	79/50	.08	-	4	48
YEAR	77/49	7.0	4	-	-
# days 32° or below: 66			# days 90° or warmer: 101		

What things cost

Overview: ACCRA statistics show that the cost of living in Las Cruces is just below the national average. Utilities are 10 percent below average.

Gas company: City of Las Cruces and Rio Grande Natural Gas Association, 505-526-0246. Activation fee: $15.45; $60 deposit pending credit check. If you are in the area served by Rio Grande Natural Gas, $60 deposit required. Gas heat, cooking and hot water average $110 monthly. Gas is common and pre-ferred here.

Electric company: El Paso Electric Company, 505-526-5555. Turn-on charge: $7. Deposits are typically not required. All-electric homes average $130 monthly.

Phone company: The area is served by US West, 800-244-1111. No deposit if credit is established. Hook-up: $30; service: $18 a month.

Water and sewer: City of Las Cruces, 505-526-0246, operates both. $15.45 activation fee (which also covers gas); $60 deposit required pending credit check. Charges average $25 to $45 monthly.

Cable company: Las Cruces Cable TV, 505-523-2531; TV West, 505-524-7625.

Car registration, license: Driver's license, $13, renewable every four years. People over 75 must renew annually, but there is no charge. Written, vision and road tests required. Plate costs depend on the year, make and model of car; rates range from $16 to $46. The excise tax on titles of new and used cars is 3 percent. Motor Vehicle Department, 505-524-6215.

The tax ax

Sales tax: New Mexico has a gross receipts tax of 5 percent, which is different than a sales tax because it is paid by the seller instead of the purchaser. Tax is applied to all services, groceries and pre-scription drugs. Las Cruces adds to the tax for a total of 6.3125 percent.

State income tax: Graduated from 1.8 to 8.5 percent depending upon income bracket. There is no deduction for federal income tax paid. Social Security benefits subject to federal tax are not exempt.

Retirement income: $1,000 to $8,000 deducted per person for married couples filing jointly, both over 65, with adjusted gross income of $51,000 or less.

Property taxes: Homes are appraised at 90 percent of market value, and taxed at one-third of the assessed value. Recently, the tax rate in Las Cruces totaled $2.7097 per $100 of assessed value; taxes on a $100,000 home would be approximately $813. Assessor's office, 505-647-7400.

Local real estate

Overview: Housing is not usually "up for grabs," so homes typically sell for about 98 percent of the asking price. There has been a steady but reasonable increase in property values recently; for the past several years, homeowners have seen 5 to 6 percent appreciation annually. Most retirees move to the area permanently. This is not a second-home market.

Average price for a 3BR/2BA home: $87,000 for a resale; $120,000 for a new home.

Average price for a 2BR condo: A new condo on a golf course can be purchased for $120,000 to $140,000. Resales run slightly less at approximately $90,000 to $120,000.

Common housing styles and features: Southwestern and Spanish architecture dominate, featuring adobe exteriors, tile roofs, courtyards and elegant archways inside and out.

Rental housing market: Rental homes are hard to come by in this market, and will cost about $750 to $950 monthly for a 1,500 to 1,700 sq. ft. home. Apartments are typically (but not always) available.

Average rent for a 2BR apartment: The range is $325 to $510 monthly.

Communities or developments most popular with retirees: Seniors blend with the rest of the community in Las Cruces. The only retirement apartment community is University Terrace Good Samaritan Village; minimum age is 62.

Nearby areas to consider: In this area of the country, you can't do much better than Las Cruces, but you also could look at nearby Deming.

Earning a living

Business climate: The area's economy is based on agriculture, commerce, New Mexico State University and defense/aerospace technology. The county, which has been somewhat vulnerable to military cuts, has directed much of its efforts to converting defense operations (such as White Sands Missile Range, the area's largest employer) to commercial applications (reusable rocket development). Most of the businesses to locate here in the last decade have been small enterprises with a limited employee base, but retail and restaurant business has grown substantially. A recently opened border crossing 30 miles south of Las Cruces is helping to develop international trade.

Help in starting a business: The City of Las Cruces, 505-526-0000, assists start-up companies by providing information and acting as a liaison with the New Mexico Department of Labor and other agencies that screen employees. The Las Cruces-Dona Anna County Economic Development Council, 505-524-1745, provides business relocation information.

Job market: Area employment is very much dependent upon the military, government, education and medical sectors; nine of the area's 10 largest employers fall into these categories. The unemployment rate ran between 7 and 11 percent for the three years prior to 1995, at which time it dropped to 6.6 percent. Seniors seeking part-time work are in competition with students, although the stability of older workers is considered a plus. Businesses and organizations that make an effort to hire senior citizens include Wal-Mart, Grandy's and Gila National Forest. Employment Commission, 505-524-6250.

Medical care

Las Cruces is a the regional medical hub for a five-county area in southern New Mexico. Proximity to El Paso, Texas, adds to the range of medical services available in the region. Memorial Medical Center, 505-522-8461, is a public hospital with lower patient costs than most hospitals in the region. The 286-bed county hospital has open-heart surgery operations, magnetic resonance imaging, a state-of-the-art cardiovascular lab and a unit offering nonsurgical techniques to eliminate kidney stones. The hospital also has a diagnostic sleep lab, an urgent care center, a skilled nursing facility, a pain management clinic and the Ikard Memorial Cancer Treatment Center. Mesilla Valley Hospital, 505-382-3500, offers psychiatric and chemical dependency programs. There are also two VA medical facilities: William Beaumont Army Hospital in El Paso, 915-569-2220, and a new VA Outpatient Clinic in Las Cruces, 505-523-2490.

Services for seniors

Munson Senior Center, 505-526-2492, is the hub of senior information, referral and activity. It offers recreation, educational programs, travel opportunities, health and wellness programs, a craft shop and a thrift shop. It also hosts a large Senior Olympics program and offers classes in Spanish, creative writing, dance and more. AARP, 505-522-8848. RSVP, 505-526-0605. *Sun Country Senior Living* magazine, 505-522-4383, publishes one of the most comprehensive area retirement guides we encountered, the *Mesilla Valley Retirement Guide*. Area Agency on Aging, 505-525-0352.

Continuing education

New Mexico State University Community Education, 505-527-7527, offers: the "Weekend College" (classes at an economical rate for those not pursuing a degree); the Academy for Learning in Retirement, a scholarly mini-series featuring such subjects as local history and appreciation of opera. The Academy also offers Internet access for $10 a month, and an Elderhostel with a commuter option.

Crime and safety

Local police offer information on security against home burglary and auto theft and help set up Neighborhood Watch programs. Most violent crime in the area is attributed to drugs and gang activity, and rarely affects law-abiding citizens. Las Cruces reports a crime index of 99 incidents per 1,000 population, with Dona Ana County at 61 incidents. Both are higher than the national average of 55 incidents.

Getting around town

Public transportation: Roadrunner Transit, 505-525-2500, offers seniors a half-price fare of 25 cents. The City of Las Cruces Senior Citizens Department of Bus Transportation transports seniors to and from Munson Senior Center, grocery stores and medical appointments.

Roads and highways: I-10 (east-west intercontinental route); I-25 (north-south) connects Las Cruces to Albuquerque and Denver; US 70.

Airports: Las Cruces International Airport is served by Mesa Airlines. El Paso International Airport, 52 miles south, provides direct flights to more than 70 cities.

Let the good times roll

Recreation: The weather in Las Cruces is almost always perfect for golf, and three nearby public golf courses let you take advantage of it. Dipping Springs and La Cueva offer hiking trails and great beauty. Nearby Aguirre Springs Campground offers hiking, camping, mountain biking and picnicking, and boating and kayaking enthusiasts enjoy Leasburg Dam State Park. Within a day's trip are White Sands National Monument, Elephant Butte and Caballo Reservoir and Sunland Park Race Track (quarter horses). If you like spectator sports, New Mexico State University has several Division 1 NCAA teams.

Culture: The Las Cruces Symphony offers six concerts annually, featuring nationally known performers. The American Southwest Theater Company presents several productions a year. Las Cruces Community Theater features local talent. The New Mexico State University Museum features rotating exhibitions of historic Native American culture, while the Branigan Cultural Center displays works by local artists. Many of the cultural offerings focus on the area's history, including Old Mesilla, a nearby town that looks almost exactly as it did at the turn of the century. Also check out the Mesquite and Alameda Depot historical districts.

Annual events: New Mexico Mesilla Valley Annual Balloon Rally features hot-air balloons, food and fun (Jan.); the Annual Feria de Arte Picante celebrates Hispanic and Native American folk art (April); the Cinco de Mayo Fiesta and the New Mexico Wine and Chile War Festival (May); the Juneteenth Celebration honors African-American history and culture (June); the Diez y Seis de Septiembre Fiesta features a parade, costumes, food and festivities (Sept.); the Renaissance Craftfaire (Nov.); the Fiesta of Our Lady of Guadalupe, a festival of lights from candles and bonfires on a mountain near the University (Dec.).

When the kids come: Fort Selden State Monument, 15 minutes north, will build appreciation for the hardships of young men who settled the area. On summer weekends rangers dress in uniforms of the time and demonstrate what it was like to be a 19th-century soldier. Carlsbad Caverns National Parks is three hours away and features incredible caverns. Silver City (two hours away) is home of Billy the Kid.

For more information

Chamber
Greater Las Cruces Chamber
  of Commerce
P.O. Drawer 519
Las Cruces, NM 88004
505-524-1968

Newspapers
El Paso Times
225 E. Idaho
Las Cruces, NM 88001
505-525-5444

Albuquerque Journal
206 S. Main St.
Las Cruces, NM 88005
505-527-0089

Realtor
Patricia K. Kirkpatrick
Sunstate Realty Inc.
1240 Telshar, Suite A
Las Cruces, NM 88011
505-521-3252
800-541-7251
Fax: 505-521-3307

34. Santa Fe, New Mexico

Nickname: The City Different
County: Santa Fe
Area code: 505
Population: 59,840
County population: 107,182
% of population over 65: 12
Region: North Central New Mexico
Closest metro area: Albuquerque, 60 mi.
Median home price: $173,750
Best reasons to retire here: Cultural opportunities, fabulous ski country, diverse ethnic backgrounds, low taxes, even lower humidity.

Santa Fe at a glance

Nestled at the foothills of the Rocky Mountains, Santa Fe is indeed a different city. The oldest capital city in the country boasts a rich blend of Spanish, Native American and Anglo cultures. Santa Fe has been discovered time and again, first by the Pueblo and other native peoples, in the 1600s by Spanish conquistadors, in the 1800s by American traders, in the late 1900s by artists and writers, and now, by the rest of the world. Without a doubt, Santa Fe is an art lover's and sports enthusiast's paradise. Skiing in Santa Fe and nearby Taos is considered the best in the Southwest, at elevations of 10,000 to 12,000 feet and with more than 225 inches of annual snowfall. For the art lover, there are more than 150 galleries and several outstanding museums, and the nearby ancient ruins and historical landmarks are also fascinating. The sovereign Pueblo nations who continue to live in the dwellings of their ancestors invite visitors to respectfully view dances, feast days and the ceremonial kivas—underground structures at the heart of their culture and religion. Santa Fe's finishing touch is its wonderfully dry climate. Relative humidity averages 45 percent, and the sun shines at least 300 days a year. Winters are chilly but not frigid, allowing for outdoor activities. One retiree said, "If someone comes here and is bored, there's no place that would excite them."

Possible drawbacks: In spite of the down market, real estate is still some of the most expensive in the state. Retiring here can be costly, with food and health care taking a big bite. The job market is very tough, and the wages are low, so you'd better off here if you have deep pockets.

Climate

Elevation: 1,257'	Avg. high/low:	Avg. inches		Avg. # days precip.	Avg. % humidity
		rain	snow		
Jan.	42/15	.4	6.0	6	60
April	6030	1.1	1.0	6	45
July	83/51	2.4	-	10	60
Oct.	70/32	1.1	.5	6	55
YEAR	63/32	14.0	29.0	-	45
# days 32° or below: 137			# days 90° or warmer: 33		

What things cost

Overview: ACCRA shows the cost of living here is 10 percent higher than the national average. Housing, utilities and health care are the major culprits, with housing nearly 25 percent more and the other categories 14 percent above.

Gas and electric company: PNM Electric and Gas Services, 505-473-1600. Connect fees: $15 for electricity; $8 for gas (unless the gas is off, in which case it's $22 and an inspection is required). Deposits ($10 and up) can be waived with a letter of credit. Average gas bill: $15 to $45 monthly. Average electric bill: $180 monthly for all-electric homes; $60 per month if gas heat. (All-electric homes are rare.)

Phone company: Contact US West, 800-244-1111. Deposit (if required): $105. Set-up fee: $30. Basic service: $20 monthly.

Water and sewer: Sangre De Cristo Water Company, 505-982-3700. No connection charge unless water has to be turned on ($7.50). Deposits are waived with a letter of credit. Water costs $30 to $45 monthly, sewer is about $12, and trash removal is about $11.

Cable company: TCI Cablevision of Santa Fe, 505-438-2600.

Car registration, license: Driver's license ($13) is renewable every four years.

Persons over 75 must renew annually, for no charge. Written, vision and road tests required. Registration: Plate costs vary, ranging from $16 to $46. There is an excise tax of 3 percent on title of new and used cars. License/registration information, call 505-827-7600.

The tax ax

Sales tax: New Mexico has a gross receipts tax of 5 percent (different than a sales tax because it is paid by the seller instead of the purchaser), which applies the tax to all services, groceries and prescription drugs. Santa Fe County and city combine to add an additional 1.25 percent, for a total of 6.25 percent.

State income tax: Graduated from 1.8 to 8.5 percent depending upon income bracket. There is no deduction for federal income tax paid. Social Security benefits subject to federal tax are not exempt.

Retirement income: $1,000 to $8,000 deduction per person for married couples filing jointly, both over 65, with adjusted gross income of $51,000 or less.

Property taxes: Homes are assessed at one-third of the market value, and the tax rate of .018089 is applied. The tax bill on a $108,000 home would be $652. Assessor's office, 505-986-6300.

Local real estate

Overview: Santa Fe's real estate market is in a period of slowdown, and the inventory of available homes is substantial. Sellers are dropping their prices, slightly or substantially, depending upon the price range. Property taxes are low compared to other states, but on the rise. Retirees choose Santa Fe as a permanent home and a second-home locale in about equal numbers.

Median home price: $173,750 for the city; $185,000 in the south of the county; $385,000 in the north.

Average price for a 3BR/2BA home: New homes start at $120,000; resales at $160,000 (new construction aims for a lower end of the market). The upper-middle range for new and resales is $350,000.

Average price for a 2BR condo: New condos are $180,000 to $300,000; resales average $150,000 to $300,000.

Common housing styles and features: Spanish Pueblo and Spanish Territorial design dominate the architecture, with adobe exteriors, tile roofs, courtyards and archways. The city has strict architectural, historic preservation and zoning controls.

Rental housing market: Growth in new apartment construction has increased supply and lowered prices. The availability of apartment rentals is very good.

Average rent for a 2BR apartment: $600 to $700 monthly, which includes all utilities except gas and electric.

Communities or developments most popular with retirees: The historic area on the east side is popular with seniors.

Nearby areas to consider: El Dorado, Pecos.

Earning a living

Business climate: The number-one industry is tourism; and the number-one employer is state government. The city has a strong commercial retail market, with 18 shopping centers. The economy experiences seasonal fluctuations based on tourism. Current political trends within the community are to slow the rate of expansion, and a great deal of the promotional literature stresses the difficulty of this job market. Many residents commute to work in Albuquerque or Los Alamos, the once-secret city atop a 7,400-foot mesa northwest of Santa Fe, where the Los Alamos National Laboratory is located. To find out more, request a copy of *Santa Fe Business*, 505-982-3508.

Help in starting a business: Free assistance to small businesses is provided by the Small Business Development Center, 505-438-1343. Counselors will arrange to work with clients in their place of business. Other sources of help are SCORE, 505-988-6302, and Santa Fe Economic Development, Inc., 505-984-2842.

Job market: Santa Fe is a tough job market—lots of competition and not a lot to compete for. Unemployment has been about 3.5 percent for two years. Most jobs are in state government or tourism-related businesses, and much of the economic activity is based on tourism, horse racing, skiing and the Santa Fe Opera summer season. A surplus of applicants vie for jobs, and wage rates for many jobs are lower than the national average. Contact the Santa Fe Labor Service Center, 505-827-7434, for a daily listing of job openings by private employers. You can also call Tele-guide Santa Fe Jobs Line at 505-820-2020, category 8000.

Medical care

Santa Fe has good health care facilities for a city its size, and it also has a developing respect for alternative medicine used in conjunction with traditional approaches. Many area doctors contract with chiropractors, acupuncturists and other alternative practitioners to treat their patients. Massage therapists are licensed by the state; the American Massage Therapy Association, 505-268-8702, can offer a referral. St. Vincent Hospital, 505-983-3361, New Mexico's first hospital, has grown into a 286-bed regional medical center with state-of-the-art facilities. It has a Level II trauma center, diagnostic services that include MRI, CAT scan, ultrasound and radiology, intensive care and cardiac units, a comprehensive cancer services center, same-day surgery center and the Margaret Strong Pain Management Center. In Albuquerque, 60 miles away, the St. Joseph Healthcare System, 505-244-8000, specializes in cancer treatment, cardiovascular care, physical rehabilitation and laser surgery.

Services for seniors

The Santa Fe Senior Citizens Program, 505-984-6731, is a county-operated agency that oversees 25 different programs and services for senior citizens including nine senior centers, classes, recreational offerings, the Senior Olympics and more. The centers offer transportation, meals, entertainment, health screenings, companions and a Foster Grandparent program for special-needs children. The Arts with Elders Program, sponsored by Open Hands, 505-982-4258, brings professional artists to conduct workshops at senior centers. RSVP, 505-662-8203.

Continuing education

Santa Fe Community College Office of Continuing Education, 505-438-1251, offers 400 to 500 classes a semester. Topics include Southwest explorations, cooking, music, dance and computers. The University of New Mexico North, 505-662-5919, has a peer learning program for seniors 50 and up. St. John's College, 505-984-6000, is the Southwest counterpart of the Annapolis, Maryland, campus. It offers a community series for reading and discussion of great books.

Crime and safety

Oddly, Santa Fe city and county do not report crime rates to the FBI. Unofficially, the crime rate for the city appears to be high. According to the Santa Fe Police, there were 5,481 crimes in 1995—approximately 92 incidents per 1,000 population, higher than the national average of 55 per 1,000. But total reported crimes include those committed against travelers, and tourism is big here. More than 60 percent of all crimes reported are larceny. Violent crime is rare; in 1995 the homicide rate was 50 percent lower than the national average.

Getting around town

Public transportation: Local transit services six routes. Services for the elderly and mobility-impaired are through the city's van and taxi program.

Roads and highways: I-25; I-40 traverses I-25 in Albuquerque, 60 mi. south.

Airports: The closest major airport is Albuquerque International. Santa Fe Municipal has daily commuter service to Albuquerque and Denver.

Let the good times roll

Recreation: The beautiful environs offer hiking, hunting, bicycling, fishing and world-class skiing. Golf is available year-round at several public and private courses, including Cochita Lake, one of the nation's best. Tennis players can choose from 44 public courts, or go indoors to a private club. Camping is great from spring through fall, with national forest and state parks nearby. More than 1,000 miles of maintained trails greet cyclists and hikers, and there's plenty of whitewater rafting, canoeing and kayaking. The Santa Fe Ski Area has seven lifts, a 12,000-foot summit, 39 downhill trails and 225 inches of snow a year.

Culture: With more than 150 galleries, Santa Fe is the third largest art market in the country. To tour the weekly gallery openings, call the Santa Fe Gallery Association, 505-982-1648. The Museum of International Folk Art features historic and contemporary folk art, and the Institute of American Indian Arts Museum offers changing exhibitions of Native American art. Santa Fe has a thriving dance scene that includes Maria Benitez and her Teatro Flamenco dance company and the Prince State Ballet. The Santa Fe Opera is world-class, bringing $100 million to the local economy during its July/August season. The New Mexico Symphony Orchestra performs regularly here, and internationally known musicians come to town annually for the Santa Fe Chamber Music Festival. Theater companies include Sage Repertory Company, Santa Fe Community Theater and Santa Fe Theater Company.

Annual events: Civil War Weekend at El Rancho de las Golondrinos (May); Fourth of July Pancake Breakfast on the Plaza (July); Santa Fe Antique Indian Art Show and Sale and world-renowned Indian Market (Aug.); Fiesta de Santa Fe (Sept.); the Matachines Dance, performed at many pueblos, and neighborhood competitions to light the Christmas Eve night sky with thousands of farolitos (Dec.).

When the kids come: The Santa Fe Children's Museum offers hands-on exhibits and interactive displays, and on Thursday afternoons kids help create a miniature adobe village in the Earthworks project. El Rancho de las Golondrinos is a living history museum that kids love.

For more information

Chamber
Santa Fe County Chamber
  of Commerce
510 N. Guadalupe St.,
  Suite N
Santa Fe, NM 85704-1928
505-988-3279

Convention and Visitors
  Bureau: 505-984-6760

Newspapers
The Santa Fe New Mexican
  (daily)
202 E. Marcy
Santa Fe, NM 87501
505-983-3303

Santa Fe Reporter (weekly)
132 E. Marcy
Santa Fe, NM 87501
505-988-5541

Realtor
Nat Shipman
Nat Shipman
  & Associates, Inc.
1700 Paseo de Peralta
Santa Fe, NM 87501
505-988-7657
800-264-7657
Fax: 505-982-6468

35. Asheville, North Carolina

Nickname: Land of the Sky
County: Buncombe
Area code: 704
Population: 66,562
County population: 185,810
% of population over 65: 16.1
Region: Western North Carolina
Closest metro area: Greeneville, S.C., 65 mi.
Average home price: $122,000 to $150,000
Best reasons to retire here: Fabulous year-round climate, mountainous region, a lifestyle for seniors unsurpassed by any city this size.

Asheville at a glance

The term "quality of life" has become such a catch phrase that it has almost lost meaning. But if ever there was a place that was worthy of the expression, it's Asheville. Located on a plateau divided by the French Broad River and surrounded by mountains, Asheville draws many a vacationer who comes back for good. Residents enjoy the sophisticated city life knowing that a million-acre natural wilderness is also at their doorstep. The year-round climate is unbeatable. The culture, recreation and amenities for a city this size are remarkable, and the quality of health care gets raves (not to mention the fact that costs are well below the national average). The unique appeal of this area has long-drawn discerning individuals to call it home, including George Vanderbilt, who constructed the famous Biltmore House here, a magnificent Victorian estate that took 1,000 men five years to build. The appeal to retirees is that the city is big enough not to be stifling, but not so large that it loses its small-town friendliness. It is a regional center for manufacturing, transportation, health care, banking, professional services and shopping, but it is also the regional center for handcrafts, adding a unique and personal dimension to the economic picture. In this place where the Smokies and the Blue Ridge Mountains meet, retirees are off their rockers, morning, noon and night—if they're so inclined. It's no wonder Asheville is consistently ranked and rated as a fabulous place to live.

Possible drawbacks: People are surprised that it gets as hot as it does in the summer, but the evenings cool off considerably. The rental market for homes is as tight as a drum. If your intent is to come down for a few months, give yourself ample lead time to find a place.

Climate

Elevation: 2,175'	Avg. high/low:	Avg. inches		Avg. # days precip.	Avg. % humidity
		rain	snow		
Jan.	48/27	2.9	-	11	70
April	69/42	3.5	-	9	58
July	84/63	4.9	-	12	74
Oct.	69/45	3.3	-	8	69
YEAR	67/44	38.0	18	-	-
# days 32° or below: 104			# days 90° or warmer: 7		

What things cost

Overview: According to ACCRA, the overall cost of living in Asheville is about 2 percent above the national average. The index is driven up by utilities costs, nearly 16 percent higher than the norm. Housing is 4 percent higher, but health care costs are nearly 14 percent lower.

Gas company: Call Public Service Co. of North Carolina, 704-253-1821. No hookup charge; deposit waived for customers with letters of credit. Average bill: $60 to $75 monthly; if stove only, $15 to $25.

Electric company: Carolina Power & Light Co., 704-258-1010. Set-up charge: $17.51; deposits waived for homeowners/customers with letter of credit. All-electric service: $115 to $125 per month; partial electric: $75 to $85.

Phone company: Bell South, 704-780-2355 or 800-767-2355. Connect charge: $42.75; deposit waived with letter of credit. Basic monthly service: $15.50 to $31.50.

Water and sewer: Asheville Department of Water Resources, 704-258-0161. Hookup: $20; no deposit. Monthly avg.: $40.

Cable company: Contact TCI Cablevision, 704-255-0000, Charter Communications, 704-252-8522, or Marcus Cable, 704-667-0442.

Car registration, license: New residents must apply for a state driver's license within 30 days. Vision and written tests are required. Plates must be purchased within 30 days; cars inspected within 10 days. North Carolina Department of Motor Vehicles, 704-298-4544.

The tax ax

Sales tax: 6 percent. Prescription medicines and transportation are exempt.

State income tax: North Carolina taxable income is calculated the same as for federal income tax purposes. The tax rate is 6 or 7 percent as calculated on a graduated scale.

Retirement income tax: Retirees receive a $2,000 exclusion on private pensions and $4,000 on public pensions, and all Social Security benefits and railroad retirement benefits are exempt.

Property taxes: Residents must pay both city and county taxes. Property tax rates for the city are .57 per $100 valuation and .73 cents per $100 valuation for the county. Homes are assessed at 100 percent of market value. There is a $15,000 exemption off assessed value for persons 65 and older with gross income of up to $11,000. Sample taxes on a $150,000 home would be $1,950. Buncombe County Assessor, 704-255-5787.

Local real estate

Overview: Property taxes have not changed for several years now. Home values are rising slowly, showing an annual appreciation of 1 to 4 percent. Retirees tend to find that their housing dollars go much further with the purchase of a resale home rather than a new one. Homes in this area sell rapidly (less than 100 days).

Average price for a 3BR/2BA home: New construction on less than an acre costs $130,000 to $150,000; resales of comparable size average $122,000.

Average price for a 2BR condo: New, $75,000 to $85,000; resales, $60,000 to $80,000.

Common housing styles and features: The typical home is a 3BR/2BA unit on one level with an attached garage and a fireplace in the Great Room. Most homes have basements and yards with gardens. Lot sizes are one acre or less. Mountain views are plentiful.

Rental housing market: Apartments are plentiful. Single-family home rentals, however, are few.

Average rent for a 2BR apartment: According to ACCRA, the average rent is $530, but our sources say $700 to $800 per month is more likely.

Communities or developments most popular with retirees: Grove Park, Lakeview Park & Country Club of Asheville, Reems Creek Country Club in Weaverville and Biltmore Forest and Biltmore Park in south Asheville.

Nearby areas to consider: Hendersonville is popular with many seniors, while Brevard appeals to those seeking a "village" atmosphere.

Earning a living

Business climate: A growing number of entrepreneurs with businesses that can locate anywhere, such as mail-order and computer consulting firms, are choosing Asheville. The economy is fueled by two industries, manufacturing and tourism. Health care, electronics, service and trade round out the economic base and are the area's largest employers. Retail is one of the fastest-growing segments of the economy.

Help in starting a business: The Small Business Center at Asheville-Buncombe Technical Community College works in tandem with the Chamber of Commerce to provide free counseling, referrals and assistance to new and expanding small businesses in the Asheville area. The Small Business Center offers counseling, classes and seminars, while the Chamber assists with loan packaging, site selection and permitting processes.

Job market: One interesting, though small, component of the employment market is handcrafts, a quiet dynamo that employs 739 full-time and 3,369 part-time workers. (Hobbyists take heed!) The area's largest manufacturing employers include Champion International, which makes uncoated paper and paperboard, and Ecusta Division of P.H. Glatfelter, which makes paper for cigarette companies. Other major employers are Steelcase, Inc., Mission/St. Joseph's Health System, Grove Park Inn Resort and local government. Manufacturing employment is currently declining. Unemployment rates trend below 5 percent. Tourism in the area means seasonal jobs are available. NC Employment Security Commission, Job Service Division, 704-251-6200.

Medical care

Memorial Mission Hospital, 704-255-4000, with 502 beds, is the major medical center for Western North Carolina. It has a heart center, cancer center and women's health center. Mountain Area Cancer Center offers diagnostic and treatment services. Mission Genetics Center gives access to new information on genetics. St. Joseph's Hospital, 704-255-3100, is a 331-bed regional medical center with 370 physicians on staff. It has specialized orthopedic surgery suites, a 24-hour emergency department, intensive care and coronary units, general radiology diagnostic services and the Stone Treatment Center. The Diabetes Center is an intensive multidisciplinary treatment center. Thoms Rehabilitation Hospital, 704-274-2400, is a regional referral center. It has programs for rehabilitation after head injuries, spine injuries, stroke, chronic pain and more. Asheville VA Medical Center, 704-298-7911, provides services to veterans throughout western North Carolina and four South Carolina counties.

Services for seniors

The Buncombe County Council on Aging, 704-258-8027, acts as an information and referral agency, and provides in-home assistance, transportation services and day and overnight trips. It oversees operations at several senior centers, including the Senior Opportunity Center, 704-254-6184. A directory of services for seniors is available through Buncombe County Council on Aging and the Land-of-Sky Regional Council, 704-254-8131.

Continuing education

The North Carolina Center for Creative Retirement, 704-251-6140, is affiliated with the University of North Carolina at Asheville and offers courses on topics such as herbs, classic mysteries, opera, current events, the writings of Asheville native Thomas Wolfe and health care policy. The center's services and programs are open to persons age 55 and older.

Crime and safety

The Asheville Police Department, Buncombe County Sheriff's Department and North Carolina Highway Patrol all operate within Buncombe County, which, at 45 incidents per 1,000 people, has one of the lowest crime rates in North Carolina. Metropolitan Asheville's rate is higher, at 89 incidents per 1,000. Asheville is a "wet" city among adjacent "dry" counties, which contributes to the crime rate.

Getting around town

Public transportation: Asheville Transit Authority, 704-253-5691, operates city buses six days a week. Adult fares are 60 cents and seniors ride for 30 cents. Medicare cards are required ID for reduced fares.

Roads and highways: I-40 and I-26 (the largest interchange in the southeast), US 19, 23, 25, 70 and 74, Blue Ridge Parkway.

Airport: Asheville Regional Airport is located 15 miles south of Asheville on I-26. Several major airlines offer connector flights to Charlotte, Cincinnati and Atlanta.

Let the good times roll

Recreation: The Carolinas are known for spectacular golf, and the Asheville area is no exception. There are 14 public and semi-public courses in the area and many more private country clubs. Tennis is also extremely popular, with 23 tennis facilities available. Hiking, fishing, watersports, snowskiing are all terrific in this area, since Asheville sits in the heart of the southern highlands of the Appalachian Mountains. Hikes in the mountains offer gorgeous views of the French Broad and Swannanoa River valleys. The Western North Carolina Horse Show Complex hosts some of the top horse shows in the southeast. Minor League baseball is played by the Asheville Tourists, a Class A farm club for the Colorado Rockies. They play in the oldest minor league park in America, the historic McCormick Field. There are many options available for those who enjoy shopping. There are major malls, shopping centers, quaint market districts and outlet shops, and Asheville is a mecca for antique collectors.

Culture: Asheville is well-known for its wealth of artists and craftspeople, and the Asheville Art Museum, Folk Art Center, Asheville Art League and Arts Alliance provide varied artistic offerings.

The famous Brevard Music Center, not far from Asheville, offers a full summer program while it trains 350 gifted students from across the nation. A favorite area attraction is the 255-room Biltmore Estate, built in 1895 by George Vanderbilt. The North Carolina Arboretum has more than 2,000 types of native plants. The Asheville Symphony presents a full season of masterworks concerts, pops performances and a children's concert.

Annual events: In March, residents gather downtown for the annual St. Patrick's Day Festival. July brings Shindig-on-The-Green and the Belle Chere Festival, two of the most popular tourist events in the region, featuring dancing, traditional folk music, arts, crafts and more. In August it's time for the Mountain Dance and Folk Festival, the oldest festival of its kind in America. In September, celebrate Kituwah, honoring the area's Native Americans, including the Cherokee.

When the kids come: The Western North Carolina Nature Center is an environmental educational resource with exhibits designed to promote conservation. It has six acres of native animals and birds, including two locally famous rambunctious otters.

For more information

Chamber
Asheville Area Chamber
   of Commerce
P.O. Box 1010
Asheville, NC 28802
704-258-6101

Newspaper
Asheville Citizen-Times
P.O. Box 2090
Asheville, NC 28802
704-252-5611
800-800-4204

Realtor
Carolyn Richardson
Beverly Hanks & Associates
300 Executive Park
Asheville, NC 28801
704-254-7221 or 800-868-7221
Fax: 704-255-8994

36. Raleigh, North Carolina

Nickname: The City of Oaks
County: Wake
Area code: 919
Population: 249,079
County population: 508,735
% of population over 65: 7.8
Region: Southeast
Closest metro area: Durham, 23 mi.
Average home price: $144,280
Best reasons to retire here: Outstanding medical care, endless recreation, park-like setting, thriving economy, low crime.

Raleigh at a glance

Raleigh offers big-city benefits with the comfort of suburban living. It is convenient to the mountains and the coast, and brimming with culture, history and natural beauty. The City of Oaks has often been described as a city within a park, and indeed, majestic oaks and blooming magnolias, dogwoods and azaleas make this city very appealing. Raleigh is the South at its picturesque best, with a lush, green landscape and mild climate. It has a greenway system that spans 46 miles and connects many of the area's 156 parks and lakes. It's also a city of gardens, including Ellen Mordecai Kitchen Garden, Martin Luther King, Jr. Memorial Gardens, North Carolina State University Arboretum and Raleigh Municipal Rose garden. But flowers and trees aren't all that grows in Raleigh; so does the business community. It is the home of three nationally acclaimed research universities (the University of North Carolina, Duke University and North Carolina State) and Research Triangle Park, one of the largest planned research centers in the world. The impact of these elements on the economy is measured by the phenomenal business expansion the region continues to enjoy. Raleigh also enjoys top-flight medical facilities and cultural offerings. The community also has something of an international flair, because its educational, medical and research/business facilities draw people from all over the world.

Possible drawbacks: Wake County has grown so fast, the infrastructure is only now catching up. The roads are being widened, but when the growing pains will stop is anyone's guess. The ones who are most concerned are the newcomers—they'd hate growth to ruin this wonderful area!

Climate

Elevation: 430'	Avg. high/low:	Avg. inches		Avg. # days precip.	Avg. % humidity
		rain	snow		
Jan.	51/30	3.0	2.5	9	56
April	72/47	3.1	-	9	46
July	88/67	5.1	-	12	61
Oct.	72/48	2.8	-	7	54
YEAR	70/48	41.8	7.3	111	54
# days 32° or below: 81			# days 90° or warmer: 23		

What things cost

Overview: Living costs in the Raleigh/Durham/Chapel Hill metropolitan area are about 1 percent lower than the national average, with grocery, transportation and health care costs accounting for the savings, according to ACCRA. Housing and utilities were 1 and 4 percent above the norm respectively.

Gas company: Public Service Co. of North Carolina, 919-833-3355 or 919-833-6641. No connect charge. Deposits, based on appliances in the home, range from $105 to $130 and can be waived with a letter of credit. Average gas bill: $47 monthly; higher in winter.

Electric company: Carolina Power and Light, 919-508-5400. There is a charge of $17 to start service. Deposits may be waived. Average electric bill: $109 per month on the budget plan.

Phone company: Contact Bell South, 919-780-2355 or 800-767-2355. Installation is $42.75. Deposits may be required. Basic monthly service is $20 to $25.

Water and sewer: City of Raleigh Public Utilities Department, 919-890-3245. No deposit required on new accounts and there is no charge to establish service.

Cable company: Time Warner Cable, 919-832-2225.

Registration, license: New residents must obtain a North Carolina license within 30 days of establishing residency. Written exam required. Fee is $10, licenses are renewed every four years. Registration: title fees, $35; license plates, $25, must be purchased within 30 days. Division of Motor Vehicles, 919-733-4241.

The tax ax

Sales tax: 4-percent state tax, plus an additional 2-percent county tax.

State income tax: The tax rate is 6 or 7 percent as calculated on a graduated scale.

Retirement income tax: Retirees receive a $2,000 exclusion on private pensions and $4,000 on public pensions, and all Social Security benefits and railroad retirement benefits are exempt.

Property tax: For Wake County: Tax rate .63 cents per $100 of assessed or declared value. Raleigh: Tax rate is .544 cents per $100 of assessed or declared value. Thus, in Wake County, taxes on a $150,000 house are $945; in Raleigh (you pay a combined county and city rate of 1.174), they'd be $1,761. For more information, contact the revenue department, assessment, 919-856-5400.

Local real estate

Overview: The market is currently balanced, strong and healthy, with a lot of new home construction and continuous corporate relocation. Because the population has been growing at a strong rate, home prices are appreciating at about 5 to 8 percent annually.

Average price for a 3BR/2BA home: $144,280. New and resale homes can be found in the $80,000 to $135,000 range, but more modern amenities and space accompany homes in the $135,000 to $250,000 mid-range.

Average price for a 2BR condo: $65,000 to $150,000.

Common housing styles and features: Traditional 2-story homes and ranches are popular, but you can find almost any style. Inside the Beltway are older neighborhoods such as Oakwood, which has many Victorian-style homes. Farther out, a 10-year-old house is considered old. Here you will find the transitional and expansive ranches. Brick is a popular exterior. Homes have decks, European kitchens, master suites and split plans.

Rental housing market: Single family homes (3BR/2BA) rent between $900 to $1,800 per month. The market is tight because of the college population.

Average rent for a 2BR apartment: $573 per month, according to ACCRA, although our sources indicate that $600 and up is more likely.

Nearby areas to consider: Wake Forest, 12 miles north, is more rural, but growing fast. Chapel Hill, 23 miles northwest, is a beautiful college town but with somewhat higher prices.

Earning a living

Business climate: Retail sales are up, development is increasing, the work force is well-educated, there are numerous research universities in the area, living costs are moderate and the location is central. It's a perfect mix for conducting business at many levels. Raleigh is a great place for major corporations and high-tech business, but it's equally good for small and home-based businesses. It's also the home of Research Triangle Park, one of the largest planned research centers in the world, with more than 50 corporations and government agencies specializing in microelectronics, telecommunications, chemicals, biotechnology, pharmaceuticals and environmental health sciences. Retailing has shown a steady increase since the mid-80s and construction is healthy, too.

Help in starting a business: Wake Technical College Small Business Center, 919-715-3440, offers training, workshops and seminars. The area is fortunate to have many high-level seminar and workshop presenters. The Small Business & Technology Development Center, 919-715-7272, offers free counseling, plus classes and seminars at a nominal charge. SCORE, 919-856-4739.

Job market: Businesses continue to relocate to Raleigh. Major companies that have expanded and anticipate job growth are MCI, Motorola, Midway Airlines, First Union Mortgage, Corning Bio and PennCorp Financial, Inc. Raleigh's unemployment rate is only 2 percent. Job Information, 919-890-3305. Employment Security Commission, 919-733-3941.

Medical care

Raleigh has one of the finest and most respected medical schools, teaching and research hospitals in the country—Duke University Medical Center, 919-684-8111. Its Heart Center boasts one of the largest cardiac groups in the country, performing major cardiac surgery. Duke has a cancer center and Alzheimer's research center, and a world-renowned diet center as well. University of North Carolina Hospitals are known for treatment of cystic fibrosis as well as a comprehensive transplant program for heart, lung, liver and kidney. Columbia-Raleigh Community Hospital, 919-954-3000, is a 230-bed facility that offers general medical and surgical services including intensive care, a diabetes treatment center, a same-day surgery center and a cardiac rehabilitation program. Wake Medical Center, 919-250-8000, is a 739-bed, six-hospital system with 24-hour emergency care, 45 outpatient clinics and a specialty in treating heart disease. And Rex Healthcare, 919-783-3100, is a 394-bed hospital known for cancer care, a heart center and a palliative care center.

Crime and safety

Raleigh has the lowest per-capita crime rate of North Carolina's five largest cities, with both the lowest violent crime rate and lowest property crime rate—more than half of all crimes are larcenies. Raleigh reports 73 incidents per 1,000 population, while Wake County reports 55 crimes per 1,000 people—exactly the national average. Generally, there's a feeling of safety here; even the downtown area is safe at night, as long as you know which areas to avoid.

Continuing education

ENCORE (at North Carolina State), 919-515-5782, is a learning in retirement program that offers more than 50 different classes, plus trips. Membership is $35 annually, and classes are $35 each. Topics covered include world religions, Shakespeare, genealogy and contemporary moral problems. Duke Institute for Learning in Retirement, 919-684-6259, offers life enrichment and liberal arts classes. It costs $100 per semester to attend any and all classes, or $65 to attend one class. More than 1,000 seniors are enrolled.

Services for seniors

The Whittaker Mill Senior Center offers exercise classes, line dancing, bingo, ceramics, a chorus and more. The Golden Years Association, 919-831-6850, is a club offered through the Parks and Recreation Department. RSVP, 919-831-6295. Resources for Seniors/Council on Aging 919-872-7933, can offer information and referrals.

Getting around town

Public transportation: Capital Area Transit Buses, 919-828-7228, and Triangle Transit Authority, 919-549-9999, provide extensive bus service, and Raleigh Trolley provides light rail service to the city.

Roads and highways: I-40, I-85 and I-95; US 1, 64, 70 and 401; NC 50 and 54.

Airport: The Raleigh-Durham International Airport is a hub for American Airlines and is served by five additional major airlines.

Let the good times roll

Recreation: Choose from 150 parks with 3,600 acres, 23 community centers and 900 acres of lakes. Outdoor activities range from picnicking, paddleboating and playgrounds to swimming lessons, jogging and fitness trails, tennis complexes, an 18-hole Frisbee golf course, volleyball and more. There are 18 golf courses in the county. Or you can take a trip to the nearby Falls Lake or Jordan Lake for skiing, swimming and boating. Raleigh is a great place for sports fans, especially college basketball fans. The University of North Carolina, N.C. State, Duke and N.C. Central play home games here. The Durham Bulls and Carolina Mudcats (minor-league baseball), Raleigh IceCaps (minor league hockey) and Raleigh Flyers (professional soccer) offer great spectator action.

Culture: The North Carolina Symphony performs at the refurbished Raleigh Memorial Auditorium and outdoors in the summer. The Raleigh Civic Symphony, the Chamber Music Guild, the North Carolina Bach Festival and the National Opera Company offer more musical entertainment. North Carolina Theatre Memorial Auditorium brings large-scale Broadway musicals to the area, while Raleigh Ensemble Players specializes in contemporary plays and musicals. Duke's American Dance Festival performs each summer. The North Carolina Museum of Art is noted for its collection and a popular film series. The Moore Square Arts District in downtown Raleigh features nine private and nonprofit galleries. A First Friday Gallery Walk is held each month.

Annual events: Raleigh is one of the South's greatest festival cities. Enjoy the Antique Extravaganza (Jan.), the Spring Herb and Lamb Day (May), Tarheel Regatta (June), Farmers Market Festival (July), Hot Hoops Basketball Tournament (Aug.), Pops in the Park, Artsplosure Jazz and the Heritage Music Festival (Sept.) and North Carolina State Fair (Oct.).

When the kids come: Playspace offers creative and educational experiences for children 7 and under. Blue Jay Point, a 236-acre center for environmental studies, focuses on conservation and environmental education. The North Carolina Zoological Park in Asheboro is an hour away.

For more information

Chamber
Greater Raleigh Chamber
  of Commerce
800 S. Salisbury St.
Raleigh, NC 27601
919-664-7000

Newspaper
The News and Observer
215 S. McDowell
Raleigh, NC 27602
919-829-4500

Realtor
Pat Earnhardt, Reloc. Dir.
Russell Gay & Associates/
  Century 21
215909 Falls of Neuse Rd.
Raleigh, NC 27609
919-848-5609
800-451-5592

37. Eugene, Oregon

Nickname: Green Eugene
County: Lane
Area code: 541
Population: 121,905
County population: 301,900
% of population over 65: 13.7
Region: Western Oregon
Closest metro area: Portland, 110 mi.
Average home price: $110,000 to $150,000
Best reasons to retire here: Laid-back lifestyle, great continuing education, proximity to the ocean and the mountains.

Eugene at a glance

More retirees are discovering that this Oregon oasis and its sister city Springfield are delightful places to hang their hats. The town prides itself on its very laid-back approach to living. Some attribute this to the many 30- and 40-year-olds who left the big bad world and have come here for the city's high quality of life. Others say that the moderate year-round climate and spectacular surroundings would "de-hyper" anyone. With the Pacific Ocean an hour to the west and the Cascade Mountains an hour to the east, it's easy to get away from it all. Snow in the valley is rare, but world-class skiing is nearby (at Mount Bachelor Ski Area in Bend). There's respect here for the healthy mind/healthy body connection; young and old alike are out on the trails and in the classroom. Residents thrive on outdoor recreation (river rafting, hiking, fishing) and educational pursuits (the University of Oregon and Lane Community College have terrific continuing education programs). Nestled at the southern end of the Willamette Valley, Eugene is part of a 100-mile stretch of lands that's considered one of the most productive agricultural areas on earth. The timber industry had been the mainstay of the local economy for many years, but now Eugene is actively recruiting high-tech business. Though the economy has been sluggish, the unemployment rate just hit its lowest mark in 30 years. This city is a find.

Possible drawbacks: Eugene's air quality is not up to par. Between winter air inversions, particle build-up from wood-burning stoves and veneer drying, there are days when the air quality doesn't meet EPA standards. There's no sales tax in Oregon, so state operating revenues come from income and property taxes. Medical costs are fairly high, but facilities are excellent.

Climate

Elevation: 366'	Avg. high/low:	Avg. inches		Avg. # days precip.	Avg. % humidity
		rain	snow		
Jan.	46/33	7.1	-	18	90
April	61/39	2.3	-	13	78
July	83/51	.3	-	2	80
Oct.	64/42	4.0	-	11	85
YEAR	63/42	41.0	7.1	-	-
# days 32° or below: 54			# days 90° or warmer: 15		

What things cost

Overview: According to ACCRA, the overall cost of living index is 5.4 percent higher than the national average. Health care and housing costs account for most of the higher cost of living, at 17 percent and 29 percent above the norm respectively. Groceries and utilities costs were substantially below the norm.

Gas company: Northwest Natural Gas Co., 541-342-3661. Bills average $45 to $50 monthly. No deposit and no charge to turn on service. Publicly owned electric utilities generate some of the least expensive power in the nation, so electricity is used for heat by most. Gas range and water heater, $45 to $50 month.

Electric, water and sewer company: Call Eugene Water and Electric Board, 541-484-2411. Average electric bill: $82.82 for all-electric. Water and sewer average about $67 monthly.

Phone company: US West Communications 800-244-1111. Installation charges are $12 to $25. Basic service averages $20 monthly.

Cable company: TCI Cablevision of Oregon, Inc., 541-484-3000.

Car registration, license: License and registration must be obtained immediately upon establishing residency. License, $26.25 (renewed every four years).

Registration fees are $30 and valid for 24 months. A used vehicle brought to Oregon from another state requires physical inspection of identification by the Department of Motor Vehicles. Fee is $4. No state sales or property tax on vehicles. Oregon Motor Vehicles Division, 541-687-7855.

The tax ax

Sales tax: Oregon has no sales tax.

State income tax: The state income tax is graduated from 5 to 9 percent depending upon income bracket. There is a deduction for up to $3,000 of federal income tax paid.

Retirement income: Federal, state and private pensions are not exempt from income tax. Social Security benefits are exempt. There is a $5,000 standard deduction for married couples 65 and older filing jointly.

Property taxes: Property taxes have been changing as a result of a law called Measure 5. Under this law, property is assessed at 100 percent of real market value. The tax rate has decreased as the law has been phased in. In 1995 it reached its final cap of $15 per $1,000 of assessed value. Lane County Assessment and Taxation, 541-687-4314.

Local real estate

Overview: Eugene now enjoys a buyer's market, after many years of sellers reaping profits from California's "equity immigrants" (house-rich Californians who snatched up anything, driving prices up and inventory down.) The savings and loan crisis affected the mortgage market and commercial loans, slowing new construction. New housing is affordable, but resales greatly outnumber new units. Most retirees in this area relocate permanently.

Average price for a 3BR/2BA home: $140,000 to $150,000 is the average price for a new home, while existing homes average $110,000 to $120,000.

Median price for a single family home: $104,900.

Average price for a 2BR condo: New condos cost an average of $120,000 to $140,000; existing units sale prices are in the $90,000 to $110,000 range.

Common housing styles and features: Newer homes are spacious and airy, with skylights and many windows. (Light is an important feature during the winter rainy season.) Contemporary and ranch styles are predominant.

Rental housing market: The area offers an abundant supply of duplex rentals and many new apartment complexes to choose from, but single family home rentals are scarce. The vacancy rate is less than 1 percent. The typical range of rental prices is from $525 to $750 monthly.

Average rent for a 2BR apartment: $641 a month, according to ACCRA.

Nearby areas to consider: Springfield, Santa Clara.

Earning a living

Business climate: In the past few years Eugene has tried, with a fair degree of success, to diversify what was once a timber-dependent economic base. Key areas for new development and nontimber manufacturing are high technology and food products; the city's unemployment rate recently dropped below 5 percent for the first time in 15 years. New business development has been steady, and the recent additions of SONY and Hyundai to the area promises that the trend will continue. Eugene/Springfield also is a regional retailing hub.

Help in starting a business: Lane Community College has a Business Development Center, 541-726-2200, that assists business owners through a variety of programs including "First Year in Business," "Small Business Management," "Farm Business" and "Advanced Business Management." The center also offers classes, workshops, business counseling and a resource library. The program is so strong that it was awarded an SBA grant to create Small Business Development Centers at 15 sites around the state. SCORE, 541-465-6600, offers free counseling to start-up and existing businesses.

Job market: A recent unemployment figure of 4.9 percent is the lowest since the early 1960s. Growth is expected in the food products, printing, publishing and computer software industries. Major employers include the University of Oregon, Sacred Heart Medical Center, Symantec Corporation, Guard Publishing Company and Sony. Oregon Employment Division, 541-686-7601.

Medical care

Two main medical facilities serve the Eugene/Springfield area. Sacred Heart Medical Center in Eugene, 541-686-7300, is one of the busiest hospitals in the state. The 470-bed facility is the regional center for several specialties including the Oregon Heart Center, the Cancer Care Center and the Oregon Rehabilitation Center. McKenzie-Willamette Hospital in Springfield, 541-726-4400, is a 151-bed acute-care surgical and outpatient facility offering pulmonary care, cardiology, oncology, vascular and neurosurgery and older adult services. There are more than 500 doctors and 150 dentists practicing in the Eugene area.

Services for seniors

The Trudy Kauffman Senior Center is in a historic house and has a comfortable, home-like setting. The center offers many special social events including Victorian garden brunches and old-fashioned barbecues, as well as health screenings (blood pressure checks) and a variety of classes including sign language, painting, exercise, Spanish and more. The only charges are for day trips, meals or supplies. Call 541-687-5231. The Campbell Senior Center, 541-687-5318, is a modern facility that offers many of the same programs, but has outdoor programs including hiking, cross-country skiing, canoeing and more. The center also has a golf league and a large, fully equipped woodshop. Senior and Disabled Services Division of the Lane Council of Governments, 541-687-4038, provides information and referral.

Continuing education

Lane Community College, 541-726-2200, has a strong business emphasis but also offers personal enrichment classes that help develop hobbies, leisure interests and talents. It is recognized as one of the top community colleges in the U.S. The University of Oregon, 541-346-3111, has an Elderhostel program as well as continuing education programs for persons over 65. Many regular classes can be audited at no charge.

Crime and safety

The metropolitan area is covered by city, county and state law enforcement agencies. Community policing efforts are also strong and visible, including a high-profile bicycle patrol unit. Eugene's crime index is 87 incidents per 1,000 population; Lane County's is 67 per 1,000. Both are above the national average of 55 crimes per 1,000 population. But violent crimes are rare; it's the property crimes that are a little higher than average.

Getting around town

Public transportation: Lane Transit District, 541-687-5555, provides a full service regional bus line that connects all parts of the community. Adult fares are 80 cents; seniors 62 and over pay 40 cents.

Roads and highways: I-5 (north-south), Highways 58 and 99, I-105 (east-west), Rt. 126.

Airport: Eugene Airport is served by five national and regional carriers, with more than 30 flights per day connecting to major destinations.

Let the good times roll

Recreation: If you like big numbers, you'll love Eugene: there are 13 golf courses in the area, along with 1,996 acres of park land and 50 developed parks, 98 miles of bike paths, 21 miles of off-street jogging trails (this is considered the running capital of the world) and 23 tennis courts. Eugene boasts year-round recreational activities for all ages, from fishing, boating, swimming, water skiing, kayaking, canoeing and windsurfing to ice skating in the Lane County Ice Pavilion. The nearby Cascade Mountains offer cross-country skiing and three developed downhill skiing areas, including Mt. Bachelor, the training area for the U.S. Ski Team. If you enjoy spectator sports, the A-division Eugene Emeralds are affiliated with the Atlanta Braves, and Eugene hosts many world-class track and field events.

Culture: The Oregon Bach Festival at University of Oregon Eugene is an internationally acclaimed annual event sponsored by the school of music. The Hult Center, with its state-of-the-art acoustical system, attracts top-name performers from around the world. The Silva Concert Hall features the Eugene Ballet Company and Eugene Opera Company. The Music School at University of Oregon offers a series of performances. There are seven area museums, including the University of Oregon Art Museum.

Annual events: The Oregon Bach Festival happens in late June, followed in July by the Oregon Country Fair in Veneta where Renaissance-era arts and crafts meets 1960s activism and whimsy. Art and the Vineyard on the Fourth of July features works by more than 100 West Coast artists, wine tastings from Oregon wineries, music and international foods. The Lane County Fair in August has rides, livestock shows, homemade foods, exhibits and local entertainment. Eugene Celebration in September is a three-day city block party with street performers, music, food and parade featuring the newly crowned Slug Queen.

When the kids come: Lane Education Service District Planetarium has year-round shows, touring the solar system with seasonal night skies and other cosmic adventures. The Willamette Science & Technology Center has "user-friendly" approaches to science, math and technology designed to captivate young minds. Also try the Lively Park/Splash, Fifth Street Public Market or scenic drives up the McKenzie River.

For more information

Chamber
Eugene Area Chamber
    of Commerce
1401 Willamette St.
Eugene, OR 97401
541-484-1314

Newspaper
The Register-Guard
975 High St.
Eugene, OR 97402
541-485-1234

Realtor
(Team David) David
    McJunkin or Michelle Jones
ERA Charles Ellis Realty
2001 Franklin Blvd., Suite 3
Eugene, OR 97403
541-729-2923 or 800-753-3270
Fax: 541-687-2327

38. Medford, Oregon

Nickname: The Pear City
County: Jackson
Area code: 541
Population: 53,280
County population: 146,389
% of population over 65: 16.2
Region: Rogue River Valley of Southern Oregon
Closest metro area: Eugene, 165 mi.
Average home price: $90,000 to $130,000
Best reasons to retire here: Friendly, small-town atmosphere, fabulous cultural and continuing education offerings.

Medford at a glance

Gold was first discovered in the Rogue River Valley in 1852, but more than 100 years later there's a new rush going on as people seek out Medford and nearby Ashland for a golden retirement. This part of southern Oregon offers a low cost of living, low property taxes, no sales tax, high-quality health care, outstanding recreational and educational opportunities, and world-class cultural events. Was there something else you were looking for? With the Cascade Mountains to the east of Medford and the Siskiyou Mountains to the south, this is an exceptionally beautiful region. Medford is also a very livable town. The rural environment has been laid out for the ease of getting around, and thanks to long-range planning, the business and residential areas are uncongested. House hunting in Medford is a dream come true—pine trees, mountain views, farmland, city living, incorporated towns, riverfront sites—it's all here, and at prices that are affordable, considering the amount of house and property you get. No wonder Californians are crossing the border in caravans. The trouble is, there's so much to do here, you may begin to wonder why you bought such a lovely home. Spend your days skiing, golfing, fishing, hiking, or enjoying the mountains or the beautiful Oregon coast. Culture abounds with the nearby Ashland's annual, world-renowned Shakespeare Festival. It's also a fruit lover's paradise—75 percent of the nation's Bosc pear crop grows here (this is the home of Harry & David). Medford is indeed a sweet place to be.

Possible drawbacks: If you want the hustle and bustle of city life, you will not find it here. Medford is a small, laid-back town. Also, air travel to and from this small community is somewhat limited.

Climate

Elevation: 1,380'	Avg. high/low:	Avg. inches rain	snow	Avg. # days precip.	Avg. % humidity
Jan.	44/29	3.2	-	14	88
April	64/37	0.98	-	9	70
July	90/54	0.25	-	5	63
Oct.	67/39	2.1	-	8	74
YEAR	66/40	20.0	8.1	-	-
# days 32° or below: 91			# days 90° or warmer: 48		

What things cost

Overview: Current comparative data on the cost of living in Medford was not available, but the ACCRA composite index for Klamath Falls, about 78 miles to the east of Medford, is 4 percent below the national average overall.

Gas company: Call W.P. Natural Gas, 541-772-5281. No deposit is required, and there are no hook-up fees. Gas heat and appliances costs average $50 to $60 a month; for appliances only, average bills are closer to $30 monthly.

Electric company: Call Pacific Power, 541-776-5420. No connect charges, and no deposits for new residential customers. Monthly bills for all-electric homes run $60 to $80 monthly depending upon usage. If the home has only electric appliances, bills run $20 to $30.

Phone company: Contact US West, 800-244-1111. Service connection fee is $12; deposits are not required pending a credit check. Basic service is $16.30 per month.

Water and sewer: Medford Water Commission, 541-770-4511. Renters pay a deposit of $40. No deposit for homeowners.

Cable company: Call TCI Cablevision, 541-770-1851.

Car registration, license: Licenses are $26.25 and are renewed every four years. New residents must obtain a license and registration immediately upon establishing residency. Registration fees are $30 and valid for 24 months. A used vehicle from another state requires physical inspection of identification by the Department of Motor Vehicles. Fee is $4. No state sales or property tax on vehicles.

The tax ax

Sales tax: Oregon has no state sales tax.

State income tax: Graduated from 5 to 9 percent depending upon income bracket. There is a deduction for up to $3,000 of federal income tax paid.

Retirement income: Federal, state and private pensions are not exempt from income tax. Social Security benefits are exempt. There is a $5,000 standard deduction for married couples 65 and older filing jointly.

Property taxes: Property taxes have been changing as a result of a law called Measure 5. Under this law property is assessed at 100 percent of real market value. The tax rate has decreased as the law has been phased in. In 1995 it reached its final cap of $15 per $1,000 of assessed value. Tax assessor's office, 541-776-7077.

Local real estate

Overview: Rural properties are showing 10 to 15 percent appreciation annually, with taxes currently stable. Medford is both a permanent residence market and a second home market. Many people purchase land with a mobile home or house of lesser value on it until they are ready to build their dream home, a strategy that has advantages with double-digit appreciation in rural areas. Look realistically at the amount of acreage you truly need, and find an agent familiar with zoning regulations.

Median price for a single family home: $118,000.

Average price for a 3BR/2BA home: New homes, $100,000 to $130,000; resales average $90,000 to $120,000.

Average price for a 2BR condo: New condominiums average about $115,000, while resales average $80,000.

Unique housing features: Retirees often choose rural properties in forested areas, finding that the land can be left in its natural state, making a nice, low-maintenance property. Log homes are popular in Applegate Valley, located west of Medford.

Rental housing market: Rentals for apartments and duplexes range from $350 to $700 per month, while homes range from $500 to $850 per month. The vacancy rate has been about 5 to 7 percent.

Average rent for a 2BR apartment: $450 to $600 monthly.

Communities or developments most popular with retirees: Sun Oaks is a gated community close to medical services, golf and shopping.

Nearby area to consider: Ashland.

Earning a living

Business climate: Medford fosters an entrepreneurial spirit. The city has one of the highest per capita small business establishment rates in the nation. Retail growth has been booming here for five years, and the growth rate has surpassed that of Eugene and Portland. Medford is the industrial, trade and service center of southern Oregon and northern California. Agriculture is a significant part of the economy, with more than 75 percent of the nation's Bosc pears coming from this area. Medford is also the regional medical center for southern Oregon and northern California.

Help in starting a business: Southern Oregon Regional Economic Development Incorporated (SOREDI), 541-773-8946, is the economic development council that serves Jackson and Josephine counties. SOREDI also provides some start-up loans. Southern Oregon State College hosts a Small Business Development Center, 541-772-3478, helping new and existing small businesses through confidential counseling, courses, seminars and workshops and employee training services. There is also a resource center and computer lab.

Job market: Part-time opportunities are plentiful in retail and service businesses. Major employers are Harry & David, Rogue Valley Medical and Boise Cascade Corporation. Unemployment has been on the high side for a decade in both Jackson and Josephine counties, ranging from a low of 6.3 percent to a high of 9.4 percent. The good news: The trend has been steadily downward since 1992, and the 6.3 rate is the most recent figure.

Medical care

The largest, most comprehensive facility in the area is Rogue Valley Medical Center, 541-773-4900. It is part of a large medical system in Medford that includes the Rogue Valley Medical Center Hospice, Home Solutions, and a skilled nursing facility called Hearthstone. The hospital includes the Heart Center and the Cancer Treatment Center. It's a regional referral center that also offers Asante Senior Advantage, 541-770-5233, a free membership program for people 55 and over that offers discounts from area merchants, transportation to medical appointments, the Lifeline System, free fitness screenings and a quarterly newsletter and magazine. Providence Medford Medical Center, 541-773-6611, has heart care, rehabilitation, and the 55 Plus program for seniors, 541-770-1366, which offers travel and activities, free and low-cost health care screenings, lectures on health topics, support groups and Lifeline personal emergency response.

Services for seniors

Medford Senior Center, 541-772-2273, offers health screenings such as blood pressure checks and hearing checks, as well as educational seminars and entertainment. The center also hosts line dancing classes, clogging, square dancing, a senior writers' group, billiards, crafts and a sing-along club. It's also a weekday noon meal site that offers live music during lunch Monday through Thursday. Senior and Disabled Services of Jackson County, 541-776-6222, offers information and referral services, case management and in-home care, among other services.

Continuing education

Southern Oregon State College has more interesting programs for seniors than any other institution of higher education found. The Extended Campus Program includes an Elderhostel, 541-552-6677, which offers a Lectures and Lunches commuter option and courses on the Oregon Shakespeare Festival. The college also has Senior Ventures, 800-257-0577, offering educational and travel opportunities throughout the West, as well as internationally. The college also has developed a program called SOLIR (Southern Oregon Learning in Retirement), 541-522-6048. Seniors plan curriculum, select instructors and assist with administration. Annual membership costs $75, which covers all of the instructional and administrative expenses for noncredit courses.

Crime and safety

Medford reported 99 crimes per 1,000 population, and the county rate dropped to 61 crimes per 1,000 population. However, violent crime is rare in Medford and countywide.

Getting around town

Public transportation: Rogue Valley Transportation District, 541-779-2877, offers fixed-route regular bus service and a one-call private taxi service that connects individuals to the routes.

Roads and highways: I-5, Highway 62 (Crater Lake Highway).

Airport: Rogue Valley International Airport (10 minutes from downtown) is served by United Airlines and Sierra Expressway.

Let the good times roll

Recreation: With its moderate climate and beautiful landscapes, recreation centers around outdoor activities. One does not have to travel far to camp at Crater Lake National Park, fish on Diamond Lake, raft on the Rogue River or ski on Mount Ashland. There are numerous golf courses, snowmobiling for those who enjoy winter sports, and hiking and wildlife viewing all year long. For bikers and hikers, the Bear Creek Greenway offers two bike and nature trails. Cross-country skiing is great on Mount Ashland and Hyatt Lake, and snowmobiling, snowshoeing and cross-country skiing are available at Crater Lake, Diamond Lake, Fish Lake and Lake of the Woods. Sports spectators will enjoy minor league baseball with the Southern Oregon Athletics.

Culture: This area is one of the best places in the world to learn about the theater. The internationally acclaimed Oregon Shakespeare Festival operates eight months of the year in nearby Ashland. Fully staged Shakespearean productions and other classic and contemporary plays can be enjoyed here. Five miles from Medford, in the historic town of Jacksonville, the summer months bring the Peter Britt Festival, featuring world-class performers of classical, jazz, country and folk music. Other performing arts groups include Actors' Theatre, Craeterian Theatre, Lyric Theatre and the Cygnet Theatre Group.

Annual events: February begins the Oregon Shakespeare Festival, which continues through October in Ashland; the Pear Blossom Festival in April features pageants, a 10-mile run, a street fair, golf tournament and much more. In June, it's time for the Peter Britt festivals of music in nearby Jacksonville, and in July, enjoy the Jackson County Fair with livestock shows, entertainment and carnival rides. August brings the Medford National Air Show, and October brings the three-day Medford Jazz Jubilee.

When the kids come: Oregon Caves, a series of limestone rooms and galleries located 80 miles southwest of Medford, makes for a spectacular and educational day trip. Visit Butte Creek Mill in Eagle Point—it is said to be the last original operating water-powered grist mill in the west. In Ashland the Pacific Northwest Museum of Natural History is open every day, except for Thanksgiving and Christmas.

For more information

Chamber
Medford/Jackson County
   Chamber of Commerce
101 East 8th St.
Medford, OR 97501
541-779-4847

Newspapers
The Mail Tribune
111 N. Fir
Medford, OR 97501
541-776-4455

The Ashland Daily Tidings
1661 Siskiyou Blvd.
Ashland, OR 97520
541-482-3456

Realtor
Jeff Vinyard
Ramsay Realty
7604 Highway 238
Jacksonville, OR 97530
541-891-1184
Fax: 541-899-1772

39. Charleston, South Carolina

Nickname: The Holy City
County: Charleston; also Berkeley; Dorchester
Area code: 803
Population: 80,414
County population: 295,039 (Charleston)
% of population over 65: 10
Region: South central coast
Closest metro area: Savannah, Ga., 105 mi.
Average home price: $70,000 to $120,000
Best reasons to retire here: Great climate, culture and graciousness of the Old South, luxurious retirement and resort areas.

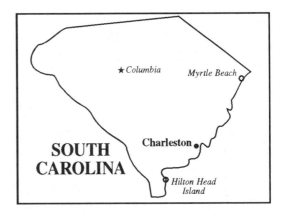

Charleston at a glance

Charleston is one of the most charming and picturesque coastal cities in the South. Originally the state capital, it has the feel of a 17th-century European town. Known as the "Holy City," Charleston has always guaranteed religious choice, and the city is the home of the nation's oldest existing Reform Jewish congregation. Historic areas lure residents and visitors alike with the promise of a stroll into the past. Quaint, narrow streets and stately antebellum homes tell the story of Charleston's rich Southern heritage. (As the first U.S. city to serve as a model for preservation, Charleston boasts 1,000 historic homes, gardens and buildings, circa 1670 to the 1840s.) Residents enjoy antiquing in the King Street shops, and there are many restaurants to enjoy, featuring everything from Southern barbecue to five-star French cuisine. With 90 miles of Atlantic beaches, it's an ideal year-round spot to soak up the great outdoors. Cool off in the summer with a morning ocean swim, then get in the car and, within hours, enjoy the cool Blue Ridge Mountain air. For the upscale buyer, the barrier coastal developments of Wild Dunes, Kiawah and Seabrook are gorgeous resort communities with fabulous amenities. As for taxes, South Carolina offers welcome relief. It has one of the lowest per-capita tax rates (combined state and local taxes), which contributes to a low cost of living.

Possible drawbacks: Living in a low-lying area means being on standby to batten down the hatches during hurricane season, and in recent years, residents have had to "batten" more than once. The humidity in the summer will have you reaching for mint juleps or anything else you can find to cool you off. Then you'll turn around and reach again.

Climate

Elevation: 46'	Avg. high/low:	Avg. inches		Avg. # days precip.	Avg. % humidity
		rain	snow		
Jan.	60/37	3	10	10	75
April	76/537	3	7	7	70
July	89/71	8.2	14	14	80
Oct.	77/55	4	6	6	79
YEAR	75/54	50.0	-	-	-
# days 32° or below: 39			# days 90° or warmer: 51		

What things cost

Overview: ACCRA statistics show that the overall cost of living in Charleston is 2.5 percent below the national average, with most major categories well below average except utilities, which are almost 25 percent more expensive than the national norm. Medical costs in Charleston are slightly above average.

Gas and electric company: South Carolina Electric and Gas Co., 803-554-7234. There is no charge to connect to service, and deposits can be waived after a credit check. Average gas and electric bill: $127 monthly.

Phone company: Contact Bell South, 803-780-2355 or 800-336-0014. The service connection fee is $40 and deposits are only required pending a credit check. Basic monthly service costs about $23.

Water and sewer: City of Charleston, 803-727-6800. There is an origination fee of $25 for water service and $15 for sewer service. Deposits are not required.

Cable company: Comcast Cablevision, 803-554-6618.

Car registration, license: New residents may use a driver's license from another state for 90 days, but then must obtain a South Carolina license by taking a written test. All new residents have 45 days after establishing residency to purchase South Carolina license tags. Before getting the tag, you are required to file a motor vehicle tax return in the county of residence. After taxes are paid, tags may be obtained from the South Carolina Highway Department. For driver's license and registration information, 800-442-1368.

The tax ax

Sales tax: 6 percent (Charleston); 5 percent (Dorchester and Berkeley).

State income tax: South Carolina has a tiered indexed personal income tax that ranges from 2.5 percent to 7 percent on all income above $11,250. There is no deduction for federal income tax paid.

Retirement income: There is a deduction of up to $10,000 per person adjusted gross income for federal, state and private pensions received by people 65 and older. Social Security benefits are exempt.

Property taxes: To estimate taxes, multiply the home value times 4 percent and multiply again by the current millage rate. The average rate in Charleston County in 1996 is .2571. Thus, tax on a $100,000 home would come to approximately $1,030 a year. Assessor's office, 803-723-6718.

Local real estate

Overview: This region has it all: antebellum mansions, beachfront property, townhouses, condos and new houses on the links. James Island and West Ashley are mostly older homes on or near laid-back Folly Beach. Summerville (Dorchester County) attracts the military and Goose Creek (Berkeley County) is rural with lower-priced homes. Overall, there is much to choose from in the under-$110,000 range, although condos and townhouses are somewhat limited.

Average price for a 3BR/2BA home: $70,000 to $90,000 covers the lower-end range for new and resale homes. A larger home (3 or 4BR/2BA with 2-car garage, in a development with tennis, pools or hiker/biker trails) goes for $120,000 to $200,000. Median home price: $114,000.

Average price for a 2BR condo: New and resale units range from $80,000 to $125,000.

Common housing styles and features: New colonials and capes are popular inland, with contemporaries found on the beachfront. Older resales are mostly 3BR/2BA with garages. Don't expect to find basements. Exteriors are mostly brick, wood and vinyl siding. Interiors show cathedral ceilings, wrap-around porches and gracious master suites.

Rental housing market: Where available, 3BR houses are $700 to $850 monthly. Townhouse apartments and condos average $600 per month.

Nearby areas to consider: With the the new bridge and I-526 open, Daniel Island and Cainhoy will see a construction boom. Also try Summerville, Isle of Palms, Mt. Pleasant and Kiawah.

Earning a living

Business climate: The economy has strengthened in recent years, as the area has attracted new investment and jobs. Beginning with Nucor's announcement that it would invest $500 million to build a mini-steel mill in Berkeley County, the region attracted $1.2 billion in investment and 7,845 jobs during 1995 alone. In total, 248 new firms and 92 existing companies joined Nucor by the end of that year.

Help in starting a business: The Small Business Resource Center, 803-853-3900, assists current and prospective business owners with marketing, advertising, human resources, financial management and loan information, and other issues. SCORE, 803-727-4778, presents seminars every six weeks in the SBRC offices. The Small Business Development Center, 803-727-2020, at Trident Technical College, offers free, one-on-one counseling.

Job market: The region's employment picture has brightened recently. Total civilian employment had a net gain during the year when operational closure occurred at the Naval Base and Shipyard and eliminated active duty positions and civilian jobs. Nonetheless, the area's total employment rose by 1.3 percent. The services sector experienced the largest gain, expanding by 26 percent. Part-time jobs are available in retail and in the burgeoning hospitality industry. Unemployment is approximately 4.5 percent. Charleston County Job Line, 803-724-0694. South Carolina Employment Security Commission Job Service, 803-792-7046.

Medical care

There are 10 major hospitals in the region. Four are within an eight-block radius: St. Francis Xavier, 803-402-1200; Roper Hospital, 803-724-2000; Charleston Memorial, 803-577-0600; and VA Medical Center, 803-577-5011. The Medical University of South Carolina Medical Center, 803-792-1414, is the state's largest teaching center and has a well-respected organ transplant program. It has the only tertiary care and Level I trauma center in the area. Trident Regional Naval Hospital is a private facility in Charleston, specializing in coronary care and renal dialysis.

Services for seniors

The Senior Citizens Center, 803-722-4127, offers free exercise and crafts classes, as well as legal assistance, blood pressure checks, an escort service to medical and dental appointments and an employment service that matches seniors looking for jobs with potential employers. The Trident Area Agency on Aging offers Elderlink, 803-745-1710, which provides information on services and referrals to other agencies throughout the area.

Crime and safety

Charleston is as safe as any area this size. In fact, there's less crime today than 20 years ago, because public safety awareness has become a top priority. Charleston proper has the highest ratio of police for every 10,000 citizens of any city in the U.S. The crime rate for both the city and the county is about 75 incidents per 1,000 population, but violent crime is rare. Crime Stoppers, 803-554-1111.

Continuing education

The College of Charleston has the Center for Creative Retirement, 803-953-5822, which offers personal enrichment and liberal arts classes plus tours and discussion groups to persons 50 and over. Classes can last from one day to a semester and fees vary. The College of Charleston also hosts an Elderhostel and offers noncredit continuing education courses on various topics, including computers, photography, fiction, personal finance, literature, writing, architecture and foreign language. The Shepherd's Center of Charleston, 803-722-2789, has life enrichment, liberal arts and wellness classes that last from four to eight weeks. The classes are offered free of charge to people who are 55 and over. The Trident Technical College division of Continuing Education and Economic Development, 803-572-6152, offers computer classes for seniors. Fees are $10 and below.

Getting around town

Public transportation: Charleston City Bus Lines, 803-747-0922, offers service throughout the city and to the nearby barrier islands. Adult fares are 75 cents and seniors can ride for 25 cents during midday, after rush hour and on the weekends.

Roads and highways: I-26, I-95, I-526, US 17, 52, 78, 176 and 701.

Airport: Charleston International Airport, which is 8 miles from downtown, is served by several national and regional carriers.

Seaport: The Port of Charleston is the second-largest container port on the Atlantic coast.

Let the good times roll

Recreation: The many waterways and barrier islands off Charleston make it an ideal place to enjoy water sports. Sailing is popular, and the freshwater fishing on Lakes Marion and Moultrie (Berkeley County) are excellent. There are 15 major parks and gardens in the Trident area, including: Cypress Gardens; the 600-acre James Island County Park with bike and hiking trails; Magnolia Plantation Gardens and Palmetto Island County Park, a 900-acre family-oriented nature facility. The Charleston area is also a golfer's paradise, with dozens of courses, including the spectacular Wild Dunes in Isle of Palms. Sports fanatics enjoy the Charleston Rainbows (minor league team of the San Diego Padres) and collegiate sports. A gorgeous new coliseum, which will likely attract a professional hockey team, is under construction in North Charleston.

Culture: The Charleston Area Arts Council and the Charleston Cultural Affairs Committee bring music, theater and art to the region. They boast their own symphony orchestra, a community repertory theater, and ballet and recital groups. Historic museums include the Gibbes Museum of Art (which offers a splendid showcase of American art and Southern history, as well as one of the finest collections of miniatures in the world), the Charleston Museum (the oldest in North America) and Patriot's Point (the world's largest maritime and naval museum). Dock Street Theater, which is one of America's first playhouses, offers free performances.

Annual events: In January, enjoy oysters, roasted or raw, at the Lowcountry Oyster Festival. February brings the Southeastern Wildlife Exposition, featuring wildlife arts, crafts and collectibles. The Spoleto Festival USA is a celebration of music and art that attracts thousands from around the world for 17 days in May and June. In September and October its time for Candlelight Tours of Homes and Gardens in historic downtown Charleston.

When the kids come: Edisto Beach State Park is the perfect place for camping and watersports (one of the most popular on the coast). Favorite stops for kids are the waterfront park at the foot of Vendue Range (there are huge water sprays to cool off in) and boat rides through Cape Romain National Wildlife Refuge (an exciting wilderness experience).

For more information

Chamber
Charleston Metro Chamber
  of Commerce
P.O. Box 975
Charleston, SC 29402
803-577-2510

Newspaper
The Post & Courier
134 Columbus St.
Charleston, SC 29403
803-722-2223

Realtor
Shirley Gilbert, Broker
Century 21-Limerick
  East, Inc.
389 Johnnie Dodds Blvd.,
  Suite 103
Mount Pleasant, SC 29464
800-531-6030

40. Austin, Texas

Nicknames: Silicon Hills, River City
County: Travis
Area code: 512
Population: 527,600
County population: 656,200
% of population over 65: 7.2
Region: Central Texas on the Colorado River
Closest metro area: San Antonio, 80 mi.
Average home price: $120,000 to $150,000
Best reasons to retire here: Mild winters, great outdoor recreation, reasonable cost of living, university influence.

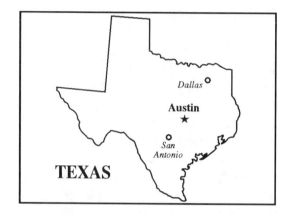

Austin at a glance

To live deep in the heart of Texas Hill Country is to have the privilege of nature's grandeur at your doorstep. The first thing that strikes newcomers is the sparkling lakes and gently rolling terrain. Austin has never needed to spruce things up with a manmade skyline (the Colorado River meanders through the center of town), and yet it has developed as much in the corporate, political and educational arenas as the largest cities in the country. In fact, it's now the second-fastest growing city in the U.S. It's the capital of Texas, and true to Texas form, the state capital building is seven feet higher than the U.S. Capital building. As home of the University of Texas, there is more "intelligence" here than in the CIA. The attitude is progressive, and the technology is cutting-edge, but the city also know how to get back to the basics: a high quality of life is first and foremost. For retirees, the great appeal is the great outdoors—12 months of waterfront fun, hiking and fishing. The great *indoors* isn't so bad, either, with the university having so much to share with the community such as the Learning Activities for Mature People (LAMP) program and extensive cultural programs and activities. The climate is mostly mild, services for seniors are good (take a free ride on the bus anytime), housing is abundant and affordable, the health care facilities are impressive and, compared to many other big cities, living costs are within reason. The extra bonus is no personal income tax. Austin is indeed a "capital" city.

Possible drawbacks: The summers can be extremely hot, and there is almost no rain. Housing prices and property taxes are on the rise, and the housing and rental markets are very tight.

Climate

Elevation: 634'	Avg. high/low:	Avg. inches		Avg. # days precip.	Avg. % humidity
		rain	snow		
Jan.	60/50	1.8	-	8	71
April	79/69	3.5	-	7	65
July	95/85	1.9	-	5	62
Oct.	81/70	3.0	-	6	65
YEAR	79/68	32.0	-	-	-
# days 32° or below: 24			# days 90° or warmer: 116		

What things cost

Overview: According to ACCRA, prices in Austin are about 4 percent below average overall, with housing 7 percent below. Health care costs are 3 percent below normal, while transportation runs 8 percent higher.

Gas company: Southern Union Gas Co., 512-477-6461. A deposit of $50 is required for all new customers, unless a letter of credit is provided. Connection fee is $25. Gas appliances only run approximately $30 monthly. Gas heat is not available.

Electric, water and sewer: City of Austin Utility Department, 512-476-7721. Turn-on fee of $20 and deposit required, ranging from $60 to $170 (can be waived with letter of credit), will get you started on electricity, water, sewer and trash removal. Typical all-electric bills for a single-family home run approximately $150 a month; water, sewer and trash removal averages $75 monthly.

Phone company: Southwestern Bell Telephone Co., 512-609-3333. The installation charge is $50. Deposits are not required if you have record of previous service. Basic rate is $13.03.

Cable company: Austin Cablevision, 512-418-4000; CableMaxx of Austin, 512-346-6299.

Car license, registration: New Texas residents must obtain a Texas driver's license within 30 days after establishing residency. A 4-year license costs $16. Renewals are done by mail. Automobiles must also be registered within 30 days. Vehicles must pass an inspection and proof of insurance is required. Registration fees vary depending upon model year or weight in pounds, but are generally less than $75.

The tax ax

Sales tax: Texas sales tax is 6.25 percent. Austin adds 1 percent, and the Metro Transit Authority adds another 1 percent, for an 8.25-percent total. Prescription drugs, groceries and medical services are exempt.

State income tax: There are no state, county or city income taxes in Texas.

Retirement income: There are no estate taxes and no inheritance taxes.

Property taxes: Austin property tax is $2.394 per $100 assessed value, and homes are assessed at 100 percent of their market value. Taxes on a $120,000 home would run approximately $2,873 with no exemptions. Tax assessor's office, 512-473-9473.

Local real estate

Overview: Housing prices and property taxes in Austin have both been on the rise in recent years. Most retirees who move to Austin stay permanently, although some opt to move to smaller towns in the surrounding area. Austin is becoming known as Silicon Hills because of the tremendous growth of the electronics and high-tech industries. As a result of the population growth, the housing market is very tight and homes moves fast.

Average price for a 3BR/2BA home: New homes average $130,000 to $150,000, while resales run about $120,000.

Median price for a single family home: $101,400.

Average price for a 2BR condo: New, $120,000, resales, $110,000.

Unique housing features: Most homes are on concrete slabs, and virtually all of them have central air conditioning. Siding is usually in stone, and design emphasis is on porches, decks and patios to enjoy the warm weather.

Rental housing market: Despite about 4,700 new multi-family units added since 1991, most such units are about 98 percent occupied, driving rental prices up. According to our sources, average rent for a 2BR apartment runs about $1,000, although the Chamber of Commerce reports numbers considerably lower, at $650. Houses run $800 to $1,400 per month and rentals are scarce.

Communities or developments most popular with retirees: Sun City, north of Austin.

Nearby areas to consider: Dripping Springs, Wimberly and Lockhart.

Earning a living

Business climate: Austin has become a high-tech research and development center after an extensive recruitment effort mounted by city leaders is the 1960s and 70s. Its reputation as a high-tech business center has led to the development of many jobs. The city's advanced telecommunications system has helped to spur this growth. To get in touch with the business community, pick up the *Austin Business Journal,* 512-328-0180.

Help in starting a business: The Small Business Administration and SCORE can be reached at 512-442-7235. Call the Small Business Development Center at 512-326-2256, which offers a workshop, "Essentials for Starting a Small Business." The workshop is offered monthly, and participation makes you eligible for free, one-on-one business counseling, including assistance with business plans, marketing, loan applications and more.

Job market: Many high-tech manufacturing businesses have plants or headquarters here, including IBM, Texas Instruments, Dell Computer, Unisys, Sematech and Lockheed. In 1994, there were 32 corporate relocations to Austin, which are a small part of the 27,700 new jobs created in the city that year, making it the top-ranked city in Texas for job growth. The service industry has surpassed government as the number-one employer in the area. Experience Unlimited, 512-480-3006, is a city-run referral system that puts senior adults wanting full- or part-time employment in touch with businesses and individuals that need work to be done. Job Services of the Texas Employment Commission, 512-478-8734.

Medical care

Options in health care are abundant in Austin, with 12 major hospitals, more than 2,500 beds and 1,500 licensed physicians. Major facilities include the Austin Diagnostic Medical Center and Clinics, 512-901-1000, specializing in skilled nursing, cancer treatment and rehabilitation. Brackenridge Hospital, 512-476-6461, a regional referral center and teaching hospital offering standard care and investigational drug therapies, cardiology and the Texas Cancer Center. Columbia South Austin Medical Center, 512-447-2211, a medical and surgical hospital with CT scanning, cardiovascular care center and wellness classes.

Continuing education

The University of Texas-Austin offers the Learning Activities for Mature People (LAMP) program, 512-471-8030. The volunteer-run program for persons 55 and older includes lectures and discussions led by university faculty. Subjects include arts, business, technology, public affairs, history and lifestyles. There are three 6-week sessions annually, and the cost is $125 per year. Austin Community College's Center for Career and Business Development, 512-223-7542, has courses in art and crafts, communications, language and culture, photography and more. For persons 50 and over, Concordia University at Austin has a Lifetime Learning Institute, 512-452-7662, ext. 1139. The courses are noncredit, and cost $12 each. The City of Austin Parks and Recreation Department also offers classes for seniors. These include fitness and wellness, arts and much more.

Services for seniors

The Capital Area Agency on Aging, 512-443-7653, provides insurance benefits counseling and assistance, case management and an ombudsman service. The Senior Activity Center, 512-474-5921, provides recreational activities, classes, health and wellness programs, dancing and much more. A nominal donation is requested. A second center, Conley-Guerrero Senior Center, 512-478-7695, provides the same services. An information and referral service is offered by Family Elder Care, 512-451-0106, which can provide contact information for more than 900 listings in a five-country area.

Crime and safety

The total crime index for the county was 75 incidents per 1,000 population, while the city of Austin reported 80 crimes per 1,000. Both indexes are higher than the national average of 55 incidents per 1,000. The Austin Police Department has 20 community awareness programs including home security checks.

Getting around town

Public transportation: Capital Metro offers citywide service and some suburban coverage. Fares are 65 cents and seniors 65 and over ride free. A Senior Card can be purchased for $3, or a driver's license can be used for ID.

Roads and highways: I-10, I-35, US 183, 290, Loop 360.

Airports: Robert Mueller Municipal Airport is serviced by 10 airlines, but by the end of 1998, the new Austin-Bergstrom International Airport is scheduled to be in operation.

Let the good times roll

Recreation: City outdoor recreation facilities are vast, with more than 14,000 acres of parkland to enjoy and plenty of waterfront, too. A favorite spot is Zilker Park with its spring-fed swimming pool. Sail on Lake Travis, go rafting on the Guadalupe River, take off at the Town Lake Hike and Bike Trail, or enjoy a round of golf on one of 21 public and private courses in the area. There are also more than 200 tennis courts in Austin. Also easily accessible are hunting, sailing, water-skiing, windsurfing, rowing, canoeing and mountain biking. The University of Texas fields nationally ranked teams in a number of sports including football, basketball, baseball, swimming and track and field. The Dallas Cowboy's training camp is here at St. Edward's University. The Austin Ice Bats, a new WPHL pro hockey team begin play in October 1996. The Ice Bats are named after Austin's world famous free-tail bats that live under the Congress Avenue bridge.

Culture: Austin calls itself the "Live Music Capital of the World," with more than 120 live music venues featuring styles from blues to jazz, from hard rock to country/western and tejano. The Austin Symphony, Austin Ballet and Austin Lyric Opera have a variety of programs and concerts throughout the year. Each spring Austin hosts "South by Southwest," an international acclaimed music, film and multimedia event. Museums include the LBJ Presidential Library and Museum, the George Washington Carver Museum and the Huntington Art Museum at the University of Texas.

Annual events: February is Carnivale Brasileiro, an extravaganza with conga lines and lavish costumes; March brings Spamarama, (a festival honoring Spam) and the Kite Festival at Zilker Park, a 60-year old event featuring handmade kites that draws 10,000 spectators; in May it's time for the Liberty Mutual Legends of Golf Tournament with the Senior PGA Tour; June brings the Clarksville-West End Jazz and Arts Festival; August is time for the Austin Aqua Festival, an eight-day extravaganza of boat races and outdoor concerts; October is time for Great Tastes of Austin; December is time for the Zilker Park Tree Lighting and Trail of Lights.

When the kids come: Try the rotunda at the state capital, Barton's Spring (great swimming), the Austin Children's Museum or the Alamo in nearby San Antonio (80 miles).

For more information

Chamber
Greater Austin Chamber
   of Commerce
111 Congress Ave.
P.O. Box 1967
Austin, TX 78767
512-478-9383

Newspaper
American Statesman
305 S. Congress Ave.
Austin, TX 78704
512-445-3000

Realtor
Laura Sternthal, GRI
Coldwell Banker, Richard
   Smith Realtors
5000 Bee Cave Rd., Suite 200
Austin, TX 78746
512-328-8200
Fax: 512-328-2559

41. Brownsville, Texas

Nickname: The Tropical Tip of Texas
County: Cameron
Area code: 210
Population: 135,260
County population: 293,418
% of population over 65: 10.6 (50% in winter)
Region: Rio Grande Valley
Closest metro area: Corpus Christi, 100 mi.
Average home price: $76,000 to $135,000
Best reasons to retire here: Fascinating culture, proximity to Mexico and beaches, low cost of living, low tax burden.

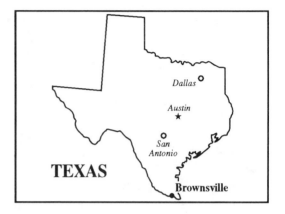

Brownsville at a glance

With the swaying palm trees, fragrant citrus groves, more than 800 species of native flowers and wide, modern avenues as a backdrop, it's easy to confuse this place with Florida! But make no mistake, the Rio Grande Valley is distinctly different. It's Mexican in its heritage and multicultural in its lifestyle. For decades, Brownsville has been the home base of winter Texans—approximately 200,000 seniors migrate from the Midwest to whoop it up for a few months. But in recent years, tens of thousands of people have made this area their year-round home, both for the interesting cultural climate and low cost of living, estimated to be as much as 14 percent below the national average. And Texas is one of only a few states with no income tax. The hot spot is neighboring Mexico, where you can literally walk across the border for fun, food and dollar-stretching shopping in Matamoros, Brownsville's sister city (it's actually five times the size of Brownsville). The fishing and hunting in this part of the country are superb, and the unspoiled beaches and gentle trade winds on nearby South Padre Island invite you to enjoy water sports. What's more, it's a birdwatcher's paradise, offering glimpses of brilliantly colored green jays and Altamira orioles in the area's many nature sanctuaries (which the birds share with ocelots and jagarundis). Brownsville truly offers something very different—"the two-nation vacation" you can enjoy year-round.

Possible drawbacks: You don't hear about "summer Texans" because it gets hot, hot, hot. From June through August the temperature is in the 90s, and the humidity is 75 percent. Also, crowds and traffic come with this territory, and being close to the border brings its share of crime, including car theft.

Climate

Elevation: 23'	Avg. high/low:	Avg. inches		Avg. # days precip.	Avg. % humidity
		rain	snow		
Jan.	70/51	1.4	-	7	77
April	83/67	1.3	-	4	73
July	93/76	1.1	-	5	73
Oct.	85/67	3.3	-	7	73
YEAR	82/65	26.0	-	-	-
# days 32° or below: 3			# days 90° or warmer: 117		

What things cost

Overview: According to the Chamber of Commerce, the composite cost of living index for Brownsville is 14 percent below the national average, with housing costs almost 25 percent below the average. Utilities costs are higher than the national average by 5 percent.

Gas company: Call Southern Union Gas Company, 210-542-3531. There's a $50 deposit inside Brownsville; $25 outside. Deposits can be waived with a letter of credit. There is a $20 connection fee. Most housing in the area is all-electric.

Electric company: Brownsville Public Utilities Department (PUD), 210-982-6100. Deposit for all utilities, including water, sewer and electricity, is $50, but can be waived with a letter of credit. Connection fees are $25 for electric and $5 for water. PUD serves 80 percent of Brownsville, the balance is split by Central Power & Light Company, 800-274-2611; and Magic Valley Electric Cooperative, 210-831-0595. Average monthly bill: $80 to $100.

Phone company: Southwestern Bell Telephone Company, 800-464-7928 or 512-967-6500. Basic installation, $38.35; basic service, $8.45 to $13.35 monthly. No deposit or advance with verifiable previous service.

Cable company: Call TCI Cablevision, 800-222-5355.

Car registration, license: New Texas residents must obtain a Texas driver's license within 30 days after establishing residency. A four-year license costs $16. Renewals are done by mail. Automobiles must also be registered within 30 days. Vehicles must pass an inspection, and proof of insurance is required. Registration fees vary depending upon model year or weight in pounds, but are generally less than $75. Department of Motor Vehicles, 210-542-5301.

The tax ax

Sales tax: Texas state sales tax is 6.25 percent, and Brownsville residents pay an additional 2 percent, for a total of 8.25 percent. Drugs, groceries and medical services are exempt.

State income tax: None

Retirement income: There are no estate taxes and no inheritance taxes.

Property taxes: Homes are assessed at 100 percent of market value. The total property tax rate is about $2.45 per $100 of assessed value. Property taxes on a $100,000 home run approximately $2,450. Tax assessor's office, 210-544-0800.

Local real estate

Overview: Prices have been steady overall in recent years, with asking prices on new construction edging upward slightly. Taxes have also increased slightly. Most retirees relocate to the area permanently, although many begin with second homes in the area. For the most part, they don't purchase a home like the one they just sold. Winter Texans and other retirees head for mobile home parks and modular homes, and the RV parks are where all the action takes place. It's estimated that there are more than 500 such parks in the Brownsville/Harlingen/McAllen area.

Average price for a 3BR/1½BA home: Larger, newer homes are $108,000 to $135,000, while resales average $76,000 to 95,000.

Average price for a 2BR condo: New: $52,000; resales average $43,000.

Common housing styles and features: Most new homes are brick veneer exterior, but Spanish-style architecture with stucco exteriors is also popular. Ranch homes without basements are common.

Rental housing market: Condos are available for $450 per month and up; homes begin at $600. The rental market is very tight in winter, so make plans in advance. Off-season, rentals go for a song.

Average rent for a 2BR apartment: $425 to $475 a month.

Communities or developments most popular with retirees: Condominiums that are part of golf course communities are in high demand.

Nearby areas to consider: McAllen, Mission (Hidalgo County).

Earning a living

Business climate: The area economy is based on agriculture, labor-intensive industry (labor is inexpensive here) and tourism. In recent years, it has also become the gateway to NAFTA, but tourism is still critical, pumping $500 million annually into the local economy. The city's border location is advantageous—53 percent of Mexico's top 500 businesses have their headquarters in Monterrey, Mexico, just three hours away.

Help in starting a business: The University of Texas-Pan-American has a Small Business Development Center, 210-316-2610, as part of its Center for Entrepreneurship and Economic Development (CEED). It helps new and existing business owners by providing free counseling in financing, merchandising, marketing, advertising and international trade. The center also offers free or low-cost workshops on tax planning, computer basics, financial management, accounting and more. CEED also operates the One-Stop Capital Shop (OSCS) to create, retain and grow business and jobs within federally designated empowerment zones. The OSCS assists clients in assessing business needs, provides technical and managerial assistance and aides in finding appropriate financing. Brownsville Economic Development Council, 210-541-1183. SCORE, 210-541-4508.

Job market: Cameron County's Private Industry Council has a state-funded Job Training Placement Agency and on-the-job training programs, 210-542-4351. The unemployment rate is 11.5 percent, and wages are very low, averaging $9,824. However, Brownsville was recently the Texas leader in job development.

Medical care

There are 300-plus physicians in the area and two JCAHO-accredited hospitals. Columbia Valley Regional Medical Center, 210-831-2700, is located on the north side of Brownsville. This 158-bed hospital has a 15-bed intensive/cardiac care unit, 24-hour emergency room, rehab center and nutritional counseling for patients. The radiology department offers CT scanning, ultrasound and nuclear medicine. The hospital also has the Breast Disease and Detection Clinic. AMI Brownsville Medical Center, 210-544-1400, is a 168-bed hospital with a 24-hour emergency room, mammography, radiology and an intensive coronary care unit. The hospital periodically offers health fairs with free screenings.

Services for seniors

The Brownsville Senior Citizens Center, 210-544-2767, offers a variety of recreational activities including bingo, dances and arts and crafts. The center also offers free health screenings, utility assistance for low-income residents and more. Amigos Del Valle (Friends of the Valley) is another program that operates within the Senior Center, offering nutritious meals at the center for persons age 60 and over. Also offered are presentations on Medicare, health and social issues, the center organizes for the Senior Olympics. The Area Agency on Aging of the Lower Rio Grande Valley, 210-682-3481 or 800-365-6131, provides services including information and assistance, benefits counseling, a long-term care ombudsman and case management.

Continuing education

The University of Texas Brownsville and Texas Southmost College, 210-544-8710 or 210-544-8284, have a partnership arrangement for offering noncredit continuing education courses. Many courses are in personal enrichment areas, such as photography, cooking, bird-watching, flower arranging, CPR, guitar and more. Classes run on a monthly basis.

Crime and safety

Brownsville has a crime rate of 91 crimes per 1,000 population, although the rate drops to 68 incidents per 1,000 for the county. Both rates are higher than the national average—55 incidents per 1,000. The major culprit is drug trafficking and drug-related crime. Auto theft is also a major problem because of Brownsville's proximity to the border.

Getting around town

Public transportation: Brownsville Urban System (BUS), 210-541-4881, has 10 routes and a large fleet of buses that offer service Monday through Saturday. Fares are 75 cents per ride, but seniors with BUS ID ride for 25 cents, or can purchase a pass for 20 rides for $3.

Roads and highways: I-77, I-83, I-281.

Airport: Brownsville/South Padre Island International Airport. Continental Airlines provides connecting flights to Dallas, Houston, Mexico City and more.

Port: The Port of Brownsville, right on the border of Mexico, is America's home port of NAFTA.

Let the good times roll

Recreation: There are six golf courses in the area, including public, semiprivate and private courses. Because of the climate, hunting and fishing are excellent. Hunting seasons include whitewinged dove, wild turkey, deer, duck, geese and quail. Freshwater fishing in the *resacas*, (freshwater lakes that were left by the Rio Grande as it changed course over the years), includes bass and trout, catfish and gar. The Brownsville Ship Channel yields plenty of trout, snook, redfish and more, and the city is only 20 miles from beaches for surf fishing as well as swimming, surfing, boating and water-skiing. Laguna Atascosa National Wildlife Refuge, which is 20 miles northeast of Brownsville, is a 45,000-acre federal wildlife preserve with hiking paths, and it's a great place to watch birds.

Culture: The Brownsville Art League features permanent and changing exhibitions of art and offers a variety of art classes to the public. The Art League is housed in a new Art Center building adjacent to the historic Neale Home, believed to be the city's oldest frame house. Also, the Camille Lightner Playhouse, a community theater that offers five plays and/or musicals per season. The Brownsville Community Concert Association provides several annual performances by touring concert groups. The city is one of the most historic locations in Texas, and there are many sites to visit that are preserved because of their link to American, Mexican and Texas history, including the Stillman House Museum and Fort Brown.

Annual events: Charro Days is Brownsville's version of Mardi Gras and is celebrated each spring with four days of elaborate costuming, carnivals, parades, dances and bicultural events. Sombrero Fest (one the main events in the Charro Days festival) is when Washington Park is converted into a gathering site with food, music and entertainment. Brownsville Art League holds its International Art Show in April. December brings Christmas tree lighting ceremonies, the Fiesta of Lights and the Christmas Boat Parade.

When the kids come: The Gladys Porter Zoo is one of the top 10 zoos in the United States, known for its open exhibits that are surrounded only by natural waterways. More than 1,500 mammals, birds, reptiles, amphibians and fish reside here. Also try the Confederate Air Force Museum, Port Isabel Lighthouse and nearby South Padre Island.

For more information

Chamber
Brownsville Chamber
  of Commerce
1600 E. Elizabeth
Brownsville, TX 78520
210-542-4341
Personalized community info.
  kit, 800-522-1052

Newspaper
The Brownsville Herald
1135 E. Van Buren
Brownsville, TX 78550
210-542-4301

Realtor
Jeane Echols
Century 21 Echols Group, Inc.
2035 Price Rd.,
  Suite C
Brownsville, TX 78520
210-541-9161
Fax: 210-542-5635

42. Kerrville, Texas

Nickname: The Palm Springs of Texas
County: Kerr
Area code: 210
Population: 18,187
County population: 36,000
% of population over 65: 25
Region: Texas Hill Country
Closest metro area: San Antonio, 62 mi.
Average home price: $75,000 to $135,000
Best reasons to retire here: Panoramic surroundings, friendly, small-town charm, low crime and cost of living.

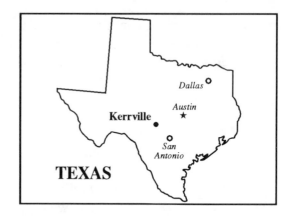

Kerrville at a glance

Kerrville is a nearly picture-perfect retirement community. Situated at the highest point of Texas Hill Country's rugged terrain, the panoramic views don't get any better than from atop the rolling hills. Unobstructed views of the Guadalupe River, which meanders through the heart of the town, are part of the charm of river-front living. People think everything in Texas is big, but Kerrville is a pleasant contradiction. It's very small, very friendly and the city is well-geared to providing services and activities for seniors. The three C's of retirement living—climate, crime and the cost of living—are at very desirable levels. The climate is warm to hot with comfortable humidity, the crime rate is low and so is the cost of living—money just goes further here, particularly in the areas of health care and housing. What makes Kerrville really special, however, is how friendly people are, and the lengths they will go to welcome visitors and newcomers. (If you call the Chamber of Commerce for relocation information or to ask a question, be prepared to talk for a while. Kerrvillites are proud of their community and would love you to join it, and they very much want you to know it.) The pace here is leisurely—stroll along the river banks and picnic in one of the parks that dot the river front, take time out to shop in a western boutique, try bird-watching (it's one of the greatest places in the U.S.) or take in a round of golf. Whatever you choose, Kerrville offers you the chance to do it in peace, taking a well-deserved rest.

Possible drawbacks: There is no public bus service, so a car is a necessity. Local shopping is limited (especially if you're partial to big department stores). Although Kerrville offers very high-quality health care for a town its size, there are still situations that may require travel to San Antonio.

Climate

Elevation: 2,000'	Avg. high/low:	Avg. inches		Avg. # days precip.	Avg. % humidity
		rain	snow		
Jan.	62/35	1.5	-	8	51
April	78/54	2.4	-	8	60
July	97/73	1.9	-	4	59
Oct.	79/54	2.9	-	6	65
YEAR	79/54	2.7	1	-	-
# days 32° or below: 23			# days 90° or warmer: 123		

What things cost

Overview: According to ACCRA, the overall cost of living in Kerrville is about 5 percent below the national average. Housing is nearly 13 percent lower, and health care runs a whopping 15 percent below the norm. Utilities are higher, however, by 8 percent.

Gas company: Contact Lone Star Gas, 800-460-3030. The turn-on charge is $25, and deposits are not required of seniors 65 and over. Deposits can be waived with a letter of credit. Monthly bills range from $10 to $100 depending upon usage.

Electric company: Kerrville Public Utility Board, 210-257-3050. $15 connect fee. Deposits are waived with a letter of credit. All-electric monthly bills run $75 to $150; partial electric, $60 to $100.

Phone company: Kerrville Telephone Company, 210-896-1111. Connection fees range from $9 to $14. Deposits are often waived. Base rate runs from $11 to $17.50 depending upon your location. Hill Country Telephone Co-op, 210-367-5333. Basic service is $10.71 monthly; additional charges may apply.

Water and sewer: City of Kerrville, 210-257-8000. Deposits, $40, are waived with a letter of credit. There is a $15 new account charge. Full service can range from $40 to $75 monthly.

Cable company: TCI Cablevision of Southwest Texas, 210-257-4700.

Car registration, license: New Texas residents must obtain a Texas driver's license within 30 days after establishing residency. A 4-year license costs $16. Automobiles must also be registered within 30 days. Vehicles must pass an inspection, and proof of insurance is required. Registration fees vary depending upon model year or weight in pounds, but are generally less than $75.

The tax ax

Sales tax: Total retail sales tax in Kerrville is 8.25 percent. Texas state sales tax is 6.25 percent of this, with 1 percent for city, half percent for county and economic development.

State income tax: Texas has no personal or corporate income tax.

Retirement income: There are no estate taxes and no inheritance taxes.

Property taxes: Total 1995 rate for Kerrville per $100 was $2.33. Homes are assessed at 100 percent of market value. Property taxes on a $100,000 home would be approximately $2,330. For more information call the Kerr County Tax Office, 210-895-5223.

Local real estate

Overview: In recent years, both new and existing homes have been selling in an average 30 to 90 days, with many new homes selling while under construction. The demand for rental housing has risen simultaneously, making this a rather hot market. Retirees in this area tend to purchase single family homes, although a number of people will choose Austin and purchase a second home in Kerrville, either for its small-town feel or for investment purposes.

Average price for a 3BR/2BA home: $90,000 to $135,000 is a typical range for a new home, while resales average $75,000 to $125,000.

Average price for a 2BR condo: New condominiums haven't been built in Kerrville for several years. Prices range from $90,000 to $135,000, and amenities vary greatly.

Common housing syles and features: Exteriors of native stone are common, and low maintenance and high energy efficiency are design factors. Most homes features casual layouts.

Rental housing market: 2BR homes in the area rent for $500 to $800 per month, and most leases are for 12 months, although shorter terms can be negotiated.

Average rent for a 2BR apartment: $425 to $575.

Nearby areas to consider: Fredricksburg is a small but beautiful town with a large German population. There are many who find it quaint, but others who say that after 10 years you still feel like a newcomer. It's a tight-knit community that's steeped in tradition.

Earning a living

Business climate: A growing residential, tourist, small industry and agricultural area, Kerrville offers good prospects in the food service, retail, wholesale, communications, retirement, hunting and finance markets.

Help in starting a business: A small business development specialist affiliated with the Small Business Development Center at the University of Texas, San Antonio, works from the Kerrville Chamber of Commerce one day per week, offering free, one-on-one counseling for all new and existing small-business owners. Appointments should be made through the Kerrville Chamber of Commerce, 210-896-1155, which also has information for startup businesses. Seminars on business topics (typical cost is $20) are available through the San Antonio Business Development Center, 210-558-2460. SCORE is also available in nearby San Antonio, 210-229-5931. Kerr Economic Development Corporation, 210-588-2460.

Job market: The major employer in the area is health care, due to a VA medical center and Peterson Regional Health Care, as well as retirement centers and community centers. Another major employer is youth camps, of which there are more than 25, including church-related and private camps with national and international clientele. This combination of factors means there are many opportunities for part-time and seasonal work in Kerrville. In recent years, the unemployment rate has varied from 2.5 to 7 percent, and wages are low because of the service economy and low unemployment rate.

Medical care

Kerrville is considered the regional and medical diagnostic center for the area, but it may be necessary to travel to San Antonio for some types of care, including open heart surgery and neurosurgery. The major health care center in Kerrville is Peterson Regional Health Care Center, 210-896-4200, which operates a 148-bed acute care hospital with a connecting professional building. There are more than 60 physicians on staff here, and some physicians from San Antonio have courtesy privileges at the hospital and maintain office hours in Kerrville. The center also operates a diabetic management program, a skilled nursing center, the Heart of the Hills Cardiac Rehabilitation Center and the Kerrville Radiation Therapy Center, offering state-of-the-art care in a compassionate environment. Also in the area is a Veterans Administration Hospital, 210-896-2020, which has 268 medical and surgical beds and 154 nursing home beds.

Services for seniors

The Dietert Claim Senior Center (named for the family that donated the land), 210-257-6228, offers a great variety of activities and classes for seniors, including line dancing, chess, folk dancing, guitar lessons, yoga, book discussion groups and more. The center also offers tax assistance and sponsors a service that, with 24 hours' notice, transports seniors to doctors' offices and to do other errands within the Kerrville city limits. (The center requests a donation for this service to help defray its expenses.) It also offers hot lunches. Many other groups and clubs, such as AARP, meet at the center.

Continuing education

Kerrville Independent School District Community Education, 210-257-1228, offers a Lifelong Learning program with more than 150 classes offered to seniors on everything from angels and antiques to fly fishing, dog obedience, sign language, piano, rock climbing, yoga and geneology. The Adult and Continuing Education division also offers many classes. Enrollment fees range from $8 to $70.

Crime and safety

Kerrville is a very safe city, with a reported crime index of 51 incidents per 1,000 population, below the national average of 55 incidents per 1,000. The Kerr County figure was 39 incidents. Crime is low in part because the town has an unusually high amount of law enforcement coverage: The city police, county sheriff's department, state highway patrol, Texas Rangers and a regional drug task force office are all located here. And the police department runs several crime prevention programs, including home safety assessments.

Getting around town

Public transportation: None.

Roads and highways: Kerrville is intersected by state highways 16 and 27 and I-10.

Airports: San Antonio International Airport, 62 miles away, is served by 14 national, international and regional carriers. It's the closest airport with commercial connections to major metropolitan areas. Louis Schreiner Field (Kerrville/Kerr County Municipal Airport) handles general aviation aircraft.

Let the good times roll

Recreation: If you're a golfer, you'll enjoy four golf courses in the area, including Lady Bird Johnson Golf Course in Fredricksburg and the private Riverhill Country Club. There is also a golf driving range in town with night lighting, automatic and grass tees, target greens and chipping and putting greens. Tennis players like the H.E. Butt Municipal Tennis Center, which has six lighted courts. Naturalists love this part of Texas. The Texas Hill Country is a birdwatchers' paradise—both for the number of species and rare birds sighted. Kerrville-Schreiner State Park is a 500-acre park on the Guadalupe River that offers fishing, camping and boating. Lost Maples State Natural Area is one-and a-half hours west of Kerrville, featuring rugged limestone canyons, plateau grasslands, wooded slopes and clear streams, and the only maple forest in Texas. You'll find great hiking and camping here. Spend a day at the Lazy Hills Guest Ranch, 210-367-5600, which offers trail rides and Texas cookouts. You can also ride at the Y.O. Ranch, 210-640-3222, by reservation. Y.O. Ranch is a native and exotic game ranch with zebra, giraffes, antelopes, registered quarter horses and longhorn cattle.

Culture: The Hill Country Arts Foundation operates the Point Theatre, an outdoor venue for summertime theater and entertainment. The foundation also offers indoor productions year-round. The Cowboy Artists of America Museum has changing exhibitions of art celebrating the American West. San Antonio offers a variety of cultural programs within an hour's drive, presented by arts groups that include the San Antonio Symphony, San Antonio Dance Theatre, San Antonio Little Theatre company and the San Antonio Museum of Art.

Annual events: Kerrville is a state qualifying site for the Senior Games, 210-896-GAME, a spring event for people age 50 and over. The Easter Hill Country Bike Tour and Easter Festival & Chili Cook-Off occur Easter weekend each year. The Kerrville Folk Festival in late spring features 25 days of musical events at Quiet Valley Ranch. The Kerrville Wine and Music Festival on Labor Day weekend is a 3-day condensed version of the Folk Festival.

When the kids come: The Riverside Nature Center blends cultural and natural history. It features walking paths, a wildflower meadow and butterfly garden. Nearby San Antonio and outdoor activities in the Texas Hill Country will keep your family coming back to visit.

For more information

Chamber
Kerrville Area Chamber
   of Commerce
1700 Sidney Baker, #100
Kerrville, TX 78026
210-896-1155

Newspaper
Kerrville Daily Times
429 Jefferson St.
Kerrville, TX 78028
210-896-7000

Realtor
Greg Bitkower
Bitkower Associates, Inc.
314 Spence St.
Kerrville, TX 78028
210-257-6592
Fax: 210-896-8886

43. San Antonio, Texas

Nicknames: River City USA, The Alamo City
County: Bexar (pronounced "Bear")
Area code: 210
Population: 1,052,900
County population: 1,282,200
% of population over 65: 10
Region: South Central Texas or edge of Texas Hill Country
Median home price: $80,800
Best reasons to retire here: A city rich in history, excellent health care and recreational opportunities, low cost of living, mild climate.

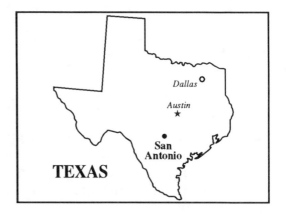

San Antonio at a glance

San Antonio is admired around the world as a modern metropolis that has nourished and maintained its old-world ambiance. The city is rich in American history, beginning with the Coahuiltecan Indians, followed by Spanish missionaries and waves of Anglo-American colonists. Founded in 1691, San Antonio has grown from a small Texas pueblo to a city of more than 1 million. But this growth has been guided; San Antonio's development has been carefully planned to maintain its unique character, from preserving the Alamo to developing the world-famous Paseo del Rio (River Walk). In fact, tourism is the second-largest industry, as visitors retrace the city's rich history and revel in its multicultural atmosphere. Military retirees have long been drawn to the area because of the presence of Lackland Air Force Base (where every Air Force pilot is trained) and Fort Sam Houston, headquarters of the 5th U.S. Army. But the city is a major draw for retirees of all types, because of its subtropical climate, proximity to the beautiful Texas Hill Country, low cost of living and excellent health care. There are more than 25 incorporated communities in Bexar County, offering newcomers an array of choices that includes everything from historic neighborhoods to modern developments with plenty of amenities. And, with more than 300 days of sunshine annually, it's no wonder San Antonio is the tenth largest city in the U.S. and growing.

Possible drawbacks: This is a major metropolitan area, with its full share of urban hassles, including traffic (although San Antonio is much easier to navigate than other cities of its size). The summers are extremely hot, and public transportation doesn't exactly meet the definition of efficiency.

Climate

Elevation: 812'	Avg. high/low:	Avg. inches		Avg. # days precip.	Avg. % humidity
		rain	snow		
Jan.	62/40	1.7	-	8	68
April	80/59	2.5	-	8	64
July	96/74	1.7	-	4	61
Oct.	82/59	2.8	-	6	66
YEAR	80/58	27.0	-	-	-
# days 32° or below: 24			# days 90° or warmer: 115		

What things cost

Overview: ACCRA statistics show overall living costs in San Antonio are about 5.5 percent below the national average. Utilities and health care are about 11 percent below the norm.

Gas and electric company: City Public Service Board, 210-353-2222. A deposit is required, which can vary from $40 to $250 or more, but it covers both gas and electric service. No service initiation fee. Most homes are all-electric. Average monthly gas bills are $19 to $24. During the winter, all-electric bills typically run $80 to $90 per month, but jump to $140 to $170 in the summer.

Water and sewer: San Antonio Water System, 210-225-5222. A minimum deposit of $55 is required of new customers, but this can be waived with a letter of credit. Average monthly bills are approximately $40 inside the city limits and $50 outside.

Phone company: Southwestern Bell, 210-360-2000. No deposit is required, although new customers may be required to pay a $49.50 advance, which is credited to the first bill. Service initiation fee is $46.10. The basic monthly rate is approximately $15.

Cable company: Paragon, 210-352-4600; CableMaxx, 210-646-7171.

Car registration, license: New Texas residents must obtain a Texas driver's license within 30 days after establishing residency. A 4-year license costs $16. Renewals are done by mail. Automobiles must also be registered within 30 days. Vehicles must pass an inspection and proof of insurance is required. Registration fees vary depending upon model year or weight in pounds, but are generally less than $75. License branch, call 210-737-2272.

The tax ax

Sales tax: 6.25 percent sales tax (food and drugs excluded). San Antonio levies an additional 1.5 percent sales tax for a total of 7.775 percent.

State/city income tax: None.

Retirement income: There are no estate taxes and no inheritance taxes.

Property taxes: Total effective tax rate inside San Antonio ranges from $2.71 to $3.15 per $100 of assessed valuation. Outside the city it ranges from $2.08 to $2.57 per $100 depending upon location. Taxes are assessed at 100 percent of current market valuation. Request a tax rate chart from the Bexar County Tax Assessor's Office at 210-220-2251.

Local real estate

Overview: Recently there has been an oversupply of housing for sale and apartments and homes for rent. Landlords and builders are offering units at a discount, making it an attractive market indeed (*caveat emptor*: markets like this can and often do change quickly). Most retirees are relocating to the area permanently.

Median price for a single family home: $80,800.

Average price for a 3BR/2BA home: $122,500.

Average price for a 2BR condo: There has been no new condo development for at least a decade. 2BR resales range between $60,000 to $120,000.

Common housing styles and features: San Antonio has an abundance of traditional homes on large lots, so often buyers have enough room for a backyard pool and deck. Many skilled contractors do beautiful stucco and tile work.

Rental housing market: Apartments have been plentiful recently—and landlords and management companies have offered reduced rents and other financial incentives. Short-term home rentals are scarce, but they're the only thing hard to come by in this rental market.

Average rent for a 2BR apartment: $528 monthly. However, prices can easily range from $600 to $900, depending upon location, amenities and terms.

Communities or developments most popular with retirees: Woodlake, Lincoln Heights, the Dominion and Timberwood Park.

Nearby areas to consider: Fredericksburg, Kerrville, New Braunfels, Seguin.

Earning a living

Business climate: San Antonio is considered the economic hub of central and south Texas, with more than 40 percent of annual trade between the U.S. and Mexico traveling through the city. The economy is based on services, tourism, manufacturing, communication and medical services. Five military installations account for the large number of government employees, but the economy has expanded for the past five years despite government cuts in military expenditures. With annual tourism of 7 million visitors, San Antonio has gained prominence as a national convention destination.

Help in starting a business: Contact the Small Business Development Center at the University of Texas, San Antonio, 210-558-2460, for free, one-on-one counseling, workshops and specialty centers for owners of new or existing small businesses. The Greater San Antonio Chamber of Commerce, 210-229-2104, and the City of San Antonio Economic Development Department, 210-207-8080, offer assistance, information, programs and referrals to local and new businesses. First Point Business Information Center, 210-554-7120, helps entrepreneurs obtain the necessary licenses and permits.

Job market: The average rate of job growth in San Antonio has been 3 percent annually for more than a decade, and job prospects are good in most sectors. Major employers include University of Texas Health Science Center, Taco Cabana, Builders Square, Southwestern Bell, Methodist Healthcare System, Sea World of Texas and Dillard's department store. Texas Employment Commission, 210-222-8484.

Medical care

Medical facilities in San Antonio are nothing short of awesome. With more than 30 hospitals in the area, the best care is available. The South Texas Medical Center is situated on a 700-acre medical complex and incorporates eight major hospitals plus clinics, laboratories, research and nursing facilities. Other major hospital systems include Santa Rosa Health Care Corp., 210-704-2011, which operates five hospitals in the city and provides numerous wellness programs, free screenings and the Santa Rosa Lifeline emergency response system. Methodist Health Care Systems, 210-208-4000, operates seven medical facilities in San Antonio, including five hospitals. San Antonio is also home to two U.S. Department of Defense hospitals, one V.A. hospital and two Texas State hospitals. Wilford Hall Medical Center at Lackland Air Force Base, 210-670-7412, is the largest U.S. Air Force Hospital. Brooke Army Medical Center at Fort Sam Houston, 210-916-6141, has a world-renowned burn unit that receives patients from all over the world.

Crime and safety

San Antonio experienced 88 crimes per 1,000 population in 1994, and Bexar county was near to that figure, with 79 crimes per 1,000. Both are higher than the national average of 55 per 1,000 for the same year. Senior Citizens Against Crime, 210-520-8401, is a program organized by the Bexar County Sheriff's Department that offers seniors volunteer opportunities in administrative areas as well as in police substations.

Continuing education

A variety of noncredit courses, from one-day workshops to several weeks of regular meetings, are offered by Our Lady of the Lake University, 210-434-6711. San Antonio Public Schools' office of adult and community education, 210-299-5500, offers adult personal enrichment classes, including computer classes. Call OASIS, 210-647-2546, for information on life enrichment, liberal arts and wellness programs at minimal or no charge.

Services for seniors

Assistance in locating services for seniors is available from the Senior Information Center, 210-222-1845, an information and referral agency. Senior Centers of San Antonio, 210-227-3157, is operated under the auspices of the city through the nonprofit Senior Community Services, Inc. There are 13 centers providing local activities, information, referrals, assistance in letter writing and basic banking and a monthly newsletter. Call the Area Agency on Aging of Bexar County, 210-225-5201 or 800-960-5201, or the Retired Senior Volunteer Program, 210-222-0301.

Getting around town

Public transportation: VIA Metropolitan Transit, 210-227-2020, provides bus service. Basic fare is 75 cents; seniors 62 and older (with VIA ID) ride for half price.

Raods and highways: I-35, I-10, I-37; US 90 and 281; Loops 410 and 1604.

Airports: San Antonio International Airport is served by 14 national, international and regional carriers, and Stinson Field Relief Airport handles general aviation aircraft.

Let the good times roll

Recreation: Spectator sports are great, from basketball to baseball to golf. The NBA Spurs have a big following, while crowds flock to see the San Antonio Missions, a Class AA farm team of the L.A. Dodgers. San Antonio has eight public golf courses and many private and semiprivate links. Also, check out the La Cantera Texas Open, part of the PGA Tour. The 343-acre Brackenridge Park features picnic areas, a golf course, driving range and more, while Friedrich Wilderness Park has trails for hiking and nature study. Boaters and fishermen enjoy the 15 lakes that lie within 150 miles of San Antonio.

Culture: The Guadalupe Cultural Arts Center is one of the finest Hispanic cultural centers showcasing local, national and international artists. Its Cinefestival is the oldest and largest film festival in the United States. The San Antonio Symphony offers 120 performances per year. San Antonio Dance Theatre is a performing ballet company offering two major performances annually and summer dance workshops. San Antonio Little Theatre (SALT) is an 83-year old community theater that presents Broadway musicals, dramas and comedies. SALT Cellar offers intimate productions of classical plays and works by new playwrights. The San Antonio Museum of Art features Chinese porcelain creations, Mexican folk art, Greek and Roman antiquities and contemporary art.

Annual events: Asian Lunar New Year is celebrated in January. In February enjoy the San Antonio Stock Show and Rodeo. On St. Patrick's Day the city dyes the San Antonio River green. In April its Fiesta San Antonio, featuring 10 days of festivals, sporting events, concerts, art shows and elegant balls. October is Greek Fun Festival with a Greek market, dancing, food and live music. November is Wurstfest in nearby New Braunfels, and the Lighting Ceremony and River Walk Holiday Parade in which Santa arrives by floating river parade. December hosts Fiestas Navidenas, with piñata parties and the blessing of the animals.

When the kids come: The Alamo attracts young historians. San Antonio Zoological Gardens and Aquarium is the largest zoo in the world. Splashtown Waterpark entertains little *and* big kids. (Seniors over 65 are admitted for free.) Sea World of Texas is the world's largest marine life showplace. Fiesta Texas is a 200-acre theme park.

For more information

Chamber
The Greater San Antonio
   Chamber of Commerce
602 E. Commerce
P.O. Box 1628
San Antonio, TX 78296
210-229-2100

Newspapers
San Antonio Express News
Avenue E & 3rd St.
San Antonio, TX 78205
210-225-7411

Daily Commercial Recorder
6222 NW IH 10
San Antonio, TX 78201
210-736-4450

Realtor
Luci A. Cockrell
Cockrell Inc.
15519 River Bend
San Antonio, TX 78216
210-545-7600
Fax: 210-829-4499

44. Provo, Utah

Nickname: America's Freedom City
County: Utah
Area code: 801
Population: 92,630
County population: 303,241
% of population over 65: 5
Region: Western
Closest metro area: Salt Lake City, 44 mi.
Average home price: $150,000
Best reasons to retire here: Fabulous mountain scenery, perfect year-round climate for outdoor enthusiasts, economic growth.

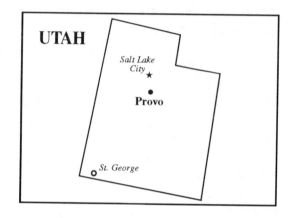

Provo at a glance

Who says beauty and brains don't mix? Not anyone who's ever been to Provo! Situated at the foot of the majestic Wasatch Mountain Range and overlooking freshwater Utah Lake, Provo is surrounded by beautiful landscapes: Gold-streaked canyons, turquoise streams and green forests are centuries-old wonders that await you. As for the brains, this once-poor farming community (colonized by the Mormon founder Brigham Young) is now (alongside sister city Orem) a booming high-tech business community that consistently earns a spot on "most livable city" lists. Why is Provo attracting all this attention? Perhaps it's because the cost of living is in-line, and housing, though more expensive than the national average, is available and affordable. The environment is mostly clean and healthy (Utah is the second healthiest state), and you'll find great recreation here—you haven't lived until you've skied at Snowbird or visited Robert Redford's Sundance resort. In addition, the continuing education opportunities are extensive, promising that this beautiful environment will keep your brain in tune, too. When the quality of life is as high as the city (4,500 feet), you've got a winner!

Possible drawbacks: The idea of moving to a sheltered city with strong family values can be very appealing. However, lifestyles can also be restrictive. The few liquor stores in town are state-owned and only fine restaurants will serve liquor on request. Provo's valley location causes temperature inversions and poor air quality in winter. When this happens, outside activities can be canceled (three to four times a year) as it can pose risks to young children and those with respiratory problems.

Climate

Elevation: 4,550'	Avg. high/low:	Avg. inches		Avg. # days precip.	Avg. % humidity
		rain	snow		
Jan.	37/18	.1	15	4	66
April	62/35	1.4	7	8	37
July	93/59	.7	-	4	18
Oct.	66/37	.9	3	-	37
YEAR	64/37	8.7	65	66	40
# days 32° or below: 135			# days 90° or warmer: 53		

What things cost

Overview: ACCRA shows the overall cost of living slightly above the national average (by less than 2 percent), with housing at 8 percent more and health care 19 percent more.

Gas company: Mountain Fuel Supply, 801-373-7400. $30 charge to turn on gas; $8 if gas is already on. Deposits are not usually required. Avg. bill: $42 monthly.

Electric, water and sewer company: City of Provo Utilities, 801-379-6820, provides water, sewer and electric service. Start-up service fee: $20. Deposit ($70 for gas and $30 for water) can be waived with letter of credit. Average electric bill: $60 a month.

Phone company: Contact US West, 800-244-1111. Hook-up charge: $25. Deposits not required pending credit check. Monthly charge for basic service: $16.

Cable company: TCI Cablevision of Utah, 801-377-8600; Provo Cable Co., 801-377-1360.

Car registration, license: Driver's license, $15, valid for five years. Seniors 65 and over renew for $5. Written exam, driving and eye test required. License must be obtained immediately upon becoming a resident. New residents have 60 days to register their vehicles. Registration fee: $25.50, includes plate, registration and new titling fee. A personal property tax is assessed, based on make and model year of the car. For example, in 1996, the personal property tax on a 1995 Honda Accord 4-door was $247.52. Taxes decrease with depreciation. Driver's license, 801-227-5002; registration, 801-451-6496.

The tax ax

Sales tax: 6.25 percent (medicine exempt); fast food taxed an extra 1 percent.

State income tax: No local or county income tax. State income taxes start at 2.55 percent and increase to 7.2 percent for all taxable income over $7,500 per person. Exemption of one-half of federal income tax paid, and an exemption of up to $7,500 of federal, state and private pensions for persons 65 and older.

Retirement income: State exemption for homeowners/renters age 65 and older with gross income of up to $17,850. State inheritance taxes range from .8 percent to 16 percent. No tax on estates of less than $640,000.

Property taxes: 6.7 percent of the market value times millage rate (.014444) per $1,000 of value. The average tax on a $150,000 home would be $1,250. Tax assessor, 801-370-8276.

Local real estate

Overview: Provo is very heterogeneous. Less expensive starter homes are found in the same neighborhoods as larger, luxury homes. Homes up to $120,000 are selling the fastest, but there aren't enough to meet demand. One of the biggest building booms in the last 15 years started in 1990. (The growth of the computer industry has attracted thousands of employees.)

Average price for a 3BR/2BA home: $85,000 to $95,000 represents the lower end of the market, which ranges up to $250,000 for homes with many modern amenities. ACCRA shows the average selling price is about $150,000.

Average price for a 2BR condo: New condos sell for $93,000, while resales average $98,000. The lower price for new units reflects a high inventory of lower-priced condos currently on the market that have been built for the married student housing market.

Common housing styles and features: Older homes can be ramblers (ranches), split entry, split levels or 2-stories. Exteriors are often brick; some are finished in stucco or aluminum siding. Newer homes feature dormers, open spaces, vaulted ceilings and, often, decks.

Rental housing market: Houses are difficult to find because of the high number of married students at Brigham Young. Where available, 2BR/1BA fourplexes go for $400 to $800 per month; 3BR/2BA homes for $650 per month. Average rent for a 2BR apartment is $550 a month.

Nearby areas to consider: Pleasant Grove, Alpine, Springville, Mapleton.

Earning a living

Business climate: The Utah Valley economy is healthy, with a job growth rate of 7 percent. An aggressive program to create new jobs at a rate of 30,000 a year is in place, and companies and individuals from across the nation are eager to be a part of Provo/Orem's economic boom. The area is a high-tech powerhouse—home to the largest concentration of software companies in the nation and the third-largest concentration of high-tech companies, including Novell, Geneva Steel, Ameritech Library Services and more than 230 others. The climate is also right for small business development. *Home Office Computing* recently ranked Provo the fourth-best city in which to operate a home-based business. In the retail and service areas, there's room for development in outdoor recreation services and restaurants.

Help in starting a business: Utah Valley State College has a Small Business Development Center, 801-222-8230.

Job market: According to an article in *Time* magazine, Utah now boasts the nation's youngest, best-educated and most productive work force. The unemployment rate is at a low 3 percent, which is much lower than the national rate of 5.5 percent. Nonetheless, the market is tough if you're looking for part-time work, because you'll find yourself in competition with the student population. Plan to be patient. LDS Employment, 801-229-2496, is a free service of the Church of Latter Day Saints, available to everyone. The service has job listings from businesses throughout the community. Utah Department of Employment Security, 801-373-7500.

Medical care

Utah Valley Regional Medical Center, 801-373-7850, is a 409-bed facility with a staff of 400, and is the busiest emergency center in the area. It also acts as a referral center for other nearby hospitals and is known for oncology, intensive/coronary, open heart surgery, rehabilitation and its wellness center. It's an IHC (Intermountain Health Care) facility. A regional health care provider, IHC was given the Health Care Forum/Witt Award, the health care industry's most prestigious honor, in recognition of quality health care. Columbia Mountain View Hospital, 801-465-9201, is located in nearby Payson, and is the only hospital in the U.S. to be named among the nation's top 100 hospitals, receive accreditation with commendation from JCAHO and to be among the top 50 hospitals in managing costs and maintaining quality in the same year. The hospital has breast care services, cardiology, an osteoporosis center, magnetic resonance imaging, a sleep lab, a critical care unit and wellness programs.

Services for seniors

The Division of Aging and Adult Services, 801-377-2262, oversees 90 percent of the services offered to seniors in the Utah County area. It is a great source for information and referral, and is also home to the community's RSVP program. The Provo Senior Citizens Center, 801-379-6620, offers a variety of free and low-cost activities, including ceramics, dancing, billiards, quilting and day trips. The center also has a weekly health clinic, which offers blood pressure checks and other basic services.

Continuing education

Utah Valley State College continuing education, 801-222-8450, offers three programs to seniors: noncredit classes, Elder Quest and Elderhostel. Noncredit offerings include arts and crafts, business, computers, home and garden, languages and woodworking. Elder Quest is a peer learning membership program for persons age 55 and up. The Elderhostel offers a commuter option. Brigham Young University's division of continuing studies, 801-378-4146, offers correspondence and evening classes in genealogy, American history, theater and film, psychology and more Also, seniors can audit almost any class on campus on a space-available basis for $10.

Crime and safety

Provo is one of the safest communities we researched. It reports a total crime index of 36 incidents per 1,000 population, which is 34 percent below the national average. The Utah County rate is slightly higher, at 40 crimes per 1,000, but it's still well below the national average. There is little violent crime, with an average of one homicide a year in Provo.

Getting around town

Public transportation: Utah Transit Authority, 801-375-4636. Adult fare is 85 cents; seniors 65 and over pay 35 cents. Seniors can purchase a monthly pass for $11; persons under 65 pay $27.

Roads and highways: I-15 (north-south) and US 50, 89, 91 and 189.

Airport: Salt Lake International, 40 miles away, is served by national and regional carriers.

Let the good times roll

Recreation: Provo's location at the foot of the Wasatch Mountain Range guarantees plenty of outdoor recreation. It has 18 city parks and one state park—Utah Lake State Park, the east shore of Utah's largest natural freshwater lake. It's perfect for fishing, swimming, water-skiing and power boating in the summer, and ice skating, snowmobiling and sledding in winter. Speaking of snow, Utah boasts the "greatest snow on earth." The city is an hour's drive from a number of major ski resorts: Brighton, Alta, Park West, Snowbird, Deer Valley, Solitude and Sundance (owned and operated by Robert Redford), which has one of the state's most popular summer outdoor theaters. The resort and the National Forest surrounding it offer numerous hiking, horse and mountain biking trails. Seven Peaks Resort Center offers a water park, an 18-hole golf course and ice-skating. Provo is only about an hours' drive from Great Salt Lake State Park, with a marina, paddle boats and a sandy beach. Brigham Young University is known for its basketball, football, golf and baseball teams.

Culture: The Harris Fine Arts Center features paintings by American and European artists and displays student and faculty artwork. The Museum of Peoples and Cultures features art and artifacts of the Mayan, Anasazi and Casa Grande Indian cultures, as well as Egyptian, Polynesian and Mesopotamian works. The Utah Valley Symphony is a 90-member community orchestra. Brigham Young University hosts theater events, concerts, sports, dance and arts. McCurdy Historical Doll Museum is an award-winning museum with more than 3,000 dolls.

Annual events: America's Freedom Festival in June and July is a three-week celebration with sports, parades and concerts. In August in nearby Springville, World Folkfest, the largest folk festival in North America, attracts dancers from 13 countries. The Children's Celebration of the Arts is a free arts and crafts day in July, designed for hands-on experience and entertainment.

When the kids come: The Earth Science Museum has one of Utah's largest collections of dinosaur bones from the Jurassic period. The Monte L. Bean Life Science Museum has mounted wildlife specimens from around the world. Peppermint Place is a candy factory and outlet store featuring observation tours and more than 600 types of candy. Sundance Resort sponsors a children's summer theater.

For more information

Chamber
Provo Chamber of
  Commerce
51 S. University Ave.
Provo, UT 84601
801-379-2555

Newspaper
The Daily Herald
1555 N. 200 W.
Provo, UT 84604
801-373-5050

Realtor
Jeff Mendenhall, Broker
Osmond Real Estate
424 S. State
Orem, UT 84058
800-925-6059

45. St. George, Utah

Nicknames: Utah's Dixie, Utah's Hot Spot
County: Washington
Area code: 801
Population: 42,000
County population: 68,500
% of population over 65: 16
Region: Southwestern Utah
Closest metro area: Las Vegas, 125 mi.
Average home price: $125,000 to $200,000
Best reasons to retire here: Spectacular scenery, endless sunshine and dry air, unbelievable golfing, affordable housing.

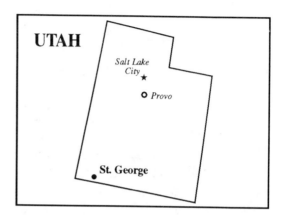

St. George at a glance

There are few areas in the United States as beautiful and full of natural wonders as southern Utah. To live in St. George is to find yourself at the gateway to some of the earth's most spectacular and varied landscapes. From 2,000 feet below sea level at the bottom of Virgin Gorge to 10,000 feet above sea level at the peak of Pine Valley Mountain, this is a land of vibrant colors: gold-streaked canyons and cliffs, brilliant red mountains, turquoise lakes and lush green forests. It is also near an incredible concentration of national parks, including Zion, Bryce and Grand Canyon National Parks, Cedar Breaks and Pipe Springs National Monuments, Snow Canyon State Park, Kolb Canyons, Lake Powell and Lake Mead. St. George was founded by the Mormon prophet-colonizer Brigham Young. What began as an idyllic religious community has now grown into a haven for snowbirds and retirees, lured by the breathtaking scenery, year-round recreation and relatively mild climate (featuring dry desert air, palm trees and, yes, snow). When they arrive, they find beautiful new communities with golf courses, Southwestern-style homes and abundant recreational opportunities. Property taxes are low, and so is the crime rate. Best of all, with the vast majority of the land administered by the Forest Service and the Parks Department, most of the county will remain preserved for future generations.

Possible drawbacks: St. George is still a small town (with fewer cultural activites than big-city transplants are used to). But population growth has been phenomenal, from 11,000 in the early 1980s to more than 40,000 today. Residents fear this is too much strain on services. Finally, there is no public transportation, and air connections are somewhat limited.

Climate

Elevation: 2,880'	Avg. high/low:	Avg. inches		Avg. # days precip.	Avg. % humidity
		rain	snow		
Jan.	50/20	.7	-	6	60
April	70/40	.7	-	6	36
July	95/58	.9	-	6	38
Oct.	75/40	.7	-	5	42
YEAR	66/42	8.0	18	-	-
# days 32° or below: 149			# days 90° or warmer: 80		

What things cost

Overview: According to ACCRA, St. George is slightly above the national average overall, with housing about 11 percent higher and groceries 4 percent more. Utilities are nearly 17 percent lower.

Gas company: Mountain Fuel Supply, 801-673-7514. Deposits are usually not required. If gas is on, connect charge is $8; if off, charge is $30. Homes with gas heat can average $50 to $100 monthly. Appliances only run $20 to $40.

Electric companies: Within the city limits, St. George City, 801-634-5800. No connect charge; $75 deposits required of renters. These fees also cover water and sewer provided by the city. Outside city limits: Dixie Escalante Rural Electric Co., 801-637-3297; Washington City Power System, 801-628-1666; or Utah Power, 801-628-7514. All-electric homes average $90 to $150 monthly.

Phone company: The area is served by US West, 800-244-1111. Basic service connection is $25. Deposits waived pending credit check. Basic monthly service is about $15.

Water and sewer: St. George City, 801-634-5800. No turn-on charge. Renters: $75 deposit. Avg monthly bill: $40.

Cable company: Falcon Cable TV, 801-628-5750. Sky-View, 801-674-0320.

Car registration, license: Driver's license must be obtained immediately upon becoming a resident, $15 (valid for five years). Seniors 65 and over renew for $5. Written exam, driving and eye test required. New residents have 60 days to register vehicles ($25.50 includes plate, registration and titling fee). A personal property tax is assessed on automobiles, based on make and model year.

The tax ax

Sales tax: 5.875 percent.

State income tax: No local or county income tax. State income taxes start at 2.55 percent and increase to 7.2 percent for all taxable income over $7,500. There is an exemption of one-half of federal income tax paid, and an exemption of up to $7,500 of federal, state and private pensions for persons 65 and older.

Retirement income: Exemption for renters/homeowners age 65 and older with gross income of up to $17,850. Inheritance taxes are .8 percent to 16 percent. No tax on estates of less than $640,000.

Property taxes: St. George millage rate is $11.92 per $1,000 of assessed valuation, and homes are assessed at 55 percent of market value. Washington County Tax Assessor, 801-634-5703.

Local real estate

Overview: Prices have increased 10 to 15 percent per year in recent years, but seem to be stabilizing. The area attracts permanent retiree residents, but it is also a popular second-home market for people from northern Utah, Idaho and Wyoming.

Average cost of a 3BR/2BA home: New homes average $150,000 to $200,000, while resales with amenities average $125,000 to $175,000.

Average price for a 2BR condo: New, $125,000 to $150,000; resales average $115,000 to $140,000.

Unique housing features: Patio homes, which are one-level detached townhomes, are very popular in this area. Design styles tend to be Mediterranean or contemporary Spanish, with stucco exteriors and tile roofs. Most homes offer spectacular views (after all, this is not the neighborhood you moved from!). Most condominium developments feature pools and tennis courts. Southwestern-style landscaping is popular, and it requires little maintenance.

Rental housing market: There is good availability for apartment rentals in the $700 to $900 month range. The market for condominiums and homes is tight, because of seasonal rentals. Plan your stay well in advance, and you'll be able to choose what you want.

Average rent for a 2BR apartment: $400 to $700.

Nearby areas to consider: Bloomington Hills, which is actually the part of St. George near country clubs, and Santa Clara, a picturesque rural area with great views of the snow canyons.

Earning a living

Business climate: Although St. George is still a relatively small town, the population increased 8 percent in 1995 alone, a figure typical of the growth the city has seen since the 1970s. (The population has increased sixfold in 35 years, and job growth was 500 percent for the same period.) That kind of growth is good for small businesses, services and the construction industry, and it's expected to continue into the next century.

Help in starting a business: The Dixie Business Alliance, 801-652-7741, is operated in partnership with Washington County Economic Development and Dixie College. It offers a Small Business Development Center with free counseling for start-up or small businesses, business plan counseling, marketing analysis and feasibility studies. The Alliance also makes demographic studies available, provides information on government contracts, and offers custom-fit training in business leadership, Total Quality Management, workplace communications and more. You can reach local offices of SCORE through the Dixie Business Alliance.

Job market: Call the Utah Department of Employment Security, 801-633-3588. There are also several temporary services and employment services in town. During 1994, the county's unemployment rate dropped to 3.4 percent, the lowest in almost 20 years. During the same year, the county had an 18.4-percent increase in jobs and an 8.4-percent increase in population. But wages are low in Washington County, only 78 percent of Utah's overall. The major employers are federal, state and local government.

Medical care

Serving the needs of 100,000 in the tri-state area of Utah, southern Nevada and eastern Arizona, Dixie Regional Medical Center, 801-634-4000, is a 137-bed regional referral facility. The hospital has a 24-hour emergency center and Life Flight, intensive and critical care, respiratory care, same-day surgery, home health care, oncology, physical therapy and more. It recently added a cardiac catheterization lab, permitting angiography and more accurate diagnosis. Dixie Regional also offers cancer services, nuclear medicine, CT scanning and magnetic resonance imaging.

Continuing education

Dixie College hosts the Institute for Continued Learning, 801-652-7670. This chartered club on the Dixie College campus is directed by retirees and semi-retired volunteers. It provides an outlet for creative energies and involvement in college life—without tests, grades or credits—offering lectures, study groups, educational trips, luncheons and special events for $30 per year. Classes include archaeology, French, bridge, photography, Spanish and t'ai chi. There is also an Elderhostel, offering noncredit classes with special events, field trips and other group activities. Dixie College/Washington School District/City of St. George Community Education, 801-652-7675, offer an extensive array of classes, which vary according to the host institution. These include personal enrichment in the arts, motorcycle riding, fly-tying and swimming. Call for a catalog.

Services for seniors

Senior Citizens Centers, 801-634-5716, are operated throughout Washington County and provide free health screenings, bingo, dancing, classes and more. The St. George Leisure Services Department, 801-634-5850, provides activities for area residents, including arts, dance, quilting, computers, crafts, framing and photography, historical lectures, hikes and much more. *The Senior Sampler* is a weekly publication available free of charge in grocery stores, libraries and other public places throughout Washington County—it's a good source of information on activities and jobs.

Crime and safety

The most recent crime index available for St. George showed 58 crimes per 1,000 population, slightly higher than the national average of 55 incidents per 1,000 population. But the index dropped to 39 incidents for the total county. Violent crime is rare. This is a safe place to live, and Neighborhood Watch programs have helped to keep it that way.

Getting around town

Public transportation: No public transportation service is offered in St. George.

Roads and highways: I-15 connects St. George with Salt Lake City to the north and Las Vegas and San Diego to the south. I-70, accessible to Denver, joins I-15 about 125 miles north of St. George.

Airport: St. George Municipal Airport has daily commuter flights to Las Vegas and Salt Lake City via the Delta Connection Sky West.

Let the good times roll

Recreation: St. George is a great place for golfers, offering eight courses with more in the planning stages. Tennis is also popular in public parks, private clubs and as part of housing developments. The city has two trails for hiking and bicycling, and four more are being developed. But the real bonanza is found in the fabulous landscapes. Canyon State Park, which has picnic areas and campgrounds, is set apart by magnificent color. Zion National Park is among the most awesome spectacles on the earth, with massive cliffs, deep canyons and monoliths. It's full of surprises—such as a desert swamp and a petrified forest. Dixie National Forest offers hiking, biking, cross-country skiing, camping, horseback riding and hunting. Fishing is popular at Baker Reservoir, Enterprise Reservoir, Gunlock, Kolb Reservoir, Pine Valley and Quail Creek Reservoir. Zion and Bryce Canyon National Parks are close by. Also, visit Cedar Breaks and Pipe Spring National Monuments, Glen Canyon National Recreation Area and the North Rim of the Grand Canyon. Ski resorts within a day's drive include Brian Head and Elk Meadows.

Culture: *Utah!*, a nightly outdoor musical covering Utah's history from Kit Carson to Brigham Young is held in Tuacahn Amphitheater, 801-674-0012. The Heritage Arts Foundation operates a school for the performing arts and has arts and entertainment events year-round. The Dixie Center is a major convention, arts and entertainment complex offering concerts by the Southwest Symphony and others.

Annual events: The Dixie Invitational Art Show is held in spring at the Dixie College Fine Art Center; the Gunlock Rodeo happens in July; the Lions Dixie Roundup Rodeo occurs in early September. The St. George Marathon is the 13th largest in the nation and is a qualifier for the Boston Marathon. It's held the first Saturday of October. The Huntsman World Senior Games features athletes 50 and over participating in 17 world-class events over a two-week period in October. More than 2,000 participants from 47 states and six countries attend.

When the kids come: Zion National Park (42 miles) has horseback riding, guided tram tours, a nature center for children and camping. In Snow Canyon State Park (8 miles) you can hike to Johnson's Arch, see lava caves and a volcano. Lake Powell (154 miles) is a huge manmade lake with boating, fishing, water skiing, Native American cliff dwellings, marinas and camping.

For more information

Chamber
St. George Area Chamber
  of Commerce
97 E. St. George Blvd.
St. George, UT 84770
801-628-1658

Newspaper
The Spectrum (daily)
275 E. St. George Blvd.
St. George, UT 84770
801-674-6200

Realtor
Kent Frei
Realty Executives
590 E. St. George Blvd.
St. George, UT 84770
801-628-1677
Fax: 801-628-7480

46. Burlington, Vermont

Nickname: New England's West Coast
County: Chittenden
Area code: 802
Population: 39,435
County population: 138,700
% of population over 65: 8.1
Region: New England
Closest metro area: Albany, N.Y., 147 mi.
Average home price: $125,000 to $140,000
Best reasons to retire here: Lake Champlain,
cosmopolitan college town, year-round
recreation, excellent cultural opportunities.

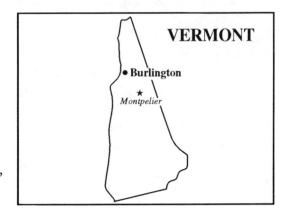

Burlington at a glance

Burlington is a beautiful town on the eastern shore of Lake Champlain, and it's enjoying a renaissance, appealing to people of all ages who thrive in a robust climate. Located 20 miles from the crest of the Green Mountains, the town is also blessed with an entrepreneurial spirit (call it Yankee ingenuity), the most notable example of which are town heroes Ben and Jerry of ice-cream parlor fame. Burlington is considered a small business mecca. In fact, the only uphill challenges are to be found on the ski slopes: Stowe, Jay Peak, Smuggler's Notch, Sugarbush and Bolton Valley are a few of the world-class ski areas in this winter wonderland region. The real estate market has its advantages too, with a high inventory of new homes available, many with spectacular views of gorgeous Lake Champlain. Sometimes called "the west coast of New England," Lake Champlain stretches from Middlebury, Vermont in the south more than 120 miles into Canada. There's even an American version of the Loch Ness monster (lovingly called "Champ") who is said to inhabit the lake and is spotted from time to time. Life in Burlington is laid-back but lively—it's a town filled with dreamers and free-thinkers (This is a place where many residents buy sheep to mow the lawn!) In fact, there's a joke that goes: "What's green and goes backward?" The answer—"Vermont."

Possible drawbacks: Frosty the Snowman spends a lot of time here. The 30-year average for annual snowfall is 81 inches, and winters are longer than many places in the U.S. If you don't fancy downhill skiing, try cross-country or snowshoeing, or consider a warmer climate. It's also expensive to live here, proving you can be on the west coast of New England and still pay East Coast prices.

Climate

Elevation: 330'	Avg. high/low:	Avg. inches		Avg. # days precip.	Avg. % humidity
		rain	snow		
Jan.	26/8	.9	19.1	9	64
April	53/33	2.2	3.6	11	53
July	81/59	3.5	-	12	54
Oct.	59/35	2.7	.3	11	63
YEAR	54/35	24.6	81	130	60
# days 32° or below: 160			# days 90° or warmer: 9		

What things cost

Overview: According to ACCRA, Burlington's composite cost of living index is about 15 percent above the national average, with housing 31 percent higher than the norm. Utilities and health care costs are also significantly higher.

Gas company: Vermont Gas Systems, 800-639-2112 or 802-863-4511. Deposits, only required of renters, can run between $15 and $300. No charge to initiate service. Winter bills average $140; summer, $20. Although gas and oil are common, some areas do not have natural gas.

Electric company: Burlington Electric Company, 802-658-0300. No deposit required; an initial service fee of $10.35. Winter bills can run $250 a month, dropping to $50 in the summer. Partial-electric bills average $75 monthly in winter.

Phone company: NYNEX, 802-658-7200. No deposit required. Cost to start service is $35.55, and basic service runs $16.25 to $22.85, depending on options.

Water and sewer: City of Burlington, 802-865-7265. No deposit and no service initiation fee. Water bills are transferred with property titles. The average water bill for a family of four is $55.60. Our sources say total costs for city services run $80 to $100 monthly.

Cable company: Adelphi Cable Communications, 802-658-5030.

Car registration, license: Driver's license costs $12 (2-year renewal) or $20 (4-year). Registration is $43. New residents have 60 days to 6 months to register cars and obtain a Vermont driver's license, depending upon the state moved from. A 5-percent tax is charged to new residents on the current market value of each car owned, unless you can prove you paid 5 percent or more in your state of origin. DMV, 802-828-2017.

The tax ax

Sales tax: 5 percent. Prescription drugs, groceries, medical services and supplies are exempt.

State income tax: Graduated from 28 percent to 34 percent of federal income tax.

Retirement income: There is a homeowner and renter rebate claim and a property tax credit certificate available to residents age 62 or older with an adjusted household income of up to $45,000.

Property taxes: Real estate taxes average $2.021 per $100 of assessed value; homes are assessed at 100 percent of market value. Property tax assessor, 802-863-7292.

Local real estate

Overview: It's a buyer's market, mainly because new businesses have flooded into the area. There is a large inventory of homes, and prices have come down since the 1980s, stabilizing in the past three years. The greatest activity is in the $115,000 to $180,000 range. Property taxes have increased slightly in recent years. Most retirees are purchasing vacation homes, and tend to prefer condos (after all, you don't have to worry about shoveling all that snow!).

Average price for a 3BR/2BA home: New homes average $135,000 to $140,000; resales, $125,000 to $135,000.

Average price for a 2BR condo: New condos range from $120,000 to $130,000; resales average $100,000 to $115,000.

Common housing styles and features: A wide variety of home designs are available, including ranches, Victorians and split-level types. This is snow country, so most homes have "mud rooms" between the garage and kitchen for wet boots, coats and hats. Most homes also have basements. Homes with 4-star energy ratings are sought after.

Communities or developments most popular with retirees: Condominiums on Lake Champlain are popular, such as the Terraces in Shelburne.

Rental housing market: Rental prices are average to above average. There are ample condominiums and apartments for leasing, but the supply of single family homes is very limited.

Average rent for a 2BR apartment: $600 to $750 per month.

Nearby areas to consider: Shelburne, South Burlington, Colchester.

Earning a living

Business climate: The mainstays of the Burlington economy are companies like IBM, IDX Systems Corporation, Lockheed Martin and the University of Vermont, but they don't offer a lot of hope to those relocating. In fact, necessity is the mother of invention—and entrepreneurship is an art form in Burlington, a great place for home-based businesses. It's also the gateway to New England for Canadian commerce.

Help in starting a business: The Small Business Development Center (SBDC) assists persons who are thinking of starting a business or who are currently in business. The center offers one-on-one counseling in marketing, finance, securing loans, developing business plans and more; call 802-658-9228. The SBDC works in conjunction with the Small Business Administration office in Montpelier, and services are offered free of charge. The SBDC also offers listings of private, for-profit business consultants. SCORE is located in East Essex; call 802-951-6762.

Job market: Burlington has one of the lowest unemployment rates of any city in the nation—2.7 percent, but it also has a relatively low per-capita income. A popular bumper sticker says, "Moonlight in Vermont—or starve." Vermont Associates for Training & Development in Essex Junction, 800-439-3307 or 802-879-7647, offers training and employment services to older Vermonters who wish to enter or reenter the job market. The Department of Employment and Training can be reached at 802-658-1120. Job Search Line, 800-464-4473.

Medical care

Fletcher Allen Health Care is the major health provider in the area, operating three hospitals with a total of 585 beds and 250 resident physicians. It is the integration of the formerly separate Fanny Allen Hospital, Medical Center Hospital and University of Vermont Health Center campus. It is a regional referral center with state-of-the art cardiology services, rehabilitation and physical therapy. Other areas of excellence include 24-hour emergency services, cardiology services, oncology, orthopedics, kidney dialysis and transplant, rehabilitation and occupational and physical therapy.

Services for seniors

The Senior Helpline for Information and Assistance, 800-642-5119, is a great resource. It can help in locating Medicare, Medicaid and Medigap assistance, and inform you about activities and services in the area. The Champlain Senior Center, 802-658-3585, on Main Street in Burlington, offers activities, exercise programs, health seminars, trips and many social opportunities. Programs and services are available to people 60 and older; most are offered free of charge or for a small fee.

Crime and safety

Burlington's crime index is about 81 incidents per 1,000 population. The rate drops to 55 incidents per 1,000 people for Chittenden County, which is the same as the national average. Violent crime is rare. Burlington has adopted community-based policing, assigning officers to specific sections of the community. Crime prevention programs include Crime Stoppers.

Continuing education

St. Michael's College, 802-654-2100, has enrichment programs and classes for adults, and continuing education credits in all regular degree areas. The Elder Education Enrichment Institute (EEE) program is an offshoot of Elderhostel that meets at St. Michael's. Classes are offered in fall and spring, and the program costs $75 annually or $40 per semester. Look for schedules in area libraries or write EEE at P.O. Box 64817, Burlington, VT, 05406-4817. The University of Vermont has an extensive selection of courses through its continuing education division, 802-863-3489, in areas such as anthropology, art, economics, environmental studies, Hebrew, music, political science and more. Seniornet, 802-878-9530, is the Vermont affiliate of a national group that specializes in friendly, hands-on computer training for seniors.

Getting around town

Public transportation: Nine intercity and local bus routes are available, and passenger/auto ferries traverse Lake Champlain. Chittenden County Transportation Authority (802-864-CCTA) is a regional public transit system serving greater Burlington. Fares are 75 cents; seniors age 65 and over pay 35 cents.

Roads and highways: I-89 connects to I-91; US 7 and US 2.

Airport: Burlington International Airport is served by four national carriers and several regional carriers. Direct service and international connections are available to and from major cities east of the Mississippi.

Let the good times roll

Recreation: In the warm months, enjoy one of six golf courses in the area or sailing, boating, fishing and romantic dinner cruises on Lake Champlain. There are plenty of places to hike and bike in the area—after all, Vermont is a state that boasts four million acres of forest and no billboards. Shopping is fun at the Church Street Marketplace, featuring more than 100 stores and outdoor cafes in a four-block, pedestrians-only area. Baseball lovers enjoy watching the Vermont Expos, an AA farm team for the Montreal Expos. Moving into the winter season, you'll find yourself in a skier's paradise, with eight downhill areas and 21 cross-country areas within 50 miles. Snowshoeing, sleigh riding, ice fishing and ice boating are other popular winter activities.

Culture: The Shelburne Museum, located on 45 acres just outside nearby Shelburne, is known as "New England's Smithsonian." It features American folk art, architecture and artifacts, including children's items, quilts, scrimshaw and ship carvings, old master and impressionist paintings, tools and trades of the Revolutionary period, seven furnished historic New England homes and much more. The Robert Hall Fleming Museum houses one of New England's finest art collections of American and European art. You can also see the Vermont Ballet, Vermont Symphony Orchestra, and take in musical and dramatic performances at Flynn Theater. The Champlain Shakespeare Festival presents classical works.

Annual events: The Burlington Winter Festival in February features dog sled rides and ice and snow sculptures. October brings the Vermont International Film Festival and annual Essex Craft Show, with more than 330 juried traditional and contemporary crafts and food specialties from across the country and Canada. In November, enjoy the Church Street Marketplace Lighting Ceremony and Holiday Windows. First Night Burlington rings in the New Year at more than 40 downtown venues, with music, magicians, dancers and storytellers.

When the kids come: The Lake Champlain Basin Science Center, 802-864-1848, is a favorite place to take the grandchildren. The center educates on the history, culture and environment of the Lake Champlain region. Other ideas include a tour of Ben and Jerry's Ice Cream Factory or a visit to Cold Hollow Cider Mill to watch cider making (free samples).

For more information

Chamber
Lake Champlain Regional
  Chamber of Commerce
60 Main St.
Burlington, VT 05401
802-863-3489

Newspaper
Burlington Free Press
191 College St.
Burlington, VT 05401
802-865-0940
800-427-3124

Realtor
Vicki Hall
Coldwell Banker Hicock
  & Boardman
346 Shelburne Rd.
Burlington, VT 05401
802-863-1500
800-639-5520
Fax: 802-658-7616

47. Charlottesville, Virginia

Nickname: Home of Thomas Jefferson's University
County: Albemarle
Area code: 804
Population: 42,906
County population: 71,845
% of population over 65: 9.6
Region: Central Virginia
Closest metro area: Richmond, 70 mi.
Median home price: $120,000 to $200,000
Best reasons to retire here: Fantastic scenery, mild climate, outdoor recreational activities, superior health care.

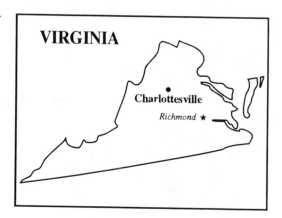

Charlottesville at a glance

Suburban dwellers who are looking for a complete change of scenery will warm to Charlottesville immediately. This pretty city to the east of the Blue Ridge Mountains is a perfect setting for retirement. Sharing its home with the University of Virginia (one of the most beautiful college campuses in the country), Charlottesville offers many intellectual, cultural and recreational activities year-round. The largest health care providers are affiliated with the university, and the medical facilities and research are state-of-the-art. Albemarle County is often referred to as "Mr. Jefferson's Country." The spectacular natural beauty of the place led him to write, "These mountains are the Eden of the United States." Charlottesville was home to three of our country's early presidents, and their estates are maintained for the enjoyment of residents and visitors. The past blends easily with the present here as vintage buildings house modern businesses. The area is also developing a thriving wine industry, and local vineyards often open their gates to visitors for tastings in a pastoral setting. There is no heavy industry here, and the landscape is beautiful; flowers bloom almost year round, and homes are surrounded by azaleas, rhododendrons and camellias. When you're in the mood to take in beautiful scenery, the Blue Ridge Parkway, Skyline Drive and Shenandoah National Park are at your doorstep.

Possible drawbacks: The humidity in July is enough to make you visit relatives you don't even like. The rural character is beautiful, but it's not without expense. If you're used to big-city living, you may go through culture shock. Charlottesville is cosmopolitan but small.

Climate

Elevation: 644'	Avg. high/low:	Avg. inches		Avg. # days precip.	Avg. % humidity
		rain	snow		
Jan.	46/26	3	6	12	67
April	66/41	3.5	.2	10	69
July	86/66	5	-	11	70
Oct.	71/44	3	.1	8	67
YEAR	67/45	43.0	19	-	-
# days 32° or below: 79			# days 90° or warmer: 29		

What things cost

Overview: Housing costs are 24 percent above the national average, and utilities costs are about 3 percent higher. Food, health care and transportation are about 4 percent below average.

Gas company: City of Charlottesville, 804-971-3211. Gas heat is available but heat pumps are more common. Connect charge: $20; $50 deposit waived with letter of credit. Avg. bill: $50 monthly.

Electric company: Virginia Power. Call 804-980-6900. Startup charge: $15. The deposit ($90-$180) may be waived with letter of credit. Avg. bill: $100 monthly.

Phone company: The area is served by Sprint, 804-977-0550. Connect charge is $23.85 to $30.69. Deposit waived with letter of credit. Basic service: $17 monthly.

Water and sewer: Public Works Department, 804-971-3211. A $50 deposit is required of all customers, but it can be waived with a letter of credit. There is a $20 service fee to establish the account.

Cable company: Contact CSW Cable, 804-977-6111; Adelphia, 800-835-4949.

Car registration, license: New residents must obtain a Virginia driver's license within 30 days. Cost is $2.40 annually. New residents must register and title vehicles within 30 days. Titles are $10. Registration fees are $26.50 for automobiles 4,000 lbs. or less; $31.50 if more than 4,000 lbs. Department of Motor Vehicles, 804-296-5851.

The tax ax

Sales tax: 4.5 percent. Food away from home is taxed at 7.5 percent. Drugs and medical services are exempt.

State income tax: $720 plus 5.75 percent of taxable income over $17,000.

Retirement income: Virginia offers an elderly income credit of $6,000 for those ages 62 to 64 who are not receiving Social Security. For those 65 and over it's a $12,000 credit. Double exemptions after age 65 ($800 per person). There are no estate or inheritance taxes.

Property taxes: Albemarle County tax is 72 cents per $100 of assessed valuation; Charlottesville tax is $1.11 per $100 of assessed valuation, both based on 100 percent of fair market value. There is a homestead exemption of a portion of property tax due for homeowners over the age of 65 with gross income of less than $15,000 and assets of less than $50,000, excluding home value. Sample taxes on a $150,000 home in Charlottesville (without exemptions) would be $1,665. Assessor's office, 804-296-5856.

Local real estate

Overview: Virginia's home sales figures are rising. In June 1996, area homes were on the market an average of only 80 days. Charlottesville has many condos, duplexes and townhouses ranging from about $50,000 to $150,000 as well as a large mix of single family homes from about $62,000 to more than $500,000. Taxes have decreased slightly in recent years.

Average price for a 3BR/2BA home: $120,000 to $180,000 for resale; new homes, $200,000. Luxury homes are available in the $350,000 to $500,000 range.

Average price for a 2BR condo: $75,000 to $90,000.

Common housing styles and features: Traditional designs such as Cape Cods, ramblers and colonials predominate. Many offer formal foyers, living and dining rooms along with spacious master bedroom suites; most homes have fireplaces. Kitchens offer eat-in areas and pantries.

Rental housing market: Charlottesville has a large rental market, but there is competition because it is a college town. A luxury 1BR in a clubhouse development would be $570. Homes average $900 to $1,200 per month.

Average rent for a 2BR apartment: $550 to $750 per month.

Communities or developments most popular with retirees: Lake Monticello (Fluvanna City) is a 26-acre luxury lake development. Wintergreen (Nelson City) is great for those who love skiing and horseback riding.

Nearby areas to consider: Western Albemarle (Highlands); Crozet (Weston); Palmyra.

Earning a living

Business climate: Charlottesville is the commercial and marketing center of a 10-county area. Higher education, light manufacturing, tourism, agriculture and retail trade constitute the economic base. The city's labor force consists of professional (engineers, teachers and lawyers) and more than half are white collar. The hospitality industry is important, as Charlottesville is a popular place for conventions, meeting, sporting events and religious gatherings.

Help in starting a business: The University of Virginia Small Business Development Center, 804-977-6917, offers counseling to owners of new and existing small businesses. The SBDC also offers low-cost seminars and has an extensive resource center. The SBDC has a Micro-Business development program intended to help all who desire training in small business management, but it is targeted especially to lower-income individuals, women and minorities. The local chapter of SCORE, 804-295-6712, works from the SBDC offices, offering free consultation to business owners. City of Charlottesville Economic Development Office, 804-971-3110.

Job market: The unemployment rates are 3.9 percent in the city itself and 2.9 percent for Albemarle County. Job competition is typically heavy in this university town, given that many students seek service jobs. A surprising number of international banking/brokerage firms are in town as well as medical and legal services where opportunities may be available.

Medical care

University of Virginia Health Sciences Center, 804-982-3683, has 651 beds and acts as a health care service provider to surrounding cities and counties as well as throughout the state. Services include neurosciences, cardiac care, a comprehensive epilepsy program, diabetes research and care, a burn center and a Level I trauma center. The Medical Center also has heart and lung transplant programs and women's services including a menopause clinic. Martha Jefferson Hospital, 804-982-7000, is a smaller, full-service facility with 201 beds, emergency and critical care units and a Cancer Care Center with radiation and medical oncology. It also has a Women's Health Center with specialized medical-surgical care, and the Cardwell Ambulatory Care Center, with day surgery, mammography, cardiopulmonary rehabilitation and physical therapy. It is a nonprofit community hospital.

Services for seniors

The Senior Center, 804-974-7756, has approximately 3,000 members and offers many physical fitness programs, including t'ai chi, hiking in the Blue Ridge mountains and water aerobics. The center also offers art classes, book clubs, lectures, picnics, out-of-town trips, games, musicals and travelogues. Membership is $35. The Jefferson Area Board for Aging, 804-978-3644 or 800-277-5222, provides information and services to all families and individuals dealing with the aging process. The Chamber has a resource directory listing more than 100 services and products.

Continuing education

The University of Virginia Continuing Education division, 804-982-5313, offers noncredit day and evening classes on such diverse subjects as the Internet and literature. Many of the classes are one or two days in length; some meet twice a week for up to four weeks. Piedmont Virginia Community College, 804-961-5351, offers special tuition status to seniors. Classes can be audited at no charge, or taken for credit at a nominal charge. Credit courses include art, computers, business, humanities technology and more.

Crime and safety

There are community watch programs and other active crime prevention programs initiated through schools. Most people lock their doors and take reasonable precautions but nothing more. The city reported 64 crimes per 1,000 people in 1994 (the most recent year for uniform reporting of statistics), somewhat higher than the national average of 55 per 1,000.

Getting around town

Public transportation: Charlottesville Transit System, 804-296-7433, operates six days a week through the city and parts of the county. Adult fares are 75 cents; seniors 65 and over ride for 35 cents with CTS ID.

Roads and highways: I-64, SR 250, SR 29.

Airport: Charlottesville-Albemarle Regional Airport has flights connecting to cities east of the Ohio Valley through Comair, The Delta Connection, United Express and US Air Express.

Let the good times roll

Recreation: Shenandoah National Park provides a spectacular setting for scenic drives, hiking, camping, horseback riding and photography. Chris Green Lake and Mint Springs Lake offer boating and fishing. As the center of the Monticello wine growing region, Charlottesville has 10 licensed farm wineries, some of which are open to visitors by appointment. There are 10 municipal and private golf courses in the area. Within the city there are 20 parks, four swimming pools (two indoors), tennis courts and ball parks. The best spectator sport in town is the annual Foxfield Races—steeplechase horse races that inspire fabulous tailgate parties. Pro sports in the Washington D.C./Baltimore area include the NFL Washington Redskins, the NBA Bullets, the Washington Capitols of the National Hockey League and the new soccer team, the D.C. United.

Culture: Major performance groups include the Charlottesville and University Symphony Orchestra; the Miki Liszt Dance Company, a professional modern dance company and the Heritage Repertory Theatre, a professional summer theater. Ash Lawn-Highland, home of President James Monroe, regularly hosts operas, concerts and entertainment. On the arts scene, Lynchburg Fine Arts Center, McGuffy Art Center, Jordan Art Gallery, the Virginia Museum of Fine Arts and Bayly Art Museum provide new exhibits. A walk through Historic Downtown Charlottesville provides a day's entertainment with sites such as the Lewis & Clark Monument, Levy Opera House, Old Eagle Tavern and Tarleton Oak.

Annual events: The annual Antiques Show and Sale (January) features fine 18th- and 19th-century furniture; the Dogwood Festival features a Pro-Am golf tournament, queen's coronation, dance, barbecue, carnival and fireworks (April); the Albemarle County Fair (Aug.); the Foxfield Steeplechase (Sept.); the Virginia Blues Festival (Sept.); the Virginia Festival of American Film (Oct.).

When the kids come: Adventureland Family Fun Park features batting cages, bumper boats, go-carts and miniature golf. Skate or play hockey at Charlottesville Ice Park on the historic downtown promenade. Children from toddlers to age 12 can enjoy the indoor playground at Jungle Max. The Museum of American Frontier Culture depicts four authentic working farms. Virginia Discovery Museum has interactive exhibits.

For more information

Chamber
Charlottesville-Albemarle
   Chamber of Commerce
Fifth & Market Sts.
Charlottesville, VA 22902
804-295-3141

Newspaper
The Daily Progress
P.O. Box 9030
Charlottesville, VA 22906
804-978-7201

Realtor
Donna B. Marshall
Coldwell Banker Bailey Realty
   Company
1455 East Rio Rd.
Charlottesville, VA 22906
804-973-9555
Fax: 804-973-9557

48. Bellingham, Washington

Nickname: Let Us Surprise You
County: Whatcom
Area code: 360
Population: 55,480
County population: 140,900
% of population over 65: 12.6
Region: Pacific Northwest (Puget Sound)
Closest metro areas: Seattle, 89 mi.;
Vancouver, British Columbia, 60 mi.
Average home price: $145,000 to $150,000
Best reasons to retire here: Beautiful
scenery, friendly neighbors, relaxed lifestyle.

Bellingham at a glance

Located on Bellingham Bay with Mount Baker as a backdrop, Bellingham is the last major city before the Washington coastline meets the Canadian border. Situated between Seattle and Vancouver, British Columbia, Bellingham is on the way to big places, but it's enough out of the way to maintain its small-town charm. People move here for the natural beauty and outdoor recreation, with the Pacific Ocean and Cascade Mountains nearby. The awesome evergreen rainforests, saltwater coves, blue lakes, green valleys and snow-capped peaks of the Cascade mountains are still home to Native American peoples, including the Lummi, the Nooksack and the Semiahmoo, who originally chose this region for its tremendous bounty of salmon, crab and shellfish and huge tracts of ancient cedar inland. Today, Bellingham offers a bounty of outdoor pleasures, including fishing, skiing, rafting, kayaking, golf and almost any other activity you can imagine. There are many interurban trails for jogging and walking, plus huge parks, 14 public and 10 private golf courses, tennis clubs and more. This small and very friendly community is also a university town (Western Washington University) with a very relaxed attitude; no one is in a hurry here. The quality of medical care is good, and the cultural offerings are diverse for such a small community. (And if you need more, you can easily travel to Seattle or Vancouver.) The magnificent beauty of the Pacific Northwest would convince almost any skeptic that this is truly a fabulous place to retire.

Possible drawbacks: The climate, though very mild, is too wet for many people. (It rains 170 days a year.) Job opportunities also could be better.

Climate

Elevation: 150'	Avg. high/low:	Avg. inches		Avg. # days precip.	Avg. % humidity
		rain	snow		
Jan.	42/31	4.79	5	22	75
April	56/39	2.43	0.1	15	58
July	72/53	1.11	-	8	49
Oct.	59/42	3.49	-	13	68
YEAR	57/42	35.26	14.3	170	62
# days 32° or below: 68			# days 90° or warmer: 0		

What things cost

Overview: ACCRA has no statistics for Bellingham, but according to the local Chamber of Commerce, the cost of living is 13 percent higher here than the national average. Housing is 40 percent above the norm. According to ACCRA, health care costs in metro areas of Washington run 20 to 50 percent higher than the national average.

Gas company: Cascade Natural Gas Corp., 360-354-5615 or 800-552-0615. Deposit waived for good credit. No hook-up fee. Avg. bill: $24 monthly. (Most homes do not have gas heat.)

Electric company: Call Puget Power, 206-455-5120 or 800-321-4123. Connect charge: $5. Deposits waived for good credit. Avg. monthly bill: $150 for all-electric; $40 with gas heat.

Phone company: Contact US West, 800-244-1111. Service charge: $31. No deposits. Basic monthly service: $14.

Water and sewer: City of Bellingham, 369-676-6900. No deposits within city limits. Single family homes: $80 within the city and $120 outside. Apartments, duplexes and other multiple family housing is metered service.

Cable company: TCI Cablevision of Washington, Inc., 360-734-5522; Telcomm Island Cablevision, 360-384-6860.

Car registration, license: New residents have 30 days to obtain a license. Written, road sign, vision and physical test required for original license. Driver's license: $14; exam fee: $7. New residents must register cars within 60 days. Initial registration: $28; $23.23 annually after that. There is a 2.2 percent annual excise tax based on manufacturer's retail price with standard depreciation. Department of Motor Vehicles, 360-676-2096.

The tax ax

Sales tax: State sales tax: 6.5 percent; local: 1.3 percent. Total: 7.8 percent. Groceries are exempt.

State income tax: No state income tax. The last governor who attempted to enact one was voted out of office.

Retirement income: Seniors over 61 who have lived in their home for a year or disabled persons are exempt from some taxes depending upon their personal income.

Property taxes: Homes are assessed at 100 percent of market value. The average tax levy rate in Whatcom County is approximately $13 per $1,000 of assessed value. Taxes on a $150,000 home, for example, might run $1,950. Assessor's office, 360-676-6790.

Local real estate

Overview: A large inventory of available homes has softened prices, and Bellingham should remain a buyer's market for some time. Most retirees relocate permanently, but some spend the winters in Arizona. Retirees tend to choose secure, gated developments from the abundance of appealing townhouse and condominium communities.

Average price for a 3BR/2BA home: New homes, $150,000; resales, $145,000.

Average price for a 2BR condo: New condos, $199,000; resales, $109,000.

Common housing styles and features: Contemporary designs with wood exteriors and open floor plans. Cedar is a common material inside and out.

Rental housing market: There is a lot to choose from in terms of both houses and apartment complexes.

Average rent for a 2BR apartment: $550 to $750 monthly.

Communities or developments most popular with retirees: Village at Cordata, Birch Bay Village, Sudden Valley, Festival Square.

Nearby areas to consider: The town of Ferndale, 10 minutes north of Bellingham, offers lower prices. Located in a fertile valley near the Nooksack River, Ferndale offers spectacular views of Mt. Baker and the San Juan islands. Birch Bay is a resort community just six miles south of the Canadian border. It is known for its shallow, warm waters, sandy beaches and fabulous sunsets. It's just right for those who love small-town friendliness, the great outdoors and plenty of privacy.

Earning a living

Business climate: Bellingham's economic base could use some strengthening, being heavily dependent on sectors that have limited growth potential, including education, medical and the timber industry. It has an active waterfront port that supports fishing, cold storage, boat building, shipping, paper processing and marina operation, and it's a major connection between Seattle and Vancouver, British Columbia.

Help in starting a business: Call the Small Business Development Center, 360-650-3899, which offers no-cost consulting on every phase of small business operations and management, assists with SBA loans, business plans, market research, cash flow analysis, hiring and more. The program is funded by Western Washington University, the state of Washington and the SBA. The Washington State Business Assistance Center, 800-237-1233 or 360-664-9501, is a hotline for business information and has a business ombudsman service that acts on behalf of business owners in resolving disputes with government entities.

Job market: Major employers in this area include Western Washington University, St. Joseph's Hospital, Georgia Pacific wood products, Haggen's Inc. and Consumer's Choice, Inc. (grocery stores) and Fred Meyer department store. The unemployment rate is 7.5 percent. For more information, contact the Employment Security Department Employment Service, 360-676-2060. The Senior Community Service Employment Program, 360-733-1941, provides income-qualified seniors with training and job search help.

Medical care

A 253-bed acute care facility, St. Joseph Hospital Main Campus, 360-734-5400, offers diagnostic and treatment services, such as: a new and comprehensive cardiovascular services program (including balloon angioplasty and open-heart surgery), endoscopy, a mobile lithotripter for dissolving kidney stones without surgery, physical and occupation therapy, a 24-hour emergency department, respiratory therapy, radiology/imaging and a Community Cancer Center with radiation therapy and support services for cancer patients and their families. Nursing services include a critical care unit, telemetry unit for intermediate care, an approved oncology program, and in-patient physical rehabilitation programs. Also, St. Joseph Hospital South Campus, 360-734-2440, is the location of the Mental Health Unit, rehabilitation and a recovery center for alcohol and addictions.

Services for seniors

Bellingham Senior Center, 360-676-1450, offers tax assistance, health screenings, day and overnight travel and a wide variety of classes. Topics include art and ceramics, billiards, exercise, computers and more. There is a $16 annual membership fee, and a nominal charge for some classes. There is also a ballroom-style dance every Tuesday night. There are similar programs in surrounding towns such as Blaine, Everson, Ferndale and Lynden. Also call Senior Services Information Assistance, 360-398-1995, and RSVP, 360-734-3055, which places seniors as volunteers with community service organizations.

Continuing education

Western Washington University on Sehome Hill, 360-650-2841, provides continuing education programs in Bellingham. Retired students 60 and older can enroll in any class at no charge on a space available basis. It is a broad-based liberal arts program with business, education, art, music, economics, recreation, environmental studies and more. The college also offers an Elderhostel program, with a commuter option. Northwest Freedom University, 360-650-3476, is a community education program that offers quarterly classes in anthropology, t'ai chi, yoga, massage, vegetarian cooking and photography.

Crime and safety

Bellingham has a crime index of 78 incidents per 1,000 people, and Whatcom County's average is 55 incidents per 1,000, which is the same as the national average. Violent crime is rare, although there is a slightly higher incidence of rape reported, due to the university.

Getting around town

Public transportation: The Whatcom Transportation Authority, 360-354-7433. Seniors pay 15 cents per ride, or can purchase a monthly pass for $8.

Roads and highways: I-5, SR 542, 539.

Airports: Bellingham International Airport is served by two regional carriers: Horizon Air and United Shuttle Express. Seattle-Tacoma International Airport is the closest major American airport.

Let the good times roll

Recreation: Bellingham was recently designated a Trail Town USA by the American Hiking Society and the National Park Service for its 29 miles of walking, biking and horseback riding trails. With 14 public courses, there's also plenty of golf to enjoy, and many of the courses offer beautiful views of Mt. Baker, Canadian mountain ranges and the Georgia Strait. Beginners to advanced kayakers love to explore the waters of Bellingham Bay and the San Juan Islands. There's great rafting on the rapids in the gorges around Mt. Baker and Mt. Shuksan, and the Mt. Baker Ski Area has Washington's longest downhill season, with an average annual snowfall of 595 inches. Nearby North Cascades National Park includes Lake Chelan and Ross Lake national recreation areas. Less strenuous outdoor pursuits include a "Look Back on Bellingham Bay" evening cruise. Or visit Peace Arch State Park, a garden on the Canadian border with a 67-foot arch that spans the international border, symbolizing peace between the nations. Larrabee State Park on Samish Bay is perfect for climbing, clamming and crabbing.

Culture: The Whatcom Museum of History and Art, housed in the original City Hall, includes a children's museum. Mount Baker, the oldest operating theater in the Pacific Northwest, was restored in 1995 and presents live Broadway shows and performances by the Whatcom Symphony Orchestra.

Annual events: Local heroes and intrepid visitors come to take a noontime dip for the Birch Bay Polar bear Swim on January 1. The Dutch community of Lynden celebrates its heritage with Holland Days (May). The Ski to Sea Race, Whatcom County's largest and most famous event, is held Memorial Day weekend. This 85-mile, multistage relay from the top of Mt. Baker to Bellingham Bay includes running, kayaking, downhill and cross-country skiing, canoeing and bike riding. The Skywater Festival salutes the start of summer with parades, arts and crafts, food, music, a beer garden and more (June). The Mount Baker Blues Festival happens in August, and September brings the Bigfoot at Baker Festival, when Mt. Baker Foothill Communities unite in furry costumes and parade through town, stage a talent show, tell tall tales and hunt for giant footprints.

When the kids come: The Whatcom Children's Museum features hands-on exhibits. Older children may enjoy (and learn from) a whale-watching expedition.

For more information

Chamber
Bellingham/Whatcom Chamber
  of Commerce and Industry
1801 Roeder Ave., #140
Bellingham, WA 98227
360-734-1330

Newspaper
The Bellingham Herald
1155 N. State St.
Bellingham, WA 98225
360-384-0878

Realtor
Chris Burton
Re/Max Whatcom County, Inc.
913 Lakeway Dr.
Bellingham, WA 98226
360-733-7383 or 800-723-1313
Fax: 360-671-8022

49. Olympia, Washington

Nickname: The City on the Sound
County: Thurston
Area code: 360
Population: 37,170
County population: 189,200
% of population over 65: 11.6
Region: Pacific Northwest (Puget Sound)
Closest metro areas: Tacoma, 30 mi.;
Seattle, 60 mi.
Average home price: $133,000 to $146,000
Best reasons to retire here: No income tax,
state capital, recreation, great senior services.

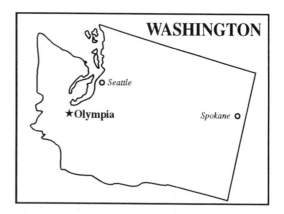

Olympia at a glance

Olympia takes a lot of heat for the amount of rainfall that blankets the area year-round, but residents get the last laugh. Yes, there are bouts of gray skies and daily drizzles, but it's all taken in stride. Despite the weather, this city on the Sound (Puget) is a wondrous place to look upon every day. It is surrounded by lakes and rivers, and it was named for its spectacular views of the Olympic Mountains (Mount Rainier's snow-capped peaks loom on the horizon). For an economy-sized city, there are giant-sized amenities. Culture, events, recreation, transportation and services for seniors in the South Sound area (including Tacoma) are so extensive that new residents should be given an orientation session. There's one thing that no one misses, though: The hassles and congestion associated with city life don't exist here. Seattle has a rush hour; Olympians like to joke that they have a rush *minute*. As both a college town and the state capital, there is a unique mix of business and basics. People are educated and ambitious but not at the expense of settling for a lesser quality of life. The single most-asked question is about the climate. Does the sun ever shine? Certainly, on average about 40 percent of each month is clear and bright with the summer season even better—mild (70 degrees) and dry. The health care is excellent, there's no state income tax, and the city is clean and affordable. All in all, Olympia has the answer if you're looking for a slow pace near great recreation and big-city culture. It offers an excellent balance of easy lifestyle and plenty to do.

Possible drawbacks: Did you say you wanted a dry, hot climate? Turn the page—Olympia is not for you. The city's economy is undergoing change, as state government scales back and stricter environmental laws affect the timber industry.

Climate

Elevation: 205'	Avg. high/low:	Avg. inches		Avg. # days precip.	Avg. % humidity
		rain	snow		
Jan.	44/30	7.4	.	20	90
April	60/37	3.1	-	15	80
July	72/46	.7	-	9	70
Oct.	61/40	5.3	-	14	84
YEAR	61/39	48.0	19	-	-
# days 32° or below: 89			# days 90° or warmer: 7		

What things cost

Overview: ACCRA doesn't provide statistics for Olympia, but the cost of living in nearby Tacoma is 3 percent above the national average. Transportation and groceries are at 6 and 8 percent above average. The real culprit throughout the state is health care, which is 20 to 50 percent above average in every metropolitan area surveyed.

Gas company: Washington Natural Gas Co., 206-464-1999 or 800-999-4964. Turn-on charge: $15-$25, plus a $10 account set-up charge. Deposits waived for good credit. Average bill is $35 to $46 a month.

Electric company: Call Puget Power, 206-455-5120 or 800-321-4123. Connect charge: $5. Deposits waived for good credit. Avg. monthly bill: $124 for all-electric; $45-56 for partial electric.

Phone company: Contact US West, 800-244-1111. Hook-up: $31. No deposit. Basic service: $14 monthly.

Water and sewer: City of Olympia Utilities, 360-753-8340. No hook-up fee or deposit. Combined rate: $45-$55 per month.

Cable company: TCI Cablevision of Washington, 360-357-3364, or Viacom Cable, 360-597-7850.

Car registration, license: License must be obtained within 30 days of establishing residency. Written, road sign, vision and physical test required. Driver's license: $14; exam fee: $7. New residents must register cars within 60 days. Initial registration: $28, dropping to $23.23 annually. There is 2.2 percent annual excise tax based on manufacturer's retail price and standard depreciation schedule. Call the Department of Motor Vehicles at 360-459-6753.

The tax ax

Sales tax: Total tax is 8 percent for most of the Olympia area.

State income tax: No state income tax. The last governor who attempted to enact one was voted out of office.

Retirement income: Seniors over 61 who have lived in their home for a year or disabled persons are exempt from some taxes depending upon their personal income.

Property taxes: Home are assessed at 100 percent of market value. There are 85 separate districts, but the average tax rate is $15.50 per $1,000 of assessed value. Sample taxes on a $150,000 home would be approximately $2,325. Assessor's office, 360-786-5410.

Local real estate

Overview: Since 1993, home price increases have leveled off to 3 to 5 percent annually. Currently, Olympia is a buyer's market and is much more stable than markets like Seattle. There are vacation homes, but most retirees in the area relocate here permanently. There is plenty of new construction, and retirees tend to choose new homes over resales.

Average price for a 3BR/2BA home: $146,000 new; $133,000 resales.

Average price for a 2BR condo: New, $127,000; resales, $166,054. Condos range from $55,000 to $285,000.

Common housing styles and features: Contemporary and California design has influenced local architecture, with more open designs, vaults and skylights. Because the winter days can be very gray, builders and buyers have been installing more windows and skylights. Designs make use of outdoor living space such as decks, sunrooms, atriums and patios.

Rental housing market: Rentals of all types are available, including houses, manufactured homes in senior parks and apartments. There is currently a glut of apartments.

Average rent for a 2BR apartment: $495 to $625 per month.

Communities or developments most popular with retirees: Laurel Oaks, Eagles Landing, Friendly Village of Olympia, Glen Terra and Golden Estates attract retirees with security, community clubhouses and/or golf courses nearby.

Nearby areas to consider: Yelm is a fast-growing community (25 minutes from Olympia), also near the Tacoma/Pierce County area.

Earning a living

Business climate: The economy in Olympia and Thurston is at a crossroads, and everyone seems to be aware of it. Government has provided up to 42 percent of the jobs and 52 percent of the wages in the county, but with new government spending controls, experts expect these numbers to decrease. Combining this with stricter environmental laws, change is definitely on the horizon for the timber industry. But the proactive economic development groups in the area continue to attract private-sector growth. Olympia is a port city, which, though smaller than Seattle or Tacoma, still attracts importing and exporting. Plans are to make the Port of Olympia a foreign trade zone, which could attract international trade. Call *The Business Examiner*, 360-956-3133.

Help in starting a business: Call the Small Business Development Center, 360-753-5616, for free business counseling as well as seminars. The Business Resource Center, 360-754-6320, offers demographics and business climate information. The Washington State Business Assistance Center, 800-237-1233 or 360-664-9501, is a hotline for business information and has a business ombudsman service.

Job market: Government remains the largest employer in the area, but the diversified economy is based on such industries as agriculture, forestry, fishing, manufacturing and construction, as well as retail and service industries. The unemployment rate is 6.1 percent. Olympia Job Service Center, 360-438-7800. The Thurston County Job Service Network, 360-786-5416.

Medical care

At Columbia Capital Medical Center, 360-754-5858, a 110-bed hospital, there is 24-hour emergency care, plus medical and surgical services, cardiac rehabilitation, imaging services, a same-day surgery center, physical therapy and a diabetes wellness center. It recently added a physician's pavilion and a nine-bed short-term care unit, and will soon complete expansion of outpatient services. Providence St. Peter Hospital, 360-491-4980, a 390-bed facility, is the largest in the South Sound area. The hospital offers a full spectrum of acute care, specialty and outpatient services, medical rehabilitation, 24-hour emergency services and outpatient surgery. Providence St. Peter also sponsors NursePLUS, 360-493-4111, offering free nurse consulting and physician referral seven days a week from 7 a.m. to midnight. Mason General Hospital, 360-426-1611, is a full-service, 68-bed hospital with an excellent oncology unit.

Services for seniors

The Senior Activity Center, 360-943-6181, is a full-service activity center that offers classes (topics include watercolor painting, current issues, foreign languages, yoga, American history, woodcarving and more). A very popular travel program plans day trips to surrounding sites such as Mount Rainier or Seattle pro sports games, as well as extended travel, such as a six-day trip to Reno. The center has health screenings, referrals and a boutique and coffee bar in addition to an on-site meal program. Senior Information and Assistance, 360-943-6188. Area on Aging, 360-786-5579. Thurston County Senior News, 360-754-2953. RSVP, 360-943-7787.

Continuing education

Evergreen State College, 360-866-6000, ext. 6170, has a Leisure Learning program of noncredit classes in areas from martial arts to financial planning. Non-degree students can also take classes on a credit or audit basis. South Puget Sound Community College, 360-754-7711, ext. 365, offers enrichment classes in business, computers, languages and the very popular "Contacting Your Guardian Angel" class. The Parks and Recreation Department, 360-753-8380, also offers classes, including languages, yoga, dog obedience, karate, sailing and more.

Crime and safety

Larceny and theft are the most frequent occurrences, and the police have stepped up neighborhood watch programs and crime prevention classes, including workshops for seniors on auto safety, telephone scams and techniques to prevent your home from being targeted. The crime index for Olympia is 67 incidents per 1,000 people, which drops to 48 crimes per 1,000 on a countywide basis, well below the national average of 55.

Getting around town

Public transportation: Intercity Transit, 360-786-1881. Seniors with ID pay half-fare (25 cents) or 50 cents for the all-day card.

Roads and highways: I-5, US 101, SR 8, 121, 510.

Airports: Olympia Airport offers commuter flights and charters. The Seattle-Tacoma International Airport is 46 miles away and is served by more than 20 carriers.

Let the good times roll

Recreation: Hiking along the edge of Puget Sound, one of the most beautiful saltwater shores anywhere, is spectacular. In the shadow of the Olympia Brewery, Tumwater falls is a great place to watch salmon leap upstream to spawn. The Nisqually Flats National Wildlife Refuge brings many visitors to its viewing platforms and photo blinds to see migrating birds. Olympia is not too far from Mount Rainier National Park, which has the largest single-peak glacial system in the U.S. and offers skiing, snowmobiling, camping, fishing and rugged terrain. Olympia also has 10 city parks that offer tennis, picnicking, jogging, boating and hiking on nature trails. Puget Sound is an ideal recreation spot for fishing and sailing. Seven golf courses are within a 20-mile radius and eight ski areas are within a few hours' drive. Seattle is home to the NFL Seahawks and the NBA Supersonics.

Culture: Washington Center for the Performing Arts hosts performances by national and regional artists including Harlequin Productions, Ballet Northwest, Capital Area Youth Symphonies, Abbey Players, the Masterworks Choral Ensemble, Olympia Chamber Orchestra, Olympia Symphony and the Puget Sounders. The Center also hosts the Washington Shakespeare Festival. Cultural events at the three local colleges are open to the public.

Annual events: The Marine Regatta in Tacoma features the nation's largest marine parade and the area's daffodils (April); don't miss the salmon bakes on Wednesday evenings in July and August on the shores at Owens Beach, Point Defiance Park; the Washington Shakespeare Festival features three plays in production over four weeks (Aug.); Olympia Harbor Days celebrate the maritime heritage of Puget Sound with tugboat races, food, arts, crafts and entertainment (Aug./Sept.); December is time for Zoolights, with more than 450,000 lights decorating the Point Defiance Zoo and Aquarium.

When the kids come: On weekend evenings in the summer, take the kids to Wolf Haven International, a 75-acre wolf sanctuary where visitors and wolves join in a duet and kids can toast marshmallows on a bonfire.

For more information

Chamber
Olympia/Thurston Chamber
  of Commerce
1000 Plum St., SE
P.O. Box 1427
Olympia, WA 98501
360-357-3362

Newspaper
The Olympian (daily)
P.O. Box 407
Olympia, WA 98507
360-754-5400

Realtor
Doug Burger
Re/Max Four Seasons Real
  Estate
2627 Martin Way E.
Olympia, WA 98506
360-459-4663
Fax: 360-459-3513

50. Sequim, Washington

Nickname: The Banana Belt of the Northwest
County: Clallam
Area code: 360
Population: 4,200; county, 62,500
% of population over 65: 26.5
Region: Pacific Northwest
Closest metro areas: Seattle, 70 mi.;
Canada, 12 mi. by ferry
Average home price: $80,000 to $145,000
Best reasons to retire here: Natural scenic
attractions, entrepreneurial opportunities,
small-town ambiance.

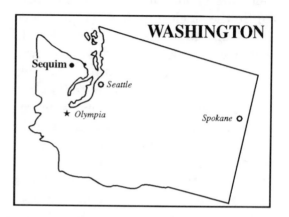

Sequim at a glance

Pronounced "skwim," this friendly small town in the Pacific Northwest has become one of the most talked-about retirement areas in the United States, in association with nearby Port Angeles. Some will tell you that the invigorating climate keeps them young. Others are drawn to the Olympic Mountains, the clean air and the gorgeous views. Sequim is especially popular because of a surprising topographical/meteorological anomaly—unlike Seattle, Olympia and many other areas of Washington State known for rainy weather, Sequim enjoys more than 300 sunny days a year. In this "micro-environment," the mountains form a barrier that creates a "rain shadow" (pilots call it "the blue hole") over the area. The result? A moderate, sunny marine climate ideal for gardeners, (not to mention golfers). The unique growing conditions have earned the area another nickname—"the banana belt." Sequim hosts many visitors each year as the gateway to the Olympic Peninsula, and more and more of them are staying. It doesn't matter that the town isn't much too look at, being neither quaint nor cute. It's affordable, with low property taxes and no income tax, and the scenery is all you need to look at. Located only four miles from the Strait of Juan de Fuca, many Sequim-area residents can see the lights of Victoria and Vancouver Island in British Columbia. Nearby Olympic National Park offers more than 600 miles of well-kept trails. Glacial mountains, wilderness beaches, sun and surf and tidepools—the landscape is as beautiful as it is varied.

Possible drawbacks: Highway 101 is the main road through town and the only one heading to Olympic National Park. In the summer, traffic jams and congestion are the norm.

Climate

Elevation: 180'	Avg. high/low:	Avg. inches		Avg. # days precip.	Avg. % humidity
		rain	snow		
Jan.	45/32	2.1	-	8	80
April	56/39	1.1	-	5	80
July	72/51	.49	-	3	80
Oct.	59/42	1.3	-	7	75
YEAR	58/41	16.0	-	-	-
# days 32° or below: 2			# days 90° or warmer: 0		

What things cost

Overview: No current comparative data is available for Sequim, but indications are that it's more expensive than the national average. Housing costs vary a great deal between urban and rural areas, and utilities costs in Washington tend to be lower than average. But health care costs are significantly higher.

Gas company: There is no supply of natural gas to Sequim.

Electric company: Clallam County Public Utility District, 360-683-4101, provides electricity to all of Clallam County and water to areas outside the city of Sequim. A $15 service charge starts electricity; $5 for water. Deposits range from $100 to $200, but can be waived with a letter of credit. A $73 monthly electric bill is typical for the area.

Phone company: Contact US West, 360-373-4468. Deposits are typically requested only by long distance providers. The basic set-up charge is $31. Basic service is approximately $14.

Water and sewer: The City of Sequim, 360-683-4139, provides water, sewer and garbage services. A $10 charge turns the water meter on, but this is rarely needed. A $135 deposit is required of renters. Combined monthly water, sewer and trash is usually about $70.

Cable company: Northland Cable TV, 360-452-8466.

Car registration, license: New residents have 30 days to obtain a Washington driver's license. Written, road sign, vision and physical test required for original license. Licenses are $14; exam fee is $7. New residents must register cars within 60 days. Initial registration is about $28, dropping to $23.23 annually after that. There is 2.2-percent annual excise tax based on manufacturer's retail price and standard depreciation schedule.

The tax ax

Sales tax: 7.9 percent.

State income tax: There is no state income tax. The last governor who tried to enact one was voted out of office.

Retirement income: Disabled persons or seniors over 61 who have lived in their home for a year are exempt from some taxes, depending upon their personal income.

Property taxes: $11.01 per $1,000 of assessed value inside Sequim; outside Sequim the rate varies from $9.87 to $10.86 per $1,000. Home are assessed at 100 percent of market value. Tax assessor's office, 360-417-2000.

Local real estate

Overview: Sequim offers a wide range of housing types, from condominiums to luxury estates, and prices of homes have been fairly steady in recent years. The rule of thumb on property taxes is that they tend to run a little more than 1 percent of assessed value. Although Sequim typically has higher real estate prices than other areas of the Olympic Peninsula, the costs compare favorably with the Puget Sound market. There is a slow but steady influx of retirees here because it is an excellent retirement location, due to climate, recreation and amenities. Most retirees relocate permanently; it is not a big second-home market.

Average price for a 3BR/2BA home: New homes range from $105,000 to $145,000. Well-maintained older homes also fall into this range, although some can be found in the $80,000 to $90,000 range. Most lot sizes are about 1.25 acres, though somewhat smaller in the city.

Average price for a 2BR condo: At the time of our survey, there were no new condos under construction or available in Sequim. Resale prices fall into a wide range from $64,500 to $239,500.

Common housing styles and features: Most single family homes are split plans or ranch styles. Lots are often wooded.

Rental housing market: Rentals range from $350 monthly for an apartment in town to $1,000 or more for one on the water. A nice, 3 BR/1½ BA home can be found within $750 to $900 per month.

Average rent for a 2BR apartment: $350 to $500 per month.

Nearby areas to consider: Port Angeles or Port Townsend.

Earning a living

Business climate: Business is thriving in Sequim's tourism, retail, agriculture and service industries. The area also is very supportive of entrepreneurs, and many retirees go into business for themselves. Happily, this often takes the form of turning a hobby into a commercial enterprise, such as woodworking, cooking or catering. Retail (boutiques) is another area that senior entrepreneurs have gone into in the Clallam County area, particularly in a redeveloped downtown area of Sequim. The monthly *Peninsula Business Journal* is a great resource to get in touch with the business community.

Help in starting a business: The Port Angeles Economic Development Council, 360-457-7793, hosts a Small Business Development Center affiliated with Washington State University. The SBDC serves Clallam and Jefferson counties, and offers business management and technical assistance, training and research to small business owners. This includes free, individualized counseling as well as skills seminars. The Council also can provide economic and demographic profiles of Clallam county communities, as well as labor force and wage statistics. You can also reach the local office of SCORE through Port Angeles Development Council.

Job market: State Employment Office, 360-457-9407. The unemployment rate is 8.7 percent. The area has been hit hard recently by restrictions in the logging and salmon fishing industries, but has seen expansion of the service and retail sectors, which combine to provide half of all employment.

Medical care

Olympic Memorial Hospital, 360-457-8513, located in nearby Port Angeles, has 126 beds and is served by more than 30 physicians. The hospital has an Education and Fitness Center in Sequim Plaza that offers programs three days a week, including weight management, cooking, cholesterol screening, muscle strengthening, back health and free lectures on health issues. A nurse is present along with the instructor for fitness training. Olympic Memorial is a surgical and acute-care public hospital that has respiratory therapy, radiology (nuclear medicine, ultrasound, CT scanning), the Sequim Radiation/Oncology Center and Mount Olympus Kidney Center. The hospital is considering expansion into Sequim, but Port Angeles is only 17 miles west.

Services for seniors

The Sequim Senior Center, 360-683-6806, with more than 1,250 members, offers many exercise and recreation activities, including billiards, yoga, art classes, health screenings, swing bands, sing-alongs and bingo. Potluck meals are held twice a month. Dues are $20 a year and the center publishes a monthly newsletter.

Crime and safety

The total crime index for Sequim is about 63 incidents per 1,000 population. This number is higher than the national average, but the index drops to 39 incidents per 1,000 in Clallam County, which is well below the average. Sequim has little violent crime. When asked about crime awareness programs, the police couldn't recall ever having one.

Continuing education

Peninsula College, 360-417-6223, offers senior classes that are open to anyone over 18, but are specifically designed for senior citizens. Classes offered in Sequim (at a variety of locations) include computer skills, painting, drawing, ceramics, art appreciation, creative writing, history, investing and "The Infinite Variety of Music," a very popular course that looks at great performances. Additional seniors classes are offered in nearby Port Angeles and Port Townsend. Courses cost $26 to $80 and up. The day and evening classes program at Peninsula College offers a much wider selection of courses, including cultural anthropology, botany, cabinet making, t'ai chi, computer applications, literature, massage therapy, philosophy and zoology. Call 360-452-9577.

Getting around town

Public transportation: Clallam Transit buses run regular routes in the city and throughout the valley, providing easy travel to Port Townsend and Port Angeles.

Roads and highways: Highway 101 is the main road into town. It is also the main road to Olympic National Park, a most visited national park.

Airport: Commuter flights are available from Port Angeles International Airport, connecting to Seattle.

Ferry service: Washington State Ferry Service runs between Port Townsend and Keystone, across the Strait of Juan de Fuca, 13 times a day. Black Ball Transport runs a ferry service to British Columbia from Port Angeles.

Let the good times roll

Recreation: Sequim is a place for those who love the outdoors. Trout fishing is excellent in streams, and salmon and cod fishing are good at Dungeness Spit. There are plenty of places to enjoy biking, hiking, sailing, skiing and canoeing, and nearby beaches provide clams, oysters, agates and driftwood. Dungeness National Wildlife Refuge is a favorite spot for birdwatchers—it is home to many sea and land birds, including eagles. Kayaking is excellent in the usually peaceful waters of the bay and the Strait of Juan de Fuca. Hurricane Ridge in Olympic National Park offers spectacular views, while Sequim Bay State Park, only three miles out of town, offers great camping. Back in town, the Sequim Aquatic Recreation Center, open to the public, includes an adult pool, hydrotherapy pool, dry sauna, exercise room, two racquetball courts and a gymnasium. There are two golf courses: SunLand Golf and Country Club's 18-hole championship course and Dungeness Golf and Country Club.

Culture: In town, enjoy the Museum and Arts Center of Sequim-Dungeness Valley, which focuses on local and natural history and the arts. Olympic Theatre Arts puts on several local production annually, and the Dungeness Bonsai Society hosts one of the finest bonsai exhibits in the Northwest. Many people travel the short distance to Port Angeles to hear the Port Angeles Symphony, see the Juan de Fuca Festival of Arts and enjoy the Port Angeles Light Opera Association. One unique area feature: Dungeness Valley is famous for its award-winning wines, and local wineries welcome visitors.

Annual events: The annual 10-day Irrigation Festival in May is more than 100 years old (the oldest in Washington state), drawing 30,000 visitors to parades, entertainment, food and more. Art Wine and All That Jazz features music, wine and a juried art show at a two-day festival in June. The festival is sponsored by the Jazz in the Olympics Society. In July it's time for the Sequim/Dungeness Valley Clam Chowder Cook-Off, when professional and amateur chowder masters put their culinary skills to the test. Other activities include live music, arts and crafts, clam gulping and more.

When the kids come: Olympic Game Farm in the Sequim-Dungeness Valley features a wide variety of animals in natural settings, many of whom have starred in Hollywood movies.

For more information

Chamber
Chamber of Commerce
  Sequim-Dungeness Valley
P.O. Box 907
Sequim, WA 98382
360-683-6197

Newspapers
Sequim Gazette
147 W. Washington St.
Sequim, WA 98382-3337
360-683-3311

Peninsula Daily News
305 W. 1st St.
Port Angeles, WA 98362
360-417-3525

Realtor
Perry Bloster/Terry
  Parenti/Glory Jones
Americus Realty Inc.
502A W. Washington
Sequim, WA 98382
360-683-3334 or 800-800-5865
Fax: 360-683-3314

Fast Facts

Location	Local population	Housing costs	Best reasons to retire here
Annapolis, MD (pp. 187-191)	34,070	Avg. $201,000-$229,000	Water recreation, culture, small-town charm with major cities nearby.
Asheville, NC (pp. 227-231)	66,562	Avg. $122,000-$150,000	Fabulous year-round climate, mountains, an unsurpassed lifestyle for seniors in a city this size.
Austin, TX (pp. 252-256)	527,600	Avg. $120,000-$150,000	Mild winters, great outdoor recreation, reasonable cost of living, university influence.
Bellingham, WA (pp. 292-296)	55,480	Avg. $145,000-$150,000	Beautiful scenery, friendly neighbors, relaxed lifestyle, outdoor recreation.
Bloomington, IN (pp. 182-186)	60,633	Avg. $120,000-$150,000	Great culture and recreation, affordable living, college-town setting, small-town charm.
Boca Raton, FL (pp. 107-111)	68,272	Avg. $135,000-$160,000	Exclusive communities, low crime rate, great recreation and culture, waterfront living.
Branson, MO (pp. 192-196)	4,454	Med. $89,979	Low cost of living, great live music and entertainment, good hunting and fishing, excellent health care nearby.
Brownsville, TX (pp. 257-261)	135,260	Avg. $76,000-$135,000	Fascinating culture, proximity to Mexico and beaches, low cost of living, low tax burden.
Burlington, VT (pp. 282-286)	39,435	Avg. $125,000-$140,000	Lake Champlain, cosmopolitan college town, year-round recreation, cultural offerings.
Charleston, SC (pp. 247-251)	80,414	Avg. $70,000-$120,000	Great climate, culture and graciousness of the Old South, luxurious retirement areas.
Charlottesville, VA (pp. 287-291)	42,906	Avg. $120,000-$200,000	Fantastic scenery, mild climate, superior health care, outdoor recreation.

Location	Local population	Housing costs	Best reasons to retire here
Clayton, GA (pp. 167-171)	1,613	Avg. $80,000-$125,000	Scenic beauty, year-round recreation, safe, affordable, small-town feel, mountains.
Coeur d'Alene, ID (pp. 177-181)	26,611	Med. $100,840	Fabulous skiing, lakes, year-round recreation, affordable housing, quality health care.
Colorado Springs, CO (pp. 97-101)	312,856	Avg. $125,000-$154,000	Ideal climate, stunning scenery, a thriving arts community, ski and sports opportunities.
Columbia, MO (pp. 197-201)	74,072	Avg. $100,000-$125,500	Rural setting, big-city culture, excellent health care, affordable housing.
Daytona Beach, FL (pp. 112-116)	62,855	Avg. $95,000-$115,000	Casual coastal lifestyle, near popular attractions, affordable housing and living costs.
Eugene, OR (pp. 237-241)	121,905	Avg. $110,000-$150,000	Laid-back lifestyle, great continuing education, near ocean and mountains.
Fayetteville, AR (pp. 57-61)	51,100	Med. $88,600	Clean environment, low crime, affordable living, college town, outdoor recreation, scenery.
Fort Myers, FL (pp. 122-126)	45,495	Med. $77,700	Gorgeous beaches, diversified real estate, subtropical climate, casual living.
Fort Lauderdale, FL (pp. 117-121)	147,678	Med. $105,900	Recreation, culture, great medical care, affordable waterfront living, solid economy.
Ft. Collins, CO (pp. 102-106)	93,600	Avg. $146,000-$187,000	Beautiful scenery, outstanding recreation and education, dry mountain climate.
Gainesville, FL (pp. 127-131)	90,753	Avg. $80,000-$90,000	University offers culture and education, affordable living costs, good medical facilities.
Hot Springs Village, AR (pp. 62-66)	12,000	Avg. $138,000	Four glorious seasons, low taxes, array of recreation, private, secure community.

Location	Local population	Housing costs	Best reasons to retire here
Jacksonville, FL (pp. 132-136)	714,300	Avg. $90,000-$150,000	Mild climate, affordable living, excellent housing prices, lots of outdoor activities.
Kerrville, TX (pp. 262-266)	18,187	Avg. $75,000-$135,000	Panoramic surroundings, friendly, small-town charm, low crime and cost of living.
Kissimmee/ St. Cloud, FL (pp. 137-141)	32,759/ 14,900	Avg. $85,000-$88,000	Comfortable climate, year-round recreation, major attractions nearby.
Las Cruces, NM (pp. 217-221)	67,000	Avg. $87,000-$120,000	Low taxes, temperate climate, recreation, healthy environment, slow pace.
Las Vegas, NV (pp. 207-211)	352,821	Avg. $119,000-$121,000	Exciting night life, good tax structure, affordable housing, dry climate.
Medford, OR (pp. 242-246)	53,280	Avg. $90,000-$130,000	Friendly, small-town atmosphere, fabulous cultural and continuing education offerings.
Melbourne, FL (pp. 142-146)	65,583	Med. $78,200	Well-managed, small city, low living costs, casual lifestyle.
Naples, FL (pp. 147-151)	21,167	Avg. $160,000-$200,000	Great golf, year-round warmth and sunshine, waterfront living, low crime.
Ocala, FL (pp. 152-156)	60,000	Med. $61,400	Low cost of living, affordable housing, mild climate, outdoor recreation.
Olympia, WA (pp. 297-301)	37,170	Avg. $133,000-$146,000	No income tax, diverse recreation, great senior services, good health care.
Palm Springs, CA (pp. 82-86)	42,050	Avg. $210,000-$245,000	Country club living, dry desert climate, world-class golf, tennis and shopping, excellent medical services.
Prescott, AZ (pp. 67-71)	30,606	Avg. $110,000-$170,000	Gorgeous scenery, great outdoor recreation, pristine environment, friendly.
Provo, UT (pp. 272-276)	92,630	Avg. $150,000	Fabulous scenery, great year-round climate, economic growth.

50 Fabulous Places to Retire in America

Location	Local population	Housing costs	Best reasons to retire here
Raleigh, NC (232-236)	249,079	Avg. $144,280	Outstanding medical care, low crime, endless recreation, thriving economy.
Reno, NV (pp. 212-216)	150,620	Avg. $100,000-$140,000	Low taxes, great outdoor recreation, entertainment and events, fabulous scenery.
Rochester, MN (pp. 202-206)	76,060	Avg. $125,000-$150,000	High-quality medical care and senior services, low cost of living, low crime rate.
San Antonio, TX (pp. 267-271)	1,052,900	Med. $80,800	Rich history, low cost of living, good health care, recreation, mild climate.
San Diego, CA (pp. 87-91)	1,149,600	Med. $171,600	Ideal climate, excellent health care, enjoyable recreation and culture.
Santa Barbara, CA (pp. 92-96)	89,200	Med. $245,000	Gorgeous climate, topography and agriculture, great recreation and culture.
Santa Fe, NM (pp. 222-226)	59,840	Avg. $120,000-$160,000	Culture, low taxes, even lower humidity, fabulous skiing, ethnic diversity.
Sarasota, FL (pp. 157-161)	52,694	Avg. $121,000	Beautiful city with great cultural offerings, lots of services for seniors.
Savannah, GA (pp. 172-176)	150,000	Avg. $120,000-$150,000	Beautiful settings, relaxed, great cultural offerings, casual living near the water.
Scottsdale, AZ (pp. 72-76)	174,490	Med.. $142,000	Great climate, outstanding medical care, recreation and services.
Sequim, WA (pp. 302-206)	4,200	Avg. $80,000-$145,000	Natural scenic attractions, entrepreneurial opportunities, small-town ambiance.
St. George, UT (pp. 277-281)	42,000	Avg. $125,000-$200,000	Spectacular scenery, endless sunshine, dry air, great golf, affordable homes.
St. Petersburg, FL (pp. 162-166)	240,318	Med. $78,300	Year-round sun, affordable, recreation, good services for seniors.
Tucson, AZ (pp. 77-81)	450,000	Avg. $100,000-$140,000	Mountain scenery, dry, sunny climate, abundant culture and recreation, excellent medical care.

About the author

Kenneth A. Stern is a nationally recognized speaker, instructor and author who is an authority on estate planning, wealth transfer and financial advice. He has appeared on hundreds of radio and television talk shows, including CNBC, *The Today Show* and CNN. He currently hosts a syndicated radio show that discusses pertinent political, financial and health issues, while revealing the latest investment tips and tax strategies.

Mr. Stern earned his Certified Financial Planner title from the College of Financial Planning. He is a registered securities principal with the National Association of Securities Dealers (NASD). Stern sits on the boards of several corporations and is president of Asset Planning Solutions, headquartered in Rancho Bernardo, California. Stern is also an instructor at various college campuses in the San Diego area.

In addition to *50 Fabulous Places to Retire in America*, Stern is the author of these popular books: *Senior Savvy, Comprehensive Guide to Social Security and Medicare, Safeguard Your Hard-Earned Savings* and *Complete Guide to Investing in Mutual Funds*. He is editor-in-chief of the *Mature American* newsletter.